MUSIC LIBRARIANSHIP

MUSIC LIBRARIANSHIP

A PRACTICAL GUIDE

BY

E. T. BRYANT

JAMES CLARKE & CO., LTD

33 Store Street, London, W.C.1

U.S.A.: Hafner Publishing Company

First published 1959
Reprinted with minor corrections 1963

© ERIC THOMAS BRYANT, 1959

PRINTED IN GREAT BRITAIN
BY LATIMER, TREND AND CO., LTD

CONTENTS

PART I

PART II

ILLUSTRATIONS

INTRODUCTION

. Librarians are well aware that the overproduction of books extends even to publications relating to their own work; before issuing yet another on a particular subject a writer should be satisfied in his own mind that there is need for it. There is no book in print on music libraries and the last one was published just over twenty years ago. Since then, and more particularly since the end of the Second World War, considerable developments have taken place in this part of our service. Furthermore, although there are many public libraries with a special interest in and knowledge of music, others admit to the need for information. The following pages may also help those who are studying for various parts of the Registration examination of the Library Association. Assistants who are working for the optional part of the Final examination on "The literature and librarianship of music" may consider this work too elementary for their needs yet still find some useful facts. The most important reason for this book, however, is that the public libraries' music sections must be developed to meet an expanding demand. The time has passed when it is possible to satisfy music-lovers with a service created and maintained by a librarian who lacks musical knowledge and is not prepared to accept advice in this field. This intensification and expansion at one and the same time call for greater specialization from public libraries and it is hoped that the second part of the book will assist the development of music stocks that are at present inadequate.

So far as I am aware this is the fourth British book to give recommended lists of music, though its layout differs considerably from its predecessors. The pioneer work was James Duff Brown's *Guide to the formation of a music library*—a pamphlet that had an effect out of all proportion to its modest size. One may smile today at some of the works distinguished by a double asterisk (those which "should form part of every public library as a foundation") but if I

vii

Introduction

thought my own selections would stand up as well to inspection some sixty-five years hence I should be extremely satisfied. After the First World War, when Brown's pamphlet was out of print, the Library Association suggested to Mr. L. R. McColvin that he should prepare a memorandum on Brown's work; the result was *Music in public libraries: a guide to the formation of a music library, with select lists of music and musical literature* (Grafton, 1924). The selection was much more generous than in Brown's work to which McColvin made handsome acknowledgement. Then, in 1937 and 1938 appeared the two volumes of *Music libraries: their organization and contents, with a bibliography of music and musical literature* (Grafton), by Lionel R. McColvin and Harold Reeves. These two volumes covered an immense range of books and scores and have proved a trustworthy standby to a generation of librarians, and I freely admit my own immense debt to that work.

Although this book has been written primarily for public librarians and their assistants, and from a British standpoint, it is nevertheless hoped that colleagues in other types of libraries, and librarians oversea, will find in it matters of interest and use—perhaps as a means of comparison with their own practice, or as an opportunity to formulate their own ideas on the topics discussed.

A highly enjoyable aspect of writing this book has been the correspondence that has been entailed with many people, checking facts and seeking information, help and advice. It says much for their forbearance that several of these correspondents are now friends. To all the people listed below, sincere thanks and acknowledgements are offered for assistance given, always generously and willingly. Because the manuscript has been several years in preparation, some people who have given help may have their names inadvertently unrecorded here and to those I offer apologies and hope they will forgive me. Finally, it must be stressed that I accept responsibility for all opinions expressed (except for those in direct quotation of others) and for any errors that have, despite the wealth of assistance, crept into the text.

The manuscript was completed in the middle of 1958, but some subsequent developments are given brief mention in the postscripts to two or three chapters.

ACKNOWLEDGEMENTS

I am deeply indebted to many people, but my greatest thanks must go to Mr. J. F. W. Bryon, Borough Librarian of Eccles, Lancashire. In 1949 we were colleagues at Beckenham, Kent, and I casually remarked one morning that I had thought, upon occasion, that there was a need for another book on music librarianship and that I had vaguely considered doing something about it myself. Those who know John Bryon will not be surprised at the result—I was prodded and persuaded into starting the work and received a constant stream of suggestions, ideas, comments and criticism. Draft versions have been torn to shreds, amended and retyped; no chapter has been written less than four times and Chapters I and V have each had more than eight versions. Despite his many other commitments, Mr. Bryon has read practically all of them and without his persistence and encouragement it is unlikely that the book would ever have been finished. Its virtues, if any, are almost entirely to his credit.

Another librarian who has read nearly all of the book, some of it on several occasions, is Mr. C. H. Turner, Borough Librarian of Woolwich, London. He most generously consented to act as critic and has improved the arrangement and coherence of much of the material to a marked degree. Mr. L. W. Duck and Miss J. Hickling, Librarian and Sub-Librarian respectively of the Henry Watson Library in Manchester, who also read most of the typescript, have made corrections and suggested additional works that I had overlooked. Their answers to queries have demonstrated both the quality of the stock and the high standard of service in their department.

The sections on music classifications have all been checked by experts in the particular schemes, though the opinions expressed remain my own. My factual accuracy is the result, therefore, of help from Mr. J. D. Stewart (formerly Borough Librarian of Bermondsey, and still actively engaged in librarianship) on Brown's "Subject"

Acknowledgements

classification; Miss Henrietta B. Schmitter (late of the Forbes Library, Northampton, Mass.) on Cutter's "Expansive" scheme; Mr. Edward N. Waters (Assistant Chief of the Music Division, Library of Congress) on the L.C. scheme; Mr. Benjamin A. Custer (Editor, Dewey Decimal Classification) on the 780 class of D.C.; the late Mr. Henry Evelyn Bliss on his own "Bibliographic" classification, and Mr. E. J. Coates (of the British National Bibliography) on the B.C.M. scheme. The chapter on gramophone record libraries owes much of its information on American practice to the magnificent help provided by Mr. Kurtz Myers, Chief of the Music & Drama Department, Detroit P.L. Other information in this chapter and on the L.C. *Catalog of copyright entries* came from Mrs. Dorothy A. Linder, Head, Music Section of the Copyright Cataloging Division of the Library of Congress. As Miss Dorothy Amesbury she was my first American correspondent, as long ago as 1937, and has remained a most helpful friend ever since.

Many British librarians have given me information, and thanks are tendered to Miss M. D. Liggett (Guildford) and to Messrs. R. K. B. Aldridge (Huddersfield), H. K. G. Bearman (West Sussex County), G. A. Carter (Warrington), R. J. M. Caul (Burnley), J. H. Haiste (Rugby), K. C. Harrison (Hendon), F. G. B. Hutchings (Leeds), E. Simpson (Coventry), the late B. Oliph Smith (West Riding County), W. B. Stevenson (Hornsey) and B. W. Wray (late Nottinghamshire, now Tasmania). In addition to these chief librarians (and others whose names I have certainly overlooked), I am pleased to acknowledge help from Miss H. M. McGill (Manchester), Mr. A. B. Craven (Leeds) and Mr. G. Shaw (Nottinghamshire).

In Part II, my chief acknowledgements must go to Mr. C. T. Haddon and to Mr. H. P. Dawson. The former taught me at school thirty-five years ago and has continued my musical education ever since; to him I am particularly indebted for my enjoyment of chamber music, for suggesting many items in miniature score and for helping me with their suggested order of priority. Mr. Dawson undertook the responsibility of checking the availability of certain editions, the provision of publishers' names for certain works and of the contents of certain volumes, and answered a host of queries. This he has done for several years; I doubt if he has been able to eliminate all my mistakes, but he has certainly done his best.

Permission to quote from my own writings and from those of others has been freely and generously given by the Library Associa-

Acknowledgements

tion and Messrs. Grafton & Co., and also by the editors or publishers of the *A.L.A. Bulletin, The Assistant Librarian, The Library Association Record, The Librarian & Book World, The Library Journal* and the *Library World*. The Deans of the Graduate Library Schools of Kent State and Chicago Universities have allowed me to quote from unpublished theses submitted at those universities. Professor Otto Luening was equally helpful, and no librarian could have had a more cordial reception to requests of this nature.

Photographs have been immediately supplied upon request by the librarians of Cincinnati & Hamilton County, Coventry, Detroit, Ilford and Liverpool, all of whom have given me a choice of pictures; the City Librarian of Manchester has allowed me to copy the rubber stamp used to indicate the number of parts available for an orchestral work. The subject headings that form Appendix I are those that appear in the catalogues of the Coulsdon & Purley libraries and are quoted by permission as are the copies of catalogue entries from Detroit's gramophone record collection.

Sections of chapters 1 and 5 of this book were extracted for use in a paper delivered at Bristol to the United Kingdom Branch of the International Association of Music Libraries in 1956; I am grateful to the Branch for allowing me to use this material again. Miss M. M. H. E. Ehrhardt of Widnes has given most practical help in reading through the final typescript, amending errors and helping in proof corrections. Finally, I must acknowledge my debt to Messrs. T. E. Callander (now Chief Librarian of Croydon) and J. L. Wilson, both of whom gave me great freedom in the selection of music at Coulsdon & Purley and at Beckenham respectively. Some of that practical experience is reflected in Part II of the book that follows.

E. T. BRYANT

Widnes
March 1959

PART I

Chapter I

MUSIC LIBRARY ADMINISTRATION

Introduction

In 1950, Ralph Vaughan Williams wrote:[1] "I am very glad to see that in late years the public libraries have woken up to the importance of music as part of our general culture. Many libraries have a good collection of music scores, but as you yourselves know, much remains to be done." It is the intention of this book to indicate what that service might be, or what could be provided. The responsibility then lies with the individual librarian and his committee members. The provision of good music is one of our more rewarding activities and an adequate collection should be an asset in any community.

Throughout the book reference is made to large, medium, small and very small library authorities. The terms are elastic and perhaps are not consistently used throughout but, generally speaking, the authority serving a population of 150,000 or more in a reasonably compact area is considered a "large" library, 75,000 to 150,000 as "medium" and from 40,000 to 75,000 as "small". County libraries in Britain often serve a wide area and the total population in the county library area may be over half a million, yet with the exception of Middlesex and Essex no single town in a county area is likely to come within the "medium" category and very few in the "small" class. For this reason, a brief section is devoted to County libraries later in the chapter.

For ease of reference, each section has its own heading, but the following are the major categories, in order: History and general; Scores; Handling problems; Accommodation and equipment; The Music Library; Staff; Other administrative problems. The chapter is intended for both librarians and students.

HISTORY AND GENERAL COMMENTS

A catalogue of standard music deposited by way of loan in the War-

3

Music Librarianship

rington Library and Museum by Mr. Marsh was printed as an appendix
to the catalogue of books published in 1850. It contained one hundred
and twenty-three items loaned by Mr. John Fitchett Marsh, Town
Clerk of Warrington, whose other claim to library immortality is that
he gave evidence before the Royal Commission of 1849; the report
of the Commissioners led to the passing of the first Public Library
Act in Britain. Liverpool, some twenty miles away from Warrington,
was apparently the second library to lend music, from 1859; the idea
slowly spread to other British libraries. Provision in the U.S.A. was
apparently first made by Brooklyn in the eighteen-eighties. Charles
Ammi Cutter, at Northampton, Mass., wrote in 1896:[2] "Following the
lead of Brooklyn, several public libraries have in the last decade put on
their shelves works of music to be circulated like books. As they have
reported that this has given their patrons great satisfaction, I seized
upon an opportunity which offered itself lately to buy on peculiarly
advantageous terms, the complete works in Breitkopf & Härtel's
well-edited and clearly printed editions, of Beethoven, Chopin,
Grétry, Mozart, Palestrina, Schubert, Schumann, Schütz, and Johann
Strauss, 312 volumes in all. Lassus, Mendelssohn and Wagner (both
pianoforte and full score editions) will soon be added. I had already
picked up the Bach Society's edition of Bach, and the Händel
Society's edition of Händel, in 119 volumes, a few shelves of miscellaneous music, and some of the publications of the Musical
Antiquarian Society, and the Plainsong and Medieval Music Society.
You will see that I have chosen for first purchase the standard composers . . ." The population of Northampton, it should be remarked,
was less than 30,000.

Although starting some thirty years later, American libraries
quickly outstripped us in the size of stock and the provision of music
departments. The penny rate limitation in Britain for library expenditure meant that very little money was available for books, and
music with its limited appeal and need for expensive binding suffered
in consequence. Some enterprising advertising agents presented
bound volumes of music, interleaved with advertisements, to certain
libraries, which must have been both disconcerting and infuriating
to the performer. In 1893 James Duff Brown wrote his pamphlet on
the *Guide to the formation of a music library*. This "tract" has 4 pages
of text and 18 pages of recommended works, arranged under 35
headings with books and scores in a single sequence. It is obvious
from Brown's comments that many libraries at that time had no

4

music stocks and the pamphlet was intended as a spur, while the subject lists were "to rectify . . . library formation on the happy-go-lucky principle of selection by instinct instead of knowledge. . . ." From this time music collections have grown steadily.

Potential users

The first and largest group of potential users is that of instrumentalists, who are usually amateurs. Although the majority of these will be pianists, a few players of the violin, organ, 'cello and other instruments may be expected. Second are the singers, either soloists or members of a group, such as a choir or choral society—a dwindling section in most southern counties of England though still important in such areas as Wales, Lancashire and Yorkshire, and parts of Scotland where the old choral tradition remains strong. The third group is usually the smallest but has an influence far outweighing its numbers; this comprises the music teachers who will normally have their personal libraries but who should find the public library valuable for its reference books and periodicals, for scores not in their own collections and for recommendations to pupils. Fourth, there are the learners who present a problem of policy upon which every librarian must reach his own decision and this question is discussed a little later. The listener, a person who may not play an instrument (though often the unwilling recipient of music lessons in childhood), or whose singing voice is untrained but who wishes to borrow a score for fuller enjoyment of a particular performance is the fifth important category of user. The novice may be able to do little more than follow the words—yet it is generally possible to get some idea of the vocal line being sung from the position of the notes on the stave. Those who have some training as singers or instrumentalists will obviously be able to follow a score with enhanced pleasure and understanding.

Students have not been included as a separate (sixth) category since many libraries will see nothing of the budding composer, conductor, professional instrumentalist or singer, unless it be out of term time when embryo professionals may descend on the library with immediate demands for scores and textbooks, often quite out of the way and unlikely to be in the library stock.

Why special treatment?

The advantages of a music department to professional musicians, students and the host of people outside those very limited numbers

B 5

who have an interest in good music needs no stressing, yet it may be justifiably asked why music should receive preferential treatment in the matter of a subject department. There are two good reasons: first, because music comes in very different shapes in books and scores (as well as in different material if gramophone records are included) and these related yet diverse forms present special problems of integration; and second, that interest in classical music is growing at an appreciable rate and can (or should) provide scope for one of our most valuable activities. On the first point, it is obviously desirable that the music section should be treated as a single unit which can take into account the special nature of the problem. On the second, good music may be ranked as a cultural force with the best literature. Gramophone and radio have brought classical music within the reach of a much greater audience than was imaginable fifty years ago, when many potential listeners had little if any chance of hearing, at first hand, good music played well.

A separate department normally confines itself (at least in Britain) to books, scores, periodicals and gramophone records. The Henry Watson music library in Manchester has on display a number of music instruments of historical interest but the provision of pianos and gramophones that may be used by members of the public is still virtually unknown in Britain. Dorothy Tilly (an Englishwoman who was for many years Chief of the Music and Drama Department in the Detroit Public Library) has written:[3] "A piano is essential for the music department. Ideally, there should be two: a concert grand for the auditorium; and a smaller grand or upright for the use of music borrowers, housed in a sound-proof room adjoining the music department." Detroit has no piano and it would appear that very few American libraries make this particular provision. In Britain, the new Central Library at Plymouth includes a concert hall with a large grand piano and a first-class sound reproducer for gramophone records but is probably unique. The late Sir Walford Davies suggested that public libraries should each have a sound-proof room, while another American writer, Alice M. Martin[4] has suggested that "If need be, it [i.e. the Music Room] can be part of the general reading room, the scores and records being shelved with other books, and the recordings being used on a portable phonograph which has earphone attachments. Such a restricted situation is not at all uncommon, nor even necessarily undesirable." The pamphlet from which that quotation is taken is still useful, though published in 1949.

6

Music Library Administration

For and against a separate music department

There can be no general agreement as to the size of a library or the population served before a separate department is considered desirable or necessary. Dr. E. A. Savage has inferred a minimum stock of between 8,000 and 10,000 books and scores and a staff of at least two members before a separate department, open similar hours to the rest of the library, can be regarded as advisable.[5] Otto Luening in his notable thesis[6] describes a model music library, and says: "It is obviously not a practical goal for communities of less than 100,000 population. It might, however, be achieved through library co-operation under a regional unit of service."

A gramophone record library would greatly increase the need for specialist staff and for separate accommodation. The matter is considered in some detail in Chapter V, where it is suggested that one assistant cannot deal comfortably or adequately with more than 150 records daily unless routine work is to suffer. If there is no separate department then staffing difficulties, inability to answer questions outside one's own special sphere and similar problems may be much less in evidence. There is still much to commend the alcove or separate area in the general lending library. Such modest provision is within the scope of a very small library if reasonable floor space is available. Because so many British libraries are housed in old, cramped and totally inadequate buildings designed to house bookstocks a fraction of their present size, floor space is frequently at a tremendous premium—but this is not the place to argue the need for a much higher rate of building new library premises.

An example of what can be done in a town of less than 50,000 inhabitants is provided by Rugby. There is a separate music section which occupies the very limited area of some 170 square feet out of a total of 2,900 for the entire Lending Library. The stock in the music section comprises over 2,600 items including some 450 miniature scores. Over 7,000 books and scores were borrowed by local library users in 1953–4 and nearly 8,000 in 1957–8. There are many music libraries elsewhere worth a visit; in the medium-sized town category one would include Burnley, Hornsey and Westminster; large towns with excellent music libraries are Bournemouth, Ilford, Newcastle-on-Tyne and Plymouth—and there are others in all three categories. The largest cities—Edinburgh, Liverpool, Manchester and the like have nearly all provided excellent music departments with adequate qualified staffs but smaller towns cannot reasonably hope to provide such a service. The librarian is likely to be more impressed by the achievements of a colleague administering a system of approximately the same size, and there are many libraries other than those mentioned above with excellent music collections.

Standards, scope and exclusions

In Britain it has always been assumed that the legal power to buy books, conferred on libraries under the 1855 Act extended to music, and this view has never been challenged. A decision to provide music is not enough; the equally important decision must be taken as to the types of music to be provided. There is no set standard for public libraries nor agreement as to what should be included. Even the largest library would probably find it beyond its resources to attempt to provide all things for all users. Even so, it would appear that some agreed policy should be possible—that librarians themselves should reach a decision as to what they can reasonably be expected to provide in their stocks and what they feel should be bought by the individual if required. Provision would increase in range and depth as the population served grew larger; some types of music (such as the ephemeral dance tune) would be considered outside the scope of any library. Other items whose musical standard is sufficiently high but which cannot reasonably be expected to be kept in the stock of a smaller library would perhaps be the responsibility of the Central Music Library or those eight cities in Britain with populations over 400,000.

The music collection, to be of permanent value, must be begun, expanded and maintained in accordance with a definite plan—modified from time to time in the light of public demand or by a change of personnel. Any collection will reflect something of the interests of the person in charge and that is not without advantages. A successor will probably have slightly different interests and another facet of the music stock may become slightly more prominent as a result. In his book selection work the librarian should not overlook *The Musical Times* and similar periodicals. The duty to read periodicals devoted to music can always be delegated if the librarian so wishes.

The competent librarian will naturally do his best to make the maximum provision possible but some types of music must be excluded and such exclusions should be consistent, if possible. The problem of providing, or refusing to provide, tutorial books and music must be faced. Books on harmony, counterpoint and musical form are not in question but with instrumental tutors the borrower is likely to require a copy for months unless interest dies quickly. One complication is that tutorial books for wind and brass instruments may include excerpts from half-forgotten sonatas and concertos that are useful for technical training when the student has acquired a fair proficiency upon his chosen instrument. The series of tutors by Otto Langey (published by Boosey & Hawkes) is of this type. There are librarians who maintain a very large collection of tutors so that teachers and pupils can try several and then perhaps choose one best suited to their needs. Many smaller libraries do not buy choral works such as the anthem, part-song and motet, partly through handling difficulties with single copies, partly because a choir is likely to require at least a dozen copies. Another general exclusion in smaller libraries is orchestral parts. Orchestras, like choirs, usually build up their own libraries; an expensive work unlikely to be played more than once in a period of years may be hired from the publishers. With many modern works the parts are not for sale so that the library itself would have no option but to hire the parts if local orchestras were supplied with music. Orchestras do not normally make application to the local public library unless it is known that scores and parts are in stock or can be borrowed through the library without difficulty. The last general exclusion to be considered here is that of music for minor instruments (i.e. those rarely learned by the amateur). Such music is only bought when there is expressed demand; the librarian who buys music for the double bass or bassoon will probably find that it receives very little use though its utility may be increased by loan to other libraries upon request.

While these exclusions are fairly general among small and medium-sized public libraries it is not suggested that they should be automatic or a fixed policy. The only rigid line drawn (so far as is possible) should be that of musical quality and every effort made to exclude the ephemeral work. A small library may receive orchestral parts and scores from a defunct local orchestra and it will naturally wish (even if not compelled under the terms of the donation) to retain these works for possible use by other orchestras. Similarly sets of anthems may be received as gifts and put into stock for loan to other choirs in the neighbourhood. In this case, a system of interloan could be organized between choirs, all copies being regarded as part of a central pool and the library acting as headquarters and clearing house. This is done most successfully at Burnley, for example.

Although music is written for so many instruments and combinations of instruments as well as for the human voice, the newly started collection is often severely restricted in scope and experience suggests that such limitation is justified. A collection of scores totalling less than a thousand usually includes vocal scores of operas, musical plays, oratorios and the like; songs, music for piano (the largest groups in the collection), organ, violin and violoncello; miniature scores and perhaps the parts of a handful of chamber music works. Such a collection is likely to answer the needs of the great majority of our library users who wish to borrow music. Instruments that have a lower proportion of players among musicians, such as the viola or clarinet may possibly have two or three local performers; for these, a token selection may have to suffice, to be increased when local demand justifies and finances permit. This is the sort of music that cries out for co-operative provision between neighbouring libraries in order to increase the selection at no greater cost to any individual library.

For orchestral scores, the dictum of Dr. Ernest Savage may be recalled:[7] "I think the following rule is reasonable: in a small library buy the miniatures of full scores by the principal composers; and in the medium library the big scores of these composers, and all the miniatures available. In the large library, such limitations are not necessary." This might be considered a rather over-generous approach to full scores for they are normally extremely expensive and often cumbersome. On the other hand, full scores are available for many works that are not available in miniature form. Dr. Savage is not, in general, in favour of the provision of orchestral parts; in his view, the small library should also omit chamber music parts but moderate provision should be made by the medium-sized library and wide coverage by the large library. He continues: "A great part of the collection will consist of vocal and piano scores or orchestral works, solo-instrumental and vocal music, and especially chamber music—quintets, quartets, trios—in which lies the strength of any music department. Miniature scores of the most celebrated chamber music are essential."

The provision of too many musical arrangements will weaken an otherwise good collection. There is so much good original music for the piano, for instance, that it is unfortunate, to say the least, if the collection of piano scores proves to consist mainly of orchestral works and operas arranged for the instrument. In the field of piano duets and organ works, the arranger seems to be even more strongly in evidence. There are certain instruments, such as the viola and oboe, which do not have a large repertory of original works and the collection will perforce have to be strengthened by the addition of arrangements but this should be a last and not the first resort.

The selection should be made as wide as possible by the inclusion of the lesser-known with the more familiar works; the contemporary with music written before the age of Bach. The librarian should remember that a standard of selection that may be regarded as too high is much preferable to the more common error of too low a standard. Quite often libraries will provide inferior music while the classics are missing. Librarians should not need to be told to buy the best, yet money is often wasted on ephemeral music. I might instance the piano selections from musical plays and films. These rarely contain music of any real merit; indeed, only a small proportion of the tunes become generally popular and after a few months the great majority are completely forgotten. There are exceptions but they are infrequent. It is not the public library's business to provide this type of music until there is a really good basic stock of original piano music and probably not even then. The smaller the section, the higher should be the standard of selection.

Where a library as yet provides no music and feels that the time has come to start a collection this may be done with a small cash allocation, but it will probably result in a delay of several years before the stock is sufficiently varied to be considered moderately adequate. Pricing a varied and comprehensive collection shows that music is not cheap but that an initial expenditure of £350 (at 1958 prices) plus £150 for binding would provide a good though limited basis for future expansion and still satisfy a reasonable proportion of normal demands for the more popular works in the general repertory. American libraries would appear to have much happier possibilities when starting a collection, for Greta Smith of the Enoch Pratt Free Library in Baltimore has suggested:[8] "Individuals may be encouraged to give money in memory of friends, an appropriate bookplate marking volumes so purchased. . . . A little friendly rivalry in gifts is an excellent device to get a new music collection off to a good start." That this is not just wishful thinking is shown by Otto Luening[6] who writes, in his *Music materials and the Public Library*: "Libraries acquire their music materials (as they do other library materials) either by purchase or by gift. Apparently neither source has, up to the present time, provided all these libraries with the resources which they say they need in order to serve their communities well. In reply to a question as to how they secured their music materials, five of the nineteen libraries having record collections had bought all of them; three had been given their entire collections. . . . The average indicates that about two-fifths of the record collections were presented to these libraries. About forty-three per cent of the scores were also given to libraries." With good publicity, a British library might receive some small donations and some scores no longer used by their owners, but gifts of money, new scores or gramophone records are very rarely forthcoming.

Development of basic stock

Unfortunately, librarians with little or no musical knowledge tend to have no settled policy for the music section however definite their ideas in other fields. With music, as with other sections of the stock, good supply will often create the demand. The present stock may be fairly large but unless it provides a wide selection of scores suitable for current demands, kept in good condition, its use will probably be disappointing. A score should not automatically retain its place on the public shelves until it disintegrates. If it is in some demand and/or is a standard work, then it should be replaced if its condition is poor; otherwise, it should simply be withdrawn. Many public libraries carry a reserve stock of books in limited demand which still deserve retention; this reserve should certainly include music.

In fact, the first step towards building up a collection may well be to remove a generous proportion of the present stock from the public shelves; some to be replaced by more modern editions and the rest to be retained in reserve, however makeshift the provision for the latter may be. Generally speaking, the score that has not been borrowed for at least twelve months should be regarded as a possible candidate for withdrawal or reserve. Placing in reserve will admittedly reduce its chances of use still further so that a check should be made to separate, as far as possible, works which appear to have no permanent place in music history—works by composers who rate but a few lines in *Grove* or do not even appear. These volumes of music may well be discarded though they should first be offered to the Central Music Library in London and, if not required by that library, perhaps to the nearest large city library. It is usually fairly safe to dispose of arrangements (the orchestral works edited for performance on piano or organ, etc.) unless the composer is of the first rank. In doubtful cases the safest plan is to retain the work in reserve stock. In areas that are cultural backwaters, the librarian may find that even excellent standard works are not used, and there seems to be no genuine answer to this most depressing problem—lowering the standard of selection is certainly not the solution.

When replacements and new editions are considered there are a number of guides to show the librarian what is available though such guides will not usually indicate the suitability of a particular edition for library use. This is an aspect of music librarianship without a textbook answer; only with wide musical knowledge and experience can one be dogmatic about the "best" edition, and even then still invite the question: "Best for whom?" The general methods of selection of classics for the library shelves, the choice between available editions of Shakespeare or Jane Austen, are also applicable to music. When there is a choice, the librarian will generally tend to adopt a cautious approach and choose an edition by a well-known publisher, perhaps with an equally well-known editor and certainly one that is well produced. Reputable publishers with an international standing cannot afford to produce poor editions and, in Part II of this book, only occasionally is a particular edition suggested in preference to rivals because the standard of alternative versions is almost equal. The first type of guide as to what is available is provided by the leaflets and catalogues of music publishers; these will often indicate works that are new to the catalogue and also ones which have been brought back into circulation after being out of print. If a library considers it worth while to be on the mailing list of a music publisher, this can usually be arranged without difficulty; in any case, such brochures can frequently be obtained through one's normal music supplier. There are some excellent second-hand dealers who will willingly send their lists to public libraries.

Lists of new music publications with reviews are to be found in many of the music periodicals discussed in Chapter II. Messrs. J. B. Cramer & Co. publish an excellent quarterly list of new music and newly available reprints, arranged in classified order. Prices are quoted but not the names of publishers, since the firm naturally expects to supply items chosen from its lists. The very large music library may find it worth while to approach the British Broadcasting

Corporation for its quarterly accession list of music. Many of the works included are difficult to trace elsewhere. The virtually world-wide selection quoted in each number of *Fontes Artis Musicae* provides a simple method of international coverage. *Notes* (also receiving comment in Chapter II) is particularly valuable both for its coverage of American publications and for the fact that its reviews are by music librarians for their colleagues.

For years music librarians in Britain have complained bitterly at the lack of bibliographical aids in tracing music scores and have had to rely upon checks in a number of sources. The appearance of *The British Catalogue of Music* in 1957, a quarterly cumulation of all music accessions in the British Museum—an equivalent for music to *The British National Bibliography* for books—is an immense stride forward, and one for which much credit must be extended to the United Kingdom Branch of the International Association of Music Libraries. These volumes are limited, as *B.N.B.*, to new works and new editions; reprints are not normally included. They will provide an excellent means of keeping a check upon current issues and, in time, will be invaluable as a means of tracing works though the file will not indicate if a score is still available. This, at last, gives British librarians a service which is roughly equivalent to that provided by the Library of Congress in its *Catalog of copyright entries*.

If music selection in general is considered it is probably true to say that here, more than in any other section of a public library stock, it is customary to buy a very large proportion of works by people who are dead. Contemporary composers represent only a small part of the output of most publishers of serious music—the classics provide their "bread-and-butter". Works by the acknowledged masters should be replaced as a matter of course when old copies wear out. Sometimes the particular volume will be out of print; in others, it will be advisable to replace by a different edition that has virtually superseded the earlier. The Novello edition of the organ sonatas of Rheinberger might be cited as a case in point. The editing (by Harvey Grace) and the layout are generally superior to those of earlier editions and should be preferred when new copies of any of the twenty sonatas are bought.

If the librarian has little musical knowledge, the problem of buying works by contemporary composers is one of very real difficulty and in general it might be suggested that no such work should be bought unless the reviews suggest it is likely to be of more than passing interest, and the librarian has some confidence that library users will borrow the work. This is particularly necessary where the allowance for new music is very small, for works covered by copyright are generally much more expensive than those which are in the public domain. However much one may desire to support a struggling composer by adding to his royalties there seems little point in buying, for example, a tuba sonata of some complexity when there is not, so far as the librarian is aware, a single player of the tuba for miles around. Though perhaps an extreme example it illustrates the point. In general, the unmusical librarian who is unable or unwilling to have any sort of assistance would be well advised to limit his initial accessions to piano music (mainly solo but with a few duets and some piano concertos, arranged for two-piano playing), solo pieces for violin, for violoncello and for organ, some songs (for all types and ranges of voice) and a number of miniature scores of the more popular classics. The stock lists in the second half of this book are intended to be of assistance here.

One of the results of a very conservative policy in selection is to increase the demand, through the Regional System, upon the Glasgows, Liverpools and Westminsters and their smaller brethren whose collections are larger and more comprehensive than average. This demand might be offset by some form of co-operative coverage of music, a possibility discussed later in the chapter.

Buying second-hand music

Money can be saved, but it can also be wasted, by buying second-hand music. This form of accession is not generally recommended for the library that does not include a fairly expert music assistant on its staff. There are certain firms which specialize in second-hand music and who circularize lists of available scores to librarians. Such reputable firms are generally reliable, but since they are experts the prices asked may be regarded as being as high as the market will accept, and one is unlikely to discover any outstanding bargains. On the other hand, the librarian will not normally be asked for more than a fair market price. This source of supply is most valuable for filling a particular gap when a work is out of print or there are difficulties in obtaining a copy through normal sources in this country. If purchase is made with the idea of increasing the size of the music stock at a reduced cost, a check should be made whenever possible on the current price of a new copy, for second-hand copies may sometimes be quoted at prices little less than that to be paid for new ones when the library discount is taken into account.

In the normal way it is not worth trying to buy music at general auction sales. The physical condition of the music is often poor and a high proportion of it not suitable for public library use. Those works that are worth adding are all too often the ones which are already represented in the stock. It does sometimes occur, however, that a sale is known to include works that the library would be pleased to have. In such a case it may be possible to secure a real bargain as music usually fetches very low prices in the auction room. This paragraph, it should be clear, refers only to the sales of furniture and effects and not to specialized sales of music. Music may also usefully be bought, on occasion, from private individuals who are local residents.

Second-hand music must be carefully collated; the last sheet would seem to be a frequent casualty and flimsy string parts can easily be lost. The bottom corners of a well-used score tend to become dog-eared, pages are likely to get torn with hasty turning over and fingering and marks of expression may have been indelibly entered on the printed page. Music that has been treated in this way or which has been extensively repaired should be bought only when there is no other apparent possibility of getting the work in better condition. Loose binding is of less importance, for the librarian would automatically send the score for rebinding before placing it on the open shelves and any weakness in the publisher's binding may lower the purchase price. The library user who marks a library copy and who fails to remove the marks neatly before returning the copy is a pest of the first order, and the librarian should try to set a good example to his patrons by ensuring that no music reaches the shelves with pencil marks of this nature.

This section can be summed up in a single sentence: Don't buy second-hand music unless you know just what is being bought; have a good idea of its current market value and check its physical condition.

Keeping the stock fresh

In a small public library the problem of providing adequate variety for the music borrower is as difficult as with any other section of the stock. Limitations of space and shortage of money for new accessions must result in a fairly small and slowly changing stock; this is a sound reason for a higher rather than a lower standard of selection compared with the larger system. No work should be bought that cannot be envisaged as a permanent asset to the stock, be it two years or thirty-two before it is in sufficiently poor condition to be withdrawn. This may appear to assume clairvoyant powers in the librarian but is not really so.

It may be possible as suggested in the previous section to eke out funds by the judicious purchase of some second-hand items but there is no satisfactory answer to the problem of maintaining and enlarging a music stock without enough money being available. It has been suggested that a certain percentage of the book fund should be earmarked for music, and where there is a separate music library a fixed allotment is highly desirable. The smaller the stock, the more obvious the new accessions become and, if shelf space is very limited, an attempt should be made to compensate for this, as far as possible, by the provision of generous shelf space in reserve. Limited display room should not be made the excuse for reducing purchases to the lowest possible level, neither should the economy of buying albums of works rather than single items blind the librarian to the fact that requests will often be for works that are not available in albums but which must be bought singly, if at all. In brief, the small library authority has a difficult task in maintaining a good and adequate stock of music that will constantly attract music-lovers, unless there is a readiness to spend regularly upon the section.

If the space for scores is very limited then the stock should be changed at intervals to give some of the works in reserve an occasional spell upon the open shelves. A number of seasonal works, such as those written for Lent, Christmas, Easter, etc., may well be removed from the shelves for nine months each year and their places taken by some of the items in stock, providing always that the physical condition of the latter justifies this temporary promotion.

The library system with branches should find it much less difficult to keep the stock fresh at its different service points. On balance it is probably better for each branch to have its own small nucleus stock of works that are in constant popular demand (those suggested for first choice in Part II of this book are recommended), particularly piano music. There are, however, good arguments against branches having any permanent music stock but to consider instead all scores as part of a general pool which serves the whole library system. Unless the branch is a large one it may be difficult to increase the stock beyond the nucleus, when the position becomes similar to that which faces the small authority without branch libraries. With no permanent music stock in the branch or a skeleton selection kept rigorously within definite limits, music can be loaned from the central library stock or a central pool for several months at a time. Where each branch has no permanent stock, all music accessions, including duplicate copies, will be added to central stock or central pool. Where a work is worth duplicating it is often worth getting a different edition for the second copy where this is possible. There are some cases, of course, where one edition is much superior to its alternative in which cases duplication of the original edition is fully justified. Where songs or song albums are to be duplicated the second copy should be bought for a different voice range, or in a different translation where the original is in a foreign language. Duplication should not be carried out automatically and without thought but the desirability of an alternative edition should be considered whenever there is such a choice. With some works it is possible to add four or five different editions and to justify such a variety without difficulty.

Unit exchanges

For the municipal system with three or more branches and for the county library branch, the interchange of stock can be organized on a much more formal basis by the creation of music "units". This system has been used successfully (for books as well as for music) in the Coulsdon & Purley libraries since 1938. A "unit" consists of a convenient number of music scores (experience suggests either twenty-five or fifty) which circulate as a collection from one service point to another, remaining at any particular library for a set period, usually six months. In this way a music score will be seen on the shelves at all libraries of the system in turn and so has an improved chance of achieving regular use than if it is in the permanent stock of one library. It is undesirable that units should include duplicates of items already in stock as this means that at least once in its perambulation of branches the unit copy will duplicate that already in stock while the other libraries in the system have no copy. If the scheme is adopted, it may be thought advisable to limit the circulation of units entirely to branches, omitting the Central Library, though this would seem unnecessary unless the stock of units is limited to duplicates of scores already at the Central Library. It may also be advantageous to call in from the branches all works not considered as basic or nucleus stock and to allocate these returned scores to units so that they will circulate, in time, to every library in the system.

If a union catalogue is maintained, a particular score is shown as part of "Unit *x*" and some sort of simple indicator would show both staff and public the current situation of each particular unit. Where there is no union catalogue, the entries for each work can travel with the scores for insertion in the branch catalogue during the time that the unit is stationed there, or a record can be kept at the central library in order to allow a particular score to be traced quickly. The unit itself should consist of a varied selection of different types of music. While collections will probably be mainly instrumental, each should contain some vocal works and it might be desirable to include a few miniature scores. Larger branches would probably have three or more units in circulation at one time; the smallest branch should have at least two, or a replacement unit should be sent before the one due to be called in is taken from the shelves. This will prevent the music stock from disappearing entirely from public view from time to time. Further details of the scheme can be found in an article by its originator, T. E. Callander, in *The Library Association Record* for June 1938 (pages 256–7).

The size of the system and of the individual music stocks should decide if the central library or any particular branch or branches should be excluded from the scheme. Where all libraries in a system have large music stocks the costs of administration and transport may be considered too high for the potential benefits to music-lovers using the library service.

Binding music

The problems of purchase and selection are closely related to that of binding. Because of its size, music binding is relatively expensive. Miniature scores are, naturally enough, much cheaper to bind but their slightness makes them a bad bargain in the eyes of many librarians—and so there is a tendency, for economic reasons, to bind as many miniature scores as possible together. This can be successful to a limited degree if restricted to related works such as Beethoven's first six string quartets (numbered opus 18, numbers 1 to 6) but it can also cause difficulties. Two patrons requiring different works that are bound in the same volume cannot be satisfied at the same time. On the other hand, a collection of very slim scores, many with spines that are too narrow to carry titling, is difficult to keep in order and troublesome to search for one particular item. Longer works, or volumes containing the scores of two or three related works, may provide guide-posts when searching for a single slim work. Scores of oblong format with the top edge greater than the height should not be bound other than singly because of their tendency to warp.

It is the custom in some libraries for all music to be sent for re-binding before it is put on the shelves, except for the occasional volumes that are issued in stiff covers by the publisher. Unless there is a loose insert (as with some Heugel and Boosey & Hawkes minia-ture scores) or separate parts (as with violin and piano sonatas, chamber music and the like) it will be possible to allow selected scores to circulate in the publisher's casing before rebinding is necessary and the original covers will often add a pleasant touch of colour to the shelves. Slim items of sheet music offer a number of alternative methods of treatment. First, the music may be sewn into a stiff brown paper or similar cover and the work arranged in a vertical file in composer or class order. This is an effective and economical method but suffers from the drawback that the casual library user is unlikely to work through a file in order to find some-thing of interest; some librarians may consider this an advantage rather than a drawback. More serious is the defect that only one person can use the file or a single drawer at a time. It also means that this vertical file provides a separate sequence away from the other scores. The second method is to sew the music into a stiff manilla cover. Libraries can do their own casing by this method, purchasing the manilla in sheets and sewing with binders' thread. Music rein-forced in this way can be shelved in the normal sequence but is liable to be overlooked since it has practically no thickness of spine and individual items can easily be misplaced on the shelves.

Where the volume is a little more substantial it may be sent to a library binder for a variant of what has generally become known as the "picture book" type of binding. The score is bound between stiff cardboard covers, with the original covers pasted on the outside and given a coat of laminated plastic. This allows the original cover to be retained and provides a surface that is grease and damp resistant. A strip of linen is used to reinforce the joint between board and score. Since "picture binding" involves oversewing which prevents the paper from remaining open and flat the method must be adapted slightly (at a somewhat higher cost) and is called by one binding firm the "quarter-flat" type of binding. The maximum thickness of a score that can be treated by this method is three-eighths of an inch; above this figure the score will require the normal type of rebinding.

"Quarter-flat" binding costs come between those of manilla and of cloth or leather and the method also may be regarded as an intermediate one. Years ago it was customary for all music to be bound permanently in quarter-leather but only a minority of scores is usually so treated today. With regular use the paper of a score would be dirty and not fit for retention whilst the leather was still firm and in its prime; where the leaves stayed clean from lack of use, the leather on the spine tended to shrivel and flake and become unattractive in appearance. Where frequent handling does not occur to keep the leather in sound condition, one of the recognized preservatives should be brushed on from time to time. During the past twenty to thirty years, quarter and half-leather have been replaced to an appreciable extent by cloth which is usually adequate and has an equally long life. This may be the place to mention that music is apparently the one type of non-fiction binding for which British public library binders have no agreed scale of charges among themselves, so that librarians are well advised to compare price schedules before deciding where to send music for rebinding.

An impressive saving in the cost of binding can result from the use of the unsewn or "perfect" method. Many librarians dislike this intensely but first-hand experience over a period of years has convinced me of its adequacy in selected cases. Prices are considerably below those ruling for rebinding by the normal sewn method and librarians may find it a useful experiment to try a small batch as a sample, choosing works that are likely to receive frequent use and carefully avoiding any printed upon a coated paper.

When a work requires parts for more than one performer, as in chamber music, the normal method is to bind the thickest part, if there is one, in the usual way, but with the spine of the binding widened in order to provide a pocket inside the back cover to accommodate the other part(s), which are cased in manilla or limp cloth. Alternatively, all parts may be sewn separately in limp covers and the binding itself consist simply of a case or box to house the individual parts. The "binding" will have the usual details of composer, title and classification on the spine and will contain the book-card, date label, etc. Whichever method is used, a note should always be written or stamped on the date label or book-card to the effect that there are x parts in the pocket or pockets, as a missing part may render the others useless. Where the work is a brief one, with a single or double sheet only for the solo instrument and a piano accompaniment of little greater thickness, it is often possible to use a manilla folder with a rear pocket made by stapling a piece of manilla inside the back cover and having the solo part covered with a transparent laminated or sprayed-on plastic or else covered by a paper or card cover. This is simple and most economical.

Dr. Ernest Savage[9] suggests that: "The lettering (always in the language of the title) on thin volumes should be up the spine, but across the spine wide enough to take legible titles." This is likely to meet with general agreement except that the use of the original title should not be made when it is a formal one, i.e. for a symphony or a sonata and similar works when English is much to be preferred to a title in French, German or other language. For operas and other vocal works, symphonic poems, etc., the use of the original title is usually justified. The title on the spine should agree with that used for cataloguing purposes and this matter is dealt with at some length in Chapter IV. Librarians as a body are much happier with titling up the spine, than down; the British Standard recommended practice is in general agreement (B.S. 1544: 1949).

It is the custom in some public libraries to bind works of a particular type in the same colour, e.g. all piano solos in red, all operas in green. This results in large blocks of colour on the shelves which may be useful in the identification of a work but it is possible that a sufficient variety of colours may be unobtainable to carry out the plan without limiting the colour classification to very broad categories indeed. Liverpool uses two colours only, red and blue, for instrumental and vocal works and attempts no further sub-division. A colour scheme may fail through use of different cloths by different binders; even the same firm may vary its colours to some degree through minor differences in dyes. A guaranteed range of colours will apparently result in a somewhat dull selection, as at Bristol. I would strongly recommend a variety of colours in binding, partly because I am not in favour of shelves of books all bound in the same colour and partly because the provision of scores in publishers' bindings and in the "quarter-flat" type of rebinding is incompatible with a set colour scheme. There is a compromise that should satisfy both schools of thought, though it adds to the expense of binding. This is to affix to each score a small strip or circle of coloured cloth at an agreed height from the base of the spine. This allows the eye of an assistant to run quickly along each shelf and discover at once if any score is mixed with members of another category, gives the same assistance to patrons that is claimed for a colour scheme of binding, yet still retains the brightness and attractiveness of variety.

Where there is a music librarian on the staff, listing and checking music binding is naturally his or her responsibility. Particular care must be taken to ensure that correct instructions are given to the binder and that the details of required lettering are precise. This may seem elementary, yet Dr. Otto Kinkeldey has told American librarians that:[10] "I could quote you several instances of otherwise well-ordered libraries in which you could have found the several instrumental parts of a chamber composition handsomely and securely bound together." I have seen copies of violin concertos, in British libraries, with the separate violin part bound in with the piano accompaniment thus completely defeating the object of issuing a separate part for the soloist. When two or more items are bound together in a single volume there should always be a strong and easily apparent link between the individual items, e.g. songs should always be by a single composer and preferably for a particular type of voice. The spine title should either list the individual items or, if room is insufficient, be given a generic title that covers the contents, such as "Songs for soprano", "Piano pieces from op. 10 and op. 12". In the chapters of Part II of this book indications have been given of those cases where it seems suitable to bind separate items into a composite volume. The separate items in such a volume may not all be printed on pages of the same size; the single volume is of unorthodox appearance, though perfectly practical, and the binder will need to be warned against trimming too closely the sheets of the largest item in the volume. This problem does not arise when the works or a selection of them by a single composer are published in album form.

The music department in county libraries

County libraries often serve large populations scattered over a very much wider area than any municipality serving an equivalent number of people. Some county branches are larger than the central libraries of some very small authorities but the general picture is of small units of population receiving full or part-time service from a limited number of permanent branches, of villages and small clusters of houses served by mobile libraries or else by centres run by voluntary "librarians", and there is a consequent need for a much greater

23

flexibility in service than is required in the municipality. The county library headquarters may not be open to the public particularly if situated in a town that provides its own municipal service. It is probable that a large proportion of the music stock, certainly multiple copies of anthems, orchestral parts, etc., and works of which the county has but a single copy, will be kept at headquarters. Permanent branches sometimes have music stocks of their own though it is contrary to general practice in the counties to recognize any stock as being permanent at any one branch. The "unit" system, discussed earlier, offers many advantages to the county that has a number of full-time branches.

Whether the branch music stocks are large or non-existent, requests for loans of books and scores come regularly from local residents who may write direct to headquarters and have their requests satisfied by post or who may make their enquiries through their nearest service point and have the copy sent there for collection. Societies will usually apply direct to headquarters though loans may be made through the nearest branch.

Because county libraries come within the local Education service, the County Music Adviser may help officially or unofficially with stock selection, enquiries outside the abilities of the headquarters staff, and as a liaison officer between local music societies and schools and the library. This may be admirable, yet for the service to flourish to full advantage requires a music librarian and every county library serving a population of some 150,000 or more should have this post on its establishment. The music librarian would control purchase, location and duplication of stock, would integrate the service with educational activities both in the selection of stock and in co-operation with schools, classes and choirs. A well-chosen stock has its influence upon all groups, particularly when the music librarian is recognized as a valuable guide to the choice of work for performance, for he can persuade groups to raise their standards and to attempt unfamiliar works that they might well shun in the normal way even if their existence was known. On his side the librarian will learn what types of music to provide to satisfy the different groups within his area.

With so much scope for a dynamic approach it seems unfortunate that only two or three counties should have the post of music librarian on their establishment. In one Midland county such an appointment has been an unqualified success and, with an assistant of the right calibre, the same results could be achieved elsewhere.

Music Library Administration

Most county library headquarters are housed in cramped and adapted buildings but efforts could be made to provide a separate music section; in any design for new premises the provision of a music library should be considered a necessity, even where the headquarters are purely administrative and not open to the public.

Co-operation

Since the Second World War a number of the Regional Systems in Britain have introduced various forms of subject specialization under which particular libraries are responsible for purchasing books published on particular subjects. All these Regional schemes, whatever their other differences, agree in excluding music. Libraries still buy new scores regardless of those bought or in stock elsewhere, and there is no guarantee that a newly published work will be available in at least one library within the Region—on the other hand, twenty librarians may have decided to buy the score. Some libraries partly remedy the shortages and limitations of their own stocks by taking out subscriptions with the Henry Watson Music Library in Manchester and/or the Liverpool Music Library. Requests for multiple copies of a work, or for a score not in the local stock that is not thought a justifiable purchase, can then be forwarded to one of these large libraries with a very strong likelihood of a satisfactory response.

That some scheme of co-operation is desirable is obvious from the following figures, which were kindly supplied by the then Honorary Secretary of the North-Western Regional Library System in 1954 (Mr. Charles Nowell). In 1953 there were 840 requests for music made through the Regional system: 570 of these were satisfied within the Region but no less than 270 (or 32 per cent) were not— 159 of these unsatisfied requests were for multiple copies of a work; and since the National Central Library does not accept requests of this nature, only the remaining 111 enquiries were forwarded. The N.C.L. was unable to satisfy 68 (or 62 per cent) of these enquiries. Out of the year's 840 requests, therefore, only a total of 613 were satisfied—and this in a Region that includes both Manchester and Liverpool and such other good music libraries as Bolton and Burnley. Requests forwarded to the National Central Library are passed on by that library to the Central Music Library in Westminster for satisfaction and if that library cannot help, then the request is circulated among the other public, university and special libraries in the normal manner. This large percentage of failures is disturbing but is not quite so bad as it might at first appear, nor is the Central Music Library nearly so weak a link as the figures would suggest. The late Mr. Nowell's letter stated that "a very high proportion of music requests lack information. They are more vague than requests for books." For this, individual librarians are to blame. In addition, requests are made that are impossible to fulfil. Music-lovers hear works on the radio and request the scores, but many of these are in manuscript only and have not been published or are not available for general loan. A tremendous corpus of music is out of print and is never likely to become available again. Whereas Warrington's collection was started in 1850, the Central Music Library is a post-war innovation, opened in 1949, and despite the inclusion of several large important private libraries and Westminster's own impressive music stock, its coverage is still small compared with what it could be or would like to be. A tremendous amount of earlier music is to be found in the British Museum but that cannot be borrowed under any circumstances, and a student is not always able to go to the Museum to study the work on the spot or to afford the price of a photostat copy of a work running to more than a few pages.

An answer to part of this problem would appear to be possible both at local and at regional level. When a librarian is considering the purchase of any out-of-the-way music, it might be well worth his while to check with neighbouring libraries which perhaps already have the work in stock and would be prepared to lend it. By co-operation in this way a small local group of libraries can aim at a wider coverage than would be possible in any one of them. The idea can be carried further with the suggestion that some attempt should be made at Regional level to include music in any subject specialization scheme. There would appear to be two possible basic methods. A library would agree to collect all works and editions as published of a particular composer or composers; or, it would agree to buy all scores issued for a particular instrument or group of instruments. The larger libraries would need to accept responsibility for the more important or voluminous composers or for the more popular instruments or collections of instruments; the smaller library would collect the works of a minor master or the music for an unusual instrument. The publication of a separate cumulation of new music scores in the *British Catalogue of Music* has partly removed one of the main problems, that of discovering just what new music or new editions are available in this country.

Music Library Administration

Music in the junior library

While many children learn music, in one form or another, it is probably safe to say that the majority do so under protest. Where there is a feeling that practice is a burden, young musicians are not very likely to use the music scores provided in the library—but there are always those children who will. Piano music, together with smaller selections of violin, violoncello and recorded music and also some vocal music should be provided. This last will include nursery rhymes, settings of verses by A. A. Milne, Lewis Carroll, etc., carols and similar works. Where such a collection is inadequate for the needs of a particular child, the logical course is to send him or her to the adult music section.

Music intended for the use of children should, naturally, be reasonably simple but simplicity and the third-rate should not be confused. There are thousands of pieces allegedly portraying fairies, elves, gnomes and the like at different activities but the greater part of this material has practically no musical value.

Standards should be as high as in the adult library; music by recognized composers should be provided and selection should be made by the music librarian, though the children's librarian ought to be consulted. The reverse process is not recommended. The greatest composers have written music within the compass of many children; the music librarian will know suitable pieces while the children's librarian may be completely unaware of their existence. Books on music and biographies of composers should also be chosen in co-operation; the music librarian will know if the work is factually accurate while the children's librarian can tell if the book is written and presented in a manner likely to appeal to children; she will also check on the typography, illustrations and general layout of the book.

Local activities and local musicians

Music should have its own place in local history. There are amateur operatic societies, local choral societies, local groups, bands, orchestras and soloists who achieve a reputation that may become national or even international. All of these come within the scope of the local collection and the music librarian may well be the best person to obtain relevant material. Programmes of concerts held in the area provide useful information about artists and can give useful

27

background material if any of those mentioned on the programmes later achieve fame. Such programmes have their own place in the social history of the town indicating something of local taste at any given time.

For the local composer treatment should be as generous and comprehensive as for the local author; the public library should collect and retain all available material. The composer may be a very minor one but if the local library does not attempt to accumulate as much material as possible it is tolerably certain that no one else will. Charles Avison (1710–1770) might be quoted as an example. He is a little-known British composer of the eighteenth century and the finest collection of his works and material about him is to be found in the public library at Newcastle-on-Tyne, his home town.

Music periodicals

If possible, music periodicals should be displayed adjacent to the music section or music shelves; where there is a music library in a separate alcove this is almost automatic policy. Most music periodicals include reviews of new music scores, books on music and of gramophone records of standard music. Comments on some of these periodicals and the scope of their reviews will be found in Chapter II.

HANDLING PROBLEMS

These will vary immensely with the type of music or its physical format. A volume of Chopin Waltzes causes no real difficulty; it is of reasonable bulk, will rebind conveniently and can be treated almost exactly as a normal book except that it will require higher and deeper shelf space. Not all music is so convenient for the librarian and some of the more usual problems are briefly considered in this section.

Piano concertos and two-piano works

Some piano concertos are published in versions arranged for solo piano. The pianist, in such an arrangement, plays both the solo and the orchestral accompaniment with the score adapted for the limitations of two hands. The more usual and popular version is that for two pianos. One pianist plays the solo part, i.e. he plays exactly the same score as that used by a concert(o) pianist. The orchestral part is arranged for piano and this reduction is played by the second pianist.

28

Music written for two pianos is a very different matter though obviously there are certain basic similarities. Generally, the composer regards the two pianists of equal standing whereas with the concerto the solo part is normally considered paramount. It is perfectly possible (with two copies) to play piano duets at two pianos but quite hopeless to attempt two-piano works as a piano duet, since both players may be required to use a wide keyboard range. For this reason the two types of music should be classified separately (though preferably at adjoining places): in practice, as is demonstrated in a later chapter, the makers of classification schemes have rarely understood or made allowance for the important separation of two-piano music from piano duet music.

There is generally little point in attempting to play one part of a two-piano piece without its complement so that the two parts should be bound separately but housed within the same cover and automatically issued together. With piano concertos and similar works for piano and orchestra there are many people who get enjoyment by playing the solo part and, when the solo pianist is given a brief rest by the composer, continue to play the accompaniment which is usually indicated in small notes or is shown in parallel staves below that of the solo part. When the soloist re-enters, the domestic pianist returns to his part; the result being that such a one-man performance will bear some similarity to that played from a solo piano arrangement of the concerto. It will be less satisfying to any listener since the pianist using the two-piano arrangement will probably continue to play the solo part even when the melody is being given out by the orchestra; the arranger of a solo piano version would ensure that the melody was given adequate prominence here. So, although two copies of a concerto will be needed for performance at two pianos it may be thought best to bind them separately rather than include them in one cover. This would allow two separate pianists in different localities to enjoy themselves attempting the solo part. It should also result in fairly even wear on the two copies; when housed in the same cover the second copy is likely to receive much less wear than the first. The disadvantage of the complete separation of the two scores is that the user with two pianos, and a partner to play the orchestral score arrangement, may find that only one copy of the work is on the shelves and so have to wait until the second copy is returned.

Orchestral parts

Orchestral parts should be filed in pamphlet boxes or manilla folders; for convenience each work should be housed separately. On

Vl. V2. Va. Vc. C.B. Pic. Fl. Ob. C.A. Cl. Bn.
H. Tr. Trb. Tuba. Timp. Tamb. D. Cym. Harp Gl. Pf.
A.T.B.

the inside cover of the container should be pasted a printed label (or a rubber stamp may be used instead) which quotes the various instruments of the orchestra in the same order as that generally used in publishers' catalogues. A space or box is shown against the name of each instrument and in this is inserted the number of copies held. This assists quick checking upon issue and return and identifies which parts (if any) are missing. It also helps conductors or secretaries of local orchestras who can quickly see if there are sufficient parts for their members.

It is advisable before issuing orchestral parts to reinforce the edges with linen tape or similar material. It is also desirable to check, upon return, that marks of phrasing and bowing, etc., which may have been inserted by the conductor, have been satisfactorily removed.

Anthems, madrigals, etc.

Sets of copies of short choral works can be filed similarly to orchestral parts, in boxes or folders. Only one work should be filed in a box; if this is uneconomic, then there should be some connecting link between works sharing the same folder—the obvious one would be that of composer. For works in small demand the simplest and cheapest filing plan is to pack the set in cardboard and brown paper to exclude dust. A tag should be attached to each parcel showing the composer, title and number of copies. This method is only economical for the work in request not more than once or twice a year; more staff time is lost in packing and unpacking than would pay for a box or folder.

While some of these works can be issued as supplied by the publisher, items difficult to replace or likely to receive regular use, can have the spine strengthened with linen tape, may be sewn into brown paper covers for added strength or laminated or sprayed with plastic. One method may be standard in a library, or each item considered on its merits and treated accordingly.

Sheet music

Music which occupies but a few pages is sometimes avoided by librarians because of handling difficulties. The matter is discussed more fully under the heading "Binding music" (p. 20). Briefly, suitable works may be bound together to make a single volume, or single items can be treated by sewing into stiff manilla or paper covers, or else laminated or sprayed with plastic. If a work is likely to be very rarely in demand and so warrants minimum expenditure, the spine can be strengthened with linen tape and the copy filed. No opinion is ventured on the general argument between those who prefer box files and those who use vertical filing. The former method is more portable and allows more readers to consult an extensive system at the same time; the latter has the advantage of requiring less floor space, though some libraries make the best of both systems by using box files and storing them in cupboards or on open shelves beneath the ordinary shelving—since this space is usually regarded as too low for normal public use. Local circumstances and personal preferences may be allowed to influence the decision as to which method to use.

Biographies, fiction

These are questions of an entirely different type from others discussed in this section and are related to the problem of music classification. They are also administrative problems—whether to shelve books on music and musicians with musical scores or to leave them with other biographies, autobiographies and novels. Since it is difficult to write a life of a composer without some reference to his music and because music-lovers are the people most likely to be interested in these lives, it is recommended that such lives be shelved with the rest of the books on musical history. The case for fiction is weaker though the Library of Congress scheme, for instance, does make provision in its schedules for such novels to be classed separately.

Music Librarianship

Location

The question of the location of a separate music library or of a music section in a general library is an academic one for many librarians but in cases where some choice is available certain factors should be taken into account. The situation preferred should be in a quiet part of the library. There should be room for tables and chairs at which students can read music periodicals and browse. Where the library loans gramophone records, the collection should (where possible) be located in the same section. If music shelves and public accommodation are simply part of the ordinary home-reading department, the preferred position allows adequate oversight from the staff enclosure and should also be related to the daily traffic of the department.

Space required

It is difficult if not impossible to make hard and fast rules about this; it depends upon the available stock, the services offered, the provision or omission of a sound-proof room, etc. Rugby's public library may again be cited as an example. The floor space allotted is 170 sq. ft. (and could be more with advantage). There is 50 ft. of shelving for music scores, 35 ft. for miniature scores, 22 ft. for music books available for loan and 12 ft. for reference books. All sections lack breathing space but no one of them is noticeably shorter of space than the others. The librarian himself would particularly like more space for reference books in order to display them to better advantage. The proportions allotted to the different sections of music stock can vary immensely; in Widnes, for example, the figures are 42 ft., 8 ft., 24 ft. and 8 ft. of shelving respectively. Once again, more room would be welcome in all cases but only books on music (which include biographies) are seriously lacking in space. The biggest and most obvious discrepancy between the two figures is that allowed for the shelving of miniature scores; Rugby has an outstandingly good collection for a library of its size, while at Widnes there is room only for some 400 scores which may be regarded as average for a library in the 45,000 to 55,000 population group, unless there is a gramophone record library when the desirable number of miniature scores is appreciably higher.

It is equally difficult to quote statistics or averages for reserve stock shelving. If the public shelves are obviously insufficient yet space precludes their expansion then a large reserve should be built up. Even the library with space to spare on its music shelves should have some sort of stack for the scores that need to be kept but whose physical condition is no advertisement for the service. The only generalization that can be made is that music is usually certain of a long life so that it is best to plan for more stock space for scores than might appear necessary at first sight in comparison with the size of stock in other classes. Bound vocal scores will average about 15 to a foot of shelving, instrumental at about 24 for piano and organ solos and 16 for violin and other works, with a second part in a pocket for piano accompaniment. Chamber music parts will require about an inch of shelf space per work.

Shelving

The need for special shelving for scores is self-evident. Some librarians prefer adjustable shelving because of its flexibility but the extra cost may not be justified. If fixed shelves are provided, a distance of 14 in. between shelves will be sufficient for nearly all sheet music to stand upright, and a depth of 12 in. should be equally adequate. Because bound music tends to be awkward to handle and is heavy in bulk, upright partitions should be provided at frequent intervals; a minimum of 6 in. and a maximum of 10 in. between such partitions is recommended. These divisions, both with wood and metal shelving, should extend flush to the front edge to minimize possible damage to the scores. As with ordinary bookshelves, it is advisable to restrict the upper and lower shelf limits; the lowest shelf should be about 18 in. from the floor and the top shelf about 63 in., allowing three shelves to the case.

Miniature scores present their own problems and the simplest solution is to provide a special set of shelves, about 9 in. high and some 7 in. deep. This will be suitable for the great majority of scores of this type although there are a number (such as the Vaughan Williams symphonies and some of the Hawkes "pocket" scores) which are too tall for a 9-in. shelf and would have to stand on their fore-edges or be shelved separately. Floor space will be required for vertical files if sheet music is stored in this fashion; where pamphlet boxes are preferred, special shelves may be required and the boxes bought to a standard size. It has already been mentioned that some libraries, rather than waste the space between the floor and bottom shelf make the front panel hinge so that the space under the shelves becomes a cupboard. Orchestral parts and sets of anthems are usually kept in reserve. Shelving for gramophone records is discussed in Chapter V.

If the music library is housed as a separate department its catalogue will be there also. Where the collection is obviously separated from the remainder of the lending stock but is not an independent department it may be thought an advantage to have the appropriate sections of the catalogue adjoining the books and scores. With a classified catalogue this would simply entail the removal of the appropriate subject entries *en bloc*; with a dictionary catalogue a similarly self-contained unit would be easily available if the catchword "Music" is used before all subject headings for scores, but a check of subject headings would be needed for books on music. It would be much more difficult to extract individual entries for composers and writers on music and there are definite advantages in leaving such entries in the normal author sequence.

Staff enclosure

With a separate department it is unfair to expect readers to use the main desk for the issue and return of scores, while gramophone records require ample room to allow individual checking of discs for scratches and other damage. If provision is made for patrons to listen to gramophone records adequate oversight is essential, though this depends in part upon whether the staff or patrons actually handle the discs.

Periodicals, biographies, reference books

If the library has a separate music department then such works as reference books, biographies and the periodicals devoted to music will automatically be shelved in the department rather than in the other sections of the library. If the music collection has a separate alcove or a reasonably self-contained part of the home-reading department then a table and chairs might usefully be provided for the use of patrons.

THE MUSIC LIBRARY

Though the separate music library is the ideal, its provision is expensive and its implications should be considered before establishment. Earlier comments have suggested that such provision, to be

Photo by W. H. Jacques

A neat case for housing music scores, Ilford Public Libraries

To face page 34

justified, postulates a local population of 100,000 or more together with a stock of some 8,000 books, though both figures can be lower if gramophone records are included for public use. A separate department requires a music librarian and at least one assistant.

The music library may permit gramophone record recitals to be held though a library hall may be a more convenient venue. The department may be used for discussion groups, etc., at times outside normal opening hours, while the provision of a radio or television set would permit selected programmes to be heard or seen by a group and discussed afterwards.

Hours of opening present a problem. If the library is to be open for similar hours to those of the general lending library a staff of two will be inadequate without assistance; three people at least will be needed for the department to be entirely self-contained except for holiday periods and absences through sickness. Late evening hours of opening are likely to preclude the possibilities of gramophone recitals and "live" music and similar activities; early closing will be to the disadvantage of the local library user. Where gramophone records are loaned it should be stipulated that records must be returned ten or fifteen minutes before closing time to allow checking of the condition of each disc to take place.

The hours of opening are naturally affected by local demand and use. It may be said that, in general, American libraries are very much more generous in this way than those in Britain. The music library at Boston, Massachusetts, is open from 9 a.m. to 9 p.m. each week-day and from 2 p.m. to 6 p.m. on Sundays. British libraries may open as early in the day but generally close at 7 p.m. or 8 p.m. (and earlier on Saturdays) and do not open on Sundays.

STAFF

A high proportion of librarians and assistants seem to have a liking for classical music and some knowledge of it; this is true both in Britain and the U.S.A. Alice Bryan's *The public librarian*[11] has some pertinent information upon this point, for she attempted to discover the vocational interests of librarians by means of a test devised by Edward K. Strong, jr., Professor of Psychology at Stanford University. The median ratings for fifty-four professional men showed the highest preference for "Musician", though Miss Bryan cautiously points out that this surprising result might not be general if a wider sample was taken. Since musician is excluded from the choice of professions for women no comparable figure can be given. A strong interest in music among British librarians of both sexes is indicated by the answers given in Landau's *Who's who in Librarianship*,[12] since nearly 400 qualified librarians out of the 2,000 or so listed give music as a major interest. Such a high proportion seems incompatible with the equally high proportion of inadequate music stocks in our public libraries. A personal impression is that few public libraries lack at least one staff member who is interested in classical music and all professional members of the staff should be able to answer simple and direct queries.

Recruitment, standards and qualifications

The post of Music Librarian should automatically be on a professional grade, and choice may have to be made between a person with library qualifications but without a degree or diploma in music or one with a music qualification but no library experience; only in the very well paid is it reasonable to expect both. My personal preference is strongly in favour of the appointment of a Chartered Librarian whose musical knowledge should grow with experience. The musician without library qualification is much less likely to be satisfactory as a general rule unless he or she has already had public library experience. Without such experience the librarian may be slow in learning the normal routine, be of limited value if required to assist in another department in case of emergency and, most important of all, may prove to have no aptitude for music librarianship. On the other hand, the Chartered Librarian ought to know, by the time this qualification is achieved, whether work in a music library is likely to make a strong appeal; the music librarian without library qualification is unlikely to be able to move to another department of the system.

The foregoing paragraph must not be taken as an attempt to decry the assistant who possesses a music diploma such as the Licentiateship of the Royal Academy of Music but this and other similar qualifications are gained as either teacher or performer within a very limited field. It does not prove a good knowledge of music outside that specialty or that the possessor has the ability to become a good music librarian. Dr. Kinkeldey[13] may be quoted on this point: "In the first place, and above all else, a music librarian should be a good librarian. I mean by that, that he or she should be a person adapted by nature and temperament to general library work. So far as systematic training goes, he or she would have received a large part of the knowledge which we expect of anyone who is connected with a library. A music librarian who is not thoroughly acquainted with the organization and operation of a general library as we know it today, who is not reasonably familiar with the methods of book selection, ordering, classifying, cataloguing and circulating as practised today, who feels that his work is a domain in itself, and who is disinclined to make his work fit smoothly into the larger mechanism, is more likely to do more harm than all the good a great special knowledge will bring. I do not believe that it is possible to exaggerate the importance of this point." It would be less than fair not to state that there are other illustrious music librarians who feel that subject knowledge should come first and the technique of librarianship should be assimilated by experience. Such persons would often go further and deny that the reverse is true, for they consider that the necessary knowledge of music implicit in a good music librarian is most difficult to acquire.

The post of Chief of the Music Division or Department is one of acknowledged responsibility and status in the United States, particularly in the large library systems. The holder of the post will always be a graduate, though music may not necessarily have been either a major or minor subject in the degree studies. Irrespective of country, the post in any library calls for a fair knowledge of music history, an ability to read music and a willingness to increase musical knowledge both in width and depth throughout one's working life. In addition, both Doctors Savage in Britain and Kinkeldey in the U.S.A. stress the need to have a good working knowledge of French, German and Italian. The poor linguist can often manage to translate title pages and publishers' catalogues with a limited vocabulary acquired by experience plus the aid of a dictionary but this cannot be regarded as really adequate for the good music librarian. An ability to read and transliterate the Russian alphabet to a degree sufficient to catalogue a title-page correctly is an added qualification.

Dr. Kinkeldey is firm on this ability to read foreign languages, for he has said:[13] "Although we say that music is a universal language, the foreign vernacular with which it is often associated is a great stumbling-block to the linguistically deficient musician. . . . In fact, the librarian who wishes to rely for his knowledge on journals, histories, encyclopaedias and dictionaries in English only cannot go very far." On performing ability he added: "It does not seem to me to be necessary that a music librarian should be a good performer or composer. To be sure, one who sings well and plays an instrument well and one who is able to create an actual musical composition, is more likely than another to understand the peculiar nature of the material in his charge as a librarian. But he may be a wholly adequate librarian without these accomplishments. On the other hand, a reasonable acquaintance with musical theory in the widest acceptance of the word; a knowledge of its principles and technical terms is a fair requirement. A music librarian who did not recognize a fugue when he heard it, or saw it on paper, or who did not know the meaning of the term double counterpoint, would be as useful as a literary librarian who did not know the difference between an epic and a sonnet. . . ."

Status and salaries

The preceding section has indicated that the music librarian should possess a library qualification, a music qualification or, best of all, qualification in both fields. In addition he should have a working knowledge of two or more foreign languages and a good general musical background. "Such people are not to be found in the hedgerows; they must be sought after and retained by satisfactory salaries and proper opportunities." Thus Mr. McColvin wrote in 1937,[14] but the present reality can only be regarded as depressing.

The best-paid music librarians in British public libraries are all graded below certain other specialists though it may be claimed that the technical demands made upon them are equally high. Almost invariably the post is on the lowest professional scale; this is acceptable in a small or medium-sized library but can hardly be regarded as encouraging in a city with a population of nearly 300,000. It is surprising to find that British music librarians are well qualified and enthusiastic as a whole; one feels that it is more than our profession has deserved.

Taking the financial reward as a yardstick (and while not ideal, it has many merits) it can be seen that music librarians in Britain have a low status indeed. Prospects of promotion within the field are extremely slight since nearly all the posts are paid on the professional minimum. The great majority of the posts have been created since 1945 but a large number of openings with very little chance of a better-paid post in a large library is of little value to the assistant with ambition.

The American scene looks very much brighter to the British librarian, though much more dismal at first hand. There are enough music librarians for them to have their own Association which may be regarded as good for status and common interest and enthusiasm. Large cities pay the chief of the Music Department an annual salary of 5,000 dollars or considerably more and this represents a far greater reward than is at present possible in Britain, even allowing for the differences in living standards. The Music Library Association maintains a personnel file for employment opportunities; an honorary officer apparently acts as a link between music librarians who wish to move and libraries that have vacancies. A number of music librarians are well known in the musical life of the U.S.A., appear in radio and television programmes, write books and articles and generally keep the profession in the public mind.

Otto Luening, in general agreement with other writers, suggests the following criteria for qualification and knowledge:[6] "The ideal music librarian has had both library and musical training, is community minded, and is able to work effectively with community music leaders, musicians, and music-lovers. A person with all these qualifications is hard to find. It is of primary importance, however, that the music librarian be community-minded and have the ability and knowledge to meet and discuss music with professionals and laymen alike. Such a person need not have had both types of specialized training to be a music librarian, although one or the other is necessary. In a few towns which have had an active musical life for some time, an active adult education programme, and well-conducted school and college music courses, the library music department is often widely used in spite of inadequate leadership." But, Luening continues: "Because the salaries paid music librarians are so low, many qualified persons do not enter this field, or if they do, often leave it before they are fully trained. Thus, the ideal music librarian, as described above, is difficult to find, and once found, to hold. And those who do work successfully in these positions must either have some private income or be so idealistic about public service that they are willing to make considerable financial sacrifice to participate in it."

In-service training

In public libraries that possess a separate music department, junior assistants should automatically work in it for a short period under the supervision of the music librarian, on the assumption that training will include duty in each of the system's specialist departments. Such training must not be regarded as obviating the need for regular assistants to take charge when the music librarian is off duty or absent. It has already been stated that a staff of three is the minimum for a library to be open the normal hours (between fifty and sixty per week) but the staff may be limited to two plus part-time assistance from other departments—a method that has both advantages and disadvantages.

Assistants allotted to permanent duty in the department should naturally be those who have shown interest and aptitude during their training period and not those who cannot be found suitable posts in other departments. These apprentice assistants will make mistakes that are obvious to the knowledgeable enquirer, but the keen and interested junior will learn rapidly.

Training facilities outside the library

There are no real training facilities for music librarians in Britain. The full-time library schools have insufficient demand to run special courses and the potential vacancies for music librarians are so few that tutors cannot be expected to lay special stress on the bibliographical tools of music. At present, the best solution would seem to be for the interested assistant to spend some time in one of those libraries that have a separate music library and a qualified music librarian in charge, such as Edinburgh, Liverpool, Manchester or Westminster. The expense of sending the assistant to one of these libraries for three or four weeks would be well repaid in an improved service in the home library within a very short period.

At present there is a further step available for the assistant who has passed the Registration examination of the Library Association. Part 3 of the current syllabus for the Final examination is entitled "Subject approach to the literature of the Arts and Sciences", and a section, 3(f), is devoted to "The literature and librarianship of music". This examination should not be beyond the capabilities of the assistant in the public library who has had the opportunity and interest to devote time and study to the music section. The assistant living or working within easy reach of London is fortunate in that a course on music librarianship is held about every other year, under the auspices of the North-Western Polytechnic. For assistants outside the Home Counties there is a correspondence course for the examination, devised and edited by Mr. J. H. Davies, the Music Librarian of the British Broadcasting Corporation.

The L.A's Final examination, part 3(f), is probably not really adequate for the music librarian but is sufficient for the assistant who is in charge of the music section in a library with no established post for music or gramophone librarian. It is possible, though difficult, for the professionally qualified librarian to study for a music qualification in his spare time. None of the accepted music diplomas or degrees really covers the best range of subjects for a music librarian. In discussion at the first Week-end Conference of the United Kingdom Branch of the International Association of Music Libraries it was suggested that the most suitable degree syllabus for the music librarian is that of Bachelor of Arts at Durham; unfortunately, this is an internal degree only though the same university accepts external candidates both for its Bachelor and Doctor of Music; these are much less useful to the music librarian since they are intended for performers and teachers. A possible answer to this problem would be the creation of a Diploma in Music Librarianship, to be the joint responsibility of the Library Association and the U.K. Branch of the International Association of Music Libraries. A qualification of real standing, designed for this particular field, might well help to raise the status of music librarianship and could provide a most useful and helpful course for the qualified librarian who wished to specialize in this aspect of our work.

Despite the much higher number of librarians and assistants in the U.S.A. and the incomparably greater number of openings in music libraries, the problem of training has not been satisfactorily solved in that country. An article by Anna Harriet Heyer, then of the North Texas State College, entitled *Where to train in music librarianship* [15] illustrates the point. Five years later, in 1956, the position was not appreciably better. Mr. Edward N. Waters, Assistant Chief of the Music Division of the Library of Congress, in response to an enquiry on this point wrote in his letter: "For a number of years there has been a keen interest in the United States in advancing the cause of special library education. Unfortunately, not very much has been done about it, the real reason (in my opinion) being a conflict of demands which so far has defied solution. This conflict arises from a feeling that the prospective librarian must acquire library training first and the opposite view that he must

41

acquire his subject training first. I incline very strongly to the second point of view."

"The American Library Association accredits the Library schools in America, but these schools in turn cannot institute special curricula unless the number of students makes them economically feasible. . . ." This is a problem related to that facing our own library schools.

Music library organizations

In Britain there is but one organization that caters in any way for the music librarian and that is the United Kingdom Branch of the International Association of Music Libraries, which includes both individual and corporate members. Its membership is spread over the whole field of music librarianship, with representatives of national, university and public libraries, and also from music schools and the music trade. Public librarians are in a distinct minority so that the assistant from this type of library will get a useful corrective to any parochial viewpoint. Because the numbers are small, rather less than 150 at the time of writing, most of the meetings have been held in London.

The I.A.M.L. produces the periodical *Fontes artis musicae* twice yearly, and the U.K. Branch is one of the contributors to this journal, which receives comment in Chapter II. The Branch was also partly responsible for the inauguration of *The British Catalogue of Music*.

The Music Library Association makes an interesting contrast. It was founded in 1931 "To promote the development of music libraries; to encourage studies in the organization and administration of music in libraries", and has a membership of over eight hundred. Nearly all American music librarians and many professional assistants in music libraries belong to the Association which also includes a number of non-librarians—people in the music publishing and recording industries, for instance, who provide a valuable leaven. The M.L.A. is divided into "Chapters" for geographical convenience; the Los Angeles, San Francisco, New York and Washington are the most active simply because the concentration of members is heaviest in those areas. Here, on a wider scale, is a repetition of one of the difficulties facing the U.K. Branch of the I.A.M.L. There are usually two national meetings annually; one is traditionally held in association with the annual conference of the M.L.A., while the other is usually independent though it may coincide with a national meeting of a kindred organization.

The M.L.A. has over a dozen standing Committees, each dealing with a specific topic such as Copyright, Library Training and a Survey of Library Resources. A committee of the M.L.A. prepared a draft code for music cataloguing much of which was subsequently incorporated into the Library of Congress rule 9 and the *A.L.A. Cataloguing Code* rule 12. The professional journal of the Association, ambiguously entitled *Notes*, is outstanding for its comprehensive reviews of new books and scores; this periodical is given more detailed mention in Chapter II. The very strength of the M.L.A. perhaps accounts for the small number of American members of the I.A.M.L.

It seems improbable that there will ever be a sufficient number of music librarians in Britain to make possible a British version of the M.L.A., and the U.K. Branch of the International Association of Music Libraries is therefore playing a double role, and playing it well.

OTHER ADMINISTRATIVE PROBLEMS

Music tickets, charging methods

It used to be common for public libraries to issue, upon request, special tickets for use with music books or scores only. This practice is now almost obsolete owing to the continued trend towards fewer restrictions on book borrowing. Libraries that do issue special tickets for music have to ensure that their use is limited for that specific purpose and the most effective method would seem to be the adoption of a different coloured manilla or cloth from that for other types of ticket. Where the issue of students', subject or other supplementary tickets is adequate (to bring the total available to a reader up to five or six, with a higher figure on request if a satisfactory case is made) the need for separate music tickets is non-existent. With photocharging, Dickman or other methods which allow unlimited book borrowing, the problem does not arise.

It is unusual, both in Britain and the U.S.A., for ordinary library tickets to be available for the loan of gramophone records; the circulation of discs is normally restricted to special tickets. This is considered in Chapter V.

Generally speaking, charging methods for books and scores will be exactly similar to those for other types of material. It is sometimes difficult with unbound music to find a suitable place for the date label and pocket, where these are used, but the problem should not be insoluble. Volumes that include separate parts in a rear pocket, etc., will take longer to issue and discharge because of the need to check the presence of loose parts at each transaction.

Issue statistics

A separate music library will naturally keep its own statistics, probably in some detail. Where the music section is part of the general home-reading department there is still good reason to count music issues separately. It is simple enough to provide an extra column for class 780 (or its equivalent in other schemes of classification). If the figures are sufficiently large, then a case for a subject department of some type is strengthened; if they are small in relation to other use, then development and expansion of the section may well be indicated. There are examples of good collections receiving much less use by the local public than is deserved by the quality and range of the music provided, but this is not frequent. If the number of books and scores is quoted separately, a comparison with the stocks and amount of borrowing in other libraries is easily made. There is a possible discrepancy here, for some libraries count the loan of 20 copies of an anthem to a choir as "1 issue", while others inflate their figures by counting such a loan as "20 issues"; arguments can be found in favour of either method.

Stationery

In general the music department will use standard stationery; a specially printed or duplicated request form may be useful, however, to ensure that readers' requests are answered correctly and satisfactorily. When a book is requested and the reader knows the correct author and title, few problems are likely to arise; but if an assistant notes that a patron wants Beethoven's seventh symphony, without further details, several points arise needing solution. Does the reader want a miniature score, an arrangement for piano duet or for organ? If the request is for Verdi's *Nabucco* is it a vocal score that is required? Will the enquirer be satisfied with a score showing the original words only; does he want an English translation or does he require both the original Italian and a translation? Such problems can be frustrating if not correctly answered, and this type of query is very common. A special form would help to eliminate most of these possible alternatives. There are arguments both for and against such a form being completed by the enquirer or filled in by the member of the staff answering the enquiry. The type of form suggested is that devised and used in Eccles P.L. (and since copied and used in a number of other libraries). The reverse of the form, for staff use only, is used as a record of the steps taken in order to prevent duplication of effort in answering the query. Several of the questions on this particular all-purpose form[16] can serve a useful purpose with music requests:

Level. Introductory/Elementary/Intermediate/Advanced/
   Research
Language. German/French/Spanish/Italian/ . . .

while the questions relating to music only are:

Music score. Vocal/Miniature/Instrumental/Full/Parts/
   Arranged for..................

Rules and regulations

There would seem to be no particular need for different rules and regulations for the music section, except perhaps for the loan period. For individual users the standard, normally fourteen days, is probably sufficient and renewal is no more or less difficult than for any other book borrowed from the library. For societies and choirs the position is different since the sets of scores and parts are generally borrowed for the work to be learned and/or performed, and so may be required for a matter of weeks or possibly months. Most libraries that supply copies in bulk make due allowance for this. West Riding County, for instance, allows a maximum loan period of eight months without renewal and after that time the copies may usually be renewed for a further lengthy period. There is also the proviso that works on long loan may be recalled before the expiry of the period if necessity dictates. If fines are charged for bulk loans, special rates are necessary as the scale would be prohibitive if levied on each individual copy. Separate rules and regulations will be required for a gramophone record library.

The very large music library will normally accept reservations for bulk loan of copies some months ahead of the actual date required. This will help both the society and the music librarian. For a practical method of making the necessary arrangements and for the provision of a scheme that allows for some copies only of a work to be loaned, readers are referred to an article by Mr. Leonard W. Duck in *The Library Association Record* for April, 1950 (pp. 118–20) entitled "The multiple issue system in the Henry Watson Music Library". Every library, whatever its size, will normally accept reservations for individual items in its stock.

Publicity

There is, as a long-term policy, only one really successful type of publicity and that is an adequate, effective and well-administered music library. Satisfied users are our best and cheapest advertisement. It is useless, and indeed detrimental, to attract music-lovers to the library by any means of publicity unless we are sure that we have a fair chance of satisfying their legitimate needs. Outside publicity should be shunned until the section has not only a good basic stock but also a few less-popular works that are likely to interest the music-lover whose personal library includes the basic works in the fields in which he is interested or for whom the standard repertory has become a trifle hackneyed. The pianist who is well acquainted with the works of the major classical composers for the instrument may well be attracted by the works of a minor master or a modern writer with whose compositions he has no first-hand acquaintance.

Printed material provided by public libraries for the music section may be divided into three categories. First come the catalogues of the complete music stock; these may be printed in a single volume or in a series of smaller handbooks, each covering a particular section of the music stock. Secondly, there are the leaflets, pamphlets and handbooks devoted to parts of the stock—works which may well resemble the handbooks mentioned in the previous sentence. Thirdly, libraries may provide lists of recent accessions or special publicity material to celebrate an occasion such as the centenary of a composer's birth, etc. Both librarians and students would be well advised to see as many different types of publication as possible, to compare the variety of information given, the general appearance and layout, and to judge for themselves the probable impact upon the music-lovers for whom each list is intended. If at all possible some similar American lists should also be examined; the standard of paper and of printing is frequently very much superior to that employed in Britain.

The largest printed catalogue of music issued by a public library in Britain is probably that of Liverpool; it is an invaluable check list and reference aid, if a little pedestrian in appearance. Newcastle-on-Tyne has also issued a catalogue of most of its music collection, but in the form of a series of slim volumes; these are excellent for content, layout and typography and are most strongly recommended as a model. Entries include the name of the publisher, often a vital piece of information to an enquirer. Because the average user of a county library service can see but a small fraction of the entire stock, printed or duplicated catalogues may be regarded as almost a necessity for counties. The standard is usually lower than would seem desirable, though there are some good sectional lists such as the printed ones of Nottinghamshire and the duplicated ones of West Riding which include a special catalogue of Brass Band Music (arranged under composer and with a full title index).

Sectional lists published for stronger sections of the music stock or for types of music in most general demand are fairly common. They need not be too elaborate and if sold for a small sum may well recover much of the original cost. Good printed lists of miniature scores, for example, have been issued by Ealing and Hove. Any library possessing 250 or more miniature scores would be justified in publishing such a hand list; if the collection is divided between central and branch libraries a note on allocation would be useful and, as stressed earlier, the name of the publisher should always be quoted. The information concerning any individual item should always be sufficient for it to be identified beyond doubt. A far smaller collection than 250 scores would justify the publication of a list of organ music, for instance. To ensure its reception by people for whom it is intended the information should be provided together with a printed or duplicated letter and sent to the organist of every local church. The list would include the library's holdings of organ scores, books on the instrument and possibly biographies and autobiographies likely to be of particular interest. Lives of Bach and César Franck would be examples; H. C. Colles's life of Sir Walford Davies a less obvious choice. The library's collection may be too small to interest the occasional full-time professional musician though he may still consider it of sufficient merit to recommend his pupils to use it. Similar lists could be sent to local teachers of the piano and violin, to members of local choral societies, orchestras and gramophone societies.

Lists of recent additions are required by the larger library whose music accessions warrant this publicity. The quarterly bulletin published by Manchester Public Libraries is possibly the best of this type of publication. As for anniversaries, centenaries and special occasions, they are frequent and can provide the necessary excuse to draw patrons' attention to the holdings of the library in different fields of music. The bicentenary of Mozart's birth resulted in some dozens of lists, with an outstanding example produced by Sheffield. Such an event does not occur every year but the Promenade Concert season of the British Broadcasting Corporation, a local music festival or some other suitable event should not be difficult to find. Two provisos only must be observed—that the special lists are not produced so frequently that they become ineffective in their task of drawing attention to a part of the library's holdings, and that there is enough relevant material in stock to make the list worth preparing. A small but well-produced list should be within the capacity of the very small library and it is probably worth the expense of building up a section of the music stock in order to make the list one that will attract music-lovers.

A simple and permanent display may be made of music due for performance on the radio during the week ahead. Once users become used to the idea the selection should receive regular use—providing that the scores displayed are checked daily and items broadcast during the previous twenty-four hours removed and returned to the ordinary shelves and any other available works added for the week ahead. Such a scheme is operated in a number of libraries, including Eastbourne, and appears to justify the time and trouble taken.

In addition to this semi-permanent display, occasional ones would be made for particular local activities, concerts, anniversaries, etc. A notice-board should also be shown in a music library displaying posters of forthcoming concerts that are taking place within reasonable travelling range of the town (or of festivals that may be visited during holiday periods), prospectuses of gramophone societies and similar local groups, perhaps an "amateur exchange" to put instrumentalists and vocalists in touch with one another with a view to combining forces and, of course, notices of any musical functions that are being organized by the library itself. Accessions lists, already mentioned, may prove a useful reminder to users of the scope of the collection as well as providing information to individuals of additions to their own particular sphere of interest. The small and medium-sized library would probably find one or two lists a year sufficient; there is no point in producing them more frequently unless there is a large number of accessions. If the library produces a general bulletin of recent additions, then music should naturally be included. Where there is a separate music library it should receive individual mention in the annual report.

Otto Luening's ideal of what a music library should do is as follows:[6] "The department maintains a bulletin board for programme announcements, musical news, events, contests, scholarships, and so forth, and makes book lists in connection with concerts, new musical motion pictures, and radio broadcasts. It also prepares reading and listening lists for groups of clubs and for general distribution to all library agencies in the region. The library sends out music on interlibrary loan whenever this is feasible." British libraries, at least, participate in the last of these suggestions even if too many do not follow the other practices mentioned.

A library with space and sufficient local interest may consider the idea of an exhibition of music and related material. It is not usually difficult to borrow suitable items for display, and ideas may be obtained from an illustrated article by an American librarian, A. Beverly Barksdale[17], which provides much useful information to anyone staging such an exhibition, under the headings Planning, Procuring, Presenting and Promoting.

Extension work

There are a number of British libraries which hold gramophone recitals in the building, thus providing excellent publicity for both gramophone record library and the music section. The recitals may be given by a member of the library staff, by outside lecturers or by a combination of both. Busy city libraries have found lunch-hour concerts popular (Holborn provides an example) but evening meetings are the general rule. A well-printed or duplicated brochure for the series of lectures (Hornsey may be cited as an outstanding example here) and notices announcing each individual recital should provide an audience of adequate size and interest. Many British gramophone societies use the local public library as their headquarters; frequently the librarian is the secretary of the society, which may provide its own record reproducer stored at the library. Ruislip offers an example of this, but the opposite occurs at Bolton where the library authority provides both accommodation and an excellent gramophone record reproducer but otherwise has no direct connection with the local gramophone society.

Music Librarianship

Library activities need not be limited to gramophone record recitals. It may be possible to arrange listening or discussion groups in which a radio programme or a gramophone record is heard and is then the subject of group comment. On a more ambitious scale the library can provide "live" concerts, in the building or at some other more suitable venue such as the local Town Hall. Bolton, for instance, engages first-class artists who attract large audiences despite the town's proximity to Manchester and all the music-making that goes on in that city. Croydon gives a regular series of mid-week lunch-hour concerts, again with performers of high quality. In this case the Chief Librarian guarantees a commercial concert agency a sum against losses on the concerts, and this sum provides the maximum amount that the corporation will be called upon to pay at the end of a season. Plymouth's new Central Library possesses a delightful auditorium with a concert grand piano and first-class gramophone reproducing equipment; here again, the library is fulfilling a real need with both live and recorded concerts. Manchester's Henry Watson Library has given some "At homes" with singing and instrumental music provided for the enjoyment of library users and some excellent publicity in the *Manchester Guardian* the following morning. Libraries may well be able to give young local musicians a chance to display their talents in public. Concerts of any kind are usually free unless a charge for admission is made under the provisions of a local Act.

American librarians appear to have a far greater awareness of the need for extension work on a wide scale. Two American music librarians, George R. Henderson and Dorothy A. Linder, who were Chief and Assistant Chief of the Music Division in the Washington, D.C., Public Library at the time they wrote, gave some idea of what extension work can mean when they suggested that:[18] "It means emerging from the library building and taking the music division into as many activities as possible." Their proposals include record recitals and community singing (to be led by the music librarian) to be given before open-air film shows; the possibility of projecting a copy of the score on to a screen by means of a film-strip during the performance of a recorded work (as is apparently done in Philadelphia)[19]; the need for the music librarian to be prepared to act as a public speaker and to give book reviews to interested groups. In addition the authors suggest library-sponsored radio broadcasts and feel that the librarian should serve on local music committees. No

Part of a Mozart Exhibition, Cincinnati and Hamilton County Public Library, 1956

indication was given of how many libraries actually undertake any of these suggested activities.

Denver's music librarian writes programme notes for the local symphony orchestra; British amateur orchestras might be glad of a similar service. The concert notes for the Hallé Orchestra are often written by Leonard Duck, Librarian of Manchester's Henry Watson Library to supplement those of his predecessor, the late John F. Russell. Brief notes of a similar character are occasionally contributed to *The Radio Times* by J. H. Davies, the Corporation's Music Librarian. Where there are music festivals held locally, opportunities for the music librarian should certainly occur.

Finance

In Britain the discount on sheet music has apparently been progressively reduced. James Duff Brown wrote in 1893:[20] "When ordering music it will often be found of some advantage to approach the publishers directly, especially if the selection made from the list of one firm runs into a respectable amount. Discounts ranging from 25 to 50 per cent will generally be allowed on a fair order, and all the bother of employing an intermediary will be saved." Between the two World Wars it had become the custom to order from a music dealer and public libraries were allowed the same discount as that granted to professional musicians and music teachers, i.e. 2d. in the shilling. This "professional" discount has now disappeared and British public library suppliers have agreed to standardize the discount offered to public libraries at 10 per cent (with some exceptions for foreign importations), the same reduction given by booksellers. The only major difference is that it is not necessary to have music suppliers included on the licence issued to public libraries by the Publishers' Association for the discount to be operative. In the U.S.A. there is no standard rate of discount, and a library gets the best terms it can—which may be very good indeed.

A public library will have its stock and its records (catalogues, accession file, etc.) insured and the figure should be checked every two or three years to ensure that the cover is adequate. It must be borne in mind that music is expensive, binding costs represent a much higher figure than in other departments and that the provision of catalogue entries is often much more difficult and time-consuming (and therefore more expensive) than average. For these reasons the department should have a rather higher sum allotted for its annual needs for books and binding than might appear equitable at first sight.

Conclusion

This chapter has attempted to show the need for a well-developed music section, even in the very small library. It has also given some suggested answers to certain problems that are likely to arise—though there may well be other questions that have not been considered in this chapter. Finally, one point must be stressed again. Money spent on good classical music is never wasted, even though it may be a very slow process to persuade the right sort of potential user to come and take full advantage of the services offered by his public library.

FOR FURTHER READING

Students are advised to check the files of *Library Science Abstracts* for résumés of articles dealing with different aspects of music library administration in a number of countries. For a brief outline of music librarianship written for the non-specialist, the British reader would do well to read "Musical scores and recordings" by the distinguished American music librarian, Vincent H. Duckles of the University of California, in *Library Trends* for October, 1955 (pp. 164–73). A number of quotations have been taken from the *Library Journal* of 1st November 1951, a number devoted to music and the theatre. This, too, is most informative and interesting.

McColvin, L. R., *and* Reeves, Harold. *Music libraries*, v. 1 (Grafton). 1937.

Though the first chapter only is specifically relevant here, no interested reader will fail to read the other chapters that precede the lists of books. The whole work has done an immense amount of good for music librarianship both in Britain and the U.S.A.

Moore, Miss G. *A library of music scores* (Library Association Record; February, 1949) pp. 45–8.

This article gives an interesting picture of the Music Department in a large county library. It emphasizes the seasonal nature of demand by choirs, orchestras and classes, and gives brief details of some of the administrative methods used.

Music Library Administration

SAVAGE, E. A. *Special librarianship* (Grafton). 1939.

This book reprints some papers and articles by Dr. Savage. The student will find "Special librarianship in public libraries" (pp. 24–35) and "One way to form a music library" (pp. 63–84) of both value and interest. The approach is often unorthodox, it is certainly challenging, and Dr. Savage could not be boring if he tried. For those who have not access to this book, the articles may also be found in *The Library Association Record* for November and December 1937, and for October 1935 respectively.

REFERENCES

1. *The Library Assistant*. August-September, 1950, p. 111.
2. Charles Ammi CUTTER. Report for 1896 (Forbes Library, Northampton, Mass.).
3. TILLY, Dorothy. [*You and your music;*] *maintenance costs*. (New York: Library Journal; November 1st, 1951), p. 1774.
4. MARTIN, Alice M. *The Music Library—physical considerations* (Chicago: University of Illinois Library School—Occasional papers, no. 2, September 1949) [mimeographed].
5. SAVAGE, E. A. *Special libraries*. (Grafton, 1939), p. 32.
6. LUENING, Otto. *Music materials and the public library; an analysis of the public library in the field of music.*
7. SAVAGE, E. A. *Op. cit.*, p. 65.
8. SMITH, Greta. [*You and your music;*] *Selection and purchase of music*. (New York: Library Journal; November 1st, 1951), p. 1775.
9. SAVAGE, E. A. *Op. cit.*, p. 71.
10. KINKELDEY, Otto. *Training for music librarianship; aims and opportunities* (Chicago: A.L.A. Bulletin; August, 1937), p. 461.
11. BRYAN, Alice I. The public librarian (New York: Columbia U.P., 1952), pp. 124–6.
12. LANDAU, Thomas, *ed. Who's who in librarianship* (Cambridge: Bowes, 1953), pp. 257–60.
13. KINKELDEY, Otto. *Op. cit.*
14. McCOLVIN, L. R., *and* REEVES, Harold. *Music libraries*, xv. 1 (Grafton, 1937), p. 47.
15. HEYER, Anna Harriet. *Where to train in music librarianship* (New York: Library Journal; November 1st, 1951), pp. 1786–8.
16. BRYON, J. F. W. *Subject enquiries* (Librarian & Book World; January, 1954), p. 2.
17. BARKSDALE, A. Beverly. *On the planning and arranging of music exhibitions* (Washington, D.C.: Notes; September, 1953), pp. 565–9.
18. HENDERSON, George R., *and* LINDER, Dorothy A. *Library music echoes in the community* (New York: Library Journal; November 1st, 1951), pp. 1741–7.

19. KONATSKY, Harry L., *and* COHN, Arthur. *Now they see as well as hear* (New York: Library Journal; June 15th, 1949), pp. 965–8.

20. BROWN, James Duff. *Guide to the formation of a music library* (Library Association, 1893), p. 3.

[Unless otherwise indicated, the place of publication is always London.]

Chapter II

REFERENCE BOOKS AND PERIODICALS

There are hundreds of reference books on music of varying age, scope and quality. There are also dozens of periodicals dealing with different aspects of music. A limited number of the major works in English together with a selection of periodicals are described for the aid they provide towards the selection of music and gramophone records. Nearly all the reference books should be in the stock of the medium-sized library which may also usefully provide a selection of the periodicals.

The exclusion of works in foreign languages is deliberate since these are normally found only in the largest libraries, while their value must be limited for the great majority of the public. It is probable that a French dictionary of music, for example, will contain the best articles on French composers and will also include information on any musicians whose international reputation is not sufficiently high for entries to appear in British, American, German and other music dictionaries but who are regarded by their compatriots as of some standing. A selection of important music reference books in French and German is to be found listed between pages 346 and 356 of the seventh edition of *Guide to reference books*, by Constance M. Winchell (Chicago: American Library Association, 1951) and also in Appendix I of *Schirmer's guide to books on music and musicians . . .* which receives separate consideration in this chapter. Students should consult both sources.

This chapter is, in fact, primarily for the student but the librarian could find the section on bibliography, for example, of value; the notes and comments on periodicals might also provide assistance since these publications are included (as mentioned above) mainly for their value as sources of reviews of books, scores and records. Periodicals such as *Organ*, important in their chosen field but omitting book reviews, are not discussed.

The first part of the chapter deals with reference works under the following headings: (a) General dictionaries and cyclopaedias; (b) Special dictionaries; (c) Bibliography; (d) History; (e) Opera; (f) Vocal music; (g) Chamber music, and (h) Gramophone records. The second part of the chapter considers the periodicals alphabetically.

(a) GENERAL DICTIONARIES AND CYCLOPAEDIAS

Though music dictionaries and encyclopaedias may vary considerably in size the scope and arrangement is usually much the same; the primary difference is in the amount of detail and the provision (or lack) of bibliographies. The usual contents include biographies of the more important composers (though the *Harvard dictionary of music* specifically excludes biographical entries) together with full or condensed lists of their works, and possibly brief notes on minor composers and other people (such as musical publishers and impresarios) who have some importance in the history of music. There are also definitions of musical terms, descriptions of instruments both current and obsolete and perhaps some epitomes of opera plots. All dictionaries of this type will show some degree of national bias—in the choice of subjects for entry and in the relative lengths of entries. For this reason alone British librarians should try to include in stock at least one non-English work to act as a balance or corrective to the obvious choices of Grove, Scholes, etc. For small and medium libraries the choice is likely to be an American work but larger libraries might consider the inclusion of a foreign encyclopaedia such as Blume's *Musik in Geschichte und Gegenwart* which is considered by many to be the most truly international in scope but which obviously needs a working knowledge of German to be of real value.

When possible, students are advised to compare entries for the same composer or topic in different dictionaries. Not only will this bring to notice differences in treatment, scope, method of entry, etc., but may also serve to underline differences of a more material nature. Dates of birth and death of particular composers, for instance, are not always identical in different dictionaries.

BLOM, Eric. Everyman's dictionary of music, 2nd edn. 1954. (Dent)

The first edition of this work was published in 1946 in what was then the standard *Everyman* format; in the intervening period the publishers introduced a new format for this famous series by increasing the page size slightly. The second edition of this dictionary has this advantage which results in a volume that is easier to handle than its predecessor and whose pages have a less cramped appearance. The amazing amount of information included is the more remarkable when one considers the limited size of the single volume and there are some features that are not easily discovered in much larger works though these items have normally been incorporated into the latest edition of *Grove* whose editor is the compiler of this smaller dictionary. Entries for composers include forenames, full date and place of birth and death, brief biographical details and a condensed list of the most important works. Major composers are given adequate treatment: the entry for Mozart, for example, covering well over a page. Some compression is achieved by the frequent use of abbreviations, as might be exemplified by the following extract from the entry for Joseph Lanner: "Anxious to cond. an orch. he began by getting together a stg. 4tet, in which J. Strauss, sen., played va." In addition to the normal entries expected in a work of this type there is a generous sprinkling of title entries. There is also a list of national anthems showing (when known) the authors of the words and composers of the music; entries under literary figures showing which works have been used by composers (the entry for Shakespeare requires more than two pages); an entry for works that have been inspired by paintings, etc., and a useful list of "Collective works".

Details for performers are usually very limited and entries for those still living are restricted to executants with a national or international reputation. Students should note that the alphabetical arrangement is on the "nothing-before-something" principle and attention is drawn to this in the work's preface. This reference book is particularly useful in the small library which has a quick-reference selection only and not a separate reference department. The work contains no illustrations nor quotations in music type.

BLOM, Eric, *editor*. Grove's dictionary of music and musicians, 5th edn. 1954. 9 vols. (Macmillan)

This is undoubtedly the best-known British musical dictionary. Sir George Grove was the first Director of the Royal College of Music and he contributed a number of articles and the preface to the first edition which appeared in 1879 in four volumes. The second edition edited by J. A. Fuller-Maitland, was published between 1904 and

1910. The third and fourth editions were published in 1927–8 and 1940; in each case the editor was H. C. Colles. The fourth edition was a corrected reprint of the third, with the addition of a fifth (supplementary) volume. The current edition is of much greater length than its predecessors, as its number of volumes indicates, and is a radically revised work in which the type has been completely reset. Articles, generally, are longer than in previous editions and the editor has included many subjects that are new to the dictionary.

Entries are arranged in a single alphabetical sequence and there is no separate index though a limited number of cross-references are provided in the text. A list of contributors is given at the beginning of the first volume; against each name stand the initials that are used to identify the writer at the end of each article. There is also an index of initials to allow users to identify quickly the particular writer of any article without the need to work through the list of contributors.

"Grove aims at being encyclopaedic and universal. Whatever a user who possesses a general musical knowledge, or hopes to acquire one, may seek in these pages he may reasonably expect to find, if not under its own heading, then with the aid of a cross-reference that will guide him to what he wants." That is a high claim but it seems to be a justified one. The dictionary contains information upon composers, performers (many of whom are still living and active), musical instruments, form, etc. Light music and jazz receive very limited treatment but there are entries for composers such as George Gershwin and Eric Coates. Music is not confined to that of the western world for there are long contributions on "Indian music", "Indonesian music" and the like. Articles vary in length from a few lines to over thirty of the work's double-columned pages. For major composers the entries are divided into two parts: the first is limited almost entirely to biographical detail, while the second is devoted to compositions. Lengthy articles have captions at the top of each page to assist quick reference; for instance, page 300 of the first volume has as its heading "BACH (J. S.): Conditions at Leipzig", and on page 301 "BACH (J. S.): Disputes at Leipzig". The entries for the great majority of composers are rounded off by the inclusion of a list of works arranged in classified order, and a bibliography. Previous editions usually arranged compositions by opus number but the new method is probably better for most enquiries.

In addition to those entries that one would normally expect to find in a dictionary of this type mention should be made of references from librettists and poets. Shakespeare receives nearly five columns of small type and the entry indicates the many songs written to his lyrics, incidental music to his plays, operas based on his plays, etc. There are also unorthodox topics in *Grove* such as "Postage stamps" and "Gestalt psychology" (which occupies well over seven pages) and similar subjects that are not normally included in comparable works.

Despite the greatly increased size of the current edition some pruning has been done: Mendelssohn, for example, being treated at less than half the length deemed necessary in previous editions, while the searcher for information on broadcasting is referred to the article in the supplementary volume of the fourth edition. A regretted excision is that of the incipits of Haydn's symphonies. Earlier editions, in fact, continue to have appreciable value for the information they contain which has been subsequently deleted. This is particularly the case with minor composers and performers whose diminishing importance has denied them entry in later editions. Only very rarely, as in the example quoted earlier in this paragraph, is there a reference from the current edition to an article in a previous edition; this may be regarded as a weakness. Bibliographies are of much greater length than in previous editions and include periodical references as well as books. By means of an appendix in the last volume these bibliographical references are extended to include articles published in 1954, which is some two years later than those included in the main body of the dictionary.

The editor's preface is divided into the following headings: The general plan; the contents; language; the alphabet [i.e. alphabetization]; revisions; display [i.e. the method of setting out individual entries]; references; transliterations; plates; acknowledgements. "Language" comments upon the fact that the dictionary is in the English language and has a natural bias towards English composers. It also attacks some modern American musical terms that derive from continental ones, particularly German; it may well be this section that has caused at least one American critic to complain of the "chauvinism" of this edition. This preface is followed by a second—a reprint of that of Sir George Grove to the first edition and this is the only remaining item by the original editor. At the other end of the set, in the ninth volume, are two appendices. Appendix II, already mentioned, is a bibliographical one, while Appendix I provides a chronology of composers. Every composer is entered both under the year of his birth and death (when either or both can be found) and also for each tenth birthday from the age of 20 onwards. Thus, the chronology for 1705 begins: "Aldrovandini, 40; Bach (J. S.), 20; Fischer (J. C.), *c*.40" and later entries for that same year show, for example, that Löhner died on the 2nd April at the age of 59. Births are indicated by an asterisk and deaths by a dagger. At the conclusion of these entries for each year are similar entries, in smaller type, for contemporaries in other fields of art such as painting, architecture and literature. It is possible that this appendix derives from a similar one in each volume of Dent's *Master Musicians* series since Eric Blom is also the editor of that series.

There are some music illustrations in the text (though one could wish for many more) and a few plates, some coloured and the remainder in monochrome. These have been reduced in number from previous editions mainly by the excision of portraits of musicians, though this is partly offset by an increase in the number of illustrations relating to musical instruments both current and obsolete.

Neither title entries nor opera synopses are included. The latter would have increased the bulk of the work appreciably without materially adding to its value since there are numerous specialist works available. Finally mention should be made of a number of corrections of errors published in *The Musical Times* for November and December 1955, and students are strongly advised to read the important articles on "Libraries and collections" and "Periodicals, musical".

SCHOLES, Percy. The Oxford companion to music, 9th edn. 1955. (O.U.P.)

Except for the opera synopses the whole of this work was written by the author; this is an amazing feat in these days of specialization. The first edition was published in 1938 and the Companion can claim, on the number of copies sold, to be the most popular work of musical reference ever. Though intended for the amateur music-lover rather than the professional musician, the latter will still find facts of interest in topics that are not to be found in similar works, e.g. Organ of Corti, Scampata, etc.

Long articles are divided into numbered and titled paragraphs. This assists discovery of a particular aspect of a subject and also allows the author to provide specific cross-references (e.g. LAROON, see *Street music, 2*). In some cases, such as Opera, the minor headings are enumerated at the beginning of the article. Entries under composers give forenames, year of birth and of death (but not the day and the month) and a statement of his age at the time of his death, a useful device to save the reader mental arithmetic. These entries give a brief biographical outline but no list of works and, generally speaking, offer appreciably less information than can be found in the *Everyman* volume discussed a few pages back. There are several hundred illustrations arranged six or more to each plate together with a number of portraits of famous musicians drawn by Batt (Oswald C. Barrett). These are particularly noteworthy for the authentic detail of the backgrounds, the results of much painstaking enquiry and research by the artist.

The opera synopses are arranged in the general sequence under their English titles; works included are those found in the average British repertory including the "Savoy" operas of Gilbert and Sullivan. Scholes' style is extremely readable and beguiling, spiced with an attractive humour; this work, more than any other dictionary of music, can be read for pleasure as well as for information. The field covered is somewhat wider than might perhaps be expected and the article on "Ragtime and jazz" has been considered as the best on this subject in any music encyclopaedia, though it is only fair to add that many jazz enthusiasts have complained that the author obviously knows nothing about the topic.

The second edition of the work, published in 1940, included a list of books on music; this was later published separately as *A list of books on music in the English language* (O.U.P., 1940) but has unfortunately been out of print for some years. In order to avoid resetting the type when the third edition was published the second edition was reprinted together with an appendix which contained some new entries together with further information for some subjects already included in the main body of the work. Where an article had been amplified in the appendix, the original entry was marked with an asterisk as an indication to the reader that further details could be found in the appendix. War-time stringencies and those that existed during the rest of the nineteen-forties and early fifties saw the method continued. The fifth edition saw the inclusion of a second appendix, similar to the first, and reference to this from the main body of the text was by means of a dagger. It was not until the publication of the ninth edition that the material was again consolidated into a single sequence and the opportunity was taken at the same time to do a certain amount of rewriting.

In order to attract an even wider public, *The concise Oxford dictionary of music* was published in 1952. Though this is generally an abridgement of the *Companion* it adds some 3,500 entries to cover living musicians, critics, etc., who are excluded from the parent work. Mention should also be made of the same compiler's *Junior companion to music* which is intended for users between the ages of eight and sixteen, with perhaps a bias towards the upper ages.

THOMPSON, Oscar, *editor*. The international cyclopedia of music and musicians, 7th edn., edited by Nicolas Slonimsky, 1956. (Dent)

This work was originally published in the U.S.A. in 1938, the same year that *The Oxford Companion to music* first appeared, and like the British volume achieved a second edition in 1940. This second edition was reprinted in 1942 and issued in Britain; this is the one usually found in British libraries. Later editions, under the editorship of Nicolas Slonimsky, show only slight revisions and no major recasting.

The names of one hundred contributors, mainly American and British, are listed at the beginning of the book. This list is followed by a second which details the more important contributors and the articles for which they have been responsible; Eric Blom, for instance, is shown as the author of the articles on Richard Strauss, Arthur Sullivan and Vaughan Williams. These special articles are easily identified in the body of the work, for each is started on a fresh page and has the name of the subject and the author of the article printed in an appreciably larger fount than that used for ordinary contributions. This unconventional arrangement is apparently made to reinforce the editor's declaration that "the articles are for reading, not merely for reference". As with the other dictionaries considered in this section, all entries are in a single alphabetical sequence and there is no separate index.

Each article on a major composer is followed by a calendar of the events of his life and a complete list of his works; the latter is subdivided into classified groups for easy reference. Where the composer is apparently considered by the compiler to be of lesser importance only the major works are listed while little-known figures have brief articles on their lives and no list of works.

An unusual feature of this work is the large number of title entries. For example, under *Fountains of Rome* (*Fontana di Roma*) is an outline of Respighi's programme for the music detailing the movements, date of first performance, etc. The entry for Respighi himself has a brief introduction by the editor, a long article by one of the Encyclopaedia's expert contributors on the composer's life plus the calendar and classed catalogue of works.

Certain articles, such as the one on *Folk music*, are the compilation of several contributors each of whom deals with a particular aspect of the subject. The authorship of each part of the article is indicated in all composite entries by the provision of the author's name or initials at the end of the section which he has written. A limited number of articles contributed by a single writer are also signed; unsigned articles are presumably by the editor. The work has no plates and illustrations in music type are very few. Cross-references are occasionally lacking and are sometimes faulty. There is a brief article, for instance, on the *King's band of music* which concludes with a useful list of "Masters of musick" (usually called in Britain "Masters of the King's [or Queen's] musick") from 1660 to the date of publication but there is no reference in the main sequence under "Masters of musick". The whole work has a fairly strong, declared American bias which adds to its usefulness both inside the U.S.A. and in other countries. In the United States it is probably the most popular general music encyclopaedia while outside it gives information on many American composers and works that are untraceable in British, French, German encyclopaedias, etc.

There are three appendices. The first gives synopses of some 200 operas, arranged alphabetically by title. The list contains some surprises; in addition to the routine works that could be expected (such as *Faust*, *The Barber of Seville*, and similar works from the standard repertory) there are synopses of *Ivanhoe* (Sullivan), *The King's henchman* (Deems Taylor), *Lady Macbeth of Mzensk* (Shostakovich) and *Natoma* (Victor Herbert), to mention but four examples that do not appear in Kobbé. The second appendix is a pronouncing guide to the names of composers and to titles. The third consists of a bibliography of some 3,500 books confusingly arranged in a single sequence of authors and subjects. Individual entries normally quote author, title, publisher and date. Cross-referencing is again occasionally faulty. For example, there is a reference under "Borodin" to "Abraham" where the latter's biography of the Russian composer is listed. On the other hand, Cecil Gray's life of Peter Warlock has no similar reference from Warlock. Entries are made for Warlock's book, *The English ayre*, and for Philip Heseltine's *Frederick Delius*, without any reminder to the casual or uninformed user that the two books are by the same author. Such shortcomings are few and are of little importance in such a long and useful list which is particularly valuable in its coverage of American books. Students are particularly recommended to read Dorothy Lawton's article on "Dictionaries of music" and C. S. Smith's on "Libraries of music" and to compare them with the similar two articles in Grove.

A smaller, cheaper but still important American one-volume work is *Harvard dictionary of music*, by Willi Apel (Cambridge, Mass.: Harvard University Press, 1944) with some 800 pages of text. The author's declared intention is ". . . to provide accurate and pertinent information on all musical topics and that it is addressed to the musical amateur as well as to the student and scholar. To reconcile the different, if not conflicting, interests of these three groups has been one of the chief concerns of the author." The dictionary is unconventional in omitting all biographical articles, but otherwise is on similar lines to the other works included in this section of the text. Generally speaking, articles are fairly brief; there are few illustrations in music type and the major articles have short bibliographies appended.

(b) SPECIAL DICTIONARIES

BARLOW, Harold, & MORGENSTERN, Sam. A dictionary of musical themes. 1948. (Benn)

BARLOW, Harold, & MORGENSTERN, Sam. A dictionary of vocal themes. 1955. (Benn)

These two American works (originally published in New York by Crown in 1948 and 1950 respectively) are in two complementary parts. In the first half of each volume are single-stave excerpts (i.e. the theme is quoted without harmony or accompaniment) varying in length from three to ten bars; the themes are arranged first under composer and then under the actual work. In the second half is the "notation index" by which it should be possible to identify any of the themes quoted. The earlier volume limits itself to orchestral and instrumental music and will be described first. All the works indexed in it have appeared in recorded form in the U.S.A. and probably in Britain also.

Composers are arranged alphabetically by surname; forenames and the years of birth and of death are shown. The works indexed are also entered in alphabetical order and not in a chronological or classified sequence; the themes are quoted in the order in which they make their appearance in the particular work. For example, the opening of Elgar's *Pomp and circumstance march no. 1* is shown as "theme 1"; the trio (better known in its vocal form as *Land of hope and glory*) as "theme 2". To the right of these two melodies are the index numbers E 38 and E 39 respectively. A fresh sequence of numbers is begun for each letter of the alphabet, so that Elgar themes are numbered from E 1 to E 79, George Enesco items from E 80 to E 103 and those of Franz Erkel from E 104 to E 107. The next composer indexed is Manual de Falla, so themes from his work begin a fresh sequence starting at F 1. At the top left-hand corner of each page is listed the name(s) of the composer(s) represented and on the right are the running numbers of the themes on that page, so that page 178 shows "Elgar-Enesco" and "E 77–95" respectively.

In order to index the various tunes all are treated as though they were written in the key of C. The time value of the notes is ignored; for the purpose of the index long and short notes are of equal importance and no differentiation is made. To exemplify the result one may cite the Elgar trio mentioned in the previous paragraph. Though actually written in the key of G major it is indexed as "C B C D A G—E 39". Normally the first six notes of a theme are given in the index but a duplication between the notes of two or more tunes may cause a longer entry to the point of difference, with a maximum entry of eleven notes.

This excellent dictionary suffers from two obvious drawbacks; the user must be able to understand music notation sufficiently to be able to write out the tune or to work out the notes in it (and there is a "transposition key" to assist in the task of rewriting the theme in the key of C), and secondly the enquirer must start the tune on the same note and beat as the compilers if he is to run it to earth in the index. With most tunes the starting note is definite enough but this is not always so, particularly when the theme is a subsidiary one that appears in the middle of an orchestral movement. This is fortunately an infrequent problem and for the librarian or enquirer whose musical knowledge is up to the standard indicated the dictionary is a wonderful instrument for identifying tunes, as I have personally found.

The range of composers represented is extremely wide; for instance, such comparatively unfamiliar names as Aubert, John Bull, Platti, Paradis and Locatelli are indexed in addition to the obvious classics. The representation of contemporary American composers is excellent though many of them and their works are still unfamiliar in Europe. The dictionary's limitation to works that had, at the time of compilation, appeared on disc has produced some strange results upon occasion. Minor works may occasionally be found with major ones omitted. *The holy boy* of John Ireland is included but his more important *Mai Dun* does not appear since it was not available on gramophone records at the time of the dictionary's compilation.

The *Dictionary of vocal themes* "includes the salient and remarkable themes from operas, cantatas, oratorios, *Lieder* and art songs, as well as many miscellaneous vocal pieces not belonging to the above categories". In this volume over 8,000 themes, together with their words, are quoted. There is a separate index of first lines and of titles in addition to the musical index. Folk songs are included only where the music has been edited and arranged by a recognized authority such as Béla Bartók or Vaughan Williams.

In compiling this dictionary the two musicians found the gramophone record repertory of the period insufficient for their purpose—the long-playing record was only just in the market when the work was written, or that complaint would not have been valid for more than two or three years—so that works that are found with some regularity in recital programmes, though not then available on disc, are included. Many of these extra items have subsequently appeared in recorded form, but recital programmes governed the choice of items to be included in the case of composers such as Bach, Handel, Schubert and Wolf. The inclusion of the complete vocal works of these and some other important composers in the field of vocal music would have resulted in a volume that would have been twice the size of the actual dictionary. The listing of the individual themes is carried out in simpler fashion than in the earlier volume. In this newer work each page starts with the first theme lettered "A", the second "B", and so on. The notation index then simply refers to a page number followed by the appropriate letter of the theme. Because of copyright difficulties a number of works are indicated in the first half of the book by blank staves (tunes from *Porgy and Bess*, *Merrie*

England, etc.) but the missing tunes are duly indexed in their proper places. Listing the notes only in the key of C, it would seem, does not infringe the copyright.

The two volumes may be regarded as parts of a single work, and the need for such an index has long been recognized but no really satisfactory solution has been provided until these two particular indexers came together. The time and labour involved was obviously immense and music-lovers owe a large debt to the authors.

(c) BIBLIOGRAPHY

The British Catalogue of Music (The British National Bibliography).

This annual was first issued in 1957; it is published in three interim issues (covering January to March inclusive, April to June and July to September), supplemented by a bound volume which cumulates the three issues and adds information on works published during the last quarter of the year. At the time of writing the annual subscription for the three paper-bound numbers and the annual volume is £4. The catalogue is officially described as "A record of music and books about music recently published in Great Britain based upon the material deposited at the Copyright Receipt Office of the British Museum, arranged according to a system of classification with an alphabetical index under composers, title, arrangers, instruments, etc., and a list of music publishers". In addition to the Council of the B.N.B. the following bodies are quoted as associate publishers: the Music Department of the British Museum, the U.K. Branch of the International Association of Music Libraries, the Music Publishers Association and the Central Music Library. "Published in Great Britain" includes foreign music imported into Britain under single-agency arrangements by which a single firm handles all (or mutually agreed) works of one or more foreign publishers.

This catalogue therefore covers somewhat similar ground in Britain to that of the Library of Congress in the U.S.A. whose *Catalog of copyright entries* is considered below, but there are some important differences. First, because of differences in copyright laws of the two countries the British work limits itself to published music while L.C. includes unpublished music also. The second and most important difference is that the London publication is arranged in classified order while main entry in the Washington work is under title. Thirdly, B.C.M. lists books in a separate sequence, L.C. in the same sequence as the scores; fourthly, the B.C.M. index precedes the main tables and is extremely full while L.C. has a name index only which follows the main entries; fifthly, B.C.M. entries give no indication of what new material has been incorporated into a work to allow a fresh copyright registration to be made and L.C. does.

As mentioned in the previous paragraph, the index is found before the main body of the work and contains in a single sequence fairly brief entries for composers, arrangers and editors, titles, series, authors of works and also subjects with their appropriate class marks. All entries (but not references) show the classification symbol, and the index entries for authors and composers also give the serial number allotted by B.C.M. Since the books on music will already have appeared in the normal weekly B.N.B. catalogue, the same number is quoted on its reappearance in B.C.M. to avoid confusion; for music scores the annual sequence starts at 50,000. Thus in the index to the first interim issue, Hugo Leichtentritt's *Music of the western nations* is quoted as B57–1234 which is the number allotted to this book earlier in the year when it first appeared in the weekly list published by the British National Bibliography. The next item in the index to this issue is Kenneth Leighton's *Concerto for violin and small orchestra* and its number (B57–50243) at once indicates that the item is a score and not a book. Running numbers are allotted, not according to the date received in the Copyright Office, but by the work's place in the classified sequence; this means that for each quarter's accessions the individual works are first classified, then arranged in classified sequence and given numbers as they appear in this sequence. This results in the first item appearing in the April to June issue taking the next number to that given to the last item in the January-March issue, though some weeks may have elapsed between actual dates of deposit of the two works.

The general arrangement and layout is very similar to that used in B.N.B. which must obviously be regarded as the parent work. One important difference is that the height of the page is not quoted but that the score is shown as *8vo*, *4to* or *fol.* for works up to $10\frac{1}{2}$ in. in height, between $10\frac{1}{2}$ and 12 in., and over 12 in. respectively; this is much less satisfactory than the more precise measurement given for books in B.N.B. The abbreviation *"obl."* is used for works whose width is greater than the height, and *"s.sh."* is used for a single sheet. Authors and composers are listed in accordance with British Museum practice, which means that all forenames whether used or unused are quoted except for certain composers, such as Mozart, for whom a popular form is chosen. B.C.M. tries to quote full names, indicating those not generally used by inclusion within brackets, e.g. Dolmetsch, Carl [Frederick], but this is not consistent because B.C.M. relies upon the B.M. entry which gives no indication as to which of the composer's forenames are actually quoted on the title-page.

Two examples are quoted to show the method of entry and the information given:

MS—Works for Light Orchestra
MSG—SUITES.
  VAUGHAN WILLIAMS, Ralph
    Folk songs of the four seasons: a suite for small orchestra arranged from the cantata of the same name by Roy Douglas. London, Oxford U.P., Piano-conductor 7/6. ᶜ1956. *24 pt. 4to.* (B57–50151)
    Prices of orchestral parts on application.

VT—Oboe
VTP—OBOE & PIANO
VTP/T—VARIATIONS
  WORDSWORTH, William Brocklesby
    Theme and variations for oboe and piano. Op. 57. [Score and part]. London, Lengnick, 4/–. ᶜ1956. *2pt. 4to.* (B57–50285)

The classification scheme used is one specially prepared for use with this catalogue and is discussed in Chapter IV. Although no separation is made between domestic issues and works of foreign publishers imported under agency arrangements (as is made in the L.C. publication), works are generally quoted under the original publisher, so that the catalogue is completed by a useful list of publishers together (when appropriate) with their English agents.

The British union-catalogue of early music, printed before the year 1801; a record of the holdings of over one hundred libraries throughout the British Isles. Editor: Edith B. Schnapper. 2 vols. Butterworth. 1957.

The preface is careful to explain that although this work represents the stock of many British libraries in its particular field, representation is not confined to British composers nor are foreign publications excluded. Some 60 per cent of the items listed are in the stock of the British Museum so that this national library's catalogue was taken as a starting point, with its two volumes of *Catalogue of printed music published between 1487 and 1800 and now in the British Museum*, published in 1912 and with the supplement published in 1940.

The general arrangement of Schnapper is alphabetical by composer; volume 1 covering the letters A–K and the second volume the remainder of the alphabet together with a title index for anonymous songs. Not only does this work contain scores, it includes music which appeared in books or periodicals; liturgies which bear the name of a composer or editor are also within its scope. Under each composer the titles are arranged alphabetically and at the end of each entry appears the appropriate symbol or symbols to indicate the library or libraries that hold the work. The great majority of the hundred or so libraries whose collections are included are national, university or colleges of music. About one dozen are public libraries and there are one or two special collections such as the Shakespeare Memorial Library at Stratford-on-Avon and the Bedfordshire Archaeological Society's library.

For fairly prolific composers a classified arrangement is adopted, entry under each heading being alphabetical, so that for T.A. Arne there are six major headings and some sub-divisions, as under:

1. Sacred music.
2. Operas, cantatas and dramatic music:
   (a) collections;
   (b) single works.
3. Songs, glees, etc.:
   (a) collections;
   (b) single works.
4. Instrumental works.
5. Doubtful and spurious works.
6. Appendix.

An actual example of an entry may be taken from the third section of Arne's works—"Songs, glees, etc., (a) collections"; the volume is entitled "British Amusement":

British Amusement. A favourite collection of songs sung at the publick gardens. . . . Book I. *Thompson and Sons: London* [*c.* 1762]. fol. M.

It can be seen that the form of entry follows that of the British Museum fairly exactly, particularly in the somewhat vague description of size. The final "M" indicates that the only available copy reported is to be found in the Manchester Public Library. Another example may be taken from the same composer:

Love and wine in alliance, *etc.* [Song]. *R. Falkener: London.* [*c.* 1777] *s.sh.* fol. Le.

The location here is that of Leeds Public Library and the music consists of a single sheet. The third example is for an anonymous work, entered under title:

On a primrose bank. *The Blush* [Song]. [*c.*1750]. *s.sh.* fol. L.

Here the only copy known is in the British Museum. The title index at the end of volume II of Schnapper contains an entry for "The Blush". When one considers the arrangement of entries under the heading "Psalms" something of the remarkable range of the work is revealed since there are no less than twenty-five sub-headings, starting with "Polyglot" and then proceeding alphabetically from "American", "Bohemian", "Czech", "Dutch", "Dutch and English" and "English" through to "Romansch" (which has three divisions) and "Welsh". Under each head the arrangement is chronological; if entries for the same year share the same title, then arrangement is by size. A typical entry for a psalter is:

8. French. Les psaumes de David, mis en rime françoise, par C. Marot & T. de Beze. *Anthoine Cellier: Paris.* 1645. 12°. L.

The final example is given for an instrumental work in order to show the method of cross-referencing. Under Haydn, the sub-division III is for instrumental music, which is again divided: (a) is for Symphonies and overtures, 1. Collections:

[B. & H. I No. 53, II No. 7]. Haydn's celebrated overture, *etc.* *See* infra; *Single works.*

From these examples it is hoped that students will have gained some idea of both coverage and method of entry. The value of the work to musicians of many types is likely to be very great (at the time of writing the volumes are too recent for absolute certainty on this point). Musicians and students will now be able to discover quickly the whereabouts of copies of works that they wish to study; if the distance is too great it is possible, in many cases, to obtain a microfilm of the score or the part required. Part of the potential success of this work must depend upon the possibility of supplements and lists of corrections. The methods of compilation were perforce far from ideal and it seems likely that there are a fair number of errors, while several libraries will have discovered fresh items in their collections since the catalogue went to press. The more complete the coverage, the greater the value of the work.

DARRELL, R. D., *compiler.* Schirmer's guide to books on music and musicians: a practical bibliography. 1951. (New York: Schirmer.)

This most important work should be in the stock of all libraries. Main entry for a work is usually made under the subject and there is a list of "Major subject headings" given at the beginning of the book. Author entries are mainly references to the appropriate subject(s) but are included in the same sequence, in the usual American dictionary-catalogue method. The author entry becomes the main one for autobiographies and for collections of essays that do not conveniently classify under a single heading. Examples may make the arrangement clearer. For example, under the name of Gerald Abraham is entered *Design in music*, a collection of essays; because it is a main entry, the pagination, publisher, date and price are quoted. This entry is followed in the catalogue by a number of *See also* references, beginning with "Beethoven—3. Quartets (1942). 1.00", and "Borodin. Biography. (1927). 4.00" to "Tchaikovsky— 2. Music of (1946). 3.00". Looking at the entries for Beethoven, it is found that they are divided into three categories—1. Letters, own writings; 2. Life; 3. Works. Under this last section is found the entry for "Abraham, Gerald. Beethoven's second-period quartets. 79p. mus ex, paper. Oxford 1942(1943). 1.00", and this is followed by the compiler's note—"*Musical Pilgrim*" *series of analyses: Op 59, 74 & 95. For companion booklets, see below: Fiske, Hadow.* These examples will indicate the use of abbreviations to save space, and also show that notes and explanations are given. Annotations are avoided except for such phrases as "A standard work".

It is hoped that the examples quoted have given some idea of the quality and usefulness of the book. Entry has normally been limited to works in print at the time of compilation but a number of important out-of-print works are included. Under certain headings the compiler has noted standard works that are either o.p. or not easily available. These standard works are not necessarily written in English, but works in other languages are relegated to Appendix I (see below). Prices quoted are those ruling in the U.S.A. at the time of going to press. *See also* references are shown immediately under the subject heading and precede entries for individual books. Thus "BARBERSHOP (Ballads, Singing)" is followed by: "*See also:* Amateur music, Community music, Popular music, Songbooks" before the entries for the two books on the subject of the heading.

The main body of the work is limited to books in English though reference is made as required to foreign books (e.g. under "Lute" is the reference "*See:* esp App Ia (Cabos)", and under "Mussorgsky" is "*Note: Standard works apparently O/P . . . include the letters & documents (1931, in Russian). . . .*") There are two Appendices; the first consists of five lists, arranged in each case alphabetically by author (and not by subject) of books in French, German, Italian, Spanish and Latin. Appendix II has two sub-sections, Juvenile biographies and Miscellaneous juveniles. The former lists collective biographies under the authors, followed by a sequence of individual biographies of musicians arranged under the names of the biographers. The second section lists all other works considered suitable for younger readers and includes fiction (so that one finds such works as Kitty Barne's *Musical honors*) and a variety of topics exemplified by *The child's book of musical instruments* and *The story of sound*.

The author is perhaps best known for that pioneer work, the first edition of *The Gramophone Shop Encyclopedia of Recorded Music,* and has written for this Schirmer guide an introduction and an explanation of how to use the work that should be required reading for all librarians and assistants. These two sections contain an immense fund of good sense, humour and useful information, while one cannot but admire a writer who ends his "How to use" instructions with the heading "How to proceed when you reach a seeming dead end".

DUCKLES, Vincent, & NICEWONGER, Harriet, *compilers.* A guide to reference materials on music, 3rd edn. 1955. (Berkeley: University of California.)

This work is shown as Syllabus no. 344 in the "University of California Syllabus series". It is generally referred to as "Duckles and

Nicewonger" but this third edition has added Minnie Elmer's name as a third compiler. The work is in typescript and includes 649 items, many of which are individual articles in various periodicals. The compilers promise an annotated edition in due course and this should be an invaluable tool for every reference library.

The items are divided into eleven headings, as follows: I, Dictionaries and Encyclopedias; II, Histories and Chronologies; III, Yearbooks; IV, Guide to historical musicology; V, Bibliographies of musical literature; VI, Bibliographies of music; VII, Catalogs of important libraries . . .; VIII, Catalogs of important collections of musical instruments; IX, Histories and Bibliographies of music printing and publishing; X, Discographies and XI, Bibliographies of Bibliographies. Several of these headings are divided, the largest number of subordinate headings occurring with section VI—1. General; 2. Current; 3. Bibliographies of collected editions of music; 4, Histories and bibliographies of early music; 5. Bibliographies of early music in modern editions; 6. Lists of music for performance.

Obviously enough, the number of entries under individual headings varies considerably. Books and periodical articles are entered in a single sequence as the following examples show:

642. COOVER, JAMES B. A bibliography of music dictionaries. Denver, Denver Public Library, 1952. 81p. (Bibliographical Center for Research. Special bibliographies, no. 1.)

643. DEUTSCH, OTTO E. "Music bibliography catalogues." In *The Library*, 23: 4 (March 1943) p. 151–170.

This latter entry is completed by the symbols "Z 671 L 59 ser.4 v. 22–23" which is presumably the University of California's press mark. Similarly, under Clough & Cuming's *World Encyclopaedia of Recorded Music* the first volume (which also contains the first supplement to the work, though this is not indicated here) carries the class mark ML 156.2 C 57. There is also a footnote in this section —"See also 'trade' catalogs of the various record manufacturers".

Very few libraries indeed will have in stock all the items listed in this bibliography but the smaller library will find it valuable to know what is in existence while the student should find the forthcoming edition, when published, a very useful work indeed.

THE MUSIC INDEX (Detroit, Mich.: Information Service Inc.) 1949–

The work is published monthly with an annual cumulation published as a bound volume. On the cover of each volume is a sub-title: "The key to current music periodical literature" and this may be taken as an adequate description of the work. The first number was for January, 1949, and indexed 41 periodicals, all of them published in the English language. Both individual articles and book reviews were indexed and by the end of the first year the number of periodicals included had grown to eighty, including examples in French, German, Italian and Danish. During 1950 the coverage was still further extended to 120 periodicals and this larger number included publications from Holland, Sweden, Mexico, Chile and Australia that had previously been omitted. Since that time the number of works indexed has remained fairly constant at about that figure. The first bound volume used letterpress printing but subsequent years have used the photo-offset method which was claimed (in 1951) to speed production—though the annual volume still seems to suffer a time-lag of some eighteen months. The 1949 volume contained 308 pages and by 1954 this had increased to 581.

The arrangement is that normally used in American publications, i.e. dictionary; authors, subjects and titles are arranged in a single alphabetical sequence. A specimen subject entry is:

ALPENHEIM, ILSE VON
Ilse von Alpenheim. MUS OPINION 77: 520–1 June 1954

This entry, which indexes the review of a vocal recital, is followed by a title entry for "Althalia. See HANDEL, GEORG FRIEDRICH". The reference, as can be seen from the first example, is to the name of the periodical (shown by an abbreviation), the volume number, page(s) on which the article is to be found and the date of issue. At the beginning of each volume is a list of abbreviations used for the individual periodicals, e.g.:

INT FOLK MUS COUNCIL JL Journal of the International Folk Music Council. Maud Karpeles, secretary. International Folk Music Council. 12 Clarence Gardens, London, N.W.3, Eng. 10/– annually.

INT MUSICIAN International musician. Leo Cluesmann, ed. & pub. American Federation of Musicians, 39 Division St., Newark 2, N.J. $1.00 monthly.

Naturally enough, various modifications have occurred during the years, particularly in the field of subject headings. These have been amended and expanded as required and also in the light of users' reactions. One might quote as example the case of music history. From 1949 to 1953 inclusive all articles on the history of music were entered directly under the appropriate century—"Nineteenth century", "Twentieth century", etc. In 1954 all these headings were grouped under the general heading "History" with sub-divisions each of which was still provided with its own *see also* references. For instance: "Twentieth century. See also CONCRETE MUSIC; ELECTRONIC MUSIC; EXPRESSIONISM; IMPRESSIONISM; MODERN MUSIC". Book reviews were originally indexed under that heading only, but from 1951 a second entry was made under the subject of the book. Obviously enough many headings will need many subdivisions—"LIBRARIES" has a host of such divisions by place, etc., California, England, France, and so on.

Because of its excellent coverage and its uniqueness this work should be in the stock of every large library yet only a handful of British libraries subscribe. Its tardy appearance each year is a drawback; its cost (25 dollars in the U.S.A. which apparently becomes £15 in the United Kingdom) is also a deterrent. There are occasional inaccuracies, as are almost certain to occur in a publication of this nature (one may quote the appearance in headings from 1951 onwards of "Sir Benjamin Britten" though this may well prove to be judicious prophecy) but none of these points can detract from the very real importance of this work and the very solid achievement that it represents. The value of the *Index* makes one realize afresh how unfortunate it is that it was only started in 1949. There must be a tremendous amount of earlier literature that loses most of its potential value because it is not indexed in an easily accessible form; this thought alone reinforces the need for continued and increasing support for the *Music Index*.

UNITED STATES LIBRARY OF CONGRESS: CATALOG OFFICE. Catalog of copyright entries, 3rd. series. 1947–

Printed catalogues for copyright registrations have been produced since 1891. The first volume included a section for music and this series covers the period July, 1891, to June, 1906. The second series, known as the "New series", was entitled *Catalog of copyright entries*; the music catalogue was part three of the set. The third series was inaugurated in January 1947 and retained the same title, but the music entries are now Part 5. There are two issues each year, covering the first and last six months. Until the end of 1956 there were three separate sections to Part 5: published music (5A), unpublished music (5B) and renewal registrations (5C) and each issue cost one dollar fifty cents for the first two parts and one dollar for the third. The public librarian is primarily interested in published music so that this description and comment is limited to part 5A, while the changes that took place in 1957 are detailed later. Part 5A included three categories, EF, EFO and EP; the two former are for music compositions published abroad and the latter for those published in the U.S.A. The catalogue is therefore intended primarily as a printed record of material deposited with L.C. for copyright purposes and its uses for librarians are incidental. Yet these uses are great, since the enquirer could find composer's names and dates, conventional titles of works, suggested subject headings and discover works of a particular genre in the classified list. It is, in fact, an invaluable finding and check list.

The catalogue includes music scores, selected books and pamphlets about music, and musical dramas. It is divided into four parts—a Name list, a Title index, a Classified index and a Claimant index. The first lists deposited works under the composer (in the case of music); the second is an alphabetical sequence of titles, showing both the conventional title used by the L.C. in its own catalogue together with the title actually printed on the title-page; the third is a dictionary arrangement of subjects while the last sequence lists the copyright owners of each work and so provides a source of addresses of music publishers all over the world.

Though further examples are quoted later, a specimen entry at this point may be useful for the British librarian or student who has not seen this particular publication:

CHOPIN, Frederyk Franciszk, 1810–1849
    [Preludes, piano, op. 28. Selections, arr.]
    Preludios; para guitarra por Francisco Terrega. NM: arrangement. © Union Musical Espanola, Madrid; 9 Sep 30; EF21452

Main entry is made under the composer whose name is entered in accordance with L.C. rules; transliteration of Russian names often varies considerably from that normally used in Britain. If the work deposited happens to consist of an excerpt from a larger work, then a conventional title is provided in order to relate the item to other excerpts and to the parent work. Should the title not agree with L.C. practice, then a conventional title is provided. In the example quoted above it will be seen that not all of the opus 28 Preludes have been included in the transcriptions and the conventional title makes it clear, first, that the original works were written for piano and secondly, that this particular volume is limited to selections from that particular opus. The remainder of the entry follows, generally speaking, normal cataloguing practice. The publisher's title is quoted, followed by the names of the authors of the words, joint composers, editors, etc. Imprint shows the place of publication and publisher, except in those cases where the publisher is also the copyright claimant when this information is shown later in the entry, i.e. in the copyright statement following the © symbol.

The fourth item is an indication as to whether a work is published in score and/or parts, and the pagination. Fifthly comes the series title when this is considered to be a useful aid to the tracing of the work. The medium is quoted, when necessary, as the sixth item. Seventh is the price, as printed on the copy, and this is followed by the names of any authors whose names are included in the copyright application but whose names do not appear on the music itself. These are usually arrangers who have been engaged by publishers to make special arrangements of works; are paid an agreed sum and full copyright rights are retained by the publisher. The next possible item concerns previous registration, while the tenth is most important—it indicates the new matter included in a work upon which the actual copyright claim is based—assuming that this new matter is not clearly indicated in the title. In the example quoted above the new matter is the arrangement of a piano score for solo guitar. In all entries the initials "NM" preceded this statement. Eleventh is the internationally accepted copyright symbol, a small capital "c" within a circle. The twelfth item is the name of the copyright claimant followed by the place and date of publication. This may be years earlier since the Library of Congress has a statement in its rules on delayed deposits which reads: "The Office will accept deposits for full-term registration at any time during the copyright term of 28 years after first publication"; it should be noted that copyright dates, however, from first publication and not from date of deposit. If the work is an unpublished one, the date of registration at the Copyright Office is used instead of the date of publication. The last item is the copyright registration number. Each issue of the Catalog includes a statement as to the number of copyright registrations of published music, and separate figures are quoted for domestic issues and those published abroad (the EP, EF and EFO categories).

Reference Books and Periodicals

Two further examples are quoted of main entries:

CHAIKOVSKII, Petr Il'ich 1840–1893
  Sing ye praises to the Lord; S.A.T.B. unacc, edited and arr.
  by Noble Cain, English version by Noble Cain. Score (8p)
  20c. NM: editing and arranging. © Boosey & Hawkes Inc.,
  New York; 19 Aug 55: EP93835

VAUGHAN WILLIAMS, Ralph 1872–
  Concerto accademico; in D minor, for violin and string
  orchestra. Miniature score (30p) 4/– © Oxford University
  Press, London; 15 Dec 27 EF 21632

It may be noted that imprint in both these examples is omitted
since the publisher is also the copyright claimant, and that in these
cases the publisher's name is given before the place of publication.

The full description of the title index is "An index to the titles,
including the conventional titles, of all works listed in this issue.
Below the work is given the name and conventional title (when one
has been used) under which the work will be found in the first
section." So the index will include entries for "Concerto accademico", "Sing ye praises to the Lord" and "Preludios—Chopin,
F.F. [Preludes, piano, op. 28. Selections, arr.]" for the examples
quoted.

The classified index is a list of subject heads, from Accordion to
Zither, plus any necessary *See* and *See also* references. A typical
sequence of subjects is SWITZERLAND, TELEVISION MUSIC, THANKS-
GIVING, TOPICAL SONGS, TRINIDAD, TROMBONE, TROMBONE INSTRUC-
TION, etc. A searcher for Welsh music is referred from "Wales" to
"Great Britain" by means of a *See* reference, while a typical *See also*
entry is "TUBA. *See also* Orchestra—Concertos and concert pieces—
Tuba".

The claimant index should be self-explanatory. It lists individuals
and publishers (with their addresses) in alphabetical order and under
each name quotes the works in that issue of the Catalogue for which
that particular firm or individual claims copyright. The value of the
work to a music librarian as a finding or check list should now be
clearly seen, and some of the major differences between this American
publication and its British equivalent, *The British Catalogue of Music*,
have been mentioned when considering the latter.

In 1957 a major reorganization of the Copyright Cataloging

Division took place. Since 1946 the Music Section of the Division was responsible both for copyright cataloguing and also for the L.C. printed card cataloguing. The copyright catalogue cards were designed to inter-file with L.C. printed cards in its catalogues. In 1957 two separate sections were created—one to do all L.C. music cataloguing (including the preparation of entries for printed cards) and the other to deal with copyright entries only. As a result, entries from 1957 are made under title and give a complete transcription of the title-page; the medium of performance is given only if stated on the copy or on the application for copyright registration. The three former catalogues for published music, unpublished music and renewals of music were combined into one; there are separate main lists for current registrations and renewal registrations. There is a single index only—a combined name index for the main lists. Names are given as they appear on the copy and/or application and no steps are taken to discover full forenames, etc. The statement of copyright facts is unchanged from the former catalogues.

In its new form the catalogue must be of much less value to librarians, though it may well be of greater use to copyright searchers, lawyers and publishers since there should be an appreciably reduced time-lag from the date of deposit to the date of publication. It should also represent an economy for the Library of Congress which, like all national libraries, has never sufficient funds to undertake all the tasks and duties that it would desire.

(d) HISTORY

The New Oxford History of music. 11 vols. 1954–   (O.U.P.)

This work is intended to replace the original *Oxford History of Music* which was first published in six volumes between the years 1901 and 1905 and which made a tremendous impact upon the musical ideas and thought of the time. Five authors were responsible for the entire work. Between 1929 and 1939 a second edition was published; in this an Introductory volume was included to cover music in the ancient world and to extend the information on music in the Middle Ages which had been the starting point of the original first volume. Some new material was added to volumes 1 and 2 for this new edition, while minor corrections were made to volume 3. The fourth, fifth and sixth volumes were not revised and another new volume (7) completed the scheme by carrying the history from its earlier limit of 1850 on to 1900. The second edition, therefore, had two more volumes than the first and these two were added one at either end of the original six.

After the Second World War the publishers sensibly decided that it would be better to compile an entirely new work than attempt to make a further revision of the original and in this they were probably very wise. Where the first edition was written by five men the new history has as many editors who will supervise and collate the work of a large number of specialists. Three of the editors have been given the responsibility for two volumes each, one (Professor Gerald Abraham) for three volumes and another (Eric Blom) for the tenth volume only. This will be the last to contain text as the eleventh will be devoted entirely to chronological tables, bibliographies and the index. The use, in the current *History*, of a host of experts under editorial guidance rather than a handful of writers for the entire work is some indication of the immense growth of specialization in this, as in other fields, during the past fifty years. No date has been announced for the completion of the work, in which the volumes are not appearing in chronological order but it seems that publication will cover a long period as volume 2 (the first to be published) appeared in 1954 and it was three years later that volume 1 was issued with the remaining nine still to come.

The work is straightforward musical history (so far as that can be straightforward) and is notable for the extremely large number of illustrations in music type throughout; there are some plates also. Further, since music should be heard as well as read and because an aural demonstration can illustrate a point (in many cases) much more clearly than pages of print, the Gramophone Company ("His Master's Voice") is issuing a series of gramophone records to illustrate the history. The discs were originally on shellac at 78 r.p.m. in albums, each album providing examples for a particular equivalent volume of the *History*. Later the recordings were reissued in LP form so that users could choose the type of gramophone record which was best suited to their needs. The recorded series is entitled *The history of music in sound*; there are references from the text to the discs. The gramophone records are accompanied by notes which give references in the *New Oxford history of music* so that the two works are complementary in the fullest sense. The issue of gramophone records has far outstripped the publication of the volumes of the parent work.

In conclusion, attention should be drawn to a statement in the introduction that "The history as a whole is intended to be useful to the professed student of music . . ." but adds that the interests of music-lovers in general have also been borne in mind.

SLONIMSKY, Nicolas. Music since 1900. 3rd edn, 1949. (New York: Coleman-Ross.)

The first edition of this work was published in 1937 and the second a year later; the second edition was issued in Britain by Dent. The first edition gave a chronological guide to important dates in musical history between 1st January 1900 and 31st December 1936; the second added events of 1937. The third edition retains this part of the work virtually intact except that the events of 1937 have been rewritten, and the coverage has been extended to 31st December 1948. As examples of the sort of information to be found in the work it may be stated that it includes the dates of births and deaths of composers, first performances, important articles, etc. The last page of entries for the year 1931 illustrates the variety of references in that it includes notes of the death of two composers, first production of a musical show, a ballet, a film and the conferment of honorary membership of the Santa Cecilia Academy in Rome upon four composers. This main section covers some three-quarters of the book.

In the earlier editions the second part of the work was "a concise biographical dictionary of twentieth-century musicians" which listed composers, writers on music, performers and the like in a single alphabetical sequence. The entry gave forenames, the briefest possible identification of the biographies and date of birth, death, or both. A typical entry read: "Nielsen, Carl, Danish composer, born 9 June 1865; died 3 Oct 1931." An addendum was a series of lists of corrections and additions to four famous biographical dictionaries. This second part is deleted from the third edition but Part Three, "Letters and documents", has been retained and expanded. It reprints such items as the *Moto Proprio* of Pope Pius X on sacred music (i.e. the principles that should govern the choice of music in Roman Catholic services), a letter from Arnold Schoenberg on the origin of the twelve-tone system and Zhdanov's speech at a meeting of Soviet musicians in February 1948.

The additions to chronology since 1936 are mainly American. The author defends this: "This pro-American partiality is accounted for not alone by the obvious fact that the book is published in America, and is designed primarily for American readers, but by the objective truth that during the last decade the center of creative music has gradually shifted from Europe to the United States." Many readers will dispute the alleged "objective truth" without denying the value of this book as a guide to important dates in musical history in the twentieth century. Slonimsky has apparently made particular efforts to go to original sources for dates so that, generally speaking, those quoted by him are to be preferred to different ones quoted in other books of musical reference.

(e) OPERA

KOBBE, Gustave. Kobbé's complete opera book, edited and revised by the Earl of Harewood. 2nd edn, 1954. (Putnam)

Gustave Kobbé was an American music writer and critic who died in 1918 as the result of an accident. He had left the material for this book in a fairly advanced state of preparation at the time of his death so that only a limited amount of editing was necessary for publication which first took place in 1922. Subsequent reprints included new material, as certain operas were added to the repertory, but the original synopses were retained. This second edition, published more than thirty years after the original, shows considerable alteration both in its omission of operas that have dropped from the repertory since Kobbé's day and in the inclusion of detailed synopses of works which were not included in the original or received very summary treatment. The editor's criterion of selection has been to pick "only those works that seemed certain to be seen by English-speaking audiences during, say, the next ten or fifteen years". Kobbé is the best-known book of opera synopses and in its new form seems likely to remain a standard work for a longer period than the modest estimate of the editor would suggest.

The book is divided into three main sections. The first is for opera before 1800 which is given three chapters. The second section, dealing with the nineteenth century, has eleven chapters, while the third part, on the twentieth century, has nine chapters. The arrangement is considerably better than that of the original edition (and the student might find it useful to make comparisons) but is still not conducive to quick reference. The first section has chapters on "Opera before Gluck", "Gluck" and "Mozart". The second part deals first with German opera, discussing the works of four composers, followed by a chapter on Wagner which is succeeded in turn by one entitled "German opera continued" for works by later composers. Italian opera has three similar chapters, the middle one in this case being devoted to Verdi. The remaining chapters of the second part deal with French, Russian, English and Czech operas. The third part deals with operas of the same six nations, arranged in similar order and is completed by chapters on Hungarian, Spanish and American opera.

The normal entry gives the title in capitals in its original form together with an English translation, if necessary, immediately beneath. Then follows a note in small type showing the genre (Opera in two acts; Opera in a prologue and four acts, etc.), the composer, the librettist and the source of the story if taken from a play or novel. After this are shown the date and place of first performance and of the first performance in other internationally-known opera houses; revivals of distinction may also receive mention. After these preliminaries appears the list of characters, showing the type of voice allotted to each part; this section is completed with a note as to the time and place of the opera's action. The actual synopsis is now given and for the major works there is a generous selection of themes quoted in music score. At the end of each synopsis appears the initial(s) of the compiler(s): K for Kobbé himself, F.B. for Ferruccio Bonavia who was responsible for the subsequent additions in later reprints of the first edition, K.W. for Katherine Wright who arranged the original material for publication after Kobbé's untimely death, and H. for the Earl of Harewood. The original edition contained thirty-six portraits of famous singers in roles for which they were particularly noted. The new edition contains an entirely fresh selection of plates, some of singers and others of the stage settings of actual productions; all are later than World War II. Finally, mention must be made of the very good index.

Since the work has been drastically altered in its new edition it should be bought for libraries of all sizes, even though the first edition may already be in stock. Students will find it useful to compare Kobbé with one or other of the many volumes of opera synopses available. Particular attention should be paid to the scope and arrangement of each work, the provision or lack of music quotations, the method of listing characters and the fullness or brevity of the plots.

LOEWENBERG, Alfred. Annals of opera, 1597–1940; compiled from the original sources. 2nd edn. 1955. 2 vols. (Geneva: Societas Bibliographica.)

This work was originally published in 1943 in a single volume (Cambridge: Heffer); this second edition may best be described as a considerably revised reprint but libraries possessing the first edition have no real need to withdraw that prematurely to replace by this new (and considerably more expensive) version.

The purpose and scope of the book is well described in the preface as "a skeleton history of opera, in dates and other facts. It is therefore arranged chronologically, but by means of copious indexes it can also be used as a dictionary of operas. There are no descriptions of plots, no musical analyses, no personal critical comments." The material is arranged from information obtained from the original scores and librettos, from play-bills, contemporary newspapers and similar places—hence the "original sources" in the sub-title of the work.

Some three to four thousand operas are listed and inclusion has been limited to works that have actually achieved production. Older operas have been selected, in general, if they are still in the repertory or have historical importance. For modern works the chosen criterion is usually that of performance outside its native country. The earliest work included is Peri's *La Dafne* (1597) and the last *Izaht* by Villa-Lobos (1940). Arrangement is strictly chronological by the Gregorian calendar and this has produced some apparent inaccuracies with English operas produced before 1752 (when the Gregorian calendar was adopted and eleven days were "lost") and with Russian works prior to the similar change made in 1917.

Each entry includes the composer's surname and the original title in the language in which it was first performed. Russian names are transliterated in accordance with the British Museum rules and the transliterated title is followed by its original in the Cyrillic script and an English translation. German, French and Italian titles are not translated as are those in other foreign languages; neither is translation made when the title is that of the principal or other character in the score. The date and place of first performance follow the heading of composer and title. The date and month only are quoted since the year is shown at the top of each column; there are two columns of type to a page. The remaining information concerning each opera is in smaller type. It begins with the librettist(s) and a note showing the original source of the text. First performances in other countries are then listed. Where these have been given in a different language to that of the original the name of the translator is generally quoted. Finally, important revivals are noted. Much of this information has been incorporated into the new edition of Kobbé, described above.

To make the method of entry more intelligible, three specimen entries follow:

(1) 1773 [at the top of the column of type] HAYDN: *L'Infedeltà delusa*/*26 July*. Esterháza/Librettist unknown (*Burletta per musica*). Two acts./ Revived Vienna 14 May 1930 (as *Liebe macht erfinderisch*, German version by H. Goja, music revised by G. Kassowitz).

(2) [1872] BIZET: *Djamileh*/*22 May*. Paris, O.C./Text by L. Gallet (founded on A. de Musset's *Namouna*). One act./When first produced in Paris given for 11 nights only, and revived there as late as 27 October 1938. Outside France given at: Stockholm 25 February 1889 (in Swedish, translated by E. G. Lundquist). . . . Revived London C.G. 18 December 1919 (in English). . . .

The abbreviations O.C. and C.G. in the above entry are those used throughout the work for Opéra-Comique and Covent Garden respectively.

(3) [1881] CHAIKOVSKY: *Orleanskaya Dyeva*/ [Russian title in Cyrillic script]/ (The Maid of Orleans)/ *25 February*. St. Petersburg/ Text by the composer (founded on V. A. Zhukovsky's Russian version of Schiller's tragedy). Four acts./Revived Moscow 1899 and September 1907./ In Czech, Prague, July 1882 (first opera of Chaikovsky that was heard outside Russia).

Readers will note that the use of the British Museum rules results in a comparatively unusual form of the composer's name. The date of the original performance is corrected from that of the Russian "old-style" calendar while the place of first performance is given its contemporary and not its modern name.

The second volume contains the work's four indexes. The first is that of titles, with the composer's name in brackets and the year of first performance. Since no more exact identification than this is given it may be difficult to trace a particular opera in a year that saw a large number of first performances. The second index is of composers; this gives forenames and (in brackets) the year of birth and that of death. Under each name are listed the operas included together with the year of the first performance of each. Where the composer has written the libretto, alone or in collaboration, the fact is indicated by an asterisk against the title of the opera. The third index is that of librettists and includes authors whose works have been used as the bases of librettos; examples of the latter category are quoted in italics to distinguish them from librettists proper. Christian names but not dates are given and after each name is the year in which the opera was performed. Thus, in the case of the Tchaikovsky opera quoted above, the Schiller entry includes a reference to 1881 and Zhukovsky's name is also included in the index with the same year noted. The fourth and last is a "General Index containing (a) all persons not mentioned in Indexes II and III; (b) a small selection of subjects, and (c) countries and towns; under the names of the latter only events of some significance are listed, as important first productions, openings of theatres, etc." Subject entries are made for such items as "American operas in Germany", "Ballad opera", "London promenade concerts". References from this index are to the appropriate column of the first volume where the particular item can be found; this is the only index which does not refer to the year and so is the easiest to use.

Loewenberg's is a major work in its field. The term "opera" is used in its widest sense so that one finds Smetana, Stravinsky, Sullivan and Suppé all included. The amount of research and cross-checking that preceded publication is obviously tremendous and the result is a permanent mine of information, unlikely to be superseded, for all interested in the historical aspect of opera.

(f) VOCAL MUSIC

SEARS, Minnie Earl, & CRAWFORD, Phyllis, *editors*. Song index: an index to more than 12,000 songs in 177 song collections comprising 262 volumes. 1926. (New York: H. W. Wilson Co.)
Song index supplement: an index to more than 7,000 songs in 104 collections comprising 124 volumes. 1934. (New York: H. W. Wilson Co.)

With a solitary exception the 281 collections indexed in these two volumes were published either in North America or in Great Britain. The collections do not include any devoted to the works of a single composer but are all anthologies of one type or another. The two volumes also exclude from their scope hymnals, children's and un-accompanied songs (but see the last paragraph of these descriptive notes). The major effect of the limitation to anthologies is to exclude almost all modern composers whose works are protected by copyright for these are rarely found in mixed volumes; on the other hand, there is an excellent selection of folk and traditional songs. Main entry is made under the title with added entries under the composer (shown in bold-face Roman type), author of the words (in bold-face italic) and the first line of the title which is, for clarity, always quoted in inverted commas, even in those cases when this first line is also the title of the song. The entries are arranged in a single alphabetical sequence and the volumes are typical H. W. Wilson products in appearance and layout.

The main [title] entry is followed by any alternative titles which are quoted in curves. In the case of a song which has variant versions of the first line, these are also given. Then is printed the name of the composer or, in the case of anonymous songs the nationality of the music and the words "folk air". The third item is "Words by . . ." showing the name of the poet, etc. Fourthly, where the song is not English or American there is a language abbreviation; for instance, if the words are given in Italian and English, this is indicated by the letters "i.e.". The entry concludes with the symbols indicating the collection(s) in which the song is to be found.

In those cases in which the poet wrote the music also, indication is given in the title entry; otherwise, the composer's name is shown after the title in the bold-faced italic used for the author of the words. Under each composer is listed a single alphabetical sequence of the songs indexed. In the case of these added entries, reference must be made to the title entry for other information. Foreign songs are generally given under their original title except in the case of "unusual" languages. If the title begins with an article, it is retained but ignored for filing purposes so that "The keel row" is shown in that form but is indexed under "K".

Before the index of individual songs which forms the main body of the work, the collections themselves are quoted in classified sequence under the following headings: General; National and Folk songs (divided alphabetically, e.g. English, French, German, Hawaiian, etc.); Chanteys; Christmas carols; Sacred songs; School and College songs. Those works recommended for first purchase are marked with an asterisk. Each collection is entered under its compilers, giving full names. This is followed by the title of the collection, its date, price and (in some cases) a contents note, e.g. "29 folk ballads; 66 folk songs; 5 accumulative folk songs", which is the note appended to Cecil J. Sharp's *One hundred English folk songs*. This work is indicated by the mnemonic "SO" in the "key symbols of collections indexed".

The index to individual songs follows. A search for the song "Ma belle Marianne" shows the English translation "Pretty Marianna" given in curves and the description "Folk song from Alsace". The letters "e.f. FTF" indicate that both English and French words are to be found in the album symbolized as FTF whose full name can be traced in the "key symbols" section. The supplement is arranged on the same principle as the original volume. Where new information has been found about any song this is indicated by special brackets < >

The usefulness of these volumes should be clear. One can find, within their stated scope, the authors of the words of over 19,000 songs, in what collection(s) these words can be found and (assuming that the tune is not traditional) who composed the music for any individual song. In some respects the index supplements Granger's *Poetry index*, especially for anonymous folk songs.

Two years after the publication of the supplement one of the gaps was filled by the *Children's song index* by Helen Grant Cushing (H. W. Wilson Co., 1936). This work indexes 189 collections in 222 volumes and only eleven of this total have been already included in the Sears and Crawford volumes. The layout and arrangement is on the same lines as the earlier volumes.

(g) CHAMBER MUSIC

COBBETT, W. W., *editor*. Cobbett's cyclopedic survey of chamber music. 2 vols. 1929, 1930. (O.U.P.)

These two volumes contain long, signed articles on chamber music and related subjects, profusely illustrated with musical examples. The articles on works of individual composers are fairly exhaustive; Debussy, for instance, who wrote but one string quartet and three other chamber works receives a three-page article of some 2,500 words. Works are usually criticized individually and composer entries begin with a complete list of compositions that are classed as chamber music. This term is interpreted in its widest sense from violin and piano sonatas, etc., to nonets and other works that verge upon the orchestral. Unaccompanied solo works and piano pieces are excluded.

Although the major part of the work may be regarded as biographical/critical there are also articles on such topics as "Choreography: its alliance with chamber music", "Clarinet in chamber music", "Competition festivals in chamber music", "Consorts of viols", to take a selection of headings within the compass of a few pages.

At the beginning of each volume is a list of contributors and a separate list of translators. The list of contributors is repeated at the end of the second volume and here each writer's articles are detailed. This volume also contains a supplement listing composers of chamber music whose names are not to be found in the main body of the work; this is followed by a bibliography of books, articles in newspapers and periodicals, etc., arranged under the names of the writers. The bibliography is tabulated in four columns showing, respectively, the author's name, title of the book or article, name of the publisher if a book or the title of the publication if an article and the date of publication. The work is rounded off with a contents list which simply repeats in convenient form the heading used in the two volumes plus the detailed list of contributors, already mentioned.

This work has been out of print for many years but is due for reprinting; a third volume is to be added, edited by Colin Mason and Nicolas Slonimsky. This will cover the period from 1929 onwards and will also contain addenda and corrigenda to the original work.

(h) GRAMOPHONE RECORDS

CLOUGH, Francis F., *and* CUMING, G. J. The world's encyclopaedia of recorded music. 1952. (Sidgwick & Jackson) Second supplement (1951–52). 1953. Third supplement (1953–55). 1957.

The original volume contains almost 900 pages of which the last 160 form the First Supplement, unmentioned on the title page; the Second Supplement is a comparatively slim volume of 262 pages, while the Third adds a further 564 pages of text. Within these four sequences is listed almost all music of permanent value issued on gramophone records between 1926 and 1955. In the case of items frequently recorded the compilers have omitted some of the less important versions; on the other hand, the first volume contains details of a limited number of pre-electric and historical records. Light music, unless considered to have sufficient musical value to keep its place in the repertory is generally omitted; despite the title of the work its scope is limited to western music—Oriental and African music is not included.

Each volume gives "a diagram of setting of the normal entry" and this should be studied before inspecting the main body. Entries are made under composers' names (with forenames and dates) in alphabetical order. The importance of each composer and the number of entries required in the encyclopaedia determine the layout of the material. For major composers an *ad hoc* classified order is adopted, while for lesser figures an alphabetico-classed system is usually adequate. An example of this latter method is provided in the first volume by Cyril Scott. Four songs, apparently all that have been recorded on 78 r.p.m. discs, are listed under the heading "Songs", but twelve works are arranged in a single sequence of titles. Entries under the composer begin, therefore, with an instrumental work— *A ballad told at candle-light*—and the sequence continues with other instrumental works to *Rainbow trout* when the heading "Songs" is interpolated and the four works of this type listed. These are followed by *Souvenir de Vienne* and other instrumental works to the end of the alphabet.

While the general scheme for major composers is standard, the actual arrangement of entries will vary between one and another according to the types of works written and recorded, so that the arrangement adopted is indicated (for clarity) immediately under the composer's name. Smetana's works, as an example, are arranged under six headings: I, Operas; II, Other vocal works; III, Instrumental and chamber music, and three other headings. The compilers attempt to identify every work by means of opus numbers, reference to a standard thematic catalogue and the like. All Schubert's works are listed with the numbers allotted to them in Deutsch's thematic catalogue; Beethoven's works are given opus numbers and for those works which have none the *Grove* number is shown together with the number allotted in the Breitkopf & Härtel catalogue. Bach and Vivaldi works are identified by the Schmieder and Pincherle numbers respectively and this detail in identification is of the greatest possible use.

A separate title index is provided under a composer when the compilers consider it warranted. Many individual items from the various sets of piano pieces by Debussy have been recorded so that an index to these titles is provided at the end of the list of recordings. This reminds the reader that *Clair de lune* is the third movement of *Suite bergamasque* and that the *Golliwog's cake-walk* is the sixth item in *Children's corner* and so on. The searcher can then look under the name of the appropriate suite or set of pieces for recordings of individual items. An extremely full index is provided for Liszt's instrumental works which can be extremely confusing without such a guide. This particular index quotes both the medium for which the work was written (pf. study; orch.) and *Grove's* number. Anthologies of gramophone records are listed separately with lists of contents. The first volume contains an index of composers, a second of arrangers and editors and a third of titles of operatic and other stage works.

The normal entry indicates the performer, record make and catalogue numbers. The first volume, limited to SP discs, indicated the item on the reverse of a record that contained two works but the system had to be modified for the supplements when LP discs were indexed that might contain as many as a dozen works on a single side. Older versions may be listed in smaller type; no less than thirty-four versions of the "Jewel song" from Gounod's *Faust* are tabulated in the first volume, including versions in English, Swedish, Russian and Italian and an "etc." at the end of the list shows that there have been other recordings not included. In the first volume 10-in. discs were distinguished by quoting the manufacturer's catalogue number in italics; the complication of LP discs was solved by the use of the music signs for sharp (♯) and flat (♭) for 33⅓ and 45 r.p.m. discs respectively—an answer that is not nearly as effective as that used in *The record guide*, discussed a little later in this chapter. When a recording has been issued in more than one country, particularly if those countries include both Britain and the U.S.A., the appropriate manufacturer's catalogue number is quoted according to the country of origin and only in a minority of cases are both the British and American numbers of the same disc given. Over 300 different record labels are listed and the trouble taken to identify every work has been tremendous—for the wording on labels has often been casual in the extreme; the standard today is appreciably higher but mistakes and uninformative titles still occur. Despite the efforts of the compilers, the Second supplement contains a consolidated list of errata that occupies over nine pages and a similar, though shorter, list is also given in the Third supplement. The general arrangement of the work has been copied (with due acknowledgement) from *The Gramophone Shop encyclopedia of recorded music* by R. D. Darrell, published in 1936. Libraries possessing this latter work or either of its two later editions (with different editors) should not discard any of the three volumes for they are to some degree complementary to *W.E.R.M.* (as Clough and Cuming's work has become generally known) since the newer work quotes only the briefest details when the recording has already been listed in *The Gramophone Shop encyclopedia.*

The work is unlikely to be superseded as the best reference work in its field. Its lists of standard-play (78 r.p.m.) discs in volume 1 is already acquiring historical value and took many years to compile; the story has been told by one of the two discographers. The work has been produced without any form of subsidy though the Decca Record Company of London has assisted in the publication of all volumes. Despite the spate of LP recordings in the early nineteen-fifties, Clough and Cuming have somehow kept abreast of the flood and their standard of accuracy and detective abilities have apparently remained unimpaired, thanks in part to the generous response of music-lovers all over the world who have sent in corrections and also details of records issued outside Europe and the U.S.A.

One final point must be made. The work is factual; it gives no guide to good or bad recordings nor to wonderful or horrible performances. *W.E.R.M's* sole interest is that a record has been issued to the public (since it is not unknown for a record to be announced but never appear on sale) and to give correct details of the work or works on each disc. The three volumes are of the highest importance in their own field; they are also useful in answering quite a number of questions on music. The work should be in the stock of every medium-sized library and in the small library that includes a gramophone record service.

MYERS, Kurtz, *compiler, and* HILL, Richard S., *editor.* Record ratings; the Music Library Association's index of record reviews. 1956. (New York: Crown Pub.)

"*Record ratings* is essentially a guidebook pointing the way to a tremendous body of critical writing about recordings." Thus begins the introduction to this most valuable aid to the gramophone librarian. Basically the work consists of a list of LP records arranged alphabetically under composer. Under each recording is a series of symbols indicating details of where the record was reviewed and the general verdict of each reviewer. The time involved in compiling and editing such a work must be great since each individual review has to be carefully read in order to note the reviewer's conclusions about the record. This particular volume is a collation of material that has already appeared in *Notes*, the journal of the M.L.A., which is noticed in the second part of this chapter.

The number of works collated varies slightly from time to time as some periodicals cease publication or new ones enter the field, but there are usually nearly thirty on average, the majority of them devoted entirely to gramophone records or music, and about three-quarters of them of American origin. Some half a dozen British and one French periodical are also considered. During the period covered by this volume of *Record ratings* three of the periodicals noticed (including one British) went out of existence. The actual time covered is not quoted but would seem to be from about mid-1949 to early 1955. Understandably, every record listed has not been reviewed in every periodical; all discs have been issued in the U.S.A. though not in Britain or France, but in many cases twenty or more reviews are indexed of an individual recording.

Each periodical is represented by an abbreviation, usually mnemonic. To the right of it is given the date of issue upon which the particular review appeared and this is followed by the actual page number; to the left is a symbol denoting the general tenor of the review. A plus sign indicates a good, favourable review and a minus sign the reverse. A small black circle means that the pros outweighed the cons for that particular reviewer but not by a large margin, while an open square denotes one of those maddening reviews from which it is difficult, if not impossible, to draw any definite conclusion. A double dagger sign indicates that the review contains some unusually valuable background information. The letters "(m.f.)" after an entry disclose that the review complains of technical shortcomings in the disc; it is interesting (if not curious) to find that this particular type of criticism is much more common in Britain than in the U.S.A. Finally, notes may be added after a composer's name or before a particular recording. Thus, under Schubert's name is the information: "A comparative discography 'Schubert on microgroove' by C. G. Burke will be found in three issues of HF . . ." [HF is the abbreviation for the magazine *High*

Reference Books and Periodicals

Fidelity], while later, dealing with one of this composer's chamber works, the following information is given:

Octet, F major, D.803. Vienna Octet. London LLP 1049
   (ML suggests this a reissue of 78 rpm set CE-A 104; if so, the previous reviews are as follow: . . .
   — ML 1–55 p. 15 (m.f.)
   + Na 11–27–54 p. 471
   • NYT 12–26–54 p. X8
   etc.

From this specimen entry it can be seen that the reviewer of the *Monthly Letter*, published by E.M.G. in London, was dissatisfied with both performance and recording, and suggested that the version was an LP pressing of an SP version. On the other hand, the record received a favourable review in the *Nation* while *The New York Times* gave only qualified approval. The reader will also note that the three reviews tend to cancel one another out, and also that the English user must remember that dates are quoted in American fashion with the month first and the actual date as the second item. Because of the limited range of symbols used to signify opinions and because the compiler may well have his own natural bias it is recommended in the introduction to this volume that the user should read the actual reviews when possible, in which case *Record Ratings* would be used primarily as an index. "The reasons a reviewer gives for liking or disliking a particular release are more crucial than his final decision, and often reveal that the decision should be taken with a grain of salt." The compiler and editor also suggest the need to acquire some background to reviewers and periodicals. "Having acquired such a background a user of this book may easily find that for him a plus sign associated with one critic is roughly equivalent to a minus sign associated with some other critic"—a comment that will meet with whole-hearted agreement with most readers. The position is much less simple, though, when more than one critic reviews (for example) orchestral records in the same periodical.

Financial stringency made it impossible to give analytical treatment for "recital" and other composite records which contain more than two works; such a task would have made the work much bulkier and increased the burden upon the compilers to an unbearable degree. Such records are grouped under the heading "Composite releases", first by manufacturer and then by his catalogue number in contrast to the bulk of the book where arrangement is by composer and then alphabetically the title of each work. The volume is completed by a performer index, classified into four groups. First come organizations, i.e. orchestras, chamber music groups, etc.; secondly, conductors; thirdly, vocalists and, fourthly, instrumentalists. This last group is sub-divided into four further categories— Keyboard, Strings, Winds and Miscellaneous; after each name is an abbreviation showing the actual instrument(s) played.

The foregoing paragraphs should have shown the book's importance as an aid to gramophone record selection since it allows one to see at a glance the consensus of critical opinion on a particular recording; this should be a particularly useful complement to *The record guide* (see below) which normally limits itself to a single opinion upon an individual recording. *Record Ratings* may also be used as an index to any of the periodicals listed which are filed by the library and attention must be drawn once more to the useful information given which is strictly outside the book's immediate scope. An example was given concerning a Schubert work; a second can be taken from the heading "Historical reissues" and the five discs of "50 years of great singing": "Some information on the engineering problems involved in preparing this release will be found in the column 'Music makers' by Roland Gelatt in HF 2–55 p. 51–52. Mr. Gelatt reviews the set at length in 'The Reporter' 6–30–55 p. 40–42 under the title 'On fogies and Figaro' ".

Since *Notes* is continuing its quarterly comparison of reviews, the source of the material for this book, the compilers expect to produce subsequent supplements or even new editions in due course. Here, again, is a work that should be in the stock of every library that has a collection of gramophone records; its cost is comparatively low and while its primary value is to American librarians it has considerable worth to a music librarian in Britain.

SACKVILLE–WEST, Edward, *and* SHAWE–TAYLOR, Desmond. The record guide. Revised edn. 1955. (Collins) Supplement. 1956. (Collins)

The first edition of this work was intended, according to its preface, as "A guide book to the vast available repertory of the gramophone"; the revised (i.e. the second) edition has the object "to help the music-loving record-buyer who is bewildered by the bulk and variety of the catalogues and incessant duplication of the repertory. The authors have attempted to take into full account all records of serious music currently available in England." It is generally conceded that they have succeeded admirably in their aims.

At the time of writing there have been five volumes. The original *Record guide* appeared in 1951, ran to 763 pages and listed selected records in the current gramophone catalogues up to December, 1950. There was an appendix of about thirty pages dealing with the then newly-introduced long-playing records. This volume was supplemented in November, 1952, by *The record year* which covered new issues to mid-1952. Both SP and LP discs were now merged in a single sequence and LP discs issued before January, 1951, if considered "of any worth or significance" were also included so that there was some duplication with the appendix of the original volume. The title-page adds to the authors' names "assisted by Andrew Porter". The same trio were responsible for *The record year 2* which covered releases from the middle of 1952 to mid-1953; this again covered earlier LP releases but omitted any annotations that had appeared in earlier volumes.

The revised edition appeared at the end of 1955 with William Mann's name added on the title-page, though the original two authors still appear to be mainly responsible for the work. It would also seem that works are normally selected and reviewed by one of the writers, who remains anonymous. On occasion there is disagreement between the compilers and a note as to their different opinions is given; it is sometimes possible to discover which has been responsible for the comments on a particular record when it is a more or less direct quotation from an earlier review, e.g. many of Andrew Porter's reviews in *The gramophone* are repeated almost verbatim in the volumes of *The record guide*. The new edition represents a complete revision; though primarily devoted to later releases ("towards the end of 1954" is the Introduction's definition of the last issues covered) the book includes the best of the earlier issues recommended in one or more of the three previous volumes. This is particularly the case when only one recording of a work has been available. The volume is fairly broad with 957 pages and the *Supplement*, published in March of 1956 brings the coverage up to the first half of 1955. From this fairly detailed description it is possible to infer something of the spate of new LP discs between 1950 and 1955; it was on a scale completely unknown even in the palmiest days of SP discs. This spate of new issues was paralleled by the withdrawal from the manufacturers' catalogues of longer works on 78 r.p.m. discs and then by the disappearance of almost all classical records on shellac except on the shelves of dealers specializing in second-hand discs. The three earlier volumes of the five here described will, therefore, be retained primarily for their discussion of SP discs (since most individual collectors will retain records of works not available on LP or performances that are irreplaceable) rather than for the limited coverage of earlier LP discs.

The general arrangement of the volumes is the same. Works are listed under composer, whose name is shown in capitals with one or two forenames and dates of birth and death in brackets. These particulars are all in bold-face type. There is a general introduction to the composer's music ranging from two lines to two pages; the standard of critical comment is usually excellent. The arrangement under individual composers varies according to the nature of his output and the amount of music recorded but, generally speaking, there are six headings used: Orchestral music; Chamber music; Solo instrumental music; Operas; Oratorios, etc.; Songs. The first heading has three sub-divisions—Symphonies, Concertos and Miscellaneous piano music, while the second heading is usually arranged in descending order according to the number of players, from nonets to duos. J. S. Bach may be cited as an example of how these general headings are adapted to the recorded music of a particular composer. In this case the order of headings is: Concerted instrumental music (for the Brandenburg concertos, Suites, etc.) and also—perhaps unexpectedly—for the chamber music items such as the trio sonatas and the sonatas for violin and clavier; Orchestral transcriptions; Organ music; Music for solo clavier; Piano transcriptions; Sonatas for unaccompanied violin; Suites for unaccompanied 'cello; Larger choral works; Cantatas; Motets, and Songs. The following composer, Balakirev, requires three headings only: orchestral music (which lists a symphony and a symphonic poem); Piano music (a single work) and Song.

There are often general critical comments and notes upon each of these sub-sections and, slightly less frequently, remarks upon individual works and performances. Generally speaking, one recording is recommended in preference to other versions (which are often not listed at all and may not be mentioned in the comments). Where different recordings have certain good qualities divided between them and, in the eyes of the compilers, more than one is worth recommending, then the alternative versions are listed with, possibly, comments upon their major differences, e.g. "Neither of these sets can be recommended *as a whole*, though both contain a fair measure of success". This begins a comparison of two recorded versions of Chopin's Preludes that runs to over 200 words. Outstanding performance and recording is indicated by the award of two stars before the record number(s), though the music itself may be (as the authors emphatically remarked in the first edition) "piffling". One star is given to older recordings which are technically good for their period, though in this case the star is given for outstanding interpretation. After the first volume the numbers of 12-in. discs are given capital prefix letters (LX 2222), while the prefix for a 10-in. record is in lower case (lx 2222). Long-playing records are given catalogue numbers in bold type in contrast to the ordinary type used for 78 r.p.m. discs. The introduction of the 45 r.p.m. record presented a fresh problem solved by the use of italics for their catalogue numbers. Though these variants may sound rather complicated they are easily understood in practice and the answer must be regarded as a much better solution to the same problem than that given in *W.E.R.M.*

Throughout the work, in all five volumes, the comments are written in a racy and enjoyable style, with some strong criticisms, occasional recorded disagreement between the compilers and in some cases a modified opinion of the same recording between one volume and the next (". . . we cannot help feeling that our original estimate of it [Dinu Lipatti's performance of Chopin's Waltzes] was over-enthusiastic") when a work has been played on a number of occasions between one volume and the appearance of the next one. "Collections" are dealt with in an appendix with a minimum of comment. It is obvious that all the works mentioned in this section on gramophone records have found the mixed LP anthology a difficult problem to catalogue. There is also a four-page section on tape-recordings (which may well have a very bright future if prices can be reduced) and two pages dealing with the recordings of the Coronations of King George VI and Queen Elizabeth II. Composers who are represented in an anthology or collection but who do not receive a separate entry in the main body of the book are listed in a separate index; the work is completed with another index which lists performers and quotes the page numbers on which their names will be found.

This is the work with the greatest general appeal to the average British music-lover and is also a handy guide to selection (within its period) for the gramophone record librarian, providing that its judgements are not accepted as infallible—a quick comparison with *Record Ratings* will show that some other critics and reviewers have considerably different views upon some of the recommendations. The torrent of new issues during 1953–55 obviously made the compilation of the work both difficult and tiring but one hopes that the compilers are unduly pessimistic when they describe the revised edition and its supplement as the "perhaps final edition".

PERIODICALS

Quite a number of newspapers and periodicals review some books on music and find space for brief criticisms of new gramophone records. The periodicals considered below are, however, primarily intended for the musician or music-lover and are considered in this chapter briefly for their value as aids to the selection of books, scores and gramophone records. Other contents, editorial policy and the like receive only superficial comment. Librarians may find the list of some use when revising the periodicals list and may also consider the possibility of alternative provision rather than duplication at branch libraries. Students facing examinations in book selection and assistance to readers are advised, whenever possible, to see specimen copies of the periodicals listed below. Not only will this act as an aid to memory but it is quite possible that the layout and coverage of any particular periodical may have changed, since these items are not necessarily static; the information given here may be outdated in certain particulars.

Though some of the periodicals limit their criticisms to gramophone records, others to books and scores and a third type will cover all three items, it has been thought best to deal with all magazines in alphabetical order rather than attempt to classify them.

CHESTERIAN (Quarterly)

This is the house journal of Messrs. J. & W. Chester, the London music publishing firm. It includes articles of general interest to music-lovers written by authors of both national and international repute. Reviews of new music are included; while much of the space is allotted to works published or imported by Chester, as could be expected, other music also receives mention.

Magazine Rack, Art and Music Department, Cincinnati and Hamilton Public Libraries.
Indicates the range of titles desirable in a big Music Library

Reference Books and Periodicals

FONTES ARTIS MUSICAE (Twice Yearly)

This is the review of the International Association of Music Libraries. It has been published since 1954 and is issued at six-monthly intervals. The actual printing is done by the music publishing firm of Bärenreiter in Cassell, Germany. The journal is multilingual with articles in English, French, German and occasionally in other languages. Important articles may have a translated précis at the end in the other two official languages of the journal but that is all. General announcements are also quoted in English, French and German.

For the librarian the greatest value of this periodical is almost certainly in the selective lists which appear at the back of each number. These comprise brief details of books and scores published throughout the world, arranged under country. The selections are given in five categories: I, Théâtre et films; II, Musique instrumentale; III, Musique vocale; IV, Folklore; V, Ouvrages sur la musique et ouvrages didactiques. These lists provide a simple but invaluable method of keeping some sort of check upon important foreign publications; the selection for each country is made by a local expert, e.g. for Britain the editor is Mr. A. Hyatt King of the British Museum.

THE GRAMOPHONE (Monthly)

This is the oldest and best-known publication in its field in Britain. It began publication in 1923 with Mr. (now Sir) Compton Mackenzie as its first editor. This famous author remains on the editorial board and is still as alertly interested in gramophone development as ever.

The major part of the periodical is devoted to reviews of gramophone records of standard music. The general heading "Analytical notes and first reviews" indicates the intention; reviews contain notes and comments on the music performed as well as criticisms of the quality of performance and recording. Generally speaking, the less well known the music performed the more detailed the description of the work and its place in the composer's output; the hackneyed symphonies and concertos are often "taken as read", and this sensible plan adds to the non-specialist appeal of the magazine. Reviews are normally up to 500 words in length but an important work or recording, particularly if new to the gramophone, may receive considerably fuller treatment. At the other end of the scale, a routine performance of a work regularly recorded may be dismissed in five or six lines—a matter of twenty-five to thirty words. Reviews are initialled and a list of reviewers is given with each issue. Minor variations in arrangement occur from time to time; the December 1954 issue, for example, was the last to include a complete list of the month's releases by the various companies, but the following month saw the introduction of the scheme whereby earlier recordings of a work are listed in small type together with the date they were reviewed immediately below the details of a record and before the criticism itself. This scheme allows the reader who is considering the purchase of a recording of a particular work to check back on all previous reviews and use them as an aid to selecting the version most likely to appeal. January 1956 saw the introduction of a general index to the records reviewed each month and it is quite possible that by the time these words are in print further modifications in the arrangement may have taken place.

Classical records are divided into the following categories: Orchestral (which includes concertos); Chamber music; Instrumental; Choral and song; Operatic; Poetry and diction. Arrangement within each class is alphabetical under composer; the "fill-up" on a long work, or the work on the second side of an LP disc is listed with the main work and the entire record is reviewed in the one place, even though the extra work or works may be by a different composer. This is where the monthly index is useful. The heading of each criticism gives the composer and title of the work, the name of the soloist(s), orchestra, conductor, etc., and the record number(s) and price.

Jazz and swing records have a separate section and these discs usually receive brief but reasonably comprehensive individual reviews; "Miscellaneous and dance" covers the mass of light and ephemeral music briefly but competently. Reviews are generally up to date but may sometimes be a month or two behind release. Very occasionally, reviewers get the chance of giving "second reviews" in which the alternative recordings of a particular work are compared at length though the reviewer is rarely able to say, hand on heart, that one version is clearly better than all its rivals. A new recording generally includes, during the course of the review, a brief comparison with some or all of its earlier competitors and reviewers generally indicate where (in their opinion) an earlier issue is still as good as or better than the new release.

Equipment, in the form of radiograms, loudspeakers, pickups, tape recorders and the like, is also reviewed, while new issues or reprints of miniature scores occasionally receive a brief mention. The monthly "Letter from America" helps to keep British readers abreast of the latest issues and developments in that country, though this is often frustrating; it is difficult to import an American disc into Britain and also expensive. The keen collector has to wait and hope that a British associate company will issue in this country a recording that interests him particularly. General articles are sometimes included and are usually fairly brief; they usually deal with gramophone personalities such as singers and instrumentalists, particularly those who have just died or who have sprung into prominence through the agency of the gramophone. The magazine must be regarded as essential for any library with a collection of gramophone records and it will almost certainly achieve regular use in the reading room of a library that has no collection of discs.

Finally, mention must be made of the *LP classical record catalogue*, issued quarterly. It contains a composer index with the works of each arranged in classified order and the briefest details of performer, companies' catalogue numbers and the month in which each recording was reviewed in the columns of *The gramophone*—no date indicating that the record has never been reviewed. The second part of the catalogue comprises an artist index which indicates the works recorded by a particular performer and the record number for each work. This index is used by many British gramophone librarians in lieu of including similar entries in their own library catalogues. A miscellaneous index lists the items on the LP discs of the "History of music in sound" (earlier editions included the D.G.G. "Archive" series in chronological order of "Research period"; both these series are mentioned in chapter 5); there is a list of "Music for schools" series, of individual organs with the organists who have recorded music upon them, the casts of complete operas are given and there is a "Drama and narrative" index. These miscellaneous indexes tend to vary over a period but the two main sequences are the backbone of the catalogue which is a reference work of very great value both to gramophone record librarians and to keen individuals who are building collections. There is a somewhat similar quarterly catalogue for popular records.

MONTHLY MUSIC RECORD (Monthly)

This is another house journal, in this case that of Messrs. Augener.

In addition to articles of general interest to musicians there are reviews of gramophone records, new books on music and of new scores. This magazine would appear to be intended for both the professional musician and the interested amateur. Practically all publications of the parent firm are reviewed (though one can hardly expect to find unfavourable notices) and a certain number of those of other publishers.

MUSIC AND LETTERS (Quarterly)

This is one of the most scholarly of the music periodicals published in Britain and was founded in 1920. The main body of each number consists of articles on various musical subjects and a high proportion of this information would seem to appear later in book form. References to discoveries of material relating to famous composers appears with surprising frequency and facsimiles and illustrations in music type are to be found in many of the issues. Book reviews (both of domestic and foreign publications) vary considerably in length, but 1,500 words is not uncommon and even longer reviews are found upon occasion. Because of this length only a limited number of books are selected for review in each number but those chosen are normally the most important. Initials at the end of each review indicate the writer.

Notices of music scores are generally restricted to new works or to important new editions of the classics, etc. These again are initialled. The scores are grouped according to form but headings are lacking in each group so that it is not always easy to discover if a particular work has received mention. At the end of the journal is a list of reviewers so that unfamiliar initials can be identified.

MUSICAL OPINION (Monthly)

This covers much the same ground as *The Musical Times* to which it provides a useful alternative. Although not mentioned in the title the second part of each issue is headed *The Organ world* and occupies over a third of the average issue. Organ specifications are of no interest to the majority of librarians, but when the Royal College of Organists announces the syllabus of pieces for its Fellowship and Associateship examinations each year, *The Organ world* gives brief notes on the music and these may provide useful pointers to the librarian who wishes to strengthen this particular section of the music stock.

Reference Books and Periodicals

Book reviews usually run to about 400 words and are initialled though the initials are not identified. New music is anonymously reviewed under broad headings such as "Songs", "Educational music" and the like, and a very wide field is covered. Gramophone records are reviewed by a single contributor and the selection is usually limited to orchestral, chamber music, instrumental and a few vocal records. These reviews are often comparatively late which reduces their value to the librarian. In conclusion, it must be said that the general appearance of the periodical is not attractive; the paper is of poor quality, the type is pedestrian and advertisements on every page are an irritation.

MUSICAL QUARTERLY (Quarterly)

This is probably the most important American magazine of its type and was founded in 1916. Its nearest British equivalent is *Music and Letters*. It contains fairly long articles giving (when needed) examples in music type in the text and also providing plates. Book reviews are an important feature and a single review may take 5,000 words or more, though the average is about 1,500. British and continental books receive equal appraisal with those published in the U.S.A.

Because of this international coverage book reviews are generally limited to the most important works. On the other hand, a bad musical work that has received national advertisement or the book that has been given, in the editor's opinion, unjustified critical acclaim may find itself reviewed at length in *Musical Quarterly*. As with all reviews in this periodical the critic will be a specialist in the particular subject—and the review will probably strip the offending work of nearly all its pretensions to scholarship or originality.

Reviews of gramophone records are also limited to important issues which are dealt with at length rather than giving many discs a brief mention. The notices, which are signed, concentrate on the music itself, on the edition used and on music scholarship rather than on the actual performance or the standard of recording.

MUSICAL REVIEW (Quarterly)

This periodical is similar in outlook to *Music and Letters*. As its title suggests, reviews are an important part of its content. Book reviews are initialled and average some 400 words. Gramophone records are also reviewed briefly under broad headings. Reviews tend, on occasion, to be didactic and even disputatious. Reviewers can be identified by a list given at the end of each issue.

THE MUSICAL TIMES (Monthly)

Founded in 1844, *The Musical Times* is the best-known music journal published in Britain. Since the beginning of 1951 it has been printed on art paper though the number of illustrations in any particular number is likely to be small. Book reviews (under the heading "The musician's bookshelf") vary in length to an approximate maximum of 800 words. The general policy, as with most other music magazines, would appear to favour a limited number of fairly detailed reviews rather than brief notices of nearly all music publications. Regular contributors sign reviews with initials; others with their names.

Gramophone records were formerly regularly reviewed and the notices included music quotations but changes in editorial policy and pressure on space has modified this. New music is briefly reviewed under broad headings such as "Piano", "Organ" and "Choral". Although this periodical is, strictly speaking, a house magazine it does not limit its reviews to works issued only by Novello—those of other publishers appear to receive equal representation and impartial treatment in its columns; the only obvious indication of ownership is the partsong or anthem that is to be found in the middle of each month's copy.

The Musical Times is also the journal of The Royal College of Organists and the official announcements of that body appear every month, together with reports of proceedings, etc. During recent years the emphasis on organ matters has noticeably increased while the magazine has also apparently attempted to become much more popular in appeal.

NOTES (Quarterly)

This is the magazine of the Music Library Association (of the U.S.A.). It is both surprising and disappointing that it is so little known to British colleagues for it is produced by librarians for librarians. The articles on musical matters include long and important bibliographical ones. There is an irregular feature, "Audio-visual matters" in which gramophone library affairs are discussed. Book reviews, which usually run to a maximum of some 500 words, are signed and are often pleasantly informal as well as being highly knowledgeable. British and European books of importance receive equal attention with American publications. At the end of the section devoted to reviews is a list of other works which have not been noticed for one reason or another and a second set headed "Corrections and amplifications of old listings". Reviews quote not only the publisher and price, but also the pagination and illustrations (if any). Music reviews are usually limited to new works or important new editions of old ones; here again the coverage is international. The music is classified under broad headings and reviews are signed.

Gramophone records are not reviewed as such but the findings of nearly thirty periodicals are collated; information as to how this is done is given earlier in this chapter when discussing *Record ratings*, compiled and edited by Kurtz Myers and Richard S. Hill. Many of the recordings are issued, sooner or later, in Britain so that the lists are of very real value to the British music librarian and are not for domestic consumption only.

Every British library that has a separate music department or a music librarian should subscribe to this periodical which should be filed as one of the most important music periodicals in existence.

RECORD NEWS (Monthly)

This periodical reviews gramophone records of classical music though lighter material may receive brief mention. There is a panel of reviewers, each specializing in a limited field such as Lute and guitar, Viennese classics, Organ and church music. Separate attention is given to the music, the performance and the recording; the playing time of each disc is given (indicating, it may be added, some immense variations in the amount of music that may be issued on a single LP side). The advantage of specialist reviews is great, particularly since this magazine overcame its early disadvantage of somewhat belated notices. The equipment upon which each reviewer's discs have been played is also quoted each month and this can be of assistance to the high-fidelity addict.

Since the coverage of this magazine is almost exactly that of the average gramophone record library the periodical is most useful to any gramophone record librarian and is likely to be much used by the public. Its approach with use of a specialist panel is somewhat akin to that of *The American Record Guide*, one of the best periodicals of its type in the U.S.A.

THE STRAD (Monthly)

A periodical for the players of stringed instruments, whatever their technical abilities. It contains brief, unsigned book and gramophone record reviews. Music reviews are limited to string music and to miniature scores of chamber music. The comments, though brief, are useful and often illuminating, particularly as the standard of playing ability required is normally indicated. This can be very helpful when choosing new accessions in this field.

TEMPO (Quarterly)

Yet another house journal, in this case that of Messrs. Boosey & Hawkes. The standard of production is as high as that of the music issued by this firm and illustrations add to the general attractiveness of the magazine. It contains brief book reviews.

FOR FURTHER READING

HICKLING, Jean. An account of current musical periodicals in English.

This unpublished essay was submitted to the Library Association as part of the Final examination by Miss Hickling, who was Music Librarian at Westminster at the time it was written; a copy of the essay may be seen at Chaucer House. The history and policy of a number of periodicals is discussed and the essay brings together information not easily found elsewhere.

The articles on dictionaries and periodicals, mentioned under *Thompson* and *Grove* respectively at the beginning of this chapter, should also be read by all students.

Postscript

Everyman's dictionary of music appeared in a "further revised edition" in October, 1958. There has been no major recasting but rather the usual small amendments that a dictionary of this nature periodically requires. Another revised work that deserves mention is James B. Coover's *Music lexicography* (Denver, Colorado; Denver Public Library, 1958). This provides a revision and considerable expansion of the same author's *A bibliography of music dictionaries*, quoted as an example on page 74 of this chapter. There are now listed over 1,300 items, though this total includes different editions of the same work. This bibliography is almost certainly the finest in its chosen field. Mr. Coover, who is Music Librarian of Vassar College in New York State, includes an essay on "Lacunae in music lexicography" in which he discusses the strange fact that music dictionaries for the sixteenth and seventeenth centuries are almost non-existent though earlier ones are known and the eighteenth century saw many productions of this nature.

Chapter III

CATALOGUING

This chapter falls into three divisions. First comes a brief survey of some of the problems that arise in cataloguing music; this is intended to be of general interest. Second is a section for students which deals with the various rules for cataloguing music in different Codes. The third section contains practical suggestions for music cataloguing. This part of the chapter is particularly intended to provide assistance for the cataloguer who has little knowledge of music and who lacks specialist help from his colleagues. The need for a fair degree of musical knowledge if scores are to be correctly handled is by no means as fully appreciated as it should be, but in the small library the cataloguing staff is likely to consist of a single professionally-qualified assistant only and that assistant may be completely unmusical. Since this chapter was written the position has been improved for the British librarian by the appearance of *The British catalogue of music* which should provide some assistance but which should not be regarded as a substitute for a cataloguer nor yet as being infallible and suitable for every library.

The problems

There are four special problems which face the cataloguer of music. The first concerns the title-page for, unlike normal practice, it may be largely irrelevant, since the same piece of music can be published in various countries with very different title-pages. Some provision must be made so that all the entries for the music appear together in the catalogue. The second problem relates to arrangements: the same piece of music may be available in several different forms, e.g. a library's stock could easily contain the miniature score of a Haydn symphony, an arrangement of it for piano solo, another for piano duet and a fourth for violin and piano. Good cataloguing requires that all versions be entered separately but that they are filed

109

together under the composer's name in a dictionary catalogue or appear together in the author index of a classified catalogue. Then the potential user can easily see the various available arrangements and choose the one most suitable for his purpose. The third problem concerns excerpts; separate publication of extracts from a longer work is uncommon with books but normal with music scores. It is particularly frequent in opera where single arias are available by the dozen in response to long-standing public demand. The amateur soprano who wishes to sing *One fine day* would be painfully surprised if she found herself forced to buy a complete score of *Madame Butterfly* to achieve this ambition, though she will probably be happy enough to borrow a vocal score of the complete work from her local library. The fourth problem has been the lack of standard examples of good cataloguing. The American librarian has had for some years the expert guidance of the catalogue cards issued by the Library of Congress to ensure a high standard of music cataloguing. The appearance in 1957 of *The British Catalogue of Music* has assisted the British librarian but it would be misleading to pretend that the standard is as good as its American counterpart.

The answers

The natural answer to these problems is the employment of a good cataloguer with a sufficient knowledge of music. Where there is a music librarian, cataloguing should be done by this expert or prepared under his or her supervision. Only the very largest libraries will be able to think in terms of a music cataloguing department.

The second answer would appear to be a sound code of rules applicable to music, such as that of the Library of Congress which was influenced by the *Code for cataloging music* of the Music Library Association. In addition to a code the cataloguer should have an adequate supply of source books. No two librarians will exactly agree as to how many are "an adequate supply"; it may be mentioned, without comment, that Elmer (whose thesis is included in the reading list at the end of this chapter) suggests no less than 243 books. Cataloguers should be reminded at this point that there is often value in old music dictionaries and cyclopaedias as these will frequently include entries for composers whose popularity has since declined and whose names may be difficult to trace in current books My own recommendations to the cataloguer would be the works annotated in Chapter II; most of these should be shelved in the

Reference Library. The expense of buying second copies so that the works could be at the cataloguer's elbow makes such a concession impractical.

It would appear that the problem of cataloguing music has been avoided in some American libraries by the device of putting on the shelves music that has been neither classified nor catalogued. Wallace C. Look[1] circulated a questionnaire to 200 libraries; only 18 per cent of these included music scores in their collections. Of the thirty-six libraries no less than eleven have neither catalogued nor classified their collections. These eleven libraries have book stocks ranging from 9,000 to 255,000 with an average of 70,000. These results will probably shock many British librarians, and one cannot deprecate too strongly such an "answer" to the problem.

CATALOGUING RULES AND THE STUDENT

The Anglo-American Code

The Anglo-American Code of 1908 dismissed music cataloguing in three brief rules—a possible indication that the music section in most public libraries was either very small or imperfectly catalogued; it could well have been both. The first rule, numbered 8 in the Code, is the general one that instructs the cataloguer to make author entry under the name of the composer with added entries for editor or arranger and also under the librettist when there are words set to music. Current practice in many libraries is to ignore these added entries unless the librettist is well known (such as Da Ponte or Hofsmannsthal), or unless the arranger has so modified the music as to carry it over the disputed boundary that separates arrangement from transcription. In the latter case the transcriber's name is often hyphenated with that of the original composer, so that the cataloguer meets Rossini-Respighi, Schubert-Liszt, Bach-Walton, etc., though these should not be confused with Castelnuovo-Tedesco, Wolf-Ferrari and similar hyphenated names of a single composer. There is a subsidiary rule to no. 8 that directs the cataloguer to enter variations written on a theme by a different composer under the name of the composer of the variations and not under the writer of the theme, even though that provides the starting point for the later composer. This is an obviously sensible rule; only rarely is the original theme of intrinsic interest—it is what the later composer has done with it that counts. The secondary entry may be of use when it identifies the work from which the theme is taken; it can also indicate when two or more composers have based variations upon the same theme as have Schumann, Brahms and Rachmaninov (among others) with an extract from Paganini's *Caprice no. 24.*

The second rule deals with libretti. ("Libretto" has become accepted as an English word so that the alternative plural "Librettos" may be regarded as almost equally correct.) These should be catalogued under the writer with an added entry under the composer. The added entry is of doubtful value in small libraries particularly where it suggests to an enquirer that a particular score is included in stock when in fact only the libretto is available. Yet there are at least two points in favour of such an entry; it may draw attention to the fact that the words (in the original, in a translation or in both) of an opera are available and few patrons are likely to know the name or names of the authors of the words of their favourite operas. The other advantage applies where there is a gramophone record library, for libretti are often preferred to scores by borrowers of operatic discs.

The third and last rule is no. 10, which is for thematic catalogues. These are to be entered under the composer with an added entry under the name of the compiler. Many students who learn this rule, parrot-fashion, remain unaware as to what a thematic catalogue is, so that a brief explanation may be useful. Since Beethoven's day the earliest published composition of a musician is normally given the opus number 1, the next becomes opus 2, and so on. When opus numbers are used no confusion should occur between works with the same title (such as *Sonata in F major*) by the same composer; in addition such numbers will usually indicate if the work is an early one or of the composer's maturity, etc. Unfortunately for the cataloguer, opus numbers were not given to works (with few exceptions) until the late eighteenth century; there are a number of subsequent examples up to the present time of composers refraining from identifying their compositions in this way. Important contemporary examples are Ralph Vaughan Williams and Aaron Copland. With certain composers some works are numbered and others not, though most composers who use opus numbers omit them for minor works particularly if they do not expect them to be published; with other composers the numbered sequence may have little or no connection with the chronological sequence. Thus a limited number of works by Handel and Haydn have opus numbers which were usually given, without permission, by enterprising music publishers of the time, but the majority of the scores by these two composers are not so distinguished. On the other hand, many Schubert works bear numbers that have little relation to the order of composition and in the Schubert thematic catalogue compiled by O. E. Deutsch (Dent, 1951), a fascinating introduction includes both a brief history of the thematic catalogue and outlines some of the divergencies. According to this authoritative list Schubert's opus 1 (the famous song *Erlkönig*; *The Erl king*) was written in the autumn of 1815 while the same composer's opus 117 (a setting of another Goethe poem, *Der Sänger*) was composed in February, 1815. Dvořák presents no problems of numbering but it is worth recalling that for some time he was under contract to one publisher and selling certain works to others, so he used two parallel sequences of opus numbers in order to appear to keep within the letter of his contract.

It is to deal with these and similar difficulties that thematic catalogues have come into being. To ensure distinction between one composition and another the thematic catalogue shows the opening bars of the music of each piece. Sometimes two staves, treble and bass, are shown; occasionally, the melody line only may be considered sufficient. The first, and probably most famous, thematic catalogue is that of Ludwig von Köchel in which he arranged the compositions of Mozart in probable chronological order, using the original manuscripts, correspondence, etc., as evidence. Köchel's work was first published in 1862 and has since twice been revised in the light of subsequent discoveries which have both added to the list of Mozart's works (and deleted others) and corrected some of Köchel's supposed dates—but it is still the standard catalogue for the identification of a Mozart work so that it is universally accepted that the distinguishing mark of a set of German dances should be K. 605 and not op. 605 as one would normally expect with another composer. These initial letters have now spread to use with certain other composers, such as Schubert, Vivaldi, etc.

Cutter

In Cutter's *Rules for a dictionary catalog* (4th edn, 1904) there is a single rule for music which suggests double entry under composer and the author of the words. Cutter adds a note that "short" and "medium" entries would probably dispense with the author of the words but that in the case of famous authors (e.g. Shakespeare) the double entry should continue to be made. At the end of the rules is a section entitled "Cataloging special publications and other material" in which the second sub-head is "Music". This particular section of the appendix is the work of O.G. Sonneck of the Library of Congress, and is divided into sections headed Author, Title, Imprint and Notes respectively. "Author" is a variation of the single rule already quoted; "Title" deals solely with the problem of those musical scores which have a title-page common to the whole series, the individual score at hand being distinguished by a pencilled or printed line under the appropriate entry on this multiple title-page. This form of printing was an obvious economy for the publisher but is rarely met with today when it is the custom to print a separate and distinct title-page for every piece of music issued. "Imprint" devotes a page to the dating of music; it emphasizes the importance of publishers' plate numbers (those letters and numbers usually to be found at the bottom of every piece of music published later than the eighteenth century). With rare or old music the date is often extremely valuable but it is of much less importance with modern music; patrons are not normally worried if a score was printed in 1925 or 1955 providing it contains the required music. Copyright dates, however, may be usefully added for modern composers whether or not they use opus numbers. The final section of this appendix, headed "Notes", gives some useful information to the music cataloguer particularly with its elucidation of the word "score" which is still often used in an imprecise way. Four examples are given but one may doubt if they are particularly helpful. Sonneck apparently favoured the exact transcription of the title page, a form of cataloguing that can often be misleading as is indicated later in this chapter.

British Museum

The British Museum rules deal with music cataloguing in an appendix in which is given the Museum practice of making entry normally under the composer together with added entries under the arranger or editor. In addition, title entries are made for operas and songs. This general rule is followed by four subsidiary ones—for Anonymous pieces and collections of music; for Psalms, Hymns and Christmas carols; for Programmes and for Musical periodicals.

Music Library Association

It can be seen that none of the three authorities briefly considered above gives rules for copies of the same piece of music published in different countries under apparently different titles, nor for excerpts, nor yet for other major problems that arise when cataloguing music. These difficulties were considered by the Music Library Association whose thirty-one suggested rules for music cataloguing were published in an Appendix to the *American Library Association, preliminary second American edition* (Chicago, A.L.A., 1941). These rules were subsequently issued as an offprint (numbered pages 354 to 371) and were considered as Chapter I of the Music Library Association's *Code for cataloguing music.* The thirty-one rules, slightly amended, were then codified into a single rule with a host of sub-sections and now appear as Rule 12 in the 1949 *A.L.A. Cataloging Code.* The new rule contains guidance on librettos, on pastiches (whether works written by a number of composers or medleys of one sort or another); on incidental music, ballets, liturgical music, masses, psalters, cadenzas, arrangements, fantasias, spurious works, collections, and thematic catalogues (which are to be entered under compiler with added entry for the original composer, thus bringing the rule into line with the American one for concordances). The great expansion is at once apparent and would seem to be based upon current American practice.

The second chapter of this Code was also issued in 1941 and consists of twenty-two pages of duplicated typewriter script on "Title". The previous chapter had included this important statement: "In cataloging music it is necessary to establish a conventional or standard title in every case. This title occupies the line between the author entry and the title as it is transcribed from the work in hand. In the examples given in this chapter the standard title is not shown. In preparing cards for the catalog, if for any reason the standard title is not given, a line should be left blank for its insertion."

This later chapter suggests how the conventional or standard title should be formulated. It recognizes five types—Distinctive, Generic, Indeterminate and Collective titles, Excerpts and arrangements. The distinctive title is one given by the composer if the work is an opera, cantata, song, etc., and also if the work is a symphonic poem (*Tasso; Till Eulenspiegel*, etc.) or sets or pieces with appropriate title (*Kinderscenen; Miroirs*). Generic titles are those of works which indicate the musical form or type of composition, such as Symphony and Sonata. Indeterminate title is for works which suggest a mood as well as a musical form, such as Nocturne, Serenade and Intermezzo. Collective titles may be exemplified by *Myra Hess album; from her repertoire,* etc.

The second section of this chapter suggests that there are three elements peculiar to music titles—the opus numbers, the serial numbers (e.g. *Sonata no 2 . . .*) which are liable to error, and key. The third section of the chapter deals with characteristics and points out some of the difficulties of extracting relevant information which may be hidden in scrolls and curlicues. The title-page may also be the cover (and so be liable to loss) while the page occupying the normal position of title-page is used for publisher's advertisements. The title page may be printed in more than one language so that the reader can select the one which suits him best.

The conventional, standard or filing title (three descriptive terms for the same thing) should be as concise as possible in order to avoid running on to the second line of a catalogue card, and should ignore ordinal numbers at the beginning of a title (*Second suite*, etc.). When there is choice between generic and distinctive titles, the latter should be chosen unless the work is one of a series. The quoted examples prefer *Eine kleine Nachtmusik* to *Quintett . . .* , but *Symphony no. 6* in preference to *Pastoral symphony.* The distinctive title will naturally be taken as the conventional title but should be as brief as possible, e.g. *King Olaf* rather than *Scenes from the saga of King Olaf.* When a generic title is used then the English form should be employed if possible (*Symphony*, etc.) and English should also be used for the instruments (piano rather than clavier, etc.).

The Code suggests that instruments should always be quoted in the same order. Where there are two instruments one of which is a keyboard instrument, then the other one should be named first (Violin and piano). If more than two instruments, of which one is a keyboard instrument then the latter is mentioned first (Piano, bassoon and flute). Stringed instruments are named in standard descending order but all other instruments in alphabetical order. The key should always be included (in English) if possible, though it is suggested that works written during this century may omit the key signature. Arrangements are shown by the abbreviation "arr." followed by the simplest possible indication of the medium of arrangement. Where only the accompaniment has been arranged, as with a vocal score of an opera, this is indicated by the abbreviation "acc. arr. piano", etc. This is unnecessary when the information has already been shown in the conventional title.

The third chapter of this Code, for Imprint, is of five pages only and was issued in Febrarury, 1942. The first rule is for place of publication and publisher; the second for date (a restatement of the A.L.A. rules); the third for date other than imprint date; the fourth for "Date of issue later than date of first publication—work undated" and the last for Publication number. The Introduction contains this sentence: "For the ordinary purposes of most libraries the exact dating of musical publications is unnecessarily expensive and time-consuming. . . ." It continues: "In most cases dates should be established only for first editions, special collections, and work of particular interest to the library." The chapter embodies some suggested sources of information for dates.

Chapters IV and V on Collation and Notes respectively were published in a single pamphlet of twenty-five pages during 1942. There are two general definitions:

"(a) *Score*. The written or printed form of a musical work in which the music for the participating voices and/or instruments appears on two or more staves, one above the other. For fuller definition, enquirer is referred to W. S. Pratt's *The new encyclopedia of music and musicians* . . . , new and revised edition, 1929.

"(b) *Part*. (i) The music for any one of the participating voices and/or instruments in a musical work.

"(ii) The written or printed copy of such a part for the use of a singer and/or player."

The rules in this section are divided into A, Introductory; B, Paging, and C, Volumes.

The fifth chapter suggests that Notes may include species (e.g. *ballet, cantata*) when not expressed in the title; the kind of publication (score; score and parts; parts); the medium of performance of the copy in hand with a note of the original medium if possible; the tessitura or voice range when a vocal work is available in different keys. Where there are words, the language or languages of the text should be indicated together with the name of the author and/or translator. Unusual notation (e.g. Tablature) should also be indicated and it may be helpful to quote the duration of performance of a work (a figure sometimes given by composer or publisher) and place and date of first performance of an opera.

These rules have been quoted at considerable length for two reasons. First, they are of immense practical use and importance;

secondly, copies are extremely scarce in Britain and the student's chance of seeing one is accordingly slight. Since the foregoing was written, however, the revised edition has appeared, entitled *Code for cataloging music and phonorecords*, prepared by a joint committee of the Music Library Association and the American Library Association, and published by the latter body in 1958. The new code contains five chapters. The first is a virtual reprint of Rule 9 in the 1949 A.L.A. Code; chapter II brings together aspects of description that formed chapters II to V of the 1941-2 Code (discussed above); chapter III deals with phonorecords and reprints rule 9a of the L.C. Code (see below); chapter IV is entirely new and gives simplified rules which should be of real value to all in charge of small music collections, while chapter V is concerned with filing rules for conventional titles and is likely to be of greatest use to those with very large music collections. English librarians can obtain copies from the Woolston Book Company of Nottingham and should certainly obtain a copy for the cataloguer.

Library of Congress

The *Rules for descriptive cataloging in the Library of Congress* date from 1949 and are twelve in number. Rule 9 deals with music; it is lengthy and immensely detailed. It is divided into five sections—Conventional titles; Transcription of title-page; Imprint; Collation; Notes. The rule is an expanded adaption of the earlier M.L.A. code and quotes many examples that are worthy of study. Excerpts (Rule 9: 2H) are entered under the conventional title of the complete work, as is necessary, but no suggestions are made for the order of entry if there are a number of excerpts from a single work. Alphabetical order by title is apparently the result but it would seem much more logical to arrange excerpts in the order in which they appear in the original work; groups of excerpts would precede single ones. Such a method of entry would tally with that adopted for the Bible and similar works that are available in several versions and which have excerpts and selections published also.

The very comprehensiveness of the rule makes detailed comment superfluous. The cataloguer of music will find reference to this rule is often helpful even though domestic cataloguing practice can hardly be compared with that of the Library of Congress. The printed cards issued by L.C. naturally adhere to that institution's rules. In 1952 a supplement was issued to rule 9—rule 9a, which is for phonorecords.

Cataloguing

This somewhat hybrid word was selected to cover gramophone records, wire and tape recordings, cylindrical ("phonograph" in British parlance) records and player-piano rolls. The rule is discussed at some length, under "Cataloguing", in Chapter V.

McColvin & Reeves

Though not a cataloguing code in the accepted sense the chapter on cataloguing in volume 1 of *Music libraries* has had immense influence and should be compulsory reading for every cataloguing student. Many of the points made have been incorporated in the M.L.A. rules; one of the most important concerns the conventional or standard title. It is suggested that this should normally be that originally used by the composer if distinctive, with the English translation following in brackets. This does not apply to generic titles, such as Symphonie, etc. Where the copy being catalogued has title-page in a language that is not the original nor yet in English, then the recommended form is: Original title in brackets; title of the actual copy being catalogued; English title in curves. This process, it is justly claimed, will bring together different versions of the same work whatever the language of the title-page. In all these cases the cataloguer should make necessary cross-references (so that the searcher for Wagner's *Twilight of the Gods* is referred to *Götterdämmerung*, for instance) and if this is done it would seem that the insistence on the original tongue is not always necessary or wise but that the cataloguer could, with advantage, enter under the best-known title with preference for the original in case of doubt. Musical encyclopaedias usually give titles in the form best known to the people of that country so that *Grove* or some other British music dictionary or encyclopaedia would serve for British cataloguers. It is not always easy to discover the original title of a work, particularly in the cases of vocal works of the eighteenth century and earlier when a composer may have set words in a foreign language but arranged for a translation into his native tongue for performance in his own country.

If one follows the use of the best-known form there would still be a reference from the unused title (as indicated in the preceding paragraph). As instances, it would probably be better to catalogue under *Christmas oratorio* than *Weihnachts Oratorium;* on the other hand, *Cavalleria rusticana* is much more familiar than the British *Rustic chivalry*.

Music Librarianship

Library Association

It may well come as a surprise to many students to know that there is the outline of a draft code for cataloguing music and gramophone records prepared by a committee convened by the Library Association. The committee met under the chairmanship of Mr. J. D. Stewart with Miss M. Dean-Smith as secretary, and held some nine meetings during 1944 and 1945. Professor Gerald Abraham, Mr. A. Hyatt King and Miss Valentine Britten were members of a highly-qualified team and it seems unfortunate that the rules so painfully hammered out have never been officially released. The notes on gramophone record cataloguing, in particular, contain much valuable information and suggestion in dealing with awkward problems.

PRACTICAL CATALOGUING

Composer

Entry will be made in the normal fashion. Where transliteration is needed the form used in a standard reference book should be used. British librarians may use *Grove* or the *British Catalogue of Music*; American librarians will probably follow *Thompson* or the Library of Congress headings. The difference may be quite considerable at times, as with Nicholai Andreievich Rimsky-Korsakov (*Grove*) and Nikolai Andreevich Rimskii-Korsakov (L.C.). Forenames will be treated in the library's normal fashion; one may be regarded as sufficient in many libraries for Puccini, while others will list all six Christian names. Most libraries will ignore the fact that Offenbach was born Lévy but the rest will consider it sufficiently important to include in the heading. Equally, some cataloguers will be satisfied to enter Philip Heseltine's books under that name, Peter Warlock's music under Warlock and link the two names by means of a cross-reference; others will insist upon using Heseltine for both and refer from the pseudonymous Warlock. These and similar minor problems can normally be resolved by reference to the chosen musical authority.

Title

This presents the major difficulty in much music cataloguing. The first problem has already been discussed when considering cataloguing codes—that of title-pages in different languages. The library may well possess two editions of the famous *48 preludes and fugues* by J. S. Bach. One copy has that title, the other is called *Das*

120

Wohltemperierte Clavier. The pianist who borrows the latter copy may
not know a word of German but music typography is international
so that the same works can be played with equal skill by the same
player whichever of the two editions is used. A biography of Bach,
available both in the original German and an English translation is
not comparable. The original is of no value to the man who cannot
read German while the translation, however good, is not exactly the
same thing as the original.

To catalogue music well, therefore, requires one of two methods.
Either the cataloguer must be prepared to ignore the title-page on
many occasions or, if this is too heretical, interpose between the
composer and the transcript of the title-page a standard or conventional title. Library of Congress practice and the Music Library
Association recommendation is that the conventional title should
always be used even though it is often exactly that which appears on
the title-page. The discussion of the M.L.A. rules on page 115 mentions the different types of standard title recognized and the suggestions for dealing with each. For works with a distinctive title the
McColvin & Reeves recommendation, to quote that first, in the
original language and in brackets, is the equivalent of using a conventional title. If the cataloguer ignores the printed title-page but
makes his own entry, he should be using the standard title in place
of the printed one of the work in hand. Examples at the end of this
chapter will indicate how this can be done.

In order to standardize entries a decision will have to be made
between the two possible forms of "Concerto for piano and orchestra . . .", "Concerto for violin and orchestra", etc., and "Piano
concerto . . ." and "Violin concerto . . .". The choice, it can be seen,
is between emphasizing the solo instrument or musical form in which
the work is written. The Library of Congress and the majority of
libraries favour the first form which will bring together all the concertos written by a composer. This is one form of classification and
is certainly useful to the student of musical form. My own preference
is for the minority view which seems to me to be better in all but the
largest collections used by performers rather than students. Using
this method, "Violin concerto . . ." and "Violin sonata . . ." entries
are filed in close proximity in the catalogue, so that this produces a
different form of classification with a different characteristic to the
other example. Here, the violin player will find all works by the
composer written for his instrument at the one point. Where this

method may be thought unsatisfactory is with the small number of concertos written with two solo instruments. *Concerto for violin, violoncello and orchestra* . . . is probably more direct than *Double concerto, for violin, and violoncello*, though the latter title is the one by which the work is likely to be requested.

With generic titles an English equivalent should be used and keys should also be given in the English form. Thus *Symphonie II, Do majeur* is entered as *Symphony no. 2, in C major*. For operas and other works with distinctive titles general preference is for the original title providing it is in English, French, German, Italian or Spanish. For other languages (particularly Slav languages such as Russian and Czech) an English title is usually better; where the title is given in two languages, the usual first choice is the original language, within the limits already mentioned, then the best known and thirdly the English title. Should the title-page give insufficient information or be misleading, a suitable title must be made up by the cataloguer.

If possible, the key in which an instrumental work is written should be quoted as part of the title. Where not shown on the title-page but discovered elsewhere it should be added in brackets. It must be remembered that this will apply mainly to works written in the eighteenth and nineteenth centuries; earlier works often do not have definite tonality while many twentieth-century works are in no ascertainable key. It is better to use the form "in G major" or "in G minor" rather than "in G" for the former. "In G" may be taken to mean that part of the work is in G major and part in the minor key.

When a composer has written more than one work in a particular form these works are generally numbered in sequence, e.g. *Symphony no. 5, String quartet no. 3*. This number should always be quoted *before* the key signature or the result is ambiguous. *Symphony in C minor, no. 2* may be misinterpreted to mean that the composer has written two symphonies in the same key and that this is the second of them. It is possible, though unlikely, that the composer's first symphony was in that particular key but the quotation of the series number before the key prevents any possible ambiguity. Where the work has a nickname, whether given by the composer or not, it should be quoted and is also inserted between the key and the opus number, e.g. *Symphony no. 2, in B minor* (*"The four temperaments"*), *op. 16*. In the case of Haydn symphonies there are various numbering sequences but the generally accepted one is that of Mandyczewski often called the "new" Breitkopf & Härtel list. Where applicable the "old" B. & H. number should also be shown and if the work is one of the last twelve, written in England for concerts presented by the impresario Salomon, the "Salomon" number is also required. This information is easily discovered in the larger encyclopaedias, in McColvin and Reeves, v. 2 and in Appendix "B" in Rosemary Hughes's *Haydn* ("Master musicians series") to mention a few sources. Thus the entry for a Haydn symphony might be: *Symphony no. 100 (Old B. & H. no. 11; Salomon no. 12), in G major ("Military").* There are no opus numbers for Haydn symphonies. Complicated as this entry might appear, all the information given is necessary to ensure that the work will be found by an enquirer, and one may still find miniature scores of Haydn symphonies giving the "old" and not the "new" Breitkopf numbers.

The second problem, mentioned at the opening of the chapter, concerns arrangements. Unless there is no possibility of misunderstanding, the medium for which a work has been arranged should be plainly stated, for it will normally happen that only one form will suit the convenience of a library user; very occasionally alternatives may be acceptable. The pianists who want a piano duet version of Peter Warlock's *Capriol* will have no use for a set of string parts for the same work and the catalogue entries should make it perfectly plain to which version an individual entry refers.

Excerpts present the third problem—one which is commonly encountered in music cataloguing. The simple answer is to ensure that entry is always made under the title of the parent work with a cross-reference from the title of the excerpt where desirable. The actual arrangement of excerpts from the same work may pose yet another problem; they may be filed in alphabetical order of excerpt title, or in the order in which the various excerpts appear in the parent work. The latter method is more logical and also overcomes the further difficulty of the translated excerpt where two versions of the same portion of the work may be known by two different titles.

Imprint

The name of the publisher should always be given with the main entry for a music score however simple the cataloguing practice of an individual library. Students may have to study a particular edition while the reputation of different publishers of the same work may vary considerably—and so may the editions themselves. One difficulty (which has only been partially solved in the entries for the second part of this book) is that of distinguishing between the publisher and the name of the importing agent for a work originally published abroad. Thus Dvořák's works may be shown as published by either Lengnick or Simrock in a British library, since one is the original publisher and the other is the agent who controls all imports of this composer's works into the country. This is not of great importance. The place of publication is normally of little interest and may well be omitted except for works issued by smaller publishing houses perhaps difficult to trace. Similarly the date of publication is generally irrelevant. If the opus number or copyright date (or perhaps both for twentieth-century composers) is shown the work can be successfully identified and the potential borrower is not likely to be worried if the music was printed in 1926 or 1946 providing that it is what is wanted and is in satisfactory condition. Music is rarely dated and there is little point in adding "n.d." to the imprint particularly as reprints from a single set of plates may be issued for half a century or more. Trying to discover date of publication is usually a waste of time that can be more profitably used elsewhere.

Those remarks refer to modern works. Old music, particularly that issued before 1800, is on a completely different footing; plate-numbers, advertisements, watermarks and other aids to precise dating are then invaluable.

Collation

Though the Music Library Association rules suggest that pagination and illustrations should be quoted as with an ordinary book this seems rather unnecessary. The inclusion of a frontispiece (as with many of the Philharmonia scores) may be considered worthy of mention. On the other hand, the number of parts (band, choral or chamber) should always be quoted or itemized when they are together in a folder, binder or pocket. If a work is published in more than one volume, that obviously requires quoting together with a contents note for each volume. Few things can be more frustrating than a search for one particular work among several volumes by a single composer. If a library has the complete organ works of Bach (as it should) and a reader requires the trio sonatas, the appropriate volume should be ascertainable from the catalogue rather than by a search among those volumes that happened to be on the shelves at that moment. Where a library has the complete string quartets of a composer bound in four volumes, one of which contains all the first violin parts, the second all the viola parts, etc., this fact also should be stated since it means that a quartet will require all four volumes to play any individual work.

Though possibly better entered as "Notes" rather than part of the title or collation, the type of score should always be mentioned. Clear distinction should be made between the following types:

(a) *Full score.* This is the type used by the conductor quoting each individual part on a separate stave. Consequently the page size is usually very large; this type of score is rarely in stock in any but the largest libraries.

(b) *Miniature score.* This is similar to a full score but the type has been reduced so that the page is pocket size or thereabouts. Examples of these should be found in every music collection.

(c) *Vocal score.* Here the vocal parts of a work such as an opera or cantata, etc., are shown on separate staves in normal sized music type, but the accompaniment, probably written for orchestra, has been reduced to two staves for performance upon a piano. The M.L.A./A.L.A. *Code for cataloging music* . . . refers to these as "piano-vocal scores".

(d) *Piano score.* An arrangement for solo piano of an orchestral, vocal or instrumental work.

When a work is written for several instruments, these should be individually noted unless the combination is a standard one. The usually accepted terms are String trio (Violin, viola and 'cello), Piano trio (Piano, violin and 'cello), String quartet (2 violins, viola and 'cello), Piano quartet (Piano plus string trio), Piano quintet (Piano plus string quartet) and String sextet (a double string trio, i.e. two violins, two violas and two 'cellos). The M.L.A. rules assume that a String quintet comprises two violins, two violas and a violoncello but this is not a universally accepted term as the others quoted are, and there are examples of works with one viola and two violoncellos, so that it is best to list the instruments in this case. Where the piano is replaced by another instrument, the same type of nomenclature applies so that an oboe quartet is an oboe and a string trio, while a clarinet and string quartet form a clarinet quintet. Works whose instrumentation does not agree with the standard terms must have the parts specified, e.g. String quartet for three violins and violoncello.

Analytical entries

Where an album is made up by the library, a library supplier or a publisher and contains items by different composers, analytical entries are naturally required for the individual works. If necessary the pages throughout the album should be numbered in sequence and an index provided.

Notes

The amount of information here will vary immensely according to the work being catalogued. Some indication of what may be necessary can be seen from the M.L.A. Code quoted earlier in this chapter. If the entry does not make it plain then the language or languages of the words should be shown together with the name(s) of the translator(s). Singers may well require a particular translation, and some translators are noted for their excellent work in this field; one might instance the translations of Schubert songs and Mozart operas by Richard Capell and Edward J. Dent respectively. Generally speaking, notes should follow the same lines as with book cataloguing and give such extra information or elucidate such ambiguities of the entry as may be considered necessary by the cataloguer.

How do I catalogue . . . ?

In an attempt to aid the cataloguer a list of difficult cases follows. In general the basis of the suggested answer is Rule 12 of the *A.L.A. Cataloging Rules*, the 1949 revision of the M.L.A's suggested thirty-one rules of 1941. "Wallace" refers to Chapter III of Ruth Wallace's *The care and treatment of music in a library*.

Anonymous works. Enter under the title. The first word of the title is ignored for filing purposes if it is an article.

Anthems. Under the composer with added entry under the title. If easily ascertainable the writer or source of the words should be included—in the entry if shown on the title-page, or in a note if not.

Arrangements. [*See also* Transcriptions.] Arrangements should always be noted as such. The arranger's name will usually be included with the author (composer) and subject entries but will not usually warrant a separate entry under his own name, unless the work being catalogued is a collection or one of a collection known under the name of the arranger. (A.L.A., A.10; Wallace, 3; McColvin & Reeves, p. 16.)

Ballets, pantomimes. A.L.A. rule (A.5) suggests added entry for the writer of the scenario and possibly for the choreographer but these references would seem unnecessary for the smaller collection.

Band parts. Catalogue in the normal way but include a note that this entry refers to band parts and give the number of copies of each part available.

Cadenzas. Enter under the composer and title of the original work, with an added entry for the composer of the cadenzas. Beethoven and Mozart wrote out cadenzas for some concertos and not for others; before this the performer was expected to improvise at a given point in the work upon the themes which had appeared. Handel was famous for his skill in this art, but we now have no authentic record of what was played and in addition modern musicologists can only give a vague idea as to the sort of music that was played to some of his works. Most of these early concertos now have two or three or more different cadenzas written by different composers and soloists, some of which show no sense of historical fitness. A miniature score will often indicate, where there is no original cadenza, the writer of that included in that particular edition and this information should be given in a note. Although these examples of technical skill and extemporizing ability are considered here in the context of orchestral works with an instrumental solo, it must be remembered that in early opera similar opportunities were provided for vocalists to show their skills in this way. (A.L.A., A9; Wallace, 5).

Choral parts. Treat as band parts, i.e. catalogue in the normal way under composer and title but note that these are choral parts and give the number of parts available.

Collections. Collections of the works of a single composer are entered under his name; added entry is possibly made for the compiler or editor. Collections of the works of several composers will be entered under the name of the editor, compiler or publisher; if there are few works, or one or two are of much greater importance than the others then analytical entries for all or for a limited number of works may usefully be provided. (A.L.A., E.)

Editor. There seems to be no particular virtue in making added entry for an editor unless he is famous on his own account as a composer or has some local connection with the library. Exception may also be made when it is apparent that the editor has played a major part in the production of the work, e.g. with early music that has needed considerable rewriting to make it suitable for modern use.

Fantasias. Enter under the composer of the fantasia unless the work is a medley upon certain works of a single composer, when entry is made under the latter with added entry under the composer of the fantasia. In cases of doubt, double entry may be used to solve the problem of which composer is the more responsible for the work.

Folk songs. Folk and traditional songs present great difficulty since the same song may appear in different arrangements and may be published with varying titles. In the latter case, one title must be chosen as standard and reference made from other forms. Preference should be given to that which is known to be the oldest or which stems from the original country of the song. An arrangement of a folk song or a collection of arrangements made by a named editor or transcriber is to be entered under his name with added entry under the title or titles. Thus the Benjamin Britten arrangement of *The Ash grove* would be catalogued under Britten with added entry under the title of the song. (A.L.A., A1.) Where the library possesses different versions of the same work, possibly with different words or with the accompaniment arranged for different arrangements, it is suggested that the title entry should read: "*The Ash grove.* The library has the following arrangements. . . ." (Wallace, 7.)

Hymnal. A hymnal will normally be entered under its title which will often (though not always) show the denomination for which it is intended, e.g. *The Methodist hymn book* in one case, *Songs of praise* in the other. The A.L.A. rule (A.6 and G) suggests entry under the name of the church. Cataloguers may follow this but are then faced with the problem of the collection written or compiled for no particular denomination, e.g. The *B.B.C. Hymnbook.* The answer would appear to be in the use of a heading such as "Hymnals—undenominational" and an added note that for the hymnals of a particular church the enquirer should look under its name.

Incidental music. This is entered under the composer and added entry may be made, if desired, under the author of the work for which the incidental music was written. There would seem to be good reason for making such added entries for *Peer Gynt* and *A midsummer night's dream*, etc., but little value in one for Helmine von Chézy, author of the drama *Rosamunde* (which received only two performances despite the aid of Schubert's music). The cataloguer should be able to judge, in most cases, the local need and value of any particular entry for this type of work.

Joint works. Though uncommon, such works may come before the cataloguer. In these cases the usual practice has been for one composer to be responsible for one movement, another for a second, etc. Most of the examples are by Russian composers but a modern example is the *Variations on Sellenger's Round* written by six contemporary British composers for the Aldeburgh Festival of 1953. As with a book, entry is under the composer first-named on the title-page with added entries for the others.

Librettos. Standard British practice is likely to follow the 1908 Joint Code. Section A.2 of A.L.A. rule 12 suggests entry under the composer of the music with added entry under librettist and also under title. It excepts the libretto published rather as a literary work than a libretto and offers (in a footnote) an alternative rule which suggests entry under the librettist and added entries for composer and title. Wallace (in Rule 8) has a similar dual approach for she too suggests entry under the composer in most cases but under the librettist when the composer is not named on the title-page or the librettist is himself well known. Decision must be made according to the type of library and its users but entry under librettist would seem to be the most consistent unless his name does not appear on the title-page. In this last case entry must be made under the composer, and Wallace suggests that time should not be wasted searching for the librettist's name.

The A.L.A. rule further suggests that added entry should be made under the work from which the libretto is taken but this would appear unnecessary in any but the largest music libraries. It may be recalled that this information is included in Loewenberg's *Annals of opera*. In any case, the relationship between the original work and the libretto is often fairly remote.

Liturgical music. This is music officially required by a church or other religious body. Such music will be entered under the name of the denomination except for music for Masses and Requiems which are entered under the name of the composer (A.L.A., A6). One of the reasons for this variant is that Masses and Requiems are part of the liturgy for more than one denomination·

Made-up volumes. These are volumes comprising works which are published separately but bound together in a single volume. Main entry will be under the first work in the volume with added entries for the remainder. Collation may be limited to indicating the number of pieces included rather than adding the number of pages together.

Masses. These are to be entered under the composer. Subject index entries, or a *See* reference in the case of a dictionary catalogue can usefully be made as exemplified in section A.7 of A.L.A. rule 12.

Medleys and potpourris. Enter under the arranger, etc., of the medley unless the selection is made from the works of a single composer. In the latter case the main entry is made under the composer's name with added entry for the arranger of the medley.

Motets. Enter under the composer and give the author or source of the words if possible.

Music in text. A book dealing with a topic that is not obviously musical (e.g. Folklore) may contain music in the text. When this occurs, it should be shown in a note and added entry made for the music as though it were published separately.

Overtures. When the overture is written as a prelude to a work (such as an opera or a play with incidental music) entry should be made under the composer. Where the library does not use the device of conventional title, the overture may need to have the title transposed, e.g. *Overture to "The Wreckers"* by Ethel Smyth would be entered as *The Wreckers: overture.* This would bring the overture with other excerpts or a complete score of the same opera. In the case of concert overtures, i.e. those that are entirely independent and which do not precede a longer work, entry will be made under the word "Overture" if the title begins with this word, e.g. Bax's *Overture to a picaresque comedy* which (despite its title) is a self-contained work and is not intended for performance before any particular comedy.

Pantomimes. See *Ballets.*

Paraphrases. These are to be entered under the composer of the paraphrase with an added entry under the composer whose work has been used as a basis. The line between transcription and paraphrase is not always easy to draw. Busoni's *Sonatina no. 6 (Kammerfantasie super Bizet's "Carmen")* may be regarded as a paraphrase upon tunes from the opera; Liszt's *Reminiscences de [Meyerbeer's] "Robert le Diable"* is a more obvious example.

Pastiches. The A.L.A. rule (A.3) suggests entry under the person responsible for the pastiche or, if this is not easily ascertainable, under the title. Added entries can be made for the composers (and even librettists) of the original works. The pastiche most likely to be encountered by an English cataloguer is *The beggar's opera* in which Dr. Johann (or John) Pepusch adapted popular contemporary tunes from many sources as an accompaniment to Gay's libretto. Modern editions, such as those of Frederic Austin or Benjamin Britten, will require added entry under the arranger's name.

Psalms. Psalters are to be entered under the composer's name when the volume consists of tunes by a single writer. If the collection is for use by a particular church or denomination then entry should be made under the name of the church with the sub-heading "Psalters". In the unlikely event of adding a general collection, enter under "Psalters" with a similar note as that recommended for undenominational Hymnals.

Pseudonyms. The sensible arrangement would appear to be for entry under the best-known name. Few enquirers would expect to search for the works of Sir Edward German under "Jones" (his real name); where the composer uses two names, e.g. Philip Heseltine and "Peter Warlock", there is much practical value in entering according to the title-page and making a cross-reference from each name to the other.

Requiems. These are to be entered under the name of the composer. It may be of some use to add a note of the person(s) to whom the Requiem is dedicated if this fact is easily discovered.

Rhapsodies. Enter under composer. If the rhapsody is in the form of a medley, then treat as a medley (q.v.).

Scenarios. If the scenario of a ballet is published separately it is to be treated as a libretto, i.e. enter under author with added entry under the composer of the music written for the scenario.

Songs. Enter under composer. Full cataloguing requires added entry under the writer of the words but in many libraries this decision will be at the cataloguer's discretion. It is possibly desirable when the author is famous and/or when the same verses or words have been set by more than one composer (e.g. Shakespeare's *Orpheus with his lute*). In this latter case a note would be made on the added entry: "For vocal settings of this, see under . . .". State the voice for which the song is written if it is shown on the copy. Indicate also if the setting is for "High", "Medium" or "Low" voice when this is stated by the publisher.

When a song cycle or set of songs is written by a composer to words by a single author (such as Britten's *Holy sonnets of John Donne* or his *Winter words* to verses by Thomas Hardy) there is a correspondingly stronger case for added entry under the author of the words. In the case of a volume with words by a single author but in which the settings are by various composers (such as a book of Shakespeare songs) the entry will be primarily under the author with added entries under the editor or the individual composers.

Spurious works. A.L.A. Code (6) suggests entry under the composer to whom the work is generally attributed with the addition to the author heading of the words "supposed composer" and an added entry under the real composer if the latter's name is known. This last seems rather harsh treatment for the actual composer, who should surely get the main entry; added entry would then be made under the supposed composer. Jeremiah Clarke should be shown as the composer of the *Trumpet voluntary* with added entry under Henry Purcell, to whom the work was long attributed. In contrast, Mozart's *Twelfth Mass* may be left under that composer's name since the actual writer or writers remains unknown. Similarly, much of the music attributed to Pergolesi is now thought to be the work of other composers but without definite, proved attribution, entry under the supposed composer is the best answer.

Thematic catalogues. The 1908 Joint Code specifies entry under the composer with added entry under the name of the compiler of the thematic catalogue. The 1949 A.L.A. Code reverses this ruling but most British librarians would normally follow the earlier method.

Traditional works. Treat as folk songs (q.v.).

Transcriptions. The difficulty in definition of "arrangement" and "transcription" has been mentioned. The best and most usually accepted definition is probably that to be found on page 17 of the first volume of McColvin & Reeves. The cataloguer should remember that a transcription presupposes some new material in harmony, in the style of the work, etc. Often the transcription couples the name of the original composer with that of the transcriber (Bach-Busoni; Scarlatti-Tomassini). The A.L.A. Rules (A.10), Wallace (4) and McColvin all recommended entry under the transcriber with added entry under the original composer except in doubtful cases when the reverse is suggested.

It would seem more consistent to enter all transcriptions under the original composer with "transcribed by . . ." as part of the heading. This obviates the need for decision on the part of the cataloguer. It would, on the other hand, require a filing decision. Such entries could be filed after the appropriate work (so that Liszt transcriptions of Schubert songs would follow immediately after the entries for the songs themselves) or alternatively they could be filed together at the end of the normal sequence under the composer's name. In the latter case, entries for J. S. Bach would be followed by those for transcriptions by Busoni, Walter Rummel, Liszt, etc. This is probably the better method but whichever way is selected will require added entry under the name of the transcriber.

Variations. There is general agreement between the various codes to catalogue under the name of the composer of the variations. The need for added entry under the name of the original theme is usually slight though it may be considered necessary for purposes of identification. Another use is to indicate themes that have been utilized by more than one composer.

SEQUENCE OF ITEMS

Since all works do not require the same amount of information to be given, the cataloguer may overlook the value of a standard sequence of items. The following list is suggested as a possible method; it makes no claim to perfection and there will be many alternative arrangements. The important matter is that a cataloguer should realize the value of a method, lay out his own sequence of items and see that all future music accessions adhere to it.

1. *Composer* (in the form given by Grove, L.C., or other chosen authority).

2. *Conventional title* for works with a distinctive title, particularly operas and some other vocal works. While usually given in the original language this is not invariable. When this item agrees with Title (no. 3) it may well be omitted to save both space and time.

3. *Title* of the work, as shown on the title-page of the music to hand. It may also include an English translation of the title; if this is provided by the cataloguer it should be shown in brackets.

4. *Number* of the work in a particular musical form. Although not invariably done, it is customary to number works in standard musical forms in chronological order, e.g. *Symphony no. 3 . . . , String quartet no. 7 . . . ,* etc.

5. *Key.* To be given when easily ascertainable. Key names relate particularly to music of the eighteenth and nineteenth centuries though still given to a fair proportion of works in the twentieth century. Unless uncertain, key should include the term "major" or "minor", e.g. *Sonata in G minor. . . .* In certain cases one or two movements of a work may be in the major and the remaining movements in the minor key; *Symphony in G . . .* would indicate this.

6. *Nickname* should be inserted, where applicable, between the key and the opus number. A title entry under the nickname is likely to be of definite use. The nickname, whether given by the composer or of later origin, is usually shown on the title-page. Example: *Symphony no. 3, in D major ("Polish"), op. 29.*

7. *Opus number.* This is normally shown on the title-page; alternatively (or additionally) it may be quoted just above the first line of music, on the right hand side. If not shown at all, reference should be made to musical dictionaries, etc., to see if the work has an opus number; if so, it should be quoted in brackets.

8. *Form.* This may be included as a sub-title to the work or added for informational purposes, e.g. *Opera in three acts, . . . Rondo for orchestra.* If added by cataloguer should be shown in brackets.

9. *Instruments or combination.* This information should always be included unless it is obvious from the title. If it is not shown on the title-page it may be given in the form of a note, if preferred. Examples: *. . . for soprano, tenor and bass, . . . for string trio.*

10. *Name of editor or arranger.* This can be omitted if the work done by either appears to be very slight.

11. *Language of text.* The language or languages of the text for a vocal work should be shown together with the name of the librettist(s) or author(s) of words and the name(s) of the translator(s) can also be shown here. Some cataloguers may prefer to indicate all or any of this information in a note at the end of the entry.

12. *Publisher.* While preference should be given to the original publisher it may well be that only the name of the importing publisher or agency is shown.

13. *Notes.* These should be provided as necessary. They should clear any ambiguities and provide any extra information likely to be of value to the potential borrower.

14. *Contents note.* Required for any volume containing a number of works unless they are all of the same genre by the same composer, e.g. a volume of Chopin *Waltzes.*

SUBJECT CATALOGUING

Subject headings will already be in use for libraries using a dictionary catalogue. If they are considered badly chosen, inadequate, etc., the headings for music entries may be revised and some recataloguing undertaken. The largest list of subject headings is that of the Library of Congress, published in 1952, and which runs to a total of 143 pages. Because these are the actual headings used with the immense L.C. collection they are extremely detailed. A smaller and simpler selection, based on the L.C. list, is to be found included with the headings for books on all other subjects in *Sears' List of subject headings for small libraries*.

If the L.C. headings are used (or a selection of them) care should be taken that the terminology used is modified to follow English usage when required. L.C. uses "English horn" where British libraries would prefer "Cor anglais". There are no English lists of subject headings but one that has been in use in a medium-sized British public library for over twenty years is quoted in the appendix at the end of the first part of this book. It is not necessary for any library to adopt these exactly as they stand, unless desired, but they may be used as a starting point for the cataloguer or librarian making a list for use in a library.

In subject headings a choice has to be made between wording that prefers form and that which gives preference to medium. L.C. prefers form so that entries are made for "Concertos (clarinet)", "Concertos (double bass)", "Concertos (English horn)", etc. This is in accordance with the choice of conventional title or method of main entry, "Concerto for clarinet and string orchestra", etc. If the alternative method of entry has been chosen, i.e. "Clarinet concerto . . .", then subject entries are probably better arranged by medium so that use would then be made of the headings "Clarinet (concertos)", "Clarinet (sonatas)", "Clarinet (suites)", etc. The matter is one of personal choice, but for the smaller library used primarily by amateur musicians and only secondarily by professionals and music students the second method is the one that seems most useful to me. For such libraries the simple heading "Clarinet", etc., is likely to be adequate since the total number of scores for the clarinet is likely to be few. Whichever form is used a general reference must be made from the alternative. If the second form of entry is made, a reference should be made under "Concertos" instructing the enquirer to check under individual solo instruments.

It would be less than honest to conceal the fact that the great majority of librarians favour entry under form; it brings together works by a composer in that form and allows a check to be made for gaps, yet the other method has its own advantages for checking and is quicker when one wishes to discover how well works for a particular instrument are represented. The problem has already been discussed earlier in this chapter; all that remains to be said is that a cataloguer should be consistent and not use both methods indiscriminately even if one form is used on one title-page and the other on a second.

Index entries should be provided for the medium, e.g. for "Clarinet music", "Violin music", etc. Entries should also be made for form though these will probably require explanatory notes. Thus the heading "Symphonies" will give the class number for books on symphonic form, for full and miniature scores, etc., but extra entries (or preferably a note where there are many entries) will be needed to indicate that symphonies arranged for piano solo are classed at *xxx*, for piano duet at *xxxx*, etc. A similar series of references or a "blanket reference" will be needed for other forms referring the enquirer to the appropriate class number for the medium if that is the method of classification adopted.

In order to illustrate the various points rather more fully than has been possible during the course of the chapter, the following examples have been chosen in the hope that they will demonstrate many of the points explained in the preceding pages.

The title-page of the first example reads: "Smetana/Ausgewählte Stücke/für Klavier zu 2 Händen/Herausgegeben/von Juliane Lerche"; the publisher is the Liepzig branch of Peters. The heading is obviously, SMETANA, Bedrich; the title can be shown as "[Piano] Selected piano works . . .", "Piano works" or "Selected piano works". I would regard the first as the best, the second as less satisfactory and the third, a simple translation of the title-page as least suitable, but there are certainly some music librarians who prefer this method to entry under a catchword. They argue that the classified section of the catalogue will bring all piano works of a composer together, so that entry under a conventional or similar title is much less helpful than it might appear at first. What would be wrong, in my estimation, is the obvious cataloguing response—a straightforward transcription of the title-page. No date appears in the volume, and "E.P. 11726" at the bottom of each page is likely to interest only the occasional user. The fact that there are thirty-five pages of text is of much less importance than a list of contents. The final suggested entry, therefore, is:

Cataloguing

SMETANA, Bedrich
> [Piano]. Selected piano works, edited by Juliane Lerche.
> Peters edition. *Contents:* . . .

Since the separation of the branches of the firm of Peters, there is reason for including the place of publication before the publisher's name if desired. The second example is an Italian one, with the title-page: "G. Verdi/4 pezzi sacri/Ave Maria. Scala enigmata, armonizzata a/4 voci miste, sole/Stabat Mater/a 4 voci miste, con pianoforte/ Laudi alla Vergine/Dall'ultimo canto del Paradiso di Dante/ a 4 voci femminila, sole/Te Deum/per doppio coro a 4 voci miste, con pianoforte/riduzione di G. Luporini". The publisher is Ricordi and the individual items are shown with an 1898 copyright date. It will not be difficult for the cataloguer to discover that "doppio cora a 4 voci miste" is a double chorus of mixed (i.e. soprano, contralto, tenor and bass) voices, though it may be rather more time-consuming to find that the "enigmatic" scale is not one generally used or recognized. The catalogue entry suggested would read:

VERDI, Giuseppe
> 4 sacred [choral] pieces [*c.* 1898] Orchestral accompaniment arranged for piano by G. Luporini; Latin words. Ricordi edition.
> *Contents: Ave Maria,* on an enigmatic scale, for four mixed voices, unaccompanied; *Stabat Mater,* for four mixed voices; *Laudi alla Vergine* (*Hymn to the Virgin*), from Canto XXXIII of Dante's *Paradiso,* for 4 unaccompanied female voices; *Te Deum* for double chorus of 4 mixed voices.

The third example is a miniature score whose title-page proclaims: "Philharmonia/Partituren. Scores. Partitions/Franz Schubert/Symphonie VII/C Dur C major. Do majeur", and at the bottom of the page "Philharmonia no. 92/Wiener Philharmonischer Verlag/Wien". This is the symphony now usually referred to as "no. 9" in Britain, though apparently by the earlier number in other countries.

SCHUBERT, Franz
> Symphony no. 7 (9), in C major ("The Great" C major), D.944. Miniature score. Philharmonia edition.

It may be considered necessary to quote the publisher's serial number and the fact that there is a frontispiece—a portrait of the composer. The nickname (which distinguishes this symphony from no. 6 in the same key; both are without opus number) and the Deutsch thematic catalogue number have been provided. If the work had a normal opus number, that would have been included also.

The last example is in English so that there is no need to transcribe the title-page (which is fortunate, since the composer's name is written vertically on either side of the title).

WALTON, William
> Violin concerto [*or*, "Concerto for violin and orchestra", as is shown on the title-page], [*c.*1941]. Arranged for violin and piano; violin solo part edited by Jascha Heifetz. [Score and part.] Oxford U.P.

"Score and part" indicates that there is a separate part for the violinist. The Henry Watson Library catalogue entry, incidentally, shows that the piano reduction of the orchestral score was made by Franz Reizenstein, though there is no mention of this fact on the score itself.

GRAMOPHONE RECORDS

In general, gramophone records present the same problems in cataloguing as are met in cataloguing music. Excerpts are much more common, and the titles shown on the record label are often defective or misleading. There are, naturally enough, extra complications with recordings since the artist or artists making the recording present an added factor with which the cataloguer must deal. This type of cataloguing is considered at length in Chapter V.

For further reading

AMERICAN LIBRARY ASSOCIATION. *Cataloging rules for Author and Title entries.* 1949. (Chicago: A.L.A.)

Rule 12 (for music) which occupies seven pages, should be read by all cataloguers who have to deal with music if they are unable to beg, borrow or steal a copy of the *Code for Cataloging Music and Phonorecords* (Chicago: A.L.A.), where the same rule is virtually reprinted together with other invaluable suggestions.

U.S. LIBRARY OF CONGRESS. *Rules for descriptive cataloging in the Library of Congress (adopted by the American Library Association).* 1949. (Washington, D.C. Library of Congress.)

Cataloguing

Music subject headings used on printed catalog cards in the Library of Congress. 1952 [As above].

Rule 9, which deals with music, requires over twenty pages of print. It is considerably more exhaustive than the A.L.A. Rule 12, though it too is descended from the preliminary rules of 1941. For the very large collection, this rule is probably sufficiently comprehensive to answer all queries. The *Subject headings* have been referred to in the preceding chapter. It may be noted that, in many cases, the appropriate class number in the L.C. classification is quoted against the heading.

ELMER, Minnie Agnes. *Music cataloging: with an annoted bibliography of useful references sources.* (MSS.) (New York: Columbia University.) 1946.

This thesis, submitted in the Faculty of Library Science at Columbia University, is intended "to analyze information needed on catalog cards for publications of music, and to survey reference works useful in supplying and verifying that information". It excludes from its purview manuscripts, Oriental music, the literature of music and gramophone records. The thesis provides a long and interesting survey of the problems encountered in music cataloguing and some of the possible solutions. The bibliography of 243 items contains some brief annotations. Books considered to be of basic importance are marked with an asterisk, and it is noteworthy that books so recommended include a fairly high proportion of works in French, German and Italian. A microfilm copy of this work is available in the Library Association's library.

NORRIS, Dorothy M. *A primer of cataloguing* (Association of Assistant Librarians). 1952.

Pages 147 to 152 give suggestions for music cataloguing and provide useful assistance for examination students. The section on cataloguing gramophone records (pp. 170–1) must be regarded as much less satisfactory.

RUSSELL, John F. *The cataloguing of music* ("The Library Association Record", June 1938, pp. 257–60).

An interesting article by the late Librarian of the Henry Watson Music Library, and one which contains details of practice there.

WALLACE, Ruth, *editor. The care and treatment of music in a library.* (Chicago: A.L.A.) 1927.

Music Librarianship

Chapter III of this book deals with cataloguing and gives twenty-seven suggested rules. Many of these would appear to have achieved permanent acceptance and can be seen in subsequent codes, including that published by the M.L.A. and A.L.A. in 1958. Chapter IV deals with subject headings and gives a suggested list. This, again, has been superseded by later and more detailed ones but its influence is still there. The small collection could still use these headings, though British librarians may find those in Appendix I of this book of greater use. Chapter V is devoted to "The organization of the card catalogs". The following quotation perhaps indicates the trend of the chapter: "Under Beethoven, for instance, it is helpful to divide his works into Concertos, Sonatas, Symphonies, etc., with a guide card for each form." Under each form, the work recommends the usual practice of arrangement by number rather than by key, e.g. *Symphony no. 1, Symphony no. 2* rather than *Symphony in A major, Symphony in C minor*. In short, despite its age, this small booklet, with its seventy-two pages of text is still worth reading.

REFERENCE

1. LOOK, Wallace C. *Classification and cataloging of music scores in libraries.* (MSS.) (Chicago: Chicago University). 1951. p. 33.

Postscript

The first volume of the "Code international de catalogage de la musique" (Frankfurt; Peters. 1957 [i.e., 1958]) has at last appeared. It deals with "The author catalog of published music" and is by Dr. Franz Grasberger of Vienna. The original text is shown on the left-hand side of each page. The right-hand column consists of an English translation in parallel by Mrs. Virginia Cunningham of the Library of Congress. The work deals with eight types of material—Music literature, Librettos (which are recommended for entry under title), Program notes, Music publication, Music manuscripts, Phonograph records and tape recordings, Pictorial representation and illustrations, Photocopies and microfilms.

The second section of the book considers briefly some of the earlier attempts to provide rules for music cataloguing and then lists the parts that may comprise a main entry. The actual make-up of a main entry and the items used in various libraries are quoted for Switzerland, Vienna, U.S.A. (Library of Congress), that recommended by a Norwegian and the scheme adopted for Schnapper's *British Union-catalogue.* . . . This section is followed by a brief résumé of the rules recommended by various authorities, including the "rules" given in McColvin and Reeves. Suggestions for choice of heading in a number of difficult cases are made and definitions of the headings may be found useful. This part of the new code has some resemblance to the A.L.A. 1949 Code rule no. 12. The last section of the new rules deals with the arrangement of entries within the catalogue of a library and shows the normal system used by the twenty libraries that co-operated in the provision of specimen entries. None of these twenty are American, and the only British one is the British Museum which can hardly be cited as typical.

A flap inside the back cover provides precarious protection for a pamphlet which gives a French translation of the text and for twelve folded sheets each of which contains a facsimile title-page of a score. Underneath each is a note of the particular problems posed by this particular work; the other half of the sheet provides copies of entries from some of the twenty libraries mentioned above. For reasons of space, and because some of the entries show very little difference, only certain of the entries are given as examples. Beethoven's violoncello sonatas arranged for viola receive three facsimile catalogue entries, while two other works receives as many as nine. These sheets provide a fascinating insight into differences of approach by expert cataloguers.

In illustrating these different methods, the new code is useful but it does not appear to make its own recommendations as to which are the best methods and it must be confessed that it is not an easy document to read. The two volumes, still to come at the time of writing, are a simplified code of rules for cataloguing scores prepared by Mme Yvette Féderov of Paris, and a full code—the work of a committee under the chairmanship of Dr. Kay Schmidt-Phiseldeck of Copenhagen. Until these appear it is impossible to judge the success or failure of this venture, but it is certainly a most praiseworthy attempt at international co-operation.

Chapter IV

CLASSIFICATION

Music presents many problems for the classification-maker; some of these may be noted here. First, should books and scores share the same symbol or should there be two separate sequences? Brown and Dewey (up to the 15th edition) use a single sequence but other schemes prefer to use separate numbers and letters for scores and books about music. Where the same number is used for both types of material some confusion is possible even though a prefix, such as "M" or "S", may help to reduce this. On the other hand, it is reasonable to expect a work and a criticism of it to be allotted the same number; where two sequences are used a copy of Harvey Grace's *The organ works of Bach* will have an entirely different class mark to the works themselves and may be shelved some distance from them, though it must be said that if a scheme allots the same number for the two items it is still unlikely that they will be cheek-by-jowl on the shelf. The separation will be caused by the very different formats of the two items.

A second problem concerns the choice of characteristic, or the order of division, of music scores. Should primary arrangement be by composer, by form or by medium? All the major schemes have chosen the last named thus bringing together works for the voice, for individual instruments, for orchestra, etc. There is a case for classification by form which would bring all sonatas together, be they for piano, unaccompanied 'cello or two clarinets, etc. Division by composer was chosen by Dr. Ernest Savage for the large music collection in Edinburgh Public Library. Though the Library of Congress scheme was adopted in other departments its music scheme did not find favour and on pages 74 and 75 of Savage's *Special librarianship* (Grafton, 1939) he explains how he grouped collective scores at the beginning of the sequence for each composer, with single scores following in alphabetical order and books about the composer

141

grouped after his works. An indication of the appearance of the shelves can be seen by reference to the plate opposite page 71 in that book.

The schemes that divide by medium usually choose form as the secondary characteristic. For all but the largest collections this may be a somewhat unnecessary refinement for instrumental music. It can be argued that a classified collection of piano music gives a better picture of the types of material available to the pianist than the same collection arranged by composer under a general number or symbol for piano music. That may be true, yet in a public library the would-be borrower disappointed in his quest for Chopin's *Waltzes* is surely more likely to make his second choice from other Chopin piano works than from volumes of waltzes by Brahms or Schoenberg, etc.? If considered desirable entries in the classified sequence of the catalogue, or subject entries in a dictionary catalogue can be sub-divided by form even though this sub-division is ignored on the shelves. In the chapter on miniature scores a similar procedure is recommended so that all scores of miniature size, or all piano works by individual composers would be arranged under the composer's name and then sub-divided by form. Then, if the Dewey scheme is used, the miniature scores of Brahms' works will be together with the symphonies preceding the concertos which in turn will be to the left of the chamber music. A similar arrangement would occur with piano music and by this means a simple separation of original works and arrangements could be made.

Much of the last paragraph may be regarded as a digression but it illustrates something of the logic and force of Dr. Savage's arguments in favour of primary arrangement by composer. The classification-maker has other problems to face. A schedule can allocate places for special songs such as shanties, for national songs, for songs written for male voices only, for songs written in four parts, etc., and promptly has to face a welter of cross-classification. Yet each category of song has works that fit it specifically. This problem and the other mentioned are quoted not because I can offer a perfect answer (for there is no such thing) but to draw the attention of the student and librarian to some of the difficulties that have to be faced and overcome as well as may be before any satisfactory scheme for classifying music can be produced. The student might ponder, for example, the matter of music written for the virginals, clavichord, harpsichord and other precursors of the modern pianoforte, and decide how to cope with that; it might be useful to compare his own projected solution with that adopted by the various schemes considered below.

In the pages that follow, the music classifications are considered in a very approximate order of complexity so that the "Subject" scheme is considered first, followed by outlines and criticism of the "Expansive", "Decimal" (in both 14th and 15th editions and also the McColvin modification), Library of Congress, "Bibliographical" and British Catalogue of Music schemes. A chronological arrangement would perhaps show how one scheme has borrowed from another but it poses the problem of dating those schemes which have undergone revision since original publication. Ranganathan's "Colon" scheme is omitted from this review because the music section, though perhaps adequate for an Indian library, is much too undeveloped for western music with its occidental polyphony, orchestras, etc.

Since the Dewey scheme is probably used in more libraries than all the other schemes added together some practical suggestions for the classifier are included in the last section of this chapter. As an appendix to the comparison of schemes, sixteen scores or books on music are listed and the class-mark given according to each of the six systems. This should give some impression of the general length of notation. It also helps to indicate if the schedules allot different placings for works which require the same number of players but whose instrumentation differs (e.g. a trio for violin, viola and violoncello and another written for piano, violin and 'cello). These placings have been checked by an expert in each scheme, and each outline has been read for factual errors; the criticisms are my own and do not necessarily indicate that the reader has agreed with them. Acknowledgements are made in the appropriate place in the introduction.

THE "SUBJECT" CLASSIFICATION

Music was one of James Duff Brown's greatest interests. In the years before the turn of the present century he was a pioneer in the provision of music scores in British public libraries and was the author of an excellent biographical dictionary of musicians and joint-author of another. With Alfred Moffat he produced *Characteristic songs and dances of all nations*, a work that sold many copies

in the years before the First World War. Brown's "Subject" classification was his third venture in this field and the first edition of the
work was published in 1906. The second edition was issued in 1914,
a year after Brown's death, and the third edition (revised and expanded by J. D. Stewart) in 1937. The music scheme in this latest
revision shows very little alteration except for the introduction of
placings for modern instruments, etc. The classification is still used
in a number of British libraries and students in this country are expected to know something of the author's theories and the way he
put them into practice.

The places C400 to C796 are allotted in the schedules for music
scores and books on music. The subject is treated as a branch of
physical science for it follows Acoustics and precedes Astronomy in
the scheme. All other book classifications consider music as a "fine"
or "expressive" art and there has been considerable criticism of
Brown's unorthodoxy which is sometimes felt to be perverse. Against
this one may quote the growing interest in sound recording and other
uses of electrical techniques in connection with music; these do provide a real link between acoustics and music, and the placing may be
regarded as rather more logical than Dewey's location of music
between photography and sport. Further criticism has come from
those who feel that the use of the same numbers both for music and
for books dealing with music is a mistake. It has been alleged that
Brown "did not produce a practical or well-balanced scheme"[1] and
the same writers refer to Dewey's "confusion between music and
music literature". Whatever the pros and cons of Brown's choice it
must be clear that there is a real case for the use of the same number
for a score and a book which deals with that score—though the
arguments on the other side may be regarded as just as convincing.
Music scores are usually located far from their proper place in the
shelf sequence whatever scheme of classification is used. If the books
on music are adjacent, as they should be, it is probable that few of
the users will realize that they are taking works from the "Physical
science" category. If the books on music are placed in their proper
place in the sequence of classes the reader may find it more difficult
to locate them in a library using the "Subject" classification but this
is primarily a case for adequate shelf and tier guiding. In any case
the interested music-lover will seek out the section and, finding it,
will know where to go on future visits to the library. As already im-
plied, there is much to be said for giving the same class mark to the

string quartets of Beethoven and works which comment and criticize them; ideally, it may be suggested that all these scores and books should be together on the shelves despite differences in size. It is both convention and economy in shelf space that normally places them apart.

The music section of Brown's classification opens with places for aspects of musical theory, such as Notation, Modes and scales, Melody, etc. From C440 onwards are scheduled Music forms (such as Exercises, Fantasias and Impromptus, etc.), Dance forms (Fandangos, Gaillards, Galops, Gavottes, etc.) and Vocal forms (Arias, Cavatinas, Scenas). These numbers would appear to be for books rather than scores. If all toccatas, to take one example, were classed together at C640, works in this form for organ, piano, etc., would be shelved together, which would lead to confusion and the separation of these works from others for the same instruments. A number of headings in the above examples appear to be of little practical value but such places can always be left blank until such time as the library does purchase a monograph on the Fandango, for instance. Students should note that Brown put his sub-divisions in alphabetical order rather than attempting to classify them. Cutter uses a similar arrangement in parts of his music classification.

The general order of the main headings for the rest of the class is as follows: Vocal music, Music for stringed instruments, Wind instruments, Percussion instruments, Orchestral music, Chamber music (in descending order from nonets to trios, and not in the more usual reverse order), Dramatic music (i.e. opera), and finally, a small section for Musicians (Bards, minstrels and troubadours) and Concerts; this last heading has a single and unexpected sub-division of Street-music (C796). This may be cited as a rare example of humour in music classification.

Many of the four hundred subjects listed will be rarely used in the normal public library. Some of the dance forms such as Branle [Brawl] and Polaccas (to name but two examples) are of very limited historical interest while books on the Rebec (C604), Crwth [Chrotta] (C605) or Lyras (C609) are equally unlikely to be found in any but the very largest music library. These three instruments are all shown under the section "Stringed instruments (played with bow)". Similar instances abound throughout the scheme though Brown, as a true Scot, places bagpipes under "Wind instruments (Reed blown)" and provides separate placings for the Highland, Union (Irish), Northumbrian and Spanish pipes. The four types of instrument show considerable differences and repertories that do not overlap. No other scheme allows for these divergencies. Reading through the schedules one finds places for other queer instruments such as the Enharmonic organ, Musical glasses and Bones. An example of Brown's declared intention of placing each subject "as near as possible to the science on which it is based" can be seen at C739–741 which are respectively allotted to Bells (electric, etc.), Bell-ringing and Bell-founding.

The Categorical tables provide a tremendous number of sub-divisions that can be given to any suitable subject and some are obviously specifically intended for music. There are fifteen of these (·257 to ·272 with ·262 missing, for no apparent reason), and they include such aspects as ·257 Acoustics, ·261 Scales, ·265 Forms and ·266 Dances. These numbers come consecutively since the Categorical tables follow the same sequence as the classification as a whole except that the shortest numbers are given to the most frequently used sub-divisions. For instance, ·9 ("Individual authors"), will be often used when classifying music.

The deficiencies of the scheme have often been quoted yet librarians using it have found it simple to apply and readers appear to have no particular difficulty in discovering what they require. The notation is desirably short with a single letter followed by three figures; where categorical numbers are used this will at most add another three figures to the symbol. Some subjects appear to be missing and it will be seen from the practical examples given at the end of this chapter that *The record guide* has to be classed away from music. Mr. James D. Stewart, who was responsible for the 3rd edition, is at work upon another revision which should be published in due course. Students may usefully try and find topics that ought to have places in the scheme and are omitted, and then decide just where they would insert these new subjects in the schedules. This is an excellent method of discovering some of the virtues and deficiencies of the scheme.

In the practical examples at the end of the chapter it must be remembered that alphabetical arrangement by composer should be used under each head. Strictly speaking, Brown's alphabetical numbers should be added to each work to indicate the composer's place in the sequence but most libraries have found it much more convenient to add the first three letters of the composer's surname.

Classification

In Charles A. Cutter's "Expansive" classification music is shown as a branch of the "Expressive arts" (an excellent epithet). Works about music are classed at VV and VX and scores themselves are at VY and VZ. Only the seventh and final expansion is considered here; this version differs considerably from the previous six from which it is nominally developed—it includes, for instance, a mixed notation where the earlier and more limited expansions use letters only. The seventh expansion was not properly completed at the time of the author's death and as a result the scheme was not given a final revision and the music section is one that lacks an index. Cutter indexed each class separately and there is no cumulation.

The section opens with sub-divisions reminiscent of Dewey. VV.2, for instance, is for Music Bibliography, VV.8 for Societies, while VV 1–99 (without decimal point but divided decimally) are for aspects of musical history. These examples provide samples of Cutter's mixed notation in this last expansion. His liking for simple and obvious mnemonics is also illustrated for VV 1 M is for the history of military music, VV 1 O for operatic, VV 1 OR for oratorio and VV 1 P for the history of piano music. This last section also includes the collected lives of pianists. Lives of opera singers, violinists and vocalists are dealt with in similar manner. Single biographies are classified at VVA to VVZ. The general history of music is followed by sequences arranged by period (e.g. Ancient Egyptian music, VV 1271) or country; for the latter division is by Cutter's "Local list" which is a similar device to Dewey's instruction to "divide like 930 to 999". Entries under country include accounts of music festivals and celebrations, and also concert programmes. It may be suggested, in passing, that these are valuable both in the provision of local history and as silent commentators on changing musical taste over the years. Musical biography and criticism including letters and journals of musicians are regarded as a branch of history, and the lives, etc., are arranged in a single alphabetical sequence of composers' names. At the end of this section is a place for musical fiction, VVZZ.

The succeeding sections are allotted to Acoustics, Musical theory, Composition and instruction (VW). VX is devoted to books about instruments (including the human voice) alphabetically arranged. VX also includes history, manufacture and instruction for each of these instruments and the notation for each instrument may be lengthened to show these individual aspects if so desired. As before, extra letters are added when two or more sub-sections begin with the same letters and the resulting mnemonics might clash—VXB is Bagpipe, VXBA Barrel organ, VXBAN Banjo, VXBASS Basset horn and VXBAS Bassoon. Double bass is classed at VXD. It can be seen that separate places are provided for many unusual instruments and that Cutter makes no attempt to divide instruments according to their family groups—to separate stringed instruments from woodwind, etc. The most surprising place is VXHO, Horn, English and French. The two instruments are, of course, utterly different, for the former is a woodwind instrument allied to the oboe and the latter a brass instrument. Obviously, different places should have been allotted. Cutter may be considered to have cheated in allotting VXOZ for precursors of the piano (for books on harpsichords, clavichords, etc.) but this placing brings these books immediately before those dealing with the piano (VXP) and this is useful and valuable. Four instruments, Organ, Piano, Violin and Voice have special numbers allotted for instructional books but similar subdivision could be made for any other instrument if desired.

In the sections for scores, general collections are allotted the first places in the schedules followed by collections of the works of single composers. Then comes VY 1 or VYA (Cutter leaves the user to make his own choice) for Concerted music, orchestral music. This is succeeded, rather surprisingly, by National music, Folk songs (sharing the same place), then Chamber music (which is mnemonically sub-divided) and Dance music. In a note, Cutter points out that one must decide whether to classify all dance music together, be it for piano, violin, etc., or whether to classify all piano music together, all violin music together, etc. Cutter declares that it makes "very little practical difference" and prefers the former method. If one considers the preference of form to medium to be a bad choice, so that the pianist needs to look in a number of places for music for his instrument—under Dance music, Marches, Overtures, etc., it must be remembered that this is also the solution adopted in the L.C. scheme. Music written for a particular instrument is classified by the same set of mnemonics as in VXA so that a history of the clarinet is at VXC and music for the instrument in VZC; similarly VZOZ is the place for music written for the virginals and other instruments which preceded the modern pianoforte and VZP is the mark for piano music. This last class may contain all piano music or else such works as cannot be classed elsewhere if Cutter's alternative system be put into operation. VZV is provided for Voice (collections of songs). These collections are divided according to the type of song, e.g. VZVCS Sailor and sea songs. Collections are also divided by the number of voices, as VZVF Four-part songs. Cutter notes that each library must make its choice between these two types of division; considerable cross-classification would otherwise result.

In general, the scheme has good points, particularly in the sensible use of mnemonics, but the abundant opportunities for cross-classification could well be a sad source of weakness and some of the headings use a fairly lengthy notation. It is difficult to decide without personal experience just how well the scheme works in practice, but those libraries that classify by Cutter appear to have no complaints about this particular section of the scheme.

DEWEY DECIMAL CLASSIFICATION

The Decimal classification of Melvil Dewey is undoubtedly the best-known and most widely-used system in the world today but its music section is far from being one of the more satisfactory, for it is often difficult to apply with consistency. The music classes of the 14th edition of 1942, the one generally in use at the time of writing, are an unchanged reprint of the 12th edition of 1927. The simplified 15th (Standard) edition of 1951 has amended some anomalies but is still far from satisfactory to music librarians. The 16th edition, when it appears, promises to contain some major alterations and re-allocations and to be, in general, a noticeable improvement upon its predecessors, though one may doubt if patching will ever really result in a satisfactory scheme; it would be better to follow the example of Mr. McColvin and use the numbers of class 780 adapted to an entirely fresh scheme.

Music is allotted the places 780 to 789 in the scheme, and while this makes the subject a "fine art", it places it uncomfortably between photography and amusements. A single sequence of subjects is provided for scores and books on music and this is generally held to be a disadvantage for reasons already mentioned in this chapter. The 16th edition seems likely to make separate provision by supplying adjacent places for the two types of material, but this must be at the expense of brevity. At present, in order to differentiate the two

L 149

sequences, a small note at the beginning of this section of the schedules suggests the possible use of the letter "M" for books and "MS" for sheet music. It would seem simpler to leave books without a prefix and to use either "M" or "S" as a prefix to the scores.

The Third summary of the 14th edition (to be found at the beginning of the schedules) shows the following heads for music: 780 Music, 781 Theory and technic, 782 Dramatic, 783 Sacred, 784 Vocal, 785 Instrumental ensemble, 786 Piano and organ, 787 Stringed instruments, 788 Wind instruments, 789 Percussion and mechanical: 780 and 781 are used entirely for books; the remaining places are primarily for scores though there will be a reasonable proportion of books classified between 782 and 789. There are the normal form divisions to 780, so that 780·7 is for "Education, study and teaching" and includes sub-headings for "Music conservatories, schools, courses" and for "Concerts and concert programs". One might have expected to find works dealing with music as a profession at this point (since the great majority of professional musicians learn the finer arts of their craft at music conservatories, etc.) and also analytical notes which are nearly always written for use in concert programmes. In fact, these last headings are 780·071 and 780·072—subdivisions of 780·07 which is for "Relations of individuals and public bodies", a somewhat obscure heading: 780·6, Associations, Societies, Clubs has a sub-division, 780·65, for Commercial establishments, Music stores; yet their catalogues are apparently classed at 780·85 under Commercial circulars. The history of music is classed at 780·9 with an optional place for biographies at 780·92 (though a note indicates a preference for 927·8), and 780·93–·99 for the history of music in special countries. There is, in my opinion, much to commend the use of 780·92 since nearly all biographies and autobiographies are almost compelled to include some critical sections (it is difficult to write a life of a musician without some evaluative reference to his music) but this means that music history is separated into two groups. Einstein's *History of music* will have all the musical biographies between it and Walker's *History of music in England*, since the former will be classed at 780·9 and the latter at 780·942.

781 Theory and technic, contains the expected headings such as Harmony, Counterpoint, Orchestration and Modes. 781·9, Various questions, contains a real miscellany of headings including general places for musical instruments, libretti, bibliographies of music, music printing and publishing. 781·5 is allocated to Music form,

Classification

Kinds of music, and has a sub-heading 781·508 for Different kinds of orchestral music and another for Dancing, 781·5085. This last item is sub-divided further into individual dances of the eighteenth and nineteenth centuries such as Minuets, Polonaise, Galop, etc. This heading has often been used by classifiers for modern dances and for jazz since no specific place is allotted for them, but the 15th edition makes a new head in the better place of 785·42.

782 Dramatic music, Theater music is the heading for opera, etc. Grand opera is at 782·1 and is followed by places for Epic, Wagnerian; Other German grand opera; French grand opera; Italian grand opera (782·2–782·5). 782·6 is for Comic and satiric opera, 782·7 for Opera bouffe and 782·8 for Operettes and secular cantatas, Vaudevils; 782·9 is provided for Pantomimes, Masks, etc. These numbers are almost impossible to apply without causing cross-classification. For instance, Mozart's *Magic flute* was written to a German text and *The marriage of Figaro* to an Italian one. Does one classify the first at 782·3 (Other German opera) and the second at 782·5, or should one call *Figaro* a comic opera and class it at 782·6? Operettas and secular cantatas are strange bedfellows; it does not seem adequate classification to find Bach's *Phoebus and Pan* sharing the same class mark as Johann Strauss's *Die Fledermaus*—or should the latter count as a comic opera? The most knowledgeable musicians would find it a Herculean task to use these sub-divisions as classification. A note in small type, at the head of the schedules for 782 does allow alternative provision for classing all opera under 782 arranging under that number in alphabetical order of composer; the same note makes the alternative suggestion that all grand opera should be classed at 782·1, again arranged alphabetically by composer. In this latter case it is suggested (though no reason is given) that Wagnerian operas should still be classed at 782·2. Opera and its near relatives are admittedly difficult to classify; Bliss calls it "a vague and historically complex class" and offers three alternative arrangements; students should find it useful and instructive to compare the answers given by Brown, Cutter, Sonneck (Library of Congress) and Bliss with those of Dewey to this particular problem.

783 Church music, Sacred music, is straightforward; 784 (Vocal music) provides fresh opportunities for cross-classification. There are places for solos, divided by type of voice, followed by numbers for duets, trios, etc., and for choruses (to which further sub-divisions are allotted). 784·4 is for Folk songs and includes Songs of the soil, cow-

boy songs, chanteys and drinking songs. 784·6 is for Student songs, Society songs, Choruses and Community singing (including provision for songs of special trades). 784·7 is for Other kinds of songs, with sub-divisions for National airs, songs and hymns (arranged by country), Exotic songs (whatever they may be), Gipsy songs and Negro and plantation songs. Are the folk songs discovered by Cecil Sharp in the Appalachian Mountains long after most of them had been forgotten in England, their country of origin, classed as English or American? Seafaring is apparently not a "special trade" since sailor songs go at 784·4. When does a student song become a folk song, or a national song? The possibilities for argument and error seem almost endless.

Orchestral music is the first major division of 785 (Instrumental ensemble) with sub-divisions for Symphony (a musical form), Wind instruments, Brass band, Music of the chase, etc., but no place for string orchestra. 785·2 is for music for orchestra with voices; 785·3 for Romantic, idyllic orchestral music (another place that offers many opportunities for confusion); 785·4 is blank, 785·5 is for Overtures (back to musical form again), 785·6 Concertos (form) and 785·7 Chamber music, divided according to the number of instruments involved. Thus, in 785, at least two different characteristics are used with consequent muddle.

786 (Keyboard music) is limited to music for and books on the piano and organ. 786·4 is for piano music, with sub-divisions for Sonatas, Fantasias, Artistic études, etc. 786·48 is for Variations, transcriptions (two entirely different things) and 786·49 for Arrangements; this has appended a note in small type: "Four hands and more; e.g. orchestral music arranged for piano." Orchestral music arranged for two hands presumably goes here also for want of a better place and there is no specific provision for original piano duets or two-piano works, since neither type of music is an arrangement; but a symphony arranged for piano duet and a piano concerto arranged for two-piano performance would be placed at 786·49. Once more the schedules show a lack of clear thinking. The sub-divisions of organ music (786·8) are as confusing with Fugue (786·82) preceding Preludes (786·83) and Preludes and fugues written in combination (which is common enough) apparently needing to be classed in the general number 786·8.

The remainder of the class is straightforward enough, though occasionally open to criticism in the order chosen for instruments.

Classification

787, 788 and 789 (Stringed instruments, Wind instruments, Percussion and Mekanical instruments) do not make provision for concertos, preludes and fugues, etc., which is an advantage. Sub-division when made is simply for individual instruments; the gramophone is a "mekanical" one, and shares the same number (789·9) as Mekanical pianos and musical glasses.

It will be obvious from my comments that I consider this to be a bad scheme for music classification; it is (again in my personal reaction) the worst of those considered in this chapter; how far a probable fairly drastic revision in the 16th edition will remedy its weakness remains to be seen. As an interim measure, some practical suggestions for the classifier who has to apply the 14th edition are given at the end of this chapter.

In general, the 15th edition has met with far more criticism than praise but the pruning of the music schedules appears to have improved this section in several places. 780·07 is now clarified as "Music and musicians in relation to society, the Arts". There is a reference to 656·6 for music copyright (previously omitted) and musical appreciation at 780·15 (a new number) includes analytical notes. These were previously located at 780·072—but concert programmes are still at 780·73. Both in 780 and 781 subjects are often given different emphasis, e.g. in the 14th edition 781·64 is "Adaptation; Resolution; Instrumental reduction; Arrangements; Transposition", but in the 15th edition is simply "Transposition". In 781 "Technic" becomes the more normal "Technique".

Big changes occur in 782 where it is recommended that all opera should be at 782·1 though 782·6 is shown in the schedules as an alternative (though not recommended) place for comic and satiric opera. 782·8, however, still includes both Theatre music and Secular cantatas. 783 shows minor simplification while 784 still leaves the confusion between 784·4, 784·6 and 784·7 unresolved. In fact, it adds to it for 784·6 (Student songs; Society songs; Choruses; Community singing, in the 14th edition) becomes "Community songs; Student songs; Society songs" in the later edition with a new sub-division 784·61 for Community songs; Home song books; Popular songs. "Home song books" will almost certainly include national songs, sea shanties, etc., and "Popular songs" can mean anything or nothing.

In class 785, 785·11 is amended to Symphony orchestras and symphonic music, but is still separated from Overture and Concerto though the latter placing (785·6) now specifically includes Concerti

153

grossi (previously classed here or at 785·1 according to the classifier's decision). 785·4 (previously blank) is now used for Dance, Salon, Theater and Reduced orchestras and music, with 785·42 for Jazz orchestras and Jazz—a number that libraries using the 14th edition would do well to adopt. 785·7 now becomes Chamber orchestra and there are no sub-divisions for quartets, octets, etc.

At 786·4 the sub-divisions all disappear though a note says: "May be arranged by form or number of pianos or performers." Similarly, organ music loses its sub-divisions and now specifically includes church organ music which was previously classed at 783·81. 787 is much as before, though there is now an alternative placing for string chamber music at 787·04 instead of 785·7. In 789 separate places are now allotted to phonographs ("gramophones" in British terminology), records, and catalogs of music.

This brief survey should have shown that the new version is certainly better than the old but that many of the criticisms levelled at the schedules of the music section in the 12th to 14th editions still apply.

THE LIBRARY OF CONGRESS MUSIC CLASSIFICATION

The importance of the LC scheme of music classification is generally admitted, but detailed description or criticism appears to be missing from British professional literature. In the chapter on classification in McColvin & Reeves, for instance, the comments are made that the Congress scheme is very detailed, and that for use in a medium-sized library "drastic alterations would be required". It is interesting to note that the Music Library Association in the U.S.A. has had a committee trying to work out a satisfactory condensation (*see* supplement to *Notes*, June, 1951); on the other hand, the Music Division of the Library of Congress has found the scheme insufficiently detailed in many places, and has introduced many new placings that do not appear in the printed schedules. A condensed or simplified scheme may have much to commend it, but if and when the library stock outgrows the less detailed version, considerable re-classification may be required. On the other hand, a detailed scheme has the advantage that minor sub-divisions may be ignored until required, but may require longer class numbers than the stock apparently warrants.

As with other classes in the L.C. scheme, the music classifications (Classes M. ML and MT) are published separately in a single volume, and in Great Britain this may be obtained through H.M.S.O. (at a cost of 8s. 6d. at the time of writing). For the majority of students, however, a reasonably detailed description of the schedules will probably be sufficient. From this, the method of division should be understood, and comparison with other schemes of music classification made comparatively simple. It must be remembered that the L.C. scheme dates back to 1902, when it was drawn up to deal with a collection of some 200,000 items: there are now over 2,000,000 in stock. Prime responsibility for this section of the scheme was taken by the late O. G. Sonneck, some of whose ideas on music cataloguing may be found in the second appendix to Cutter's *Rules for a dictionary catalog*. Looking back, in 1917, Sonneck declares in the introduction to Class M that the only alteration he would make, were he then to start afresh upon a scheme, would be to provide a separate classification for early music, which presents problems of its own. Just where "early music" ends is not stated, but it is understood that Sonneck had in mind the year 1800. The problem is certainly very important in the largest music libraries, but is not likely to cause many difficulties in those of smaller size.

The class lists are printed in a volume of 157 pages, some ten-and-a-quarter inches high, and the three sections are consecutive: M, Music scores; ML, Literature of music, and MT Musical instruction and theory. There is a single index to the three classes. The first class, M, divided into four major groups. M 1 to M 4 are for collections in the broadest sense; M 5 to M 1459 are for instrumental music; M 1490 is a special class, more of bibliographical than musical significance, while M 1495 to M 2199 are for vocal music, which is broadly divided into secular and religious music.

The scheme starts with places for general collections, otherwise unclassifiable, and M 3 for the collected works of individual composers. Single works, or works of a particular form for a single instrument, are classified in the places that follow. M 5 is the first number for instrumental music (miscellaneous and heterogeneous collections), and the individual instruments are then treated individually in turn, starting with organ music at M 6. M 7 to M 13 are sub-divisions of M 6; thus, M 7 is for collections of organ music, M 8 for sonatas and sonatinas, M 9 for suites and kindred cyclical works, M 10 for fugues (with or without pedals), while M 12 and M 13 are for arrangements for organ, collections using the former number, single works the latter. A set of Handel organ concertos, arranged for organ solo, would be classed at M 12, but a single concerto from the set would be at M 13. M 14 is the place for organ accompaniments to hymns and psalms.

The harmonium provides the link between organ and piano music, the latter being allotted the numbers M 20 to M 39·5, and this music again is generally arranged by type. M 35 is the place for arrangements of orchestral music, and M 37 for concertos, arranged for a single performer. Pianoforte duets, it should be noted, do not come into this section, but are to be found in M 200, with works for two instruments. After keyboard instruments, the schedule continues with stringed instruments, and the general sub-divisions are the same in each case. Five numbers are usually allotted, providing places for miscellaneous collections, collections of original works, single works written for the instrument, collections of arrangements, and arrangements of single works. String instruments are followed in turn by Wind, Plectral instruments, and Percussion and other instruments. The last begins, surprisingly enough, with Bagpipe, and includes pianola.

Duos begin at M 180, but other combinations are mnemonic, with trios having places from M 300 onwards, quartets from M 400, and so to nonets at M 900. First in the duos are pieces for organ and one other instrument, and this section continues with harmonium and one other instrument and so in parallel order with the solo section. This indicates that the earlier numbers allotted to stringed instruments are for unaccompanied works, such as the Bach *Chaconne* for unaccompanied violin; works written or arranged for violin and piano would be found between M 217 and M 223. It can now be seen why piano duets and works for two pianos are classified in this section, and not somewhere around M 35. With trios and larger chamber combinations, the general order remains unchanged. Trios begin with works for organ and two instruments, followed by works for piano and two instruments, etc. Nonets end at M 985, and M 990 and M 993 are provisional numbers for modern works which employ obsolete musical instruments.

M 1000 (itself for miscellaneous collections) begins a fresh section, for orchestral music. M 1001 is for symphonies, 1002 for symphonic poems, 1003 for suites, partitas, theme and variations, with 1004 for overtures and entr'actes. From 1005 onwards are places for concertos, arranged according to the solo instrument, beginning with organ and maintaining the same order demonstrated at the beginning of the class. In each case, two numbers are provided; one is for full score, the second for scores in which the orchestral score has been arranged for pianoforte, so that the work can be performed by a soloist together with a pianist who plays an approximation to the orchestral parts. A full or miniature score of Mozart's clarinet concerto would be classed at M 1024, and the same work arranged for solo clarinet and piano would be at M 1025. M 1045 and subsequent numbers are for orchestral pieces such as marches, pot-pourris and arrangements for orchestra. M 1100 onwards is for music for string orchestra, M 1200 for [military] band (with numbers analogous to those following M 1000), and M 1350 onwards for "reduced orchestra" and juvenile instrumental music. These divisions alone show something of the care and detail with which the schedules have been made.

M 1490, as indicated at the beginning of this description, is a number on its own. The heading is "Music (instrumental or vocal), printed or manuscript, before 1700 and preferred here, arranged by composers, in a special group instead of being assigned to special classes (as are operas, ballets, oratorios, masses, liturgical music, hymns, songs for one voice, etc.)". This provides a permissible place for libraries that wish to separate music written before the present "key" system was finally established to succeed the mediaeval "Modes".

Vocal music starts, for no apparent reason, at the odd number of M 1495. Secular music is classified first, divided by type of composition, and then by the combination for which the work is written, such as men's voices, women's voices, etc., with a further sub-division for the number of parts of different voices for which the work is written. Special places are given in the schedule to works written for unaccompanied singing. From M 1611 onwards songs are classified. Here, special numbers are allotted for songs written with lute accompaniment, concertina accompaniment, etc., but the general sub-divisions are unexpectedly meagre. This section is succeeded (from M 1627 onwards) by one for Folk and other national songs. As one would assume, there is very close division for songs of the U.S.A., and broader divisions for songs of other countries. "Society songs" is the next heading, again closely divided, and primarily of American interest. The British librarian is not likely to meet, for example, a work to class at M 1920 A 6, Collections of songs of an Anti-Cigarette League. This section concludes with places for Student songs and Juvenile songs.

The next field covered is that of Church music, at M 1999. M 2000 to 2017 provides places for Masses, Requiems, etc. These are succeeded by Anthems, which are divided by types of voices and also by the Church seasons of the year. There are special sub-divisions for such items as *Creed, Nunc Dimittis*, and a separate place for Motets that are difficult to classify elsewhere. Foreign hymnals are divided by country, regardless of denomination, but (as is natural) American hymn-books are divided closely by sect. The section then provides places for Church music, liturgy and ritual. Roman Catholic church music of this type is allocated M 2150 to 2155, with subdivisions, and Protestant churches have provision made, such as M 2164, Dutch and other reformed; M 2166·3, Scottish Episcopal church; M 2166, Irish church and Church of England. There are places for what might be called "topical" or "utilitarian" church music (gospel hymns, religious bodies with particular functions, etc.) which are analogous to the secular society songs. These special interests are allotted the places M 2198 (for collections) and 2199 (for single works). Class M is completed with M 5000, which includes "unidentifiable" works (chiefly fragments) which may be instrumental or vocal, sacred or secular. It is *not*, however, the place for anonymous works, which are classified in the normal manner, and if necessary, entered under title.

Before describing the other two sections, some comments on class M may be helpful. First, it can be seen that (except for the collected works of a composer, which are classified together as a set in M 3, and not broken up) the general scheme of division is first by medium, and then by form. Whatever criticism one might make, it must always be tempered by the fact that the scheme was devised to deal with the scores already held in the Library of Congress (and the preface does not indicate any second thoughts of the "If I had but known . . ." type), and was intended primarily for internal use rather than by other libraries. In support of the contention in McColvin & Reeves, mentioned in the opening paragraph of this outline, it may be mentioned that Edinburgh uses LC for its non-fiction stock, but that Dr. Savage rejected the music classification, and devised an entirely different one, based primarily on composer, and only secondarily on form or medium. In the music library of all but the largest cities, I feel that (to quote an example) Bach's organ works are better classed together rather than spread over eight different places, as is possible in L.C. The student of form might find the divisions by form of use, but interest is normally first by composer, with form as a secondary interest only. The argument against this is that having chosen the medium, a better view of what is available can be given if the works are divided by form, remembering that each section is divided alphabetically by composer. In LC, at least, the person primarily interested in Bach's organ works can be given the complete works, while single items are classified according to form. The student must judge for himself whether or not he agrees with this method. Mr. Edward N. Waters, Assistant Chief of the Music Division of the Library of Congress, has categorically declared in a personal letter: "I do not believe that we neglect the interest of readers seeking music by composer."

Against my criticism of these form divisions, I would balance pronounced approval for the provision of separate numbers for original works and those which have been arranged for an instrument, or combination of instruments; M 12 and M 13 (mentioned earlier) are examples of such numbers. At first sight, this has the compensating disadvantage of separating similar works of a composer. Dvořák's *Humoreskes* would be in M 25 (Pieces); a copy of the most famous of all the *Humoreskes* (no. 7 of this opus 101 set of eight) would, on the face of it, be classed at M 31 (Two-rhythm), although LC itself would apparently class it as M 25 as it is a single item from a set of pieces. An arrangement of the *New World* symphony for solo piano would be at M 35. This last place has proved useful, particularly as such arrangements are usually made by a musician other than the original composer. My own preference would be to place all original works and arrangements under the composer, and then sub-divide by form, etc., with a separate number for arrangements. The even wider separation, in LC, of piano solos from piano duets is logical, but unattractive. I am also surprised that separate numbers are not allotted for the different keyboard instruments such as virginals, clavichord, etc., as much early music was written for one or other precursors of the modern pianoforte, and many musicians consider that such pieces sound better when played on the instrument for which they were written, though this is a matter of taste. The difficulty here is that there is often no certainty, when two or three different keyboard instruments were in vogue at the same time, as to which particular one was favoured by a composer when he wrote a particular piece of music or set of pieces. Such would be the case with the Bach "48 Preludes and Fugues". Finally, it is obvious that a non-American library using this scheme would ignore the sub-divisions in a number of places, where these are peculiar to the U.S.A., and incorporate national sub-divisions for its own use. This is a difficulty that should be easily surmounted.

Though many people tend to regard Classes M, ML, and MT, as a single class, this is not really true; they are three self-contained and semi-independent classes. ML, the Literature of Music, includes such items as periodicals, almanacs, Societies, Institutions, programmes, libretti, etc. It also includes such special topics as musical prodigies (ML 81) and women and music (ML 82). Libraries that collect the writings of musicians—manuscripts, autographs and facsimiles, etc., find the scheme provides a place for these at ML 90. The numbers ML 100 to 110 are given to dictionaries and encyclopaedias; ML 111 to 158 are for bibliography, while 159 to 3795 are utilized for history and criticism, including biography. Division is normally by country, and there is a special section for Wagner, which illustrates once again how the scheme was built round the books held rather than according to abstract theory. A similar scheme could be adopted for any other composer of large output, well represented in a library. Places are provided for books on orchestral, chamber and vocal music. ML 3800 to 3920 are for subjects dealing with the philosophy and physics of music, and finally at ML 3925 is an extremely useful place for fiction. There are quite a number of novels that deal sufficiently with musical subjects to be of interest to music-lovers.

The final schedule, MT—Musical Instruction and theory, should be self-explanatory. It takes in all aspects of pedagogy, including such subjects as harmony and counterpoint, orchestration, teaching methods for various instruments, etc. These last are generally divided into four headings—General observations, Systems and methods, Studies and exercises and Self instructors. The inclusion of the third heading means that educative works and those composed particularly to exploit and illustrate technical difficulties (such as Bartók's *Mikrokosmos* and Liszt's *Etudes d'exécution transcendante*) are to be found here, and not (as would be expected) in the section of solo works in Class M. The Liszt concert studies are often heard in recitals, and are completely outside the scope of the great majority of amateur pianists, so that this placing seems somewhat unreal. This difficulty is met, in LC itself, by classing some copies in class M and others in MT.

Classification

This scheme has been dealt with at length because it is used with what is probably the largest music collection in the world. The greatest proof of its quality is the simple fact that Sonneck's scheme still meets with the approval of those who work with it, though the collection has now grown to ten times the size of that for which the classification was devised.

THE "BIBLIOGRAPHIC" CLASSIFICATION

In some respects, the "Bibliographic" classification of Henry Evelyn Bliss is the most difficult to grasp of those considered in this chapter. The student, when reading this sub-class Music, sections VV-VX, is advised to have a copy of the scheme to hand: a check of the point made should help to clear up difficulties and possible ambiguities. The Music is found in volume III of Bliss's work, but the first and fourth volumes may also be requisite—the former for certain schedules which act as common form sub-divisions, the latter for the index.

Acknowledgement should be made here of the courteous help given by Mr. Bliss in the writing of this section. On more than one occasion he replied in great detail to a long list of comments, questions and suggestions. He has virtually edited both first and second drafts of this text, and but for his assistance, this section would have contained several faults of emphasis and interpretation. There remain a number of points upon which he and I agreed to differ, and these may be evident to the reader. On others, however, Mr. Bliss generously conceded the changes and indicated his intention of revising the music schedules in accordance with suggestions made. Some of these proposed amendments are shown in square brackets.

In the introduction to volume III, pages 65-6, the author points out that the term "Music" has six different meanings, and that allowance for all of these should be made in a good classification. Another long note on the classification of music precedes the section itself. Briefly, these six aspects are musical sound itself (acoustics); the subjective "heard music"; music composition, according to the rules of harmony, counterpoint, form, etc.; the compositions shown physically, in the form of scores, gramophone records, pianola rolls, etc.; the rendition of music, and finally the hearing of such renderings—not as acoustic but as aesthetic. Bliss, in the introduction to the classification itself, points out again that music classification is extremely complex, with the problems of cross-classification occurring at almost every heading. It would appear that Bliss would provide for the shelving of criticism of a work with the work criticized, but deems that impractical because of differences of size. If most sheet music were published in a format similar to that of books, or vice versa, this mixing of the two different kinds of material might become practical.

Music is described as an Expressive art, and is shown in the schedules as part of Class V (Aesthetic arts), being allocated the divisions VV to VX. The long comment before the tables themselves should be read (as well as the two pages in the Introduction that refer specifically to music); it will be noted that Bliss combines his six aspects of music into three (each having objective and subjective aspects): heard music, the composition of music, and the rendition of music. In the scheme, VV deals with music in a general manner and with history; VW with Musicology—the science, theory and philosophy of music, and VX with Musical compositions, Scores and Records, i.e. the actual material for performance. These three sections do not, Bliss points out, correspond to the three (or six) aspects. They are practical, not basic.

Class VV, for music in general, uses the mnemonics (constant throughout the system) 1, 2, 6 and 7 for reference books, bibliography, periodicals and miscellanies respectively. VV3 is devoted to ancillary material relating to the history of music, such as Societies' reports, programmes, etc. If preferred, VV3 and/or VV5 can be used for a special collection of music. VV8 is for the history of music in general, and can be sub-divided by Schedules 1, 3 or 4 at the classifier's discretion. Schedule 1 provides a series of general topics for sub-division, Schedule 3 is for sub-division by language or nationality, and Schedule 4 for sub-division by historical periods.

VV9 is for biographies of musicians and criticisms of their works. As with VV8, this section can be divided in more than one way, according to the classifier's wishes. Once a choice is made, of course, future accessions must be classed in the same manner. The first possibility is alphabetically by composer, etc., in a single sequence, arranged by the first letter of the composer's surname and a numerical suffix; the second choice is division by nation or country, with alphabetical arrangement under each section; the third choice is chronological, using the sub-divisions given in Schedule 4. Under this scheme a sixteenth-century composer would be classed at VV9, E

162

for biographical purposes. Whichever of these methods is used, further sub-division for any individual composer can be obtained by the use of Schedule 7. Bliss himself would appear to prefer the first of these four possible methods, for in the index Bach is listed at VV9, B1; Beethoven VV9, B3; Bizet, VV9, B5; Brahms, VV9, B7, and Britten at VV9, B8. None of these names is actually shown in the main tables; it will be seen that several numbers are missed, presumably for intercalation. The intention in the index has apparently been to include examples rather than the most important names, so that there is no point in criticizing those selected or pointing out important omissions.

If the user of the scheme chooses the division by nationality or place, books on the history of music in a particular country are shelved with lives of musicians of the same country, unless the librarian prefers to have all biography at the general number of L9, which ignores special interests, but does divide by country. These are good alternatives, but the difficulty lies in deciding the nationality of composers such as Gluck, Saint-Saëns or Handel. Mr. Bliss prefers to refer always to Händel, a difference that emphasizes that composer's claim to double nationality.

"Musicology" (Class VW) is an American term of rapidly growing use, though still regarded with some caution in Britain, and includes the theoretical and critical aspects of music. Naturally, classes VV and VW are of different scope, that of VV being more general, but there are occasional similarities. For instance, VV6 is for "Periodicals relative to Music and the History of Music", VW6 for "Periodicals for Musicians, the Profession and the Art of Music". This distinction is permissive, as the word "may" shows in the note on the numeral sub-sections under the heading VW, Musicology. All the periodicals of musical interests may be kept in VV6, unless the need for VW6 becomes manifest. VWB, on the theory of music, is excellently divided, with separate sub-divisions for scales and for their antecedents, the Modes. VWC is for Consonance and Dissonance, and has a cross-reference to Acoustics. VWD is allotted to the Arts of composing and Producing Music, VWE for Aesthetics, Philosophy and Psychology of Music. VWEN is for Absolute music (i.e. music that does not attempt to paint a picture or convey a specific idea or set of ideas, but is intended to be listened to purely as music, and perhaps admired for its construction); VWEP is for its antithesis, Program music (i.e. music that attempts to render a story or picture in terms of sound, such as Richard Strauss's *Till Eulenspiegel* or Saint-Saëns *Danse macabre*); VWEO for Classical music and VWER for Romantic, Idyllic, Pastoral music. These places are provided for the more general studies, but a book discussing the *Pastoral symphonies* of Beethoven and Vaughan Williams may be placed at VWEP (Program music) or at VWER (. . . Pastoral music), at VWEO (Classical music) or under Beethoven and Vaughan Williams in VV9.

Composition of music, and Writing music is VWF, Time and Tempo is VWG, Harmony VWH, Counterpoint VWI and Musical form VWJ. All these have the necessary sub-divisions. VWK is provided for the "Literature of Musical Education and the Studies of the Musical Arts", VWL for "Private study of the Musical Arts, Self-education in" and VWM for "Music schools. . . ." These particular sections are probably more practical than those corresponding in any of the other schemes discussed in this chapter. The class continues with VWN, Voice training; VWO, Instrumental training; VWP, Musicians, including music as a profession. VWQ is allotted to the "Publication of Musical Compositions, and production of 'Records' for Mechanical Rendition". Thus, VWQC is for copyright, VQWS for recording instruments and apparatus. The fullness of these headings is obvious, and books on these topics are difficult to fit in in some of the other classification schemes.

VWR, which has no sub-divisions, is for "Rendition, Expression of Musical Compositions, General". This is succeeded by VWS Vocal music and VWT Instrumental music. These are for books on interpretation, and not on how to sing and play, but there may well be some slight confusion in practice. A note states that "The training and study may be included, instead of under VWO". VWT includes organ, and has two sub-divisions for "Pipe" and "Reed, Melodeon". No separate provision is made for the electronic organ, but the Hammond and other organs of this type will be allotted a separate sub-division, VWTLE, in any subsequent revision. VWU is for "Wind instruments in general; Reed instruments in general". The first sub-division here is for wood-wind, followed by VWUF for Accordion, concertina, barrel organ (the old church type, and not the once-familiar street piano seen in England before World War II; this instrument is neither wind nor reed), etc. The next sub-division is for brass instruments. Bliss then provides for Percussion instruments in general (neither wind or reed), which are allotted the places

VWUN to VWUR, with VWUS for Historic, Exotic, Primitive and other Instruments, VWUT is for for Chinese Cheng, Scotch [*sic*] bag-pipe, etc. It may be recalled that only James Duff Brown treats the instrument sensibly as a reed one (though Mr. Bliss was not impressed by that argument) and he also makes provision for the different types of pipes that are still extant. VWUU is for Chamber music, sub-divided into VWUV, String Quartette; VWUW, Piano and violin, and VWUY, Other groups. [This placing is open to considerable criticism, and Mr. Bliss indicated his intention of transferring VWUU–Y to VWVU–Y, where these subjects will be much more consistently placed in collocation with orchestral music. As the notation VWVW is already used for Jazz orchestras and Music, this will be altered to VWVS, to allow for the inclusion of the chamber music headings.]

VWV is for Orchestral music, and contains eight useful sub-heads [with four to be added from VWU], including Conductors; Reading orchestral scores; Program; Selection and arrangement of music, and (mentioned in the previous paragraph) Jazz orchestras and music. VWW, Religious music, etc., includes VWWM, Organ, Organists. This might be confused with VWTK, Organ, unless it is remembered that this deals with the organ in general, while VWWM is for religious music rendered on the church organ and for its structure and technical details. The smaller library would probably find it more convenient to use one rather than both places. The section for books on music is completed by VWY, Popular music and Mechanical (or Physical) rendition. This section includes places for player-pianos, Juke-boxes and Megaphones, in addition to such obvious items as gramophones.

Music scores are classed at VX. This section, as with the others, begins with the constant and the variable mnemonics for bibliographical sub-division. VX2, for example, is the Bibliography of musical scores in general, and VX28 (a decimal type of sub-division) for catalogues of dealers and music publishers. 8, one of the variable sub-divisions, whose meaning changes from class to class, is here (VX 8) used for Special collections of unbound scores; and Miniature scores. This makes provision for the works of a local composer, or some other historical or self-contained collection. The scores themselves are arranged in VX in similar sequence to the earlier sections for books on music, i.e. vocal music, instrumental music and recorded music.

Although a separate place was provided for books on Sea

shanties, in VWYB, no place for the scores is provided under VXJ, Concert and Chamber Vocal Music; [but Mr. Bliss promised to allot VXJR, now vacant, to them, thus paralleling VWYB. He suggested, as an alternative, that such scores be classed in VXJY with "Other choral scores".] Religious music is at VXK, and Dramatic and Operatic music at VXL, which may have a chronological division (e.g. VXL38, Twentieth century), national division (according to the nationality of the composer) or type division (Music drama, Mythological and heroic, etc.). Any of the three methods may be chosen by the classifier, but once chosen, should not be altered for future accessions, unless the whole section is to be reclassified. The safest method in this "vague and historically complex class", as Bliss calls it, is chronological; the date of the opera's first performance is usually easily ascertainable (from Loewenberg's *Annals of opera*, etc.), but the nationality of the composer may be debatable, and the division of opera by type soon leads to considerable difficulty. Places are provided for selections, librettos and programs. In a similar manner, Orchestral music, Scores (VXM) is divided by form, such as symphonies and suites. Orchestral music is further divided by medium (string orchestra, brass band, theatre orchestras) and this could give rise to cross-classification with the headings immediately preceding. For instance, many eighteenth-century composers (such as J. C. Bach) wrote symphonies for string orchestras, so that the latter heading might need to be restricted to arrangements for this particular type of orchestra, or for works whose form is not included under the heading, such as concertos or variations. This last is a surprising omission, but variations may be included under VXMY. VXMP, Modernistic music and VXMQ, Jazz orchestra scores appear to overlap, since Bliss apparently used "modernistic music" as a synonym for "jazz". VXMR, Recently composed music, may also provide difficulties, though it was hoped by its author to provide a convenient and practical place, albeit one requiring a time limit and frequent revision to prevent confusion with the preceding form headings.

VXN is for chamber music. VXNA to VXNJ may be sub-divided as orchestral music is, VXNK for transcriptions and arrangements, VXNL for string quartets (piano quartets apparently being placed under "other ensembles"), VXNM for trios of any sort, no separate places being provided for string trios and piano trios. VXNN is for quintets, VXNO for sestets, septets and octets, VXNP for ensembles with harp, VXNR for duets. This last head has three sub-divisions; VXNT for piano and violin, VXNV for violin and viola, and VXNW for violin and violoncello. Bliss arranges this sequence to have the commoner, most-frequently used forms first, leaving the less-used forms to follow if they are requisite. (My own opinion is that a single sequence from duets to octets, or the reverse, would have been less arbitrary.) Organ music is classed at VXO and is divided into religious and secular sub-divisions. It is surprising to an English user to find special provision made for offertories and postludes (both comparatively rare in music published in this country), whereas there is no specific place for those popular organ works, the choral prelude and the fugue [but this need should be met in the next edition, and the two forms will be included in the index].

Piano music (VXP) is closely divided, and harpsichord music is considered as an integral part. To allow for close classification, there is a special sub-division, Schedule 22, which can be utilized for this or any other section of music scores large enough to warrant such sub-division. Piano music can be divided by nationality, by chronology, or by form, such as Nocturnes, Marches, etc. Dance music (VXPT) sensibly includes Gigues, Sarabandes, Mazurkas, etc., though students should note that "Tarantula" is more usually known as "Tarantella". Waltzes are considered sufficiently important to have a separate sub-division at VXPV. VXPW for Modernist music, "New" music, is distinguished by Bliss from "jazz". [The word "Jazz" will be added in the next edition, and also included in the index. This should prevent any misconception arising as to the use of this particular place in the system.] The provision of a single place for both piano duets and works for two pianos (VXPD) is disappointing, but a separate place for the latter scores may be marked VXPDD on Bliss's own authority. No other place is available.

After piano music, the harp has a complete section to itself, though one may doubt if the average public library has any harp scores in its collection. VXR, for violin, includes places for the lute and the viol. VXT and VXU provide places for the music of wood-wind instruments. The general sequence is similar to that of class VWU, but the alterations made are open to criticism. For instance, VWUC is for oboe and English horn, but oboe music is classed at VXU and music for the English horn at VXUV, with other instruments intervening. [This separation of the two closely related instruments, the oboe and the English horn, generally known in Britain as the cor anglais, will be remedied by transferring the latter to VXUH.]

In the index are about 250 entries under the key word "Music", while those forms and kinds of musical compositions considered most important by Bliss are entered in the general sequence under their own names, and not under the general heading "Music". There are, apparently, about fifty terms so treated, making the total number of entries for music and its terms about 300 which is generous. A personal preference would be for all the entries to be grouped under "Music" or else for all terms to be scattered through the index as part of the general alphabetical sequence. The present half-and-half method seems likely to cause difficulty until familiarity is gained with both the scheme and the index. Such subjects as "Anthem" and "Piano" (which has over thirty sub-divisions) appear in the main sequence while "Chamber music" and "Scales" are sub-headings under "Music". These illustrations may give some idea of the problem.

Without practical experience to back one's judgement, it is difficult to assess any scheme fairly but this would appear to be soundly based. Bliss had a wide knowledge of music and a great liking for it; he also received some assistance in this class from Senor J. Albani of Buenos Aires to whom acknowledgement is made at the beginning of Class U. It is obvious that the problems of a music classification have been clearly seen and considered by Bliss though his solutions may not win general acceptance. The provision of alternative methods of sub-division at certain points is in line with that adopted in other classes in the system; this may be of real value to the classifier providing that the correct choice is made after taking into account both the current stock of the library and probable future accessions. Comments have been made, at one or two points, on the chances of cross-classification but if these ambiguities are settled as they arise no great difficulty should be experienced in putting the scheme to practical use. Though attention has been drawn to what may be considered defects and mistakes, this is probably the best music classification on what may now be considered to be traditional lines, in contrast to the methods of division and arrangements used in the British Catalogue of Music, discussed below.

THE BRITISH CATALOGUE OF MUSIC

The first number of the B.C.M. appeared in 1957 and listed both music scores and books on music that had been deposited in the British Museum during the preceding quarter. In general the work resembles in appearance the familiar B.N.B. but there are two major differences. The first is purely one of convenience—the index to each issue is placed before the classified section and not, as in B.N.B., after it. The second difference was more fundamental in the replacement of the Decimal Classification by a new and original scheme compiled by Mr. E. J. Coates of the staff of B.N.B. The bibliographical side of B.C.M. has been covered in Chapter II; the following pages are devoted to consideration of the classification scheme only.

An outline of this scheme is given with each interim issue and with the first annual volume, which is the only one to have appeared when these lines were written. Draft schedules of the detailed scheme were published in November 1957 and have been used for this summary. To those trained upon a numerical notation the B.C.M. scheme may appear a complicated and possibly frightening scheme for the arrangement of music but familiarity should quickly show that it is not difficult to apply and is highly effective in operation. As already indicated, provision has to be made for all music received in the British Museum (with certain fairly well-defined categories of ephemeral character excluded); this includes not only works published in Britain but also those foreign scores for which certain British firms possess sole agency rights. The best comparison is therefore with the L.C. scheme, and it may be felt that the new classification, though superficially the more difficult to understand and apply, is the more exact and precise in its relationships between subjects. This is as it should be, since ideas on classification methods have altered considerably since the L.C. scheme was introduced some fifty years earlier.

The scheme is a faceted one (based in method on that used by Ranganathan in his "Colon" classification) whereby one builds up a symbol to show all the essential constituents; though the final result may appear complicated it is usually reasonably simple to decode and it gives an exactness of meaning that is not possible with the older and more conventional schemes. With the exception of Table 7 which is used to indicate dates and duration the scheme is entirely alphabetical with a base of twenty-four letters; I and O are generally omitted for reasons of clarity, though they are used in class B when coding composers' names and it is proposed to develop an alternative scheme for chamber music as class O, though B.C.M. will continue to use N. There are two sequences, often parallel: the first, A and B, is for music literature, and the second, C to Z, for scores. As in Cutter and (to a somewhat lesser degree) in Bliss, the two sequences have a close relationship which can be quickly indicated by an example. AQS is for books on the spinet and QS is the class for music written for the instrument. These parallels will be stressed in subsequent pages as they represent an important part of the scheme.

Because scores have so great a part of the alphabetical base allotted to them, this part of the schedules will be considered first. C begins with places for educational scores of a general nature (C to C/AL) with C/AY for general collections of music (which can be divided for different localities if necessary or desirable) and C/AZ for collections from individual composers. This last has no subdivision. The remainder of class C is for collections of music, e.g. folk, incidental and religious music. Class C/A . . . is, therefore, something of a generalia class in the scheme but from CB onwards the places are for "music of particular kinds (individual works and collections)". The remainder of class C, together with classes D to H and J are all for choral music of one sort or another and K is for vocal solos. Collections of instrumental music are classed at L, orchestral music in M, chamber music and instrumental groups at N and P respectively. These are followed by piano music at Q, organ at R, violin at S, plucked string instruments at T, wind instruments at U, with sub-divisions for woodwind in class V and brass at W, percussion at X and other instruments at Y. Z is allotted to non-European music. This apparent emphasis on choral music is dictated, it seems, because this is the field in which the greatest volume of accessions is received. The use of a wider base helps to reduce the total length of necessary symbols to cope with this complexity.

The schedules also include seven auxiliary tables, somewhat reminiscent of Bliss; Table 1 is the general one for the sub-division of any particular instrument or instrumental group, while Tables 2 and 3 provide very small modifications of Table 1 for use with piano and organ music. Table 4 provides another modification, this time for books (but not for scores) dealing with instruments and instrumental groups. Table 5 quotes letters that are used as required to indicate the most frequently required religious denominations; Table 6 is a series of ethnic/locality sub-divisions and Table 7, which has already been mentioned, provides "chronological reference points".

The first stage of classification is invariably (as in all schemes) by the instrument or instruments for which the particular score in hand has been written or arranged, e.g. QP piano solo. To this are added further letters to show the particular type of music—QPE piano sonatas, QPH dances and QPHVH polkas for solo piano, which is a direct sub-division of QPH and not a division of QPHV as might be expected. This illustrates the lack of parallelism between the notation and the logical structure of the schedules. The sub-divisions of QPH are in alphabetical order and fresh subjects can be intercalated as necessary—though this is true of any part of the schedules. S is for violin, SP for violin and piano, SPM unaccompanied violin (which may be regarded as moving backwards in the schedule) and SPME unaccompanied violin sonatas.

Common form divisions are given within curves; these apply primarily to books. Arrangements are always introduced by the letter "K" and, though not logically required, this is always quoted with a stroke "/" after it in order to assist comprehension. The stroke also forms part of the notation of certain topics, e.g. "/LF" represents Christmas music and the stroke is included when this aspect is applied in any part of the schedules. Thus, carols are classed at FDP, and Christmas carols at FDP/LF, while New Year carols are FDP/LFM. In an earlier example QPH was quoted for dances for piano; QPJ is for miscellaneous piano works and QPK introduces solo piano works that are arrangements of pieces originally written for some other instrument or instruments. Remembering that K is always followed by the stroke to attract attention, we find QPK/CM is the pianoforte score of a musical play and QPK/CM/JR of a filmed musical play score; these follow QPK/CC for the piano score of an opera. The symbols that appear after the stroke are related to those of the original scoring. Earlier in this paragraph the notation FDP/LF was quoted for a volume of Christmas carols and this bears an obvious relation to a book of carols arranged for piano solo which would be classed at QPK/DP/LF. The method of building up symbols in combination to show the instrument, the form, its relationship to another work if it is an arrangement (and for collections), its nationality and its place in chronology allows an exactitude that no other scheme of music classification gives and yet the notation remains comparatively brief. It may be mentioned here that the scheme is designed to accommodate without strain new developments as they occur in the published material, and this is the primary reason for the non-hierarchical notation. It was also an important consideration in the decision to adopt a facet-type structure since this enables the classifier to see where a new subject should go; a non-hierarchical notation enables it to be placed at the desired point with a minimum of complication in the notation.

Class A, musical literature, has the same basic method and is closely related to the symbols for scores. A book on Christmas carols is ADP/LF, one on opera AC, on film music A/JR and on musical plays ACM. These placings may be usefully compared with those quoted above for piano arrangements of these particular types of music. It needs no great perspicacity to deduce that an operatic score is likely to be classed at CC and the score of a musical play at CM. The common form sub-divisions, from A(A) to A(Z) include the expected ones such as encyclopaedias A(C), bibliographies A(T), history A(X) and its related division by place A(Y), but also include a number of unexpected topics such as statistics A(HM), law A(J), lists of objects A(WT) (whose use is demonstrated in a later example) and aspects of music in relation to other subjects—branches of A(Z), e.g. music influenced by another subject, A(ZF).

These sub-divisions are followed by places for other aspects of music—A/AM the theory of music, A/CY technique (which includes A/D composition, A/E performance and A/F recording), A/FY musical character (including A/G folk music, A/H dance music, A/L religious music, etc.), A/M elements of music (including A/P pitch and A/R harmony) and A/S forms of music (which includes A/T theme and variations and A/Y fugue). Two points stand out here. First, that the sub-division may have a shorter notation than its containing head, and second, that many of these places use symbols related to those for the appropriate scores. On the first point, it is simply a matter of practical use; there are likely to be appreciably more books on musical composition than on the more general topic of music technique. As for the second, the previously quoted example of FDP/LF for a collection of Christmas carols can be connected with A/LF for books on music for Christmas.

Now follows the straightforward division of class A, from AB Vocal music to AY Other instruments. These topics are for "Works on particular kinds of music, designated by executants". AD is for choral music, ADP for carols; AL begins the sequence for books on instrumental music with ALH as the general place for dance forms, sub-divided alphabetically from ALHJ Allemande to ALHW Waltz. Somewhere in the middle is ALHVH Polka; here again, it is simple to see the relationship between this placing and that of QPHVH (quoted earlier) for a collection of polkas for piano solo.

Class B is for books on individual composers. Collective works on musicians are in A/D(M) which is made up of the symbol A/D Composition plus the common sub-division (M) from A(M) for "Persons in music". A/N is for biographies, so that general biographies of composers are classed at A/D(N). For individual composers the arrangement is alphabetical using the initial letters of the composer's surname plus other letters (on the style of Cutter and other author arrangements) to bring the names into a single sequence. Thus, a life of Bach is at BBC; the first "B" is for a work on an individual composer, the second "B" for the first letter of his surname and "C" to arrange the name among the other composers whose names also have B as an initial letter. Beethoven is BBJ, Mozart BMS, Schubert BSF and Schumann BSG. William Schuman, the American composer, would therefore be allotted a symbol such as BSFZ to bring a book on him and his works into place in the schedules immediately before Robert Schumann. This method of interpolation can be applied at any point throughout the schedules. Here is a class in which I and O have to be used—for books on John Ireland or Jacques Offenbach and others whose names begin with these two letters. Not only biographies but any books dealing with aspects of the life or works of an individual composer are classed here. The appropriate sub-division is taken from class A and added to the symbol for the composer. Thus, a biography of Schubert would be given the symbol BSF(N) and a book on Schubert's variations BSF/T, since A/T is the class mark for books on variations in general. Other amplifications can be made by using the symbols from AB to AY; a book on Schubert's Masses would be given the notation BSFADG. Such a scheme brings together works dealing with many varied topics relating to a particular composer. This simple juxtaposition of symbols, somewhat reminiscent of what is possible in the "Subject" classification, is invaluable. It might be a weakness in the hands of the unskilled classifier who could link together the various parts of a complicated notation symbol in the wrong order, unless he remembers the basic rule which should prevent this happening, i.e. that symbols should be combined in reverse schedule order (unless the schedule itself directs to the contrary). Once this is understood and practised the book on Schubert's Masses will be correctly placed at BSFADG and not at a place such as ADGBSF.

Further help in the application of the schedules is given by the instruction quoted in the 1957 volume that "A is followed by A(. . .), which is followed by A/ . . ., which is followed by AB, which is followed by AC, which is followed by B, etc.". It may be useful to demonstrate still further how some of the longer symbols indicate quite clearly the exact nature of the music. Before doing so, mention must be made of the fact that BZ is allotted to non-European music (and this can be sub-divided in exactly similar fashion to class A) and a reminder made that an arrangement of music in a form other than that originally written is introduced by the letter K followed by a stroke. The final technical point is that a subject divided by two common sub-divisions in curves has the two aspects combined by a stroke so that A(K/C) is used and not A(K)(C).

The first example chosen is an arrangement for military band of ballet music, UMMK/MM/HM. The constituent parts are U, Wind instruments, UMM Military band and K for arrangements to show the actual setting of the score in hand. M is orchestral music and MM music for symphony orchestra. A/H is the symbol for books on dance music and A/HM for books on ballet music. Used with a score the "A" is dropped so that the final symbol is /HM, completing UMMK/MM/HM.

An apparently more complicated example is AB/FD(YD/XLT 28/WT) but this too can be broken down piecemeal without difficulty. AB is for books on vocal music; A/FD is recorded music. As in the previous example, the "A" is dropped from the second symbol when combined with another, so that AB/FD is recorded vocal music. Y introduces the ethnic/locality sub-division [Auxiliary Table 6] where D is English or, in this particular context, England. X introduces a period from Auxiliary Table 7, with L indicating 1880 and T adding 18 years, so that XLT indicates 1898; 28 shows that the particular work covers a period of 28 years while A(WT) is the symbol for "Lists of objects". The symbol can therefore be dissected to indicate a list of recorded vocal music in England from 1898 to 1925 or 1926; the actual book in the schedules is, in fact, the first volume of J. R. Bennett's *The voices of the past: vocal recordings, 1898–1925.* If the reader feels that the B.C.M. class mark is too long, difficult or complicated he is invited to see what results he gets when trying to classify this particular book by any other scheme.

Generally speaking, the symbols required for scores are shorter than those applied to books since the latter have a base of two letters

Classification

(A and B) only. MSK/DW/GT is the category for a medley of hunting songs for light orchestra. M is orchestral music, MS music for light orchestra and K introduces arrangements; DW is the symbol for songs, etc., and GT comes from A/GT, a sub-division of A/G, Folk music. So the three parts of the notation show clearly the actual executant of the music (the light orchestra), the original executant (a singer) and the actual character of the composition, in this case the type of song.

VWPK/RXLF shows VW Bassoon, P, piano accompaniment, K arrangement [from] RW String instruments (R is organ and RW is therefore not a subsidiary subject but another example of a quite separate subject sharing the same initial letter for notational convenience only) and RX, Bowed string instruments. L comes from Auxiliary Table 1 (K/L) which indicates a reduction from a score for orchestra and the same instrument; in this case the interpolation of RX before the L means that the original orchestra was a string one. The final digit is F, Concertos, and the complete symbol, therefore, indicates a work for bassoon and piano which is an arrangement of a work written for bassoon and string orchestra.

Two final examples show the same sort of built-up notation. In XMK/QRGM, X represents percussion instruments, XM percussion band, K an arrangement [from] QR Harpsichord works and in Auxiliary Table 1, G is suites and GM marches: so the score is therefore an arrangement for percussion band of a march originally written for harpsichord. The last number is AC/E(YDBC/XPP 3); obviously a book about music, with AC for opera; A/E is performance, so that AC/E is operatic performance; (Y...) introduces the locality sub-division from Auxiliary Table 6, so that (YDB) is London, while (YDBC) is the place for the Covent Garden Opera. X is the "period introducing symbol" of Auxiliary Table 7, in which the first P represents 1940 and the second P an addition of 14 years, making XPP represent 1954, with a duration of three years. The actual book allotted this symbol is *Opera, 1954–1956*, the tenth of the series of "Covent Garden books". Other examples of notation are given in the comparative lists at the end of the chapter.

Unlike all the other schemes considered, this one is not part of a general classification but is limited entirely to music.* It can be used in lieu of the music classification of any scheme but would probably

---

* By no means the first. An excellent earlier American example is George S. Dickinson's "Vassar-Columbia" system (2).

be most useful with a large collection that is housed in a separate department. A large collection would benefit from the detailed sub-division and the different notation would be less noticeable in a separate department.

SOME SUGGESTIONS FOR THE CLASSIFIER USING
DEWEY 780 CLASS

In the outline and criticisms of D.C., made earlier in this chapter, some of the pitfalls for the classifier were indicated. Because Dewey's music classification is often regarded as poor, many libraries have adapted or revised the 780 section to a greater or lesser degree. The most widely used variant in Britain is that of Mr. L. R. McColvin and comment is made on this at the end of these notes. It can be said here, however, that this is not an amended version of Dewey but a complete recasting, having only the symbols 780 to 789 in common with the original. The library with a large collection may decide, if all books and scores in class 780 are to be reclassified to use the B.C.M. scheme.

The notes that follow are for classifiers who feel that this is too great a task but who find the printed tables of D.C. full of unexpected pitfalls. Libraries with small music collections, in particular, may find the following suggestions helpful both as to placings and to simplification of certain sections.

Operas, etc.

Cross-classification results if Dewey's 782 sub-divisions are strictly followed and the simplest arrangement that would still separate unrelated items would seem to be:

782·1 All GRAND OPERA, of whatever nationality, in single alphabetical sequence of composers.

782·6 COMIC OPERA, LIGHT OPERA and MUSICAL COMEDIES, i.e. music of the Gilbert and Sullivan, Franz Lehar, Noel Coward, Rogers and Hammerstein types. Mozart and Rossini would be in 782·1, Offenbach in 782·6. Comic opera is sometimes defined as that having spoken dialogue between arias, etc., but this must be regarded as a very approximate guide indeed. In cases of doubt, prefer 782·1 to 782·6.

782·8 SECULAR CANTATAS, i.e. works for soloists, chorus and orchestra in which the text is non-religious. Examples of this type of work are Bach's *Coffee cantata*, Bliss's *Morning heroes*, Coleridge-Taylor's *Hiawatha*, etc.

Masses and Oratorios

Masses, such as the Beethoven *Missa Solemnis, op. 123*, should be classed at 783·2. 783·3 is retained as the number for oratorios and 783·4 for Sacred Cantatas which differ from those in 782·8 in that the subject is usually Biblical, though the text is not usually taken from the Bible itself as is common with Oratorio. Hymnals will be classified at 783·9 and such works as the *Oxford book of carols* at 783·6, but other sub-divisions in the schedule may well be ignored.

Vocal Music

The simplest method of reducing the chances of cross-classification here is to reduce the number of headings. Ignoring the 784·0 . . . sub-divisions, 784·1 would be retained for glees and madrigals. Individual songs or albums of songs by a single composer should be arranged in composer sequence at 784·3. The boundaries between collections of folk songs, student songs and national airs are often ill defined and baffling and it could well be that the best answer is to class them all at one of three numbers, 784·4, 784·6 or 784·7, dividing nationally in the normal method of D.C. where the selection is limited to the songs of a single country. 784·8 can then be used for collections of songs for a particular type of voice, e.g. an album of baritone songs. 784·5, Festival songs is another heading that can be ignored, since solo songs can be classed at 784·3 if by a single composer (and at the chosen number of 784·4, 784·6 or 784·7 if by various composers) and at 784·1 if the songs are for choirs.

Instrumental Ensemble

Many smaller libraries find it simplest to class all miniature scores at 785, arranging the works in alphabetical order by composer. This method also separates quite clearly in the classified sequence of the catalogue the vocal score of an opera (782·1) and the miniature score of the same work, the four parts of a string quartet for use by instrumentalists for actual performance (785·74) and a miniature score of the work. If it is desired to retain full Dewey numbers for miniature scores, particular care must be taken to ensure that staff and public can see clearly from the catalogue entry which version or versions are in stock.

Piano Music

Books dealing with the piano, such as Closson's *History of the piano*, can be classed at 786·2, purely instructional works (both books and scores) at 786·3, and 786·4 used for ordinary piano pieces in a single composer sequence (as recommended earlier in this chapter and in the 15th edition of D.C.). When in doubt between 786·3 and 786·4 (as in the later books of Bartok's *Mikrokosmos*) the latter placing is preferable, so that 786·3 is used for strictly pedagogic works. Three other types of piano music deserve special provision. These are piano duet, works for two pianos and piano solo scores of country dance music and similar pieces.

Piano duet is for two players sitting side by side and sharing the same keyboard, so that one player normally monopolizes the upper half of it while the second confines his attentions to the bass end. With two pianos both players have a complete keyboard to themselves and this gives the composer much greater freedom in his writing. It is a common practice to arrange the orchestral score of a piano concerto for a piano, so that the first player takes the solo part, exactly as in the original, while the second pianist does his best to represent the orchestra.

In the nineteenth century, without the aid of radio and gramophone to make possible the regular hearing of the classics, many orchestral works were arranged for piano duet and there is a large body of good original duet material available, as is indicated in the second half of this book. Duets are played from a single copy of the music; it is customary for the two parts to be printed with the primo on the right and secondo (the bass player) on the left, so that each has his own part in front of him. Occasionally the two parts are arranged in tandem one above the other—this makes it easier to see what the other player is doing but requires some craning over the other player's shoulder during alternate pages. Works written or arranged for two pianos clearly require two copies of the score for performance. The two types of composition and arrangement are related since each requires two pianists but the differences are sufficient to make two separate placings desirable in any classification scheme, and I would recommend the use of 786·48 for two-piano works and arrangements and 786·49 for piano duet scores. The placings can be reversed, if desired, but most libraries will probably already have some piano duet material that has been classified at 786·49 for years while the number of two-piano scores is likely to be appreciably less. The occasional freak work for six or eight hands at a single keyboard would also go at 786·49 and a work for eight hands, two pianos at 786·48.

The demand for country dance music and such related works as sword dances and the like is fairly constant and such scores tend to be overlooked if filed in the general sequence of piano works. The name of Cecil Sharp may be easily remembered but other collectors and arrangers are not usually so well known and this can cause obvious difficulty in searching shelves and catalogue in response to an enquiry. There is also the point that the music itself is usually of no interest to the ordinary solo pianist so that a further sub-division of 786·4 would seem to be justified; 786·41 might be suitable. The alternative, to use the appropriate number in 793 is less satisfactory since the books and scores are unlikely to be shelved together.

Organ Music

If 786·7 is retained for instructional and pedagogic works and 786.8 (ignoring the D.C. form sub-divisions) used for organ music arranged in composer sequence, books on the organ as an instrument can be classed at 786·6. This should reduce confusion between the three types though Harvey Grace's *The organ works of Bach* should be classified at 786·8 BAC (or arranged under Bach's name in that sequence) so that the music and the criticism of it are at the same placing.

General Observations

The remainder of class 780 would seem to need neither explanation nor alteration but one or two further comments may help to clear up some possible difficulties for the classifier who knows little about music. It is vitally important to remember that music must be classified according to the medium of the score at hand, which is not necessarily that of the original. For instance, an arrangement for piano solo of a Haydn symphony should be classed with piano solos at 786·4 and not at 785·11 which would be the appropriate place for a full or miniature score of the work. If the arrangement is for piano duet, then 786·49 is the appropriate place and 787·1 for a version for violin and piano.

Where the music is written or arranged for two instruments and one of these is piano or organ the work should be classed under the other instrument, e.g. a piece for piano and flute is classified under flute music. In other cases it is usual to adopt one of two courses. The work can be classed under the less well-known of the two instruments, so that a *Duo for flute and violin* by C. P. E. Bach would be classed with flute music with an added entry under violin; the alternative method used is to classify under the instrument with the higher register; the range of orchestral instruments is easily found in many textbooks. With three or more instruments in combination, the work is classified as chamber music.

Rather more difficult for the classifier is the problem presented by an album of Oratorio songs by Handel. Choice here is between 784·3 (songs) and 783·3 (oratorio); I would prefer the former but would certainly accept the validity of the latter place. The important thing here is that the classifier chooses one answer and notes it so that future volumes of a similar nature are classified in the same manner and precedent is maintained.

McColvin-Dewey

Mention has been made on more than one occasion of the alternative scheme for Dewey's class 780 propounded by Mr. L. R. McColvin in his *Music in public libraries* and slightly modified in *Music libraries*. Though this uses the same Decimal base as Dewey the order of subjects is completely different.

Music scores are allotted places in 780 to 782 inclusive and the remaining places in the scheme (783–789) are sub-divided for music literature. The balance is in complete contrast to that chosen by B.C.M. The author has attempted to base his schedules upon musical evolution, so that 780 is for vocal music, 781 for instrumental music and 782 for chamber and orchestral music since this is the natural order of musical development. Many of the criticisms made of the Dewey scheme have been met in this new version; for instance, 780·24 is for "Special types of songs—e.g. sea-songs, chanties, hunting songs", with 780·26 for "Songs for special occasions . . .". 780·25 has been left blank so that the various types of special song are in adjoining places. Operas, arranged by composer, are at 780·7 and are followed at 780·8 by Musical comedies, light operas, etc. arranged by title. This last is unorthodox but probably highly effective as titles are usually much more easily remembered than are the composers of light operas. The major difficulty is likely to occur with operettas and the like written by Offenbach, the Strausses and others in which the library may have the work with its original title and with varying English titles (*Die Fledermaus; The bat; Gay Rosalinda,* etc.). 781 and 782 appear to be sensible and unfussy and mention should be made of the alternative placings for miniature scores. The preferred place is 782·77 (under 782 orchestral music) but libraries may like to use 782·99 which gives these works, which are almost certain to be shelved in a separate sequence, the number between scores and books on music.

783 provides places for general books on music and works on theory; 784 for "practice"—books on music that provide the written background to 780–782—books on singing, on instruments and on orchestral music. 787 is for aesthetics and appreciation, and also for music study and teaching; 788 is allotted to history and criticism while biography and miscellaneous topics use 789.

The author describes this as "a simple scheme suitable for the average public library" and the schedules have been adopted by a few British libraries as well as by one or two in the U.S.A. Those libraries that use the scheme appear to find it very satisfactory though one may doubt if there is sufficient sub-division for a really large collection. Notation is commendably brief with a maximum of six figures (i.e. three after the decimal point) and it seems likely that many more libraries would adopt this variation but for the thought of the labour involved in amending the class marks on the entire music stock. Some librarians may be hoping that the forthcoming edition of D.C. will provide radical improvements and others may not realize just how much better is McColvin 780 than Dewey 780. If the library can find the staff time to make the necessary alterations to books, catalogues and stock records, then there is a very great deal to be said for reclassifying according to this scheme.

REFERENCES

1. McColvin, L. R., *and* Reeves, H. *Music Libraries*, v. 1, p. 25.
2. Dickinson, George S. *Classification of musical compositions: a decimal symbol system* (Poughkeepsie, N.Y.: Vassar College, 1938).

FURTHER READING

Very little appears to have been written about the classification of music. The student will naturally read the appropriate chapter (the third) in the first volume of *Music Libraries*. Another interesting article is:

LINE, M. B. A classified catalogue of musical scores: some problems (*Library Association Record*, November, 1952, pp. 362–4).

In this article Mr. Line makes some criticism of the L.C. schedules and deals with a number of the difficulties in applying them in certain cases. He recommends a revision of the schedules (though no specific suggestions are made) together with an entirely new scheme for music written before 1750.

PRACTICAL EXAMPLES OF THE CLASSIFICATION OF BOOKS AND SCORES

These examples are provided for two reasons. First, they show the relative lengths of notations for the same book or score in different schemes; secondly, students can study, in so far as the necessarily limited number of examples allows, the relative merits of the schemes in showing the relationship between works that have a common factor (as in the first two examples, and the three Elgar scores), and in the provision or lack of provision for works that have some superficial relationship but for which separate places ought to be provided (as in the piano and string trios). Except for the D.C. placings, all have been checked by the appropriate expert mentioned under "Acknowledgements" at the beginning of the book.

	Brown	Cutter	Dewey (14th ed.)	L.C.	Bliss	B.C.M.
BEETHOVEN Piano sonatas	C647·9	VZP	786·41	M23(a)	VXPI	QPE
BLOM Beethoven's piano sonatas discussed	C647·9	VVB	786·41	MT145	VV9,S,I *or* VWJN, B3	BBJAQPE
DEBUSSY Preludes for piano	C647·9	VZP	786.4(b)	M25	VXPP	QPJ
ELGAR "Enigma" variations, min. score	C761	VYA	785·1	M1003	VXMY	MM/T
do. arr. piano duet	C647·9	VZPA	786·49	M209	VXPD	QNVK/MM/T
do. arr. 2 pf	C647·9	VZPB	786·49	M215	VXPD	QNUK/MM/T
SACKVILLE-WEST & SHAWE-TAYLOR The record guide	C330(c)	VXME	789·9	ML156·2(d)	VWYV	A/FD(WT)
NEWMAN Opera nights [synopses and criticisms]	C781	VV10	782·1	MT95	VWSO	AC
MOZART Don Giovanni: vocal sc.	C781	VYO	782·1(e)	M1503	VXL3(f)	CC
MOZART [i.e. Da Ponte] Don Giovanni: libretto	C781	VYOL	782·1	ML50	VXL5 *or* VWSI	BMSAC
SMETANA Bartered Bride, v.s.	C783	VYO	782·1(g)	M1503	VXL35(f)	CC
FORSYTH Orchestration	C760	VWT	781·632	MT70	VWVD	AM/D
BEETHOVEN String trios, op. 9 [parts]	C777	VYC	785·73	M351	VXNM	RXNT

Classification

	Brown	Cutter	Dewey (14th ed.)	L.C.	Bliss	B.C.M.
SCHUBERT						
Piano trio, op. 99 [parts]	C777	VZQ	785·73	M312	VXNM	NXNT
SPITTA						
Life of Bach	X BAC	VVB	927·8(h)	ML410	VV9	BBC/N
LESLIE						
Polonaise [a life of Chopin, in novel form]	N 020	VVZZ	823·91	ML3925 *or* ML410	VV9, Y *or* VV9, L	BCE(N/EG)

Notes: (a) L.C. have some editions in MT247; these would be so-called "instructive" editions. The decision between the two places can be extremely difficult.

(b) Or, perhaps, 786·43. Though there is no separate place for preludes, this number includes "descriptive" music.

(c) This number is actually outside the music class, and comes under "Acoustics".

(d) This number does not appear in earlier schedules, but is listed among the "additions and changes . . ." adopted since publication of the second edition.

(e) Written to an Italian libretto, so 782·5?

(f) Or alternatives, according to the method of division chosen for use.

(g) But some classifiers would consider this to be a comic opera, at 782·6.

(h) Legitimate alternatives are 780·92 and 92 B.

Chapter V

GRAMOPHONE RECORD LIBRARIES

This chapter attempts to provide a fairly comprehensive picture of the provision of gramophone records in public libraries, the methods of administration, the problems of cataloguing and classification, staff and their qualifications and similar related matters; the chapter is intended for the librarian who is considering the possibility of providing a gramophone record service in his library and also for the student. There is some repetition of material used earlier in this book; this is deliberately done in order to make the chapter reasonably self-contained.

The novice may well find the different playing speeds and abbreviations (which often indicate both speed and size) confusing until familiarity overcomes this difficulty. The matter of record speeds is dealt with in some detail at the beginning of the section on administration. The basic fact to learn is that the shellac disc which plays at 78 revolutions per minute has become known as the "standard playing" or SP disc, although this speed is no longer standard for classical music. The plastic disc, played at $33\frac{1}{3}$ revolutions per minute, is the "long playing" or LP record and these abbreviations (SP and LP) are used throughout this chapter to indicate these particular types and speeds. The 7-in. disc with a playing speed of 45 r.p.m. and the record which plays at $16\frac{3}{4}$ r.p.m. receive due mention later in the chapter.

Manufacturing developments of various kinds are constantly taking place so that it is only right to record that this chapter gives the picture, in general, up to the beginning of 1958. The first part of the chapter may be regarded as theoretical for it provides the background and indicates something of the field open to the librarian starting a new collection. The main headings of this half of the chapter are: History; Preliminary factors; What to provide, and for whom; What to collect—I, Musical, II—Mainly non-musical. These last two sections each have a number of sub-divisions, each of which is titled for ease of reference.

Though Britain's public libraries provided music scores long before their American counterparts (as is shown in Chapter I) the reverse is true of gramophone records. It would seem that the innovator was a resident of St. Paul, Minnesota, who gave his local library a small collection of gramophone records in 1913 or 1914. These were taken into stock and loan was restricted to schools and clubs.[1] In 1921 the Detroit Public Library collection was started; it has always been one of the biggest and best-known and its methods of administration widely copied by other American libraries. In 1939 there were seventeen towns in the U.S.A. with populations of 75,000 and over that had gramophone record collections;[2] their number was augmented by many other smaller towns that had made similar provision. In the same year there was but a single British public library that held a stock of records for loan—this was Middlesex County Library where a collection had been started in 1935 and in which loan was limited to schools within the county area. The issue of gramophone records to individuals was first made in 1946 when the Chingford branch of Essex County Library was the pioneer.

The editorial of *The Library Association Record* for June, 1949, stated that there were 37 public libraries in England with gramophone record libraries at that time. Between 1949 and the middle of 1957 the total number of collections had exactly doubled with Motherwell as the only Scottish representative. By no means all of these 74 libraries issue records to individuals; a number restrict loans to local schools and societies. It is noteworthy that gramophone record libraries are mainly provided in residential rather than industrial areas and that provision is most common in authorities with populations between 50,000 and 120,000. Gramophone record libraries were inaugurated at a much faster rate in the U.S.A., for between 1945 and 1948 another 32 libraries in American towns and cities with populations in excess of 75,000 had started collections;[2] it now seems to be a fairly true generalization that gramophone records are available from public libraries in the majority of larger American cities but that similar provision is still extremely limited in Britain particularly outside the Greater London area.

To some extent this slower rate of development of the service in Britain has been advantageous, for it has meant that librarians in this country have had a large corpus of information available from the U.S.A. about every practical aspect of gramophone record libraries and have, in consequence, been able to avoid most of the errors committed by a few of their transatlantic counterparts. During 1936 and 1937, for example, there were numerous articles in the professional press in the United States dealing with gramophone record libraries and these articles indicated immense variations in the standard of selection, methods of cataloguing, classification, loan procedure and other points. Partly through articles of this nature but also from meetings held by the Music Library Association, a considerable degree of standardization has been achieved. This is particularly true of cataloguing, for the M.L.A. adopted a code of rules for cataloguing phonograph (i.e. gramophone) records in 1942 and this code was the basis of that used by the Library of Congress. American principles and practice still seem to have much to teach many British gramophone record libraries and to offer us many interesting comparisons, so that considerable space is devoted to the American scene. Mention is also made of some American discs of types not available (except at considerable expense and trouble) in Britain in the hope that the time is not too far distant when such records can be imported without restriction.

England has seen much less variation and experiment in the service, and it is perhaps surprising that only Coventry (1950) and Leeds (1957) have adopted open-access methods for their collections. Guildford supplies the single example of a service ceasing to function. In this case a small collection was provided for use by local societies but the results did not justify the retention of the service.

The normal, if not the invariable, practice in Britain has been to keep all gramophone records together; this is not always the American method. The Enoch Pratt Free Library in Baltimore places music records in the Fine Arts Department while non-musical ones are kept in the Literature & Language Department. The large American output of literary recordings (e.g. those of plays and poetry readings) and of language instruction records may make such a division in the large city library desirable unless (as in Detroit) Music and Drama together form one department. The majority of American libraries include their record collections as part of the Art & Music Department but some consider it as an aspect of the Circulation Department's activities while others place the collection in the Reference Library.[1] A good case can be made out, in fact, for the division of the collection into lending and reference sections. The former would include the great majority of records, the latter would retain memorable performances deleted from the manufacturers' catalogues (and not reissued in long-playing form) which are irreplaceable. The reference section would also contain some of the special types of material discussed a little later in the chapter. Because, almost without exception, British gramophone record collections have to be housed in buildings that were designed and built long before this recent activity was dreamed of, the collection has had to be placed at some point where sufficient room can be found, whatever its other defects. In some cases the collection is housed with the music library or section, in many space has been cleared in the Lending Department, but a number have had to keep their records away from the normal public departments and file them in stock rooms, offices and the like, with a resultant loss of efficiency in administration.

The legal position for this kind of service in Britain is a little obscure. Westminster Corporation took up the matter with the Ministry of Health when about to start a record library, and the relevant part of the reply is quoted in *The Library Association Record* for May, 1947. It reads: "The Minister has consulted the Minister of Education in the matter and is advised that as music is both a science and an art, and a gramophone record is undoubtedly a specimen of music, the Council have power under Section 15(1) of the Public Libraries Act, 1892, to form a lending library of gramophone records as an extension of the present library service." In 1956 the Croydon Corporation presented a Local Bill before Parliament and included in it a clause that would have permitted the provision of a gramophone record library with the right to charge users a fee for each record borrowed. This clause was rejected, presumably because of the financial aspect. Yet a similar clause in a Bill promoted by the Huddersfield Corporation was accepted. Rather ironically, Huddersfield has yet to begin a gramophone record service though its powers would appear to be unique. It must also be recorded that at least two other County Boroughs and a Municipal Borough run record libraries on a rental basis without apparent qualms or local opposition, possibly under the somewhat wide and vague terms of Section 132 of the Local Government Act of 1948 by which local Councils are permitted to spend a maximum of a sixpenny rate on entertainments. Charges certainly cannot be legally made under any provisions of the 1892 Public Libraries Act. American libraries have no similar difficulties but appear to be under greater stress with reference to copyright problems, particularly with users who borrow records for the purpose of making their own tape recordings of them.

PRELIMINARY FACTORS

Before a collection is inaugurated a librarian will need to consider his local library service as a whole. A gramophone record service should certainly not be provided until that offered by the home reading and reference departments can be considered adequate; an expressed local demand for a gramophone record library is important but not over-riding. In his report to his Committee the librarian should indicate something of the factors involved, the initial outlay and the running costs required to provide a progressive rather than a stagnant service. The provision of gramophone records may well be regarded as a logical extension of the book service, as a desirable if not essential adjunct to the music section, and as an invaluable aid to musical education. The recreational side may be regarded as of minor importance compared with the cultural and educational aspects but should not be overlooked since many users will take records home primarily for enjoyment rather than for education, while "culture" is a word often regarded with some suspicion. Honesty demands that the librarian stresses the need for ample resources and the service should never be provided at the expense of the book fund. The Library Committee may well find that the gramophone record library, once started, develops into a major service. In these days when there is a wide public for good music and the gramophone turntable is to be found in an ever-increasing proportion of homes it is not just a handful of the musically sophisticated that will use the service to the exclusion of others. The tremendous output by the manufacturing companies of records and of radiogramophones, playing desks, portable gramophones and the like, indicates something of public demand today. Recordings of classical music obviously sell well or the companies would not continue to turn out version after version of the most popular classics.

In preparing a report, consideration will naturally be given to the estimated potential demand. If the opening collection is small and the librarian has remote hope of a further grant for buying more records if the public denude his shelves, then it may be best to limit loans initially to schools and societies only and not make the collection available to individuals; the latter may well stimulate their local Councillors to agree to a more generous and enlightened policy. Where individuals are allowed to borrow, permission may be restricted at first to local residents; non-resident employees and/or subscribers may be allowed to join when the stock is considered adequate to meet this extra demand. If a service for all these categories is envisaged from the start, and this is obviously a desirable aim, then the opening stock must be large enough to allow some choice to every user. The wider the scope of the collection, the greater its use is likely to be; this suggests that it is only prudent to limit the opening stock to classical music of a high standard. Light music and/or jazz should definitely not be provided unless it is certain that financial resources will allow adequate coverage, and also that provision is not made at the expense of permanent music of greater value. Jazz is considered at some length later in the chapter.

Some practical comments of a more detailed nature will be found under the heading "Initial cost and running costs" in the second half of this chapter; this section might therefore be rounded off with three relevant figures. In 1957 the amount spent on gramophone records in the twenty-three Metropolitan Boroughs of London that provide this service varied between the equivalent of 1 and 13 per cent of the book fund; the proportion of expenses recovered by way of fines and subscriptions, etc., ranged from 2 to 68·5 per cent (the latter in a system with many subscribing members and a fairly high rate of fines). It must be realized that not all the twenty-three libraries allow loans to individual borrowers. Finally, in a most interesting and useful article (listed at the end of the chapter), Mr. L. G. Lovell considered that library expenditure would need to rise about 4d. per head of population for adequate gramophone library provision. Where libraries are administered upon a rental or subscription basis, an excellent stock can be maintained at a very small cost to the ratepayers as a whole.

WHAT TO PROVIDE, AND FOR WHOM

What types of records should collections include? Two decisions must be made. The first and primary one is that of the standard of selection and of the intended scope of the collection; the second is the physical one involving record sizes and playing speeds. Both problems are dealt with at length in succeeding pages but can be summarized by suggesting (as has already been said) that the standard of selection should be no lower than that applied to music scores in the library—and may usefully and profitably be higher; the LP disc is now supreme in the field of classical music, though consideration may be given to the 7-in. disc with a playing speed of 45 r.p.m.

An American view, not necessarily representative, of what should be provided is given by Oscar Luening, Professor of Music at Columbia University, New York;[3] he wrote that in the good library "There are a sufficient number of turntables or listening rooms to make the collection available to the community, and there is a phonograph in the auditorium for the use of groups and classes. The record collection includes a number of foreign language sets, recordings of literature, history and poetry, and enough recordings of children's records to serve local users." Facilities for listening to records at the library are not regarded by British librarians as a necessary part of the service, neither is the provision of records for children.

For whom should we provide? As has been indicated, quite a number of gramophone record libraries in this country limited the use of the collection to societies and perhaps to local schools, thus providing the service only through the medium of organized bodies. Most libraries admit individual users who are resident within the library's boundaries of service, though limitation may be made to ratepayers, those over a minimum specified age, etc. One wishes that some method of checking their sense of responsibility could also be discovered. A category of library extends borrowing privileges to employees working full-time within the local area, while the final concession is to allow any person with a valid library ticket, whether he has any connection with the district or not, to use the collection. Penge, one of the smallest authorities to maintain a collection, made this generous gesture until 1957 when it modified its policy to the more usual one of allowing those who neither lived nor worked within its boundaries to become members, but as subscribers. The only collection free to all, both callers and correspondents, is almost certainly that attached to the American Library in London; this is a most enlightened form of propaganda for American music.

For what types of user should we provide? Another American

Gramophone Record Libraries

(Kurtz Myers, Chief of the Music and Drama Department of the Detroit P.L.) considered in a personal letter written in 1954 that "the public for records is in the main a youthful one, ranging from about the junior year in high school through college and up to the point where sufficient economic advantage is reached to make purchases answer needs, or where family responsibilities take up time and interest. Males predominate, but not in the degree they did formerly. Another audience for records is to be found among older men, the ones who have retired or who are about to retire. They are much like graduate students who set systematically about the business of trying to fill a cultural gap—sometimes with rewarding success." Three years later Mr. Myers modified that statement. "Record equipment has now become standard in so many homes of young married couples. I think we get more families and couples than we used to be aware of. The musical sophistication of some of our teen-age borrowers is quite terrifying. They don't listen by the book but rather listen omnivorously and sort out their impressions confidently. Bartók is a favourite composer with the young and seems to afford the bridge from the progressive jazz to serious contemporary music. The fanciers of old vocal records are becoming fewer and fewer." British experience is only partially in agreement with these statements for in this country it would seem that masculine borrowers predominate under the age of 30 but that family borrowing is common to all ages, while a number of users find it invaluable to try discs in the public library stock before buying those particular recordings for their own collections. The need for this policy, unless one is prepared to buy solely upon the recommendation of a trusted reviewer, is growing in this country and is most necessary in the U.S.A. There, many of the larger shops that sell records keep a special copy of the disc for trial purposes; the customer receives a factory-sealed copy which can only be changed if it is mechanically faulty. If no records are provided for trial purposes then the customer has to decide whether to buy the sealed package and trust that he will like the record, or else leave it and hope to hear that performance on the radio, in a friend's house or in the same recording borrowed from his local public library. It would seem that dealers are beginning to follow a similar policy of supplying guaranteed unplayed discs in British shops and this is another factor that will increase the use of the library that has a gramophone record collection and will cause greater demand for recent releases by the manufacturers.

191

Music Librarianship

In most libraries the proportion of registered readers at the library to the total population is between 20 and 35 per cent; for gramophone record libraries the figure may well vary even more, from approximately one-twentieth to one-tenth of that ratio, i.e. between 1 and 3·5 per cent, though still wider variations may be found. A higher proportion can probably be achieved (as with the percentage of readers) by lowering the standards of selection but this must be strongly deprecated. Potential users of the gramophone library will undoubtedly include many of the most intelligent and influential local residents—the types of readers who make the best use of our services and who deserve the best we can provide—but librarians must realize how comparatively limited is this number and plan accordingly.

WHAT TO COLLECT: I—MUSIC

General

The unimaginative librarian might feel that the problem of record selection is capable of easy solution; all that is needed is a collection of works of different types (orchestral, vocal, instrumental, etc.) limited perhaps to composers who are already represented in the music collection, and chosen mainly from the catalogues of the major recording companies. The question of which version to buy of a particular work might be answered by noting the consensus of critical opinion as shown in *Record ratings*, by reading the comments on the different interpretations in *The record guide*, and by checking the reviews in *The Gramophone* or other critical periodical for records issued subsequently to the period covered by the two books mentioned. Such a collection could be a very good one and even the imaginative librarian will be well advised to attempt nothing more ambitious while the collection is small in numbers for the service may be hard pressed to satisfy even the demands for standard classics until the stock is quite large. One may regard Schubert's *Unfinished symphony* and Mozart's *Eine kleine Nachtmusik* as hackneyed classics yet they will always be new to some of our users and will always be in demand, while the colourful orchestration of *Bolero* or *Scheherezade* is particularly attractive to the untutored listener who may find in such works the necessary background that enables him to progress to music of less obvious attraction but of equal if not greater value. A small collection that attempts to include the esoteric as well as certain other types of record mentioned below is opening the way for demands upon the service that may be financially impossible to satisfy. Minority groups may not appreciate the limited cash resources behind the service and may even assert that the collection should be designed to meet specialist rather than the "bread-and-butter" requests of the majority of users. An American library has a greater incentive to provide popular run-of-the-mill works, possibly in several different versions, since these are sure to provide a steady income, while the unusual composition may take a long time to earn a reasonable proportion of its original cost. It is suggested, therefore, that the early days should see the record collection covering a limited but well-rounded field and doing that job well rather than hopelessly attempting to provide something for all tastes.

That conservative policy is recommended while the collection is small, but as it grows the librarian should not miss opportunities to broaden its basis and so add enormously to its value. The average library collection will naturally consist mainly of musical items: of orchestral and chamber music works; instrumental and vocal solos; operatic and other choral works, etc. The two major difficulties here are that all the works the librarian might like to include in the collection have not been recorded, or that existing versions may be unsatisfactory in performance, in recording, or both. In fairness to the companies it must be stated that the number of important works still unrecorded is small indeed. Since the advent of the LP record the gramophone record repertory has widened to an extent that would have been quite unbelievable in 1939. Comparatively obscure works never to be heard in the concert hall may be available in alternative recordings and the spate of issues during the early nineteen-fifties was almost the despair of critics, dealers and collectors alike. On the second point it must be admitted that there are still too many discs that perpetuate unsatisfactory performances or whose technical quality of recording falls well behind the steadily advancing standards of today. Only when there is no satisfactory recording available should a disappointing disc be bought.

At this point it may be timely to add a word on the "recital" record. With 78 r.p.m. discs it was unusual to find more than two songs on a single side of a record; with LP it is not uncommon to have as many as eight to a side—and more have been known. The private collector is often annoyed because he has to buy so many items when he may wish to possess but one or two, and the companies occasionally recognize this desire by issuing some 7-in., or perhaps 10-in. "medium-play" records with one or two only of the same performances on each side. These shorter records, however, are often not issued until an appreciable time after the original LP has appeared. If the library purchases the LP disc it is certain that all borrowers will have their particular preferences among the various items on each side and many of the users may like to repeat these favourites rather more frequently than the other items on the same side. This can result in certain parts of the record becoming well worn while other sections are still in good condition. As an added difficulty, the "scrolls" (i.e. the intervening spaces between the end of one item and the beginning of the next) may be very narrow and this will make it difficult to place the needle exactly at the start of the desired piece unless it happens to be the first one on the record. It needs but one or two clumsy handlings for the grooves to become badly damaged. The incidence of this problem appears to vary unexpectedly between libraries; one with a very large collection has had to cease buying this type of record unless public demand makes accession almost imperative, yet other collections find no evidence of uneven wear. Some librarians consider the recital record to be a useful if not essential type to have in stock. It may contain the only available recording of a brief work or may contain just those separate excerpts that are most popular. The recital record presents major problems for the cataloguer, as indicated in the appropriate section, and the difficulty of discovering whether a particular work has been recorded if it is included in a disc of this type is a further handicap for the gramophone librarian. One final point worth mention is that the actual choice of music on these records, which may be vocal, instrumental or orchestral, is often inartistic and sometimes deplorable though Lieder recital records may be generally exempted from these strictures.

Alternative recordings

Once a gramophone record library has begun to function the demand for certain popular works is sure to be heavy. Rather than duplicate the particular version already in stock it is usually better to provide an alternative recording even though the second performance may be somewhat less satisfactory, in one way or another, than that already bought. Comparison of recordings can provide a source of great enjoyment to the music-lover (the B.B.C's "Composer and interpreter" series of programmes is simply a double or treble hearing of the same work with a different soloist, etc.); it is certainly a method of sharpening one's critical faculties and can give pleasure both to the interested amateur and the hardened professional musician. In any event, it is most unlikely that one particular version of a recorded work will possess all the virtues compared with its rivals; a better performance may be offset by a less satisfactory recording, etc.

Complete works and limited editions

It is generally agreed with book selection that the public library should provide the important but expensive book so far as its funds will allow. Only a minority of our readers can afford to pay a high price for books, and unless a work is required for regular use over a long period, private purchase may well be considered uneconomic. It was possibly easier for a man to buy a symphony on SP discs, record by record, than to buy the same work on LP; the total cost may be almost the same, but the newer version requires the money to be paid at one time. The shorter excerpts necessitated on 78 r.p.m. discs were advantageous to the person who wished to buy part of the work only rather than the complete composition. Another aspect of uneconomic purchase is provided by the work that one might like to hear two or three times, or perhaps once a year, but whose use does not really justify buying for such occasional performance—music, in fact, that one likes to savour occasionally rather than music to live with. Here the public library can help by including in its stock the expensive and also the unusual work, providing that the latter is not so out-of-the-way that only one or two patrons (to use the American term) will borrow it. The obvious case is opera; few people can afford to buy the six LP discs of *Parsifal*, and fewer still can find the time or would wish to play the work with any frequency. The demand for recorded opera has been growing immensely over the last few years and many works that are never staged in Britain can be heard on records. The librarian has to balance, once again, the conflicting demand of the standard repertory work that has a large body of admirers and which will be in regular demand by library users, and the less-known and often expensive sets that the minority of users feel should be provided through the library rather than bought for themselves.

Other examples of the work considered to be of limited appeal but of great musical value were the pre-war "Society" issues. The name was somewhat misleading, since it was simply an issue of works considered by the manufacturer to have small popular appeal and given the somewhat artificial stimulus of a limited circulation. An album (usually of five, six or seven records) had to be bought as a complete entity; single discs were not sold separately and the broken pieces of a damaged record had to be produced before a replacement could be bought. The records themselves were issued at the normal price, but the containing album was of superior quality and there was a ceiling (usually unspecified) on the number of sets of each work that were made available. One could buy a single volume and there was no compulsion to buy the first album in a series nor all the series. In a few cases some of the "Society" sets issued by H.M.V. did reach the permitted maximum and the company felt itself bound to issue no more. Even today, the first volume of the Hugo Wolf Society (issued in 1931 and the precursor of all "Society" issues) is at a considerable premium on the rare occasions when one can buy a second-hand set of these records. It is an interesting reflection on both public taste and demand that none of the major companies has thought it necessary to revive the limited edition with LP records despite the fact that many discs have been produced which contain music that one might have thought to be of far more specialized interest than that issued under "Society" auspices in the nineteen-thirties. Only one company, apparently, has made a condition that certain LP sets must be sold complete and that the sale of a single disc will not be permitted, but this is a most unusual (and apparently unnecessary restriction). A similar restriction was made in Britain with the issue of the Beethoven piano concertos with Rubinstein as the soloist, though no restriction was placed on buying the records separately when they were originally issued in the United States. When a public library owns any of the various sets of limited or restricted editions, the matter of damage and breakage is important, particularly with the SP sets which have now all been withdrawn from the catalogues. These records might be considered an obvious choice if a reference collection of gramophone records is being maintained, though some of the pre-war "Society" issues have been issued in 1957 in LP form and without restriction as to the number of copies available for sale.

Consideration now follows of three different types of record, all of which may be called "historical" though not necessarily for the same reason.

Gramophone Record Libraries

The composer as interpreter

It has long been realized that the printed score can give only an approximation of what the composer wishes to express, however carefully he may indicate tempi, phrasing and dynamics. Since the introduction of the phonograph and gramophone records, the composer has had the means to hand down to posterity a fairly clear demonstration of his intentions. He may play or conduct the work himself; if that is not practical he may be able to supervise the musical side of a recording so that the resultant performance is to his satisfaction. Examples of the composer as executant on gramophone records include Elgar, Richard Strauss, Rachmaninov and Benjamin Britten, while the (English) Decca version of the first six symphonies of Vaughan Williams includes a spoken tribute from the composer to the conductor and orchestra at the end of the last work—a verbal imprimatur. Records of this nature deserve generous representation in a library possibly for reference use only, unless they have been made on LP discs or have been re-made in this form. Many of these authentic performances have been available only on SP discs but a number have been reissued in LP format, using the original recordings as a starting point, and the skill of the engineers in these cases is often almost unbelievable. Almost invariably, these "re-creations" have managed to reduce surface noise to a minimum (though the original SP discs may have been very noisy in this way), they have provided excellent and unobtrusive joins where one side of the original version ended and the next began, and have rarely lost more than a tiny fraction of the original tone quality; in fact, some records appear to have gained in clarity and immediacy in their new guise. Outstanding examples of this type of record are the Rachmaninov piano concertos and his *Rhapsody on a theme of Paganini* with the composer as soloist in every case; even the *Enigma variations*, recorded as long ago as 1926 under Elgar's baton, has a tonal quality that is still acceptable today. In any case, the historical value of records such as these renders their technical virtues and vices of secondary importance.

Of a different nature, yet perhaps of equivalent value, is the recording of Mozart's *Linz* symphony under the baton of Bruno Walter. The conductor was unaware that the microphone was "live" during a rehearsal of the symphony, and the two LP discs consist of three sides of rehearsal with the fourth side devoted to the finished

O

performance. It is a most practical and enthralling demonstration of a very great conductor at work.

It seems true to say that such performances are better appreciated in Britain than in the U.S.A., where the technical standard of the recording may cause complaint despite a statement on the record sleeve quoting the actual date of the recording. The American user is apparently tending to become more interested in the actual work recorded and to pay less attention to the particular artist; the assumption is growing that any orchestra or soloist, etc., that is good enough to achieve a contract with a gramophone record manufacturer must be competent. In Britain, the relative size of the name(s) of the performer(s) compared with that of the composer on the front of the record sleeve suggests irresistibly that the companies expect to sell the disc mainly through interest in the performer and only secondarily through the composer or the actual work recorded. These comments probably do not apply with equal force to those borrowing discs from the library, where there is likely to be a much greater interest in composers—but the records one wishes to borrow are by no means necessarily those that one would wish to buy.

Musical history

There are many records which contain music whose interest for the majority of listeners is probably historic rather than intrinsic; some of the works will be played on instruments no longer in general use and many will use a harmonic language that may seem harsh and rudimentary to ears accustomed to listening to music of the seventeenth century and later. Such discs may include works by composers whose names remain in the music histories but whose compositions have long since disappeared from the concert repertory, usually rightly so. Posterity ruthlessly winnows the wheat from the chaff but is certainly not infallible. Not least of the gramophone's virtues is the opportunity it has given us to discover how much we have underrated certain composers, e.g. it has done much to rehabilitate the reputation of Boccherini and Vivaldi with many music-lovers. Works may be played on the clavichord, viol da gamba, lute and other instruments that are regarded with dubiety and suspicion by a large number of listeners. Music written before the time of J. S. Bach and his contemporaries presents almost as many harmonic problems as that of Bartók or Schoenberg to a host of untutored music-lovers. This comparatively early music is gaining an increasing representation in the gramophone record catalogues, often in wonderful performances, but is still rarely heard in the concert hall. The growing interest in "old" music, particularly in authentic performances, is almost entirely to the credit of the LP record. Many listeners are finding their interests diverted from the massive works that characterize many nineteenth-century composers in favour of the smaller scale pieces of the sixteenth and seventeenth centuries (and of the twentieth century). This trend is, at the time of writing, much more marked in the U.S.A. than in Britain.

There have been some outstanding recordings, on SP discs, before 1939 and on both SP and LP discs since the end of the Second World War. If the Dolmetsch family in Britain can justly claim to be pioneers in the revived tradition of playing music on original instruments or reproductions of them their lead has been followed in many other countries. Three well-known series before 1940 were of French origin—"L'Oiseau lyre", "L'Anthologie sonore" and "Lumen". All these discs contained out-of-the-way music, nearly all of it written before 1800. In the U.S.A. a number of records of Gregorian chant were issued under the "Kyriale" label, while another excellent series of limited scope was the French "Sept siècles de musique sacrée". All of these SP discs have now apparently disappeared off the market and a library that possesses any of them might do well to transfer them to a reference or restricted access collection. "L'Oiseau lyre" has made a welcome reappearance on LP discs with a series of new recordings, while a most important series of records (originally SP only, but later available on LP also) is that of "The history of music in sound", issued by His Master's Voice to illustrate *The New Oxford History of Music*. These valuable discs are of a generally high standard though not all achieve perfection in performance and recording.

An outstanding issue on LP discs (later supplemented by 7-in. "extended-play" records) is the German "Archive" series. These discs are produced by the "History of music Division of the Deutsche Grammophon Gesellschaft" and the music is limited to works of the eighth to eighteenth centuries. The years between 700 and 1800 are divided into nine "Research periods" which are sub-divided as necessary. There are, for instance, three divisions for both "Gregorian chant" (Period I) and the "German pre-classics (1700–1760)" (Research Period XI) compared with twelve sub-divisions for J. S. Bach, alone in Research Period IX, and thirteen for "The High Renaissance" in Research Period IV. Instead of the analytical notes usually found on the back of the record container each disc is accompanied by a card which gives details of the performers, instruments and edition used, strength of choir and orchestra, etc., and which also quotes the appropriate Research Period and its subdivision. Thus a record of organ music by J. S. Bach is shown as "Research Period IX, Series F". "Series" in this context means subdivision. This methodical classification may sound formal in the extreme but it must be emphasized that almost without exception both performance and recording are of the highest quality; it should also be mentioned that the music itself can be enjoyed by a very high proportion of music-lovers without worrying too much about the historical import of the music. There is apparently no indication of the total number of records that will complete the series (though it will obviously be extremely large), nor is there any work in book form to which the series forms a practical illustration. No analytical notes accompany these records (which is often unfortunate, particularly with some of the more obscure composers and lesser-known works), nor are the records issued in chronological order. Originally issued on 12-in. and 10-in. LP discs, the format was widened in 1956 by the inclusion of 7-in. EP discs, which usually contain pieces not otherwise available in the series, i.e. they rarely repeat any of the items already recorded on the LP discs.

Rare and early recordings

These records are historical also but in a somewhat different sense from that used in the preceding paragraphs. This is the type of record that in the nineteen-thirties could be found listed at the back of the ordinary H.M.V. catalogue as part of the "No. 2" catalogue; since the 1939–1945 war it was briefly revived in Britain as the "Archive" series (which must not be confused with the D.G.G. LP records) and in the U.S.A. as the Victor "Heritage" series. Subsequently, a number of these performances have been issued yet again, when in 1956 H.M.V. issued the first of their new "Celebrity series" on LP discs which have been devoted mainly to vocal music. The series has included, for instance, recordings of Caruso and also the Rachmaninov performances mentioned earlier. The SP "Archive"/"Heritage" series was limited exclusively to old vocal recordings made around the turn of the present century, the so-called "golden age" of singing, particularly in the operatic field. By modern standards the recording is most inadequate, the accompaniment a travesty and the surface hiss deplorable—yet, despite these drawbacks, these records can still show something of the qualities that made these particular singers world famous, particularly when played on a really good modern reproducer. Many of the records, long since deleted from the companies' catalogues and not reissued in one or other of the historical series, have a high scarcity value. The library that possesses any such discs in fair to good condition has to face the double problem of safeguarding and of wear, for replacement is likely to be impossible. These records give practical demonstrations of the great changes that have taken place during the last half-century both in singing technique and in ideas of musical interpretation and for these reasons are invaluable to the serious student of singers and singing. Here again it would seem that this type of record is better kept in a reference collection and not be issued for hearing outside the library.

The H.M.V. "No. 2 catalogue" mentioned above also contained such items as speeches by members of the Royal Family, politicians and other famous people. One may doubt if there was much demand for a "dehydrated" version of Lloyd George's Budget speech of 1909 (on H.M.V. D381) and cannot now assess the appeal of Fred Terry reciting "The charge of the Light Brigade" (on E360), but the market for old vocal discs is apparently insatiable. Catalogues compiled for those interested in these old recordings include Robert Bauer's *New catalogue of historical records, 1898–1908/9* (Sidgwick & Jackson, 1947) and John R. Bennett's *Voices of the past: a catalogue of vocal recordings* (Oakwood Press), a wonderful example of detective work. The first part appeared in 1956 and the work is still in progress at the time of writing. The day when one could discover a Patti or Plançon disc mixed up with a pile of other old but valueless records in a local "junk" shop and buy it for a few coppers is almost done and the librarian who considers providing this sort of gramophone record "incunabula" for his patrons can only really do so through the medium of the various microgroove reissues that have appeared and continue to appear during the last few years. In many cases the original matrices have been lost or destroyed so that these new copies have been made by recording the performance of an actual copy of the original disc; if the state of that is good then the new recording may be adequate or better but any blemishes acquired down the years will also appear in the new recording.

Where the gramophone company still possesses the original matrix a reissue is comparatively simple though the master may well have deteriorated sadly with age and frequent use. In 1937 and 1938 the Parlophone Company in Britain re-pressed a number of early vocal records and it was American demand that persuaded H.M.V. to search its vaults at Hayes for matrices of its early singers. Only after the "Heritage" series had been on sale for three years were the new pressings made available to British buyers in 1951, and then at a cost more than twice the price of current releases. It is an interesting and pleasing change of policy that has brought the new LP "Celebrity series" within the reach of many more music-lovers; although the white label so long associated by H.M.V. with rare recordings has been retained, the cost has been reduced to a mere two or three shillings above that charged for the standard red-label issue. Later still, the "Great recordings of the century" series (devoted mainly to issues of the nineteen-thirties) has been issued at the same price as normal new issues but in a stouter package and with an excellent booklet of very full analytical notes with each disc. In the U.S.A. this reissue policy has been carried even further in some cases, since SP recordings of famous artists of the nineteen-twenties and thirties have been reissued on a very much cheaper label; for example, almost all of Rosa Ponselle's recordings have been released on two discs by RCA-Victor in the "Camden" series at a total cost of less than four dollars.

Folk music

Though a gramophone record collection may limit itself to classical music, there should be little argument that coverage ought to be extended to folk music. There are a number of recordings of folk dances and folk songs to be found in the general catalogues of many British gramophone companies; several American companies (as indicated below) have specialized in this field and have recorded such works sung and played by indigenous musicians. There are one or two British specialist suppliers who import records of this type, though they become extremely expensive under present restrictions.

Somewhat different in scope and much more popular with British audiences are the folk dance records of England, Scotland, Ireland and the United States (Welsh music seems quite unrelated to these and represents a specialist taste of a different calibre). These records are in demand both by country dancers and by those who just like to listen to this type of music; mention should also be made of the comparatively few students for whom such records have a textbook value. The major record companies in England have special Scottish and Irish supplements wherein are listed bagpipe music, reels and strathspeys, etc. Within recent years the vogue for square dancing in Britain has added a fresh hazard for the gramophone librarian, for many of the tunes have little musical merit and are completely lacking in any genuine folk-music element.

British folk music is well represented in the catalogue though only rarely is it sung by a local singer. The usual practice is to record a professional vocalist, normally with an instrumental accompaniment and sometimes with a chorus. As with square-dance music it is difficult to decide where to limit representation in the library's stock. While there are many genuine examples of sea shanties, negro spirituals and hill-billies, there are as many synthetic examples.

American libraries are much more fortunate in their potential range. The Library of Congress has issued no less than twenty-two volumes of SP discs of *Folk music of the U.S. and Latin America*. The recordings were made "on location" with local folk singers and this helps to ensure a genuine and unedited version of the music— though some listeners find them rather too authentic for enjoyment. Many of these recordings have subsequently been transferred to LP form and further discs issued, including such rarities as traditional Red Indian songs transferred from an old collection of cylinder recordings. A number of the big American commercial companies release folk material, particularly the Decca and Capitol firms. But, since this type of material can be recorded fairly cheaply, this is the hunting-ground of many smaller companies who often make but a fleeting appearance before insolvency overtakes them. Some of the better-known minor companies are: Folkways (Folkway Record & Service Corporation, 117 West 46th Street, New York City); Riverside records (418 West 49th Street, New York, 19); Elektra Records (361 Bleecker Street, New York, 19); Stinson (Stinson Record Distributors, Inc., 27 Union Square West, New York, 3); Vanguard (Vanguard Recording Society, Inc., 256 West 55th Street, New York, 19) and Period (304 East 74th Street, New York, 21). "Folkways" is the best known and some of its issues can occasionally be bought in Britain. It apparently started life as Asch-Stinson, changed its name to Disc and again to Ethnic Folkways before adopting its present title. Before the war, under the "Disc" label, the firm issued a number of sets of 10-in. SP records, each album consisting of between three and six records, of folk music of Armenia and the adjoining Russian provinces and of similar sets devoted to Haiti and Ethiopia; the same firm issued a number of American Indian songs and dances and six sides of Cuban cult music. All were recorded on the spot and may be regarded as authentic. Modern issues of these types are sufficiently frequent and well established to receive review in the "Ethnomusicology Newsletter" and less detailed coverage in such magazines as "Western folklore", "Journal of American folklore", "New York Folklore Quarterly", etc. These recordings have been mentioned in some detail in the hope that the time is not too far distant when it will again be possible to import American records into Britain with a minimum of formality and at a reasonable cost. If and when that day arrives, the British gramophone librarian has a fruitful field of choice and can cover most of the New World and parts of the Old through these enterprising firms.

Most countries with coloured inhabitants appear to issue records for their native populations using local singers and instrumentalists. There are, for instance, Bantu records in South Africa, and a number of recording companies in India but these discs are generally extremely difficult to obtain in Britain, though Collet's in London do supply some Chinese records. A collection of African and Oriental music could well be of great interest and use to the music student and to the budding anthropologist. Occasional discs, such as those of Balinese theatre music, have been included in the British catalogues. Suitable records are listed in the *International catalogue of recorded folk music*, edited by Norman Fraser (Oxford U.P., 1954) and in *A list of American folksongs currently available on records* (U.S. Library of Congress; Music Division, 1953).

Jazz

This is a most controversial field when considering provision. The librarian is usually on safe ground when providing the normal classical repertory, though here he will have some difficulty in deciding upon the quality that separates light music from classical music —a dividing line between the permanent and the ephemeral. That must always be, to an appreciable degree, a matter of opinion. If jazz is provided a similar criterion can be used by attempting to include in the collection only jazz recordings of lasting value, and this is a considerably more difficult proposition. The question of the musical stature of jazz is an entirely different one and one upon which attackers and defenders are never likely to agree; the only common ground is the mutual dislike of "concert jazz", a hybrid that attempts to combine jazz with a symphonic style of writing and orchestration.

In Britain only one or two libraries have provided music of this type in gramophone record collections, but provision is much more frequent (though far from universal) in the U.S.A. There are various possible reasons for this; the most likely is that it is often related to the experiments connected with Youth work. A collection of jazz records is considered to have a strong appeal to adolescents, yet an investigation into the types of jazz audience (made at the expense of a firm of watch manufacturers) suggested that, in fact, the strongest appeal was to the 20 to 40 age group; the survey also found that the audience is predominantly male, is educated above average and also earns more than the national average. While this result, if correct, completely undermines the suggested provision for adolescents it may justify the inclusion of jazz records because of their growing "respectability". If jazz becomes as fashionable in Britain, then stronger demands will be made upon our libraries to include jazz records in our collections.

The essence of the case for including jazz is that it is alleged to be an important form of contemporary music which has achieved much prominence and a wide audience and which has also accumulated a large corpus of critical writing. To prove its importance the jazz enthusiast may well point to the fact that records made twenty, thirty or even forty years ago are still in the companies' catalogues in various forms—the same recording may be available as one side of a 78 r.p.m. disc and also as part of a 7-in. record and/or a longplaying record. This suggests that such works are regarded as classics in their particular field. Such artists as Louis Armstrong, Duke Ellington, Earl Hines and the like are studied seriously, their methods and techniques compared with knowledgeable fervour. Jazz has very little to do with the commercial dance band record of a "hit" tune that gets played to death for three months and then mercifully disappears; records of these tunes also disappear from makers' catalogues a year or two later. While this fate overtook many of the early jazz records, the best (or those played in a style that has revived in vogue) have been exhumed and reissued, sometimes more than once, and later appearances are provided with much detail—the names of the band personnel, the date of the recording, etc. As with classical music, the dividing line between true jazz and commercial jazz is a blurred one with plenty of border-line cases.

Since the major interest in many jazz records often centres on the improvisations of the soloists, handbooks have been issued which list the personnel responsible for particular recordings. A band may make records for a period under the same name yet change its members to a greater or lesser degree from one recording session to the next—many bands, in fact, had no corporate existence outside the recording studios but were assembled from the star instrumentalists of several regular bands. Charles Delaunay's *New hot discography* (New York; Criterion Music Corporation, 1948) is an excellent example of a type of reference book that has come into existence in order to fulfil a known need—and the growth in numbers of this type of work on jazz performers that has taken place during the nineteen-fifties may be regarded as symptomatic—while with many LP discs the note on the back of the "sleeve" (i.e. the outer envelope) will normally be expected to quote the names of instrumentalists.

Because of its wider and more popular appeal, it may be regarded as certain that the provision of any jazz records will provoke immediate demands for more; it is also likely to lead to criticism of the selection since the disciples of the different "schools" of jazz will be sure to feel that their particular interest has not received sufficient representation. Classical music has no equivalent of the "traditionalist" versus "modern" jazz battle that provokes heated arguments and claims. American libraries that allow public use of playing equipment in the library sometimes find themselves having to cope with groups of high-spirited youngsters in contrast to the rather more decorous classical music-lovers. Jazz records may be borrowed for parties and often seem to receive rougher handling, with a resultant brief useful life in the library stock. Most librarians would probably agree that it is an excellent thing to have some of the important and valuable anthology records of jazz for use in connection with the books in the music library—records that depict a phase such as the return to the beat in jazz music after the bop era, the rebirth of traditional jazz, or the trend to absorb modern classical influences; the problem, apparently insoluble, is to ensure that the records are borrowed and used only by the serious student of jazz. Even allocation to a reference collection opens the way to a fresh set of difficulties, as the American Memorial Library in Berlin found to its cost. Here, the catalogue entries for jazz records had to be removed after twenty-four hours as, during the single day that they were displayed, the listening booths were besieged by eager listeners. That, of course, may be regarded as the most convincing argument for the provision of records of this type. If the librarian does start to supply jazz records, he will have plenty of problems to solve as this section may have indicated.

Educational records

Records of an educational nature cover quite a wide field; indeed many of the types already discussed could be classified under this heading. Once again the librarian is advised to make an early decision as to what he expects to provide in this field and to try to define his limits fairly closely. Nearly all libraries, for instance, provide records intended to assist the learning of a foreign language; "Linguaphone" and "Assimil" are the best-known British examples. These records will normally require special rules for their issue, a matter that is considered in detail in the second half of the chapter.

On the musical side the *History of music in sound* and the D.G.G. "Archive" records have already been mentioned; these and other similar series may be regarded as the successors to the *Columbia history of music*, a pioneer project before World War II, of five albums containing 10-in. discs and accompanying descriptive notes by Percy Scholes. The records gave an excellent, if necessarily brief, survey of a very wide field and most of the music was well worth playing for its own sake irrespective of its importance in musical history. Few people could write so well for the interested novice as could Dr. Scholes, and the set achieved a deserved popularity with a wide audience. A somewhat similar set, though shorter and cheaper, was the *Parlophone 2,000 years of music*.

In the late nineteen-thirties the German firm of Telefunken issued a series of records under the title "Spiel mit". These records contained single movements from famous chamber works but with one performer missing in the recording. The intention was that the purchaser should perform the absent part himself and a copy of the missing part was issued with the record. Movements were selected from various works but the missing parts were limited to first violin, violoncello or piano and the recording artists were the Vienna String Quartet. By buying the appropriate record a 'cellist, for instance, could practise the Andante from the opus 99 trio of Schubert with two professional partners; the major drawback was that the record-buyer had to play his part at the same tempo as that chosen by the recording artists. Telefunken also issued some records with piano accompaniments to songs by Brahms, Wolf, etc. Here again, the live performer had to follow the recorded accompaniment rather than be accompanied, in the true sense, by the pianist. Shortly after the Second World War the American Columbia Company issued a similar series of music records under the title of "Add-a-part"; these covered a wider field than the German original and included complete works rather than single movements from records. On LP the scheme has been continued on the "Music Minus One" discs which include nearly a dozen records for pianists and more than that for violinists, as many for recorder and single discs for flute (Mozart quartets), bassoon (Beethoven/Mozart) and French horn (also Beethoven/Mozart). The same firm produced a number of jazz records with rhythm sections playing the basic accompaniment for a number of "evergreen" jazz tunes. The buyer can then improvise on his own particular instrument. A more ambitious scheme is that of Vanguard which has supplied the accompaniment to a handful of piano concertos. There will be many pianists who can get immense pleasure from playing the solo part with full orchestra provided via the gramophone.

The records considered so far in this section are intended mainly for individual use though musical history may well be studied in class. An entirely different type of record, apparently unique, was the recording (during 1929 and 1930) of one hundred lectures by eminent men and women. The recordings were made under the auspices of the International Education Society and issued by the Columbia Graphophone Company; the discs were listed as a supplement to that company's normal catalogue. The range of subjects was very wide—from "The care of the teeth" to "Ants and their habits" (this last by Professor Julian Huxley); from "Smallpox and vaccination" to "Latin pronunciation". Most of the lectures were contained on two 12-in. discs and lasted between fifteen and twenty minutes; almost all of the set survived until the general withdrawal of SP discs in the middle nineteen-fifties when they all disappeared from the Columbia catalogue. One of the "lectures" was a recording of Virginia Sackville-West reading her own poem, "The Land". Columbia also issued a series of six 10-in. discs of Morse code recordings, starting with single letters and ending with messages transmitted at comparatively high speed.

The Gramophone Company (H.M.V.) also issues periodically some records intended primarily for schools. Examples are the

Gramophone Record Libraries

Picard Bateman French course records and a number of recordings by choirs of schoolboys and schoolgirls of different age groups. The latter records provide a useful comparative standard for any particular school form and may also serve as an example when a song, available in this series, is being learned. The ordinary music-lover may also find himself getting much enjoyment from these records, overlooking their educational intent but delighting in well-chosen songs, zestful singing and a technical competence that puts many adult choirs to shame. The same manufacturers also issue records for use with percussion bands in nursery and infant schools.

Records demonstrating in turn the different instruments of the orchestra, giving each a brief solo passage to illustrate its tone-colouring and range are of obvious value though it seems that there is still no really successful British issue of this type. Benjamin Britten's *Young person's guide to the orchestra* is not exactly in this category for it is written as a continuous piece of music; certainly it is highly skilled in its combination of demonstration piece and music that is enjoyable for its own sake. For educational use the spoken commentary, originally written for the film in which the music appeared is excellent, and a recording incorporating this is therefore preferable to one containing the music only.

WHAT TO COLLECT—II: MAINLY NON-MUSICAL

Local collection

This is a field unexplored in Britain, with few exceptions, though its possibilities have been recognized in the U.S.A. for some years. Nearly every public library possesses a local collection which normally represents as many aspects of life in the town as possible. The rapid growth of private recording and the recent advances in tape-recording make possible the provision for posterity of sound pictures of local events and the voices of local celebrities. This matter is referred to again at the end of the chapter in the comments on tape-recordings, but selected recordings may be more generally useful on disc and there are many professional sound engineers and firms that will transfer a tape to disc form, so that extra copies can be made if required and the recordings can be played on gramophones.

The spoken word

One naturally associates the gramophone with music but poetry and drama have been increasingly represented since the introduction of the LP disc, particularly in the U.S.A.—which is far ahead of Britain in the numbers of records of these types available. In both countries there are a number of records which perpetuate poetry readings both by actors and actresses and also by the poets themselves. Records of this last type may be regarded as an equivalent to composers recording their own works—the results may not always equal those achieved by the professional performers, but they have the inestimable value of providing authoritative interpretations. Recordings in Britain have included T. S. Eliot and C. Day Lewis, while in the U.S.A. personal readings have been made by Robert Frost, Carl Sandburg, Archibald Macleish and W. H. Auden, to mention but a few examples. In addition to purely commercial recordings there are a number available from the Library of Congress.

Drama was for years barely recognized by the gramophone companies but perhaps the success of the excerpts from the film of Shakespeare's *King Henry V* with Sir Laurence Olivier in the title part encouraged the companies to become more venturesome. Since then a number of plays, as well as some shorter excerpts, have been issued both in this country and in the U.S.A. If any librarian is sceptical that such records will receive adequate use it may be recalled that non-musical recordings were introduced into the library of Boston, Mass., with considerable misgivings but they immediately proved a great success, particularly the play recordings. This experience has been paralleled elsewhere.

With the disappearance from the catalogues of the Columbia lectures, mentioned earlier, there is nothing in the British catalogues to compare with such American discs as the "Informal hour" series which includes authors such as S. J. Perelman, J. B. Priestley and Dorothy Parker reading selections from their own works, or the "Distinguished playwrights" series, which includes Arthur Miller "in a provocative discussion of attitudes to character portrayal, with readings from his *Death of a salesman* and *The crucible*". Westminster, the issuing company of both these series also produce the "Golden treasury of verse" series which includes readings of German verse, French verse and drama, Irish verse (read by Padraic Colum) and a selection of John Betjeman poems read by the poet himself. Finally there are the "Great artists" series (with recordings by Siobhan McKenna, Frank Petingell, Anthony Quayle, etc.) and the "Distinguished teachers" series which includes university professors of the calibre of Jacques Barzun and Robert M. Hutchins giving recorded lectures. Another label, "Caedmon", specializes in the spoken word, with "Monuments of early English drama", readings by William Faulkner, Frank O'Connor, Dylan Thomas, Edith and Osbert Sitwell, Sean O'Casey, Ogden Nash, Tennessee Williams, Colette, Thomas Mann and W. H. Auden, among others. None of these discs have been issued in Britain. Folkways have a "Literature series", while Period release an impressive number of French classics of Molière, Racine and Corneille performed by La Comédie Française and another series ("Their works and their voices") with authors such as Jean Cocteau, Paul Claudel and André Gide. Mention has been made of the poetry recordings sponsored by the Library of Congress; this national library has also issued three discs of animal tales recorded in the Gullah dialect of the coastal islands of South Caroline and two discs of "Jack tales" (in which Jack the Giant-killer, whose exploits were brought into Carolina by English settlers, has become adapted over the years into an American character), a few lectures (including "Whitman the philosopher" by David Daiches) and an unscripted and unrehearsed interview with H. L. Mencken. These are listed in the hope that these discs will, at some future date, be freely imported into Britain when they should be promptly bought by British librarians with gramophone record libraries. To conclude this section, mention should be made of an excellent discography, compiled by Henry C. Hastings, on "Spoken poetry on records and tapes; an index of currently available recordings" published in 1957 by the Association of College and Reference Libraries. It occupies no less than fifty-two pages.

Children's records

Selection in Britain is limited in numbers though fairly wide in scope. There are nursery rhymes, some children's tales, dramatized excerpts from "Alice in Wonderland", sound track recordings from Mickey Mouse films and tunes such as the *Teddy Bears' picnic*. The great majority of these recordings are likely to make little appeal to the gramophone librarian though a few are very good of their type and there is also the rare musical work for children that is also good music; the outstanding example is Prokofiev's *Peter and the Wolf*.

Once again it has to be regretfully admitted that American practice is well ahead of British. A number of children's stories, told by first-class readers, have been issued in the U.S.A. Gudrun Thorne-Thomsen recorded stories which were released under the sponsorship of the Children's Section of the American Library Association. Later, the Victor Company issued an album of children's stories under the auspices of the same Section; in this set the narrators were Ruth Sawyer, Frances Clarke Sayers and Jack Lester. On LP discs there is an impressive section of the Folkways catalogue devoted to the "Children's series" which includes folk tunes, English versions of folk tales from Indonesia and West Africa, Bible stories and the story of jazz. An indication of the importance attached to children's listening is given by the publication of at least two guides: *The children's record book: an authoritative guide to the best recorded music for children from six months to sixteen years*, by Harriet Buxton Barbour and Warren S. Freeman (N.Y.; Oliver Durrell, 1947) and *A guide to children's records: a complete guide to recorded stories, songs and music for children* (N.Y.; Crown, 1948), by Philip Eisenberg and Hecky Krasno. It will be noted from the dates of publication that both these works deal with SP discs only.

Miscellaneous records

Several recording companies have issued discs for the use of technicians or keen amateurs in search of high-fidelity sound reproduction. These records usually contain notes, briefly sustained, of given frequencies from the squeak of 15,000 cycles down to the near-grunt of 30 cycles; the lowest note on a piano has a frequency of 32 cycles. Records of this type will therefore demonstrate the effective range of a particular record reproducer or one's own hearing, whichever is the less. One of the most interesting discs of this type is that issued by Vox under the title *This is high fidelity*; issued in a special case and accompanied by an explanatory booklet, the total cost is about 50 per cent above the normal LP price. Test records of this type appear to have a shorter playing life than the normal record.

There have been one or two records issued in Britain with the sounds of motor cars of various types, but here again the Americans have been much more enterprising (though one may wonder, occasionally, who is likely to buy some of the records). There is a disc *Adventures in cacophony* with recordings of a squealing pig, chickens, cows, a dog and "a vocal family of felines". On the reverse side the sounds include watch ticks, a typewriter and tugboats. There are records of circus calliope music, of a rotary saw and hammering a nail, of rare old music boxes, of sea animals, of medicine (operation and human body sounds: "Actual operation performance on the spot . . ."), of a South African homestead and of earthquake tremors. Folkways have issued two LP discs of *Sounds of steam locomotives*, and the different types are carefully categorized; similar discs in Britain might well find an extensive sale.

American public libraries are expected to provide records which include particular sound effects, atmospheric music or items suitable for use with a particular dramatic production. English assistants might well be confounded if they were to receive normal American requests for "background music" for weddings, for family movies (Hawaiian music to accompany the pictures taken at Waikiki, etc.), for teas and various social events. The larger systems have had, in fact, to repeat the practice of the musical director or the cinema organist in the days of silent films and build up indexes of standard music that is suitable for background use in particular situations.

One other type of record of obvious value that does not seem to have been copied in Britain, though popular in the U.S.A., is that for use by shorthand students. On these, passages are read at given speeds for dictation use.

Summary

From the foregoing sections it is hoped that no librarian starting a gramophone record library will consider limiting the selection to music only. The well-rounded collection includes much other material, though this is not to suggest that every type of record mentioned in the preceding sections must be bought. Each category should be considered in the light of local conditions.

PART II: ADMINISTRATION

Before dealing with the day-to-day running of the gramophone record library some preliminary items will be considered. These are all of importance and are dealt with in the following order: Record speeds; Accessibility; Initial cost and running expenses; Free provision and rental collections. The remainder of the chapter is divided into the following headings: Selection; Accessioning; Classification; Cataloguing; Gramophone and soundproof room, and The department in action. This last head is further sub-divided and its sections listed for ease of reference.

Music Librarianship

Gramophone records are manufactured in different standard sizes and are made to play at one of four speeds. These variations compel an early decision as to which type or types should be included in the library stock and the librarian should have sufficient information before making his choice. Those who have no interest in this aspect of the subject or who already know enough about it are advised to omit the next few pages and continue with the following section.

In the early days of the gramophone the playing speeds of records varied from company to company, but in the first decade of this century the normal speed was standardized at 78 revolutions per minute. When earlier discs were reissued to satisfy public demand (as with the recordings of many famous singers) the correct speed was noted, though this was sometimes in rather vague terms, such as "over 80", "below 75". With such records the turntable speed must be adjusted accordingly or, if still revolving at the standard 78 r.p.m., the whole timbre of the vocalist's tone is altered and the music will be reproduced at a different pitch from that originally recorded. Many modern machines make no provision for slight adjustment of playing speed and upon such reproducers these old vocal records are almost useless. Even with the reissues on long-playing discs critics have occasionally questioned the pitch at which the re-recording was made; in at least one case a record was withdrawn and new copies with one item corrected in pitch were issued as replacements. Although 78 r.p.m. became the standard speed it was many years before it became universal; as late as the end of the nineteen-twenties the Columbia Graphophone Company (the "graphophone" was originally a different instrument from the "gramophone") was using 80 r.p.m. as its standard. 78 r.p.m. discs have become known as "SP" records, i.e. "standard-playing" (though it has also been claimed to mean "short-playing") since the introduction of long-playing discs at a slower speed. The usual diameters of these discs have been 10-in. and 12-in., with a playing time limited approximately to three and five minutes per side respectively. The records themselves are made from a shellac compound; this is brittle and the surface noise during performance varies from the quiet to the highly obtrusive. Much of this noise can be eliminated on the more expensive playing machines by the use of a scratch filter which cuts out the band of frequencies at which scratch is apparent.

Gramophone Record Libraries

In an attempt to overcome the disadvantages of a comparatively short playing time for each side some German records were made in the early nineteen-fifties with a maximum playing time of eight minutes. This was achieved by means of a "variable micrograde" (or "microgroove" as it would probably be called today), i.e. the width of the groove varied—the softer the music, the narrower the groove. A string quartet, for instance, would be able to utilize the maximum eight minutes without loss of tone quality but narrower grooves could only be used for quieter passages of an orchestral work, so that a shorter side would normally result. A similar idea of a variable groove was also tried with 45 r.p.m. discs but was apparently unsuccessful.

With the introduction of the long-playing record the SP disc lost very much of its earlier popularity though much light music and commercial jazz is still produced on 10-in. SP discs. For longer works the disadvantages of four-minute instalments and the break in continuity between one side and the next were obvious. The use of twin turntables and automatic couplings (in which the first side of the music is backed by the last, the second side by the penultimate one, etc.) lessened these drawbacks—twin turntables almost overcame them, but at a comparatively high cost. Machines were sold with automatic record-changers, some of which could change records at a higher speed than could be achieved by hand though the set had to be turned over by hand at the half-way stage and the machine then worked through the reverse sides of the records; such machines required automatic couplings, while the usual method of backing, whereby the first record contained sides 1 and 2, the second record sides 3 and 4 became known as "manual" couplings, for obvious reasons; the companies issued longer works in both formats using different series of catalogue numbers in separate sequences to differentiate them; only in the last days of the classical SP record, when automatic couplings were often the only type issued for long works, did the [English] Decca company use the simple device of prefixing the record numbers with an "A" for automatic couplings, e.g. manual coupling K 1332 to 1334 and automatic coupling AK 1332–4.

In 1948 the long-playing record made its first appearance in the U.S.A., where the Columbia Company (which has long ceased to have any connection with the English firm of the same name) issued 12-in. records that would play for twenty to twenty-five minutes per side. The tremendous increase in playing time has been achieved

215

partly through the reduction in playing speed from 78 to 33⅓ revolutions per minute, but mainly through the use of much finer grooves on the record ("microgrooves") which demand the use of a lightweight pick-up of not more than 10 grammes weight on the needle (and preferably nearer 5 gr.) and a needle-point of 1/1,000th inch radius compared with the three or four thousands of the SP needle. This drastic innovation was followed immediately by another. RCA-Victor, the great American rival of Columbia, produced a wafer-thin 7-in. disc with a playing speed of 45 r.p.m. and a centre-hole of some 1½-in. diameter. This new disc was also of the microgroove type but only contained about the same playing time as a 12-in. SP record, so that it was not a direct competitor of the LP disc. Both types of record were made of a plastic (vinyl) which was much lighter than shellac and almost unbreakable, it also virtually eliminated surface noise.

The Decca Record Company in England began to make discs for the American market in 1949 and these were marketed in the U.S.A. under the trade name of "London" records. The same company made its initial British issue in June, 1950, with about fifty records and quickly followed this with two further releases to bring the total number of available discs to some 140. Since then, the firm's catalogue has expanded at a somewhat slower rate and the company has also acted as British agent for both American and continental firms. The actual pressings have been made in London but the records have carried the name of the original issuing company. At a later date, this company began to issue 45 r.p.m. discs for short items (often four-minute excerpts from a long work, or separate items originally included in a "recital" disc) and introduced a new form, the 10-in. "medium-play" record which is used for items that conveniently fit a side playing for ten to twelve minutes. The medium-play (MP) discs are, perhaps confusingly, played at 33⅓ r.p.m. and not at the 45 r.p.m. that one might expect from their title. Here again, though by no means invariably, the issues were of works that had previously been released as one side of a 12-in. LP disc, and this is a particularly attractive investment for the collector who is interested in the work on one side only of an LP disc, and several issues with an ill-matched pair of sides have benefited by this form of separation. As has been already indicated, the 45 r.p.m. disc is the equivalent of the 12-in. SP and is valuable for the operatic aria, a brief overture, a song, solo instrumental piece and the like. To the collector it provides the opportunity to purchase the individual item he wants rather than the entire collection on a "recital" disc where a number of the items may be uninteresting to him or duplicate works already owned. It must be added that by no means every LP which contains a complete work on one side of a 12-in. disc, or every LP recital record, appears in MP or 45 r.p.m. form later.

The E.M.I. group (His Master's Voice, Columbia, Parlophone) made its first LP issue in October, 1952, when both LPs and 45s were put on the market. After this a minor host of companies made their appearance, many the affiliates or subsidiaries of American or continental firms, and almost all have limited their issues to 10- and 12-in. discs at 33⅓ r.p.m. The large centre-hole of the 45 r.p.m. disc soon gave way to the normal size but these records are still manufactured in a fashion that allows the centre to be pressed out easily if one's machine will only deal with 7-in. discs with the large centre-hole. A later innovation in record types, a possible counterblast to the MP, was the "extended-play" 7-in. disc which contains up to about eight minutes' playing time per side, i.e. up to double the normal 45 but appreciably less than the MP. The EMI group who introduced this type of record in Britain made four different categories (with a different colour label for each) issued at different prices to permit (it would seem) some relationship between the amount of music provided and the cost. The less music provided, the cheaper the record would appear to be as a general rule, though there are numerous exceptions. Many of the recording celebrities are invariably limited to the highest-priced category only. D.G.G., Nixa and Phillips (the latter with two price categories) have all issued EP discs but no four-minute 45s. Decca, with the introduction of EPs in October, 1957, provide both types of 7-in. record.

The five different types of record generally available are therefore:

The SP disc at 78 r.p.m., 10- or 12-in. diameter (up to 5 minutes per side). [Before 1952, all companies; now only jazz and light music on 10-in.]

The "45" disc, 7-in. diameter (up to 5 minutes per side) [E.M.I. and Decca only.]

The EP disc, also at 45 r.p.m., 7 in. diameter (up to 8 minutes or so per side) [D.G.G., Decca, E.M.I., Nixa, Philips and Cetra].

The MP disc at 33⅓ r.p.m., 10-in. diameter (up to 12 minutes or so per side) [Decca only].

The LP disc, at 33⅓ r.p.m., 10- or 12-in. diameter (up to 25–30 minutes per side and 16–18 minutes per side respectively) [All companies].

This does not complete the possibilities. For some time one was able to buy in Britain 7-in. discs at a playing speed of 33⅓ r.p.m. under the Concert Artist label and the description "Special play". Though the slower speed should have made longer playing time available the actual records issued apparently provided no more music than could be accommodated on an EP disc. French records of a similar size and type appear to be rather more successful. Russian records (available in Britain through Collet's) include some of 8-in. diameter and 33⅓ speed, and also some 78 r.p.m. microgroove records.

As though this variety of speeds was insufficient a number of gramophone motors now incorporate a fourth speed—16⅔ r.p.m. A 7-in. disc at this speed could contain the equivalent of a 10-in. LP record, but suffers from the drawback that the slower speed needs extra steadiness in motor and governor since the slightest variation in playing speed produces a most noticeable variation in the pitch of the music. Despite the production of these four-speed motors no commercial records are available at this slowest speed in Britain (though "talking books" play at 16⅔ r.p.m.) and American production was limited to similar records on the Audio Book label. At the end of 1957 Vox issued a few records, and a typical 12-in. disc included the Beethoven *Coriolan* and *Leonora no. 3* overtures, the violin and *Emperor* concertos. The makers claimed up to 120 minutes of music per disc, and some jazz recordings were also issued at this speed on the Prestige label. At the time of writing there is no sign that this lead will be followed by other manufacturers. It is noteworthy, though, that classical music in the U.S.A. is tending to appear on 12-in. LP only; the 10-in. disc has proved unpopular while 7-in. records are limited to popular use. This standardization has obvious pros and cons.

With the occasional exception, such as [English] Columbia's *Anthology of English church music*, the newly established gramophone record library may well afford to ignore the SP disc entirely since almost the entire range of classical records issued in this format have now been withdrawn from the catalogues. There appears to be no major objection to the inclusion of 45s and EPs in the collection though it has been alleged that the minute grooves of EPs cause a higher proportion of unsatisfactory copies than with other types, yet very few (if any) public libraries include them in their collections. Some excellent performances (not all available at 33⅓ r.p.m.) are to be bought on this size of record.

Accessibility

The great majority of American record libraries have been run on open-access principles but quite a number have reverted to staff service for long-playing records. In Britain, closed access (a contradiction in terms though common usage) is the rule with the exceptions of Coventry and Leeds. The three major arguments against open access are: (i) that one cannot browse with a record in the sense that browsing is possible with a book; (ii) open access is bad because LP discs are very easily damaged by careless handling, for although the material itself is nearly unbreakable, the fine grooves are extremely susceptible to finger pressure, dust, etc.; (iii) the high cost of an LP disc requires extra precautions against theft. The first argument is true for SP records but it has lost much of its force since the arrival of the LP disc with its generally attractive cover (though some of the best records have been saddled with the most appallingly designed sleeves) and the provision of notes on the composer and the music on the back of the envelope. Constant handling is undoubtedly bad for both record and sleeve but if the shelving is designed so that the records are visible face on and do not have to be withdrawn sideways from a rack for inspection, then little damage should result.

Mr. Ernest Simpson, City Librarian of Coventry, maintains that non-access by the public compels the use of some sort of indicator, which is expensive and unattractive even at its best. He also suggests that the arguments in favour of open access for books are almost as valid for gramophone records. Finally, he reports that in seven years not a single gramophone record has been stolen from the library, though there is a small but constant loss from the book stock. This happy experience, it must be admitted, has not been paralleled in the U.S.A. where losses in some cities have been appreciable. It seems that closed access has gained general acceptance in Britain for two reasons—precedent and space. Librarians have naturally tended to follow the example of established collections, and since many of the earlier British collections were for restricted issue to schools and local societies only, open access was pointless. Gramophone record libraries are, almost invariably, a post-war service operating in a pre-war library—and many of the buildings are pre-World War I. As a result, the collection has had to be sited wherever sufficient room can be found; this space may be insufficient for open access which ideally requires a rather larger area than a service in which borrowers handle records only over the staff table or counter. Librarians starting a collection should seriously consider this problem and weigh the arguments in relation to local conditions rather than assume from the beginning that the public will not have access to the available records.

Initial cost and running costs

These are the two items likely to be of paramount interest to many members of a local Authority, yet it is most difficult to quote definite figures, particularly in respect of furniture and fittings since very much will depend upon local circumstances.

The size of the opening stock in different libraries has shown immense variation; it is an obvious truism to say that the bigger it has been, the more satisfaction it has been able to give to users and the more adequate its coverage of the standard repertory. At least two British libraries opened with a stock of between 800 and 1,000 SP discs and found this barely adequate as a starting figure; another began with 600 and had issued them all to borrowers long before the first day had ended. Translating these figures into terms of LP discs it envisages an opening stock of between 200 and 250 discs. It can easily be seen how narrow a margin this will provide, for even a small town will have no difficulty in enrolling 200 users (particularly as the service will be a novelty), and works that occupy more than a single disc are normally issued together to the same user. Until 1945 a very high proportion of the opening stock in the collections of smaller American libraries were donations and the median opening stock was only 200 discs. This must surely be an important factor in the present stagnation of many of these collections. The opening stock was too small and there was not sufficient allowance in the budget (which often apparently assumed a continuing stream of donated discs) to build up the collection quickly in response to the early public demand—so public demand withered and died.

The make-up of the initial stock also varied considerably between libraries, but experience suggests that orchestral works and complete operas should provide some 30 per cent each of the stock. Recordings of complete operas have been much more popular than anticipated some years ago; on the other hand, demand for piano music has been less insistent than might have been expected, though Chopin discs are an exception to this. Chamber music, instrumental works, vocal and choral records, and plays and poetry-readings might be allotted the remaining 40 per cent in fairly even shares. Once started, there will be three factors to take into account for new monthly accessions to the library's collection—the amount of money available, the types of record that are receiving heaviest use and consideration of what has been issued by the manufacturing companies since the last batch of purchases. Organ music may prove unexpectedly popular but if the companies do not issue any organ records for some months, the library cannot increase its representation. Even though a growing proportion of the record-buying fund may have to be spent on the replacement of worn-out discs, the three factors mentioned may result in a noticeable change in the proportions of the stock once the collection is established, and such a change would be justifiable. The librarian must, however, ensure that there is as wide a variety as possible in the original stock to allow many differing tastes to find something of interest in the collection; this only reinforces the desirability of having as large an opening stock as possible. It is more expensive to buy or replace records that were first issued in mid-1955 or earlier. The Autumn Budget in that year increased the rate of Purchase Tax from 50 to 60 per cent on the wholesale price and most record companies took the opportunity to increase the basic price slightly at the same time; prices rose again in 1957 (and Purchase Tax automatically rises as the basic price increases), and the discount allowed to public libraries on the net price has been decreased from 15 to 10 per cent. At 1957 prices, therefore, an initial allowance of £500 for records will probably buy less than 300, and this total will include a small number of 10-in. discs, both LP and MP. Even the smallest library, therefore, should not start below this figure for its beginning, keeping £50 perhaps on one side to fill the immediate gaps indicated by requests for records not in stock.

One might wish, in some ways, that it was possible to emulate American practice here. Elizabeth L. Andersen's thesis[2] records that only 34 per cent of the American public libraries covered by her survey bought all their original stocks; no less than 47 per cent were started entirely on gifts, and the remaining 19 per cent bought only a proportion of their initial collection. Gifts provided the nucleus of the collections of such large libraries as Boston, New Orleans, New

York, Philadelphia and Pittsburgh. When the library at Akron, Ohio, started its collection in 1949 it was assisted by gifts totalling $1,000 and records of an equivalent value. One of the disadvantages of gifts is that the records are not necessarily those that the librarian would choose to buy, and there is the further point (already suggested) that such a start may persuade the city fathers that they need provide only a very small allowance for new records on the assumption that gifts will continue to fill the gap. Many American libraries have received large donations of SP records from residents who have "changed over" to LP, and a few have been given LP recordings—but usually in versions that have been superseded by later and better ones. British librarians may hope to receive an occasional donation of this nature but cash or new records are rare gifts indeed.

There is no standard rate of discount in the U.S.A., librarians reporting variations between 10 and 40 per cent, but the lower figure would appear to be fairly general in small libraries. If the librarian is willing to take the trouble to order from New York discount houses he can rely upon a 25 per cent. reduction on the list price. It would appear that many records are intended to be sold at less than the official list price, and *New Records* quotes two prices for many new releases—the list price and the current market price. Further variation is introduced by the availability of many recordings in two editions—a de luxe and a thrift package, the chief differences usually being the quality of the package itself and the provision of detailed notes with the more expensive version. For standard works many libraries buy the cheaper packing (since the record is exactly the same in both coverings) but for works not previously represented in the collection or for operas and other works that require a libretto for full enjoyment, the de luxe package is preferred.

The American scene also differs from the British in its much wider price range for new records; in Britain there appears to be an agreement between the companies to keep prices almost exactly in step. Sales of new gramophone records at reduced prices are a regular feature of the American scene and envy is enhanced with the fairly recent introduction of some cheaper series of records. RCA-Victor have been releasing a stream of important 78 r.p.m. recordings in skilfully engineered LP form under the series title of "Camden" records; these cost $1·98 each, just about half the cost of an ordinary current LP disc. Columbia has a similar series, originally entitled "Entré" but now called the "Harmony" series. American prices, in general, fell appreciably after the introduction of LP discs (in complete contrast to British experience) but were showing an upward trend again at the end of 1957. Only in one field does Britain offer the chance of a bargain; there are no second-hand gramophone record dealers in the U.S.A. as there are in this country.

Though the standardized price of British discs may be regarded as a disadvantage it does allow the cost of the opening stock to be worked out quite accurately before any records are actually bought. Allowance will be made for selected works that are available at the lower price level—the H.M.V. plum label and its equivalent in certain other companies—and for any SP discs that the librarian may decide to acquire. Except for the important series mentioned in the first half of the chapter (language-teaching records and other educational types of record not available at 33⅓ r.p.m.) there would seem to be no place for the SP disc in a current collection except for items in a reference collection. With some works duplicated on LP, it is more economical to buy one version than another, sometimes because a particular recording is issued on a cheaper label but more frequently because of the different amount of music that may be included in a disc. Beethoven's *Choral symphony* took four sides in the early days of microgroove; a little later the recording companies were able to get the complete work, without appearance of undue haste or the deterioration in tone quality towards the centre of the disc that is a consequence of congested grooves, on three sides—leaving the fourth side free for another complete work, such as the same composer's first or eighth symphonies. In 1957 Vox issued a highly praised version, lacking only two repeats, on a single disc containing sixty-five minutes' playing time. This reduces the cost by 50 per cent. compared with the earliest version; on the other hand, not every music-lover would choose the Horenstein version for his collection despite its economy. In other cases one company will take a complete disc over a work while a second contrives to find room for an extra piece of music. All things being equal, the second version is obviously the one to choose, but it very rarely happens that all things *are* equal and the record containing the shorter measure in terms of the actual amount of music may well be the one to buy. Another point arises with these extra works; a collection can easily include three or four versions of the same comparatively short piece because it has been used as a "fill-up" to different works by different manufacturers who have tried to give purchasers better value for their money, in terms of playing time. These extra items present a cataloguing problem, too, but that matter is discussed in the appropriate section later.

With book-buying it is often possible to await a cheap edition of a popular work while the valuable but unsuccessful (as well as the valueless and unsuccessful) book may be remaindered and, if it is a good work on its particular subject, can represent a really economical purchase. Similar conditions do not exist with gramophone records. [But see p. 241.] Though it may well show its age because of the steadily improving standard of recording, the 1950 LP is no cheaper to buy in 1958; it is, in fact, dearer because of the higher basic price and increased rate of Purchase Tax. It is the latter that causes some prices to include an odd halfpenny (and 11s. and 8d. in addition, in a total of 41s. 8½d.) and makes prices the more difficult to calculate. Records are not remaindered in Britain but are simply withdrawn from the manufacturers' catalogues, usually with a few months' notice. In short, the only alternative to buying a disc at list price, less the accepted discount, is to try to get it second-hand. There are a number of shops, particularly in the London area, which sell second-hand gramophone records, both SP and LP, but the condition of the playing surface needs to be carefully examined before purchase and the record tried over if possible. Prices vary, but average around two-thirds of the gross price of a new record. A librarian will invite adverse comment if he starts his library with a noticeable proportion of used records; in any case, it is natural that many of those offered for sale in slightly used condition are versions of works that have been superseded by later issues that offer better performance, superior recording, or both. The second-hand market may be useful as a source of replacement for a single record or a set, or of a work that has been deleted by the manufacturing company but which the librarian would still like to have in stock, such as the withdrawn recordings of Haydn string quartets made by the Schneider Quartet and released in Britain by Nixa. At least one of the largest gramophone record dealers is prepared to accept "Wants" lists and to report as and when any of the desired records become available. Generally speaking, however, the gramophone record market is not nearly as well organized, as yet, as the book market in tracing and obtaining second-hand and out-of-print works.

Having selected the opening stock (though the situation cannot be imagined where the librarian can buy every disc that he would like to have available for potential users) and kept a certain amount of money in hand for emergencies, he has to solve the question of housing. As with books, much less space will be required than would be needed to accommodate the entire stock. In fact, the fairly small collection may find itself in a very short time looking somewhat forlorn with most of its shelves empty. It is likely that shelf space for a maximum of a third of the collection will be ample, though some temporary provision will be required for discs that cannot be brought out until the first borrowers have taken out their initial choices. If the service is being run without giving members of the public access to the records themselves, then floor space must be found for an issue desk, for the shelving of the discs, for a catalogue (if one is maintained), indicator and circulation space. The last should be as generous as possible. Since the issue and return of gramophone records when properly done is a slow process, queues are likely at busy times; in addition, patrons will be checking the indicator to see which records are available; these considerations predicate plenty of floor space if users' comfort is to be consulted. If the system is open access a rather larger floor space should be provided since the records must be well spread to allow as many people as possible to browse at any given time, and also because an indicator system can function with records filed on shelves that are both higher and lower than would be desirable for public use.

Slightly more space still would be required for a method of combining, to a large degree, the advantages of open access with the safeguards of the indicator system. If the individual discs are kept in polythene "inners" which fit inside the sleeve and the sleeve in turn is issued to the borrower in a manilla or similar folder, then the disc can be kept while at the library inside the folder, with the polythene jacket protecting it from dust and handling. The sleeve can then be displayed empty (as is done in many gramophone record shops). This allows all the advantages of browsing, is a safeguard against theft and rough handling, and permits the sleeve to act as its own indicator. If the sleeve is displayed, then the record is available; the potential borrower takes it to the assistant, who finds the record on the non-public shelves, checks the condition of the disc with the borrower and then inserts it in the sleeve. The catalogue number of the disc, and perhaps brief details, can be quoted on the manilla folder which can also be used for the date label, etc. This would obviate the problem, mentioned later under "Issue methods" of deciding the best place on the sleeve to paste the label.

So far as is possible the record library should be housed in a part of the building not subject to extremes of temperature. Where the shelves are not open to the public, accommodation for the records can be made cheaply. Some libraries have successfully if not beautifully adapted old bookcases or shelving; in others, shelves consisting of a simple series of cross-slats and uprights made of softwood suffice. If the records are stored vertically, as is most common, then the uprights should be fixed at 5- to 6-in. intervals; wider intervals increase the lateral pressure as the discs lean to one side or the other and thus the likelihood of warping or, if the section is fairly full, make it less simple to insert or remove a disc from the middle of the sequence. Solid shelves are not essential, for four cross-pieces of 1-in. planed timber each 2 in. from front to rear will provide sufficient support, if firmly affixed to the uprights. The depth of the shelving should be about 13 in., and the same distance should separate one shelf from the next in order to allow an adequate margin between the top of the record sleeve and the shelf above. Ten-inch discs should be shelved separately and not intermixed with 12-in. records; three cross-slats and a vertical height of about 11 in. between shelves should be enough. Seven-inch records, if stocked, will require a third sequence of shelves. The third possible type of shelving is the metal cabinet or metal shelving made to a standard specification by suppliers of library furniture. Messrs. Libraco Ltd., for example, supply a metal cabinet that will hold about 1,200 records. It has five shelves with nine compartments in each; the individual compartments are $12\frac{3}{4}$ in. high, $3\frac{3}{4}$ in. wide and 13 in. deep. With double doors that lock (a precaution when the library may be open for longer hours than those in operation for the gramophone record collection) the current cost is about £50, while the same model without doors is rather cheaper.

There is much to commend the storage of records in a flat position as this appreciably reduces the chances of warping; at the same time it is more difficult to find an individual record unless it happens to be on top of the sequence. Leeds uses this method of shelving, with an inch between shelves and an arc cut out of the front of each shelf for ease of handling. Each compartment holds five or six records only, so that it is not difficult to trace an individual disc. The shelves themselves are $\frac{3}{8}$ in. thick and the front edges are used for guiding. Gold lettering on leather is used and for the more prolific composers the colour of the leather background denotes the particular type of music to be found on that shelf. This assistance is carried further by quoting the composer's name on some shelves, while the intervening ones carry the word "Overtures" or "Symphonies" or other appropriate form. It may be remarked here that the Music Library Association has stated that "No scientific investigation has confirmed the superiority of storage horizontally or vertically".[4]

Where SP discs are in stock, provision should be made for stouter covers than the paper envelopes provided by the gramophone companies since this protection is too flimsy to withstand much handling. The recommended type includes a top flap that will act as a dust excluder, for dust is abrasive and is probably the major enemy to the long life of records. The envelopes should be made of kraft paper, manilla or similar material. LP discs have a stouter covering; some libraries leave them without further protection, but it is advisable to strengthen the edges with transparent cellulose tape. If and when the manufacturer's jacket becomes shabby it is possible to buy a replacement if the record is still current, though the price may be considered high; alternatively the record may be kept in a plain cover. Some American libraries transfer all new records to plain jackets and split the original jacket, mounting it with a plastic adhesive on the front and back of its plain counterpart. This is an excellent idea but is expensive in time and material. The earliest British releases of LP discs, on Decca and Capitol, had thick cardboard sleeves but these were soon superseded by thinner and lighter covers, some of them quite unsuited to withstand handling with any frequency. From the first releases many of the sleeves carried varied designs upon their faces (ranging from the extremely attractive to the artistically appalling, from the apt to the incongruous) though a minority were austerely plain. At a later date the jackets were covered with a laminated plastic that was dirt-resistant and this improvement led to the introduction of some photographic covers. A further modification introduced by two or three companies was to thicken the spine of the sleeve and to print the title and artist's name there; this allowed brief details to be seen without withdrawing the record—a great boon to the dealer, record librarian and individual collector alike. The back of the sleeve is normally used to supplement the details of the items and artists shown on the front, and also to include a programme note. Some companies give the names of the writers of these notes, others maintain anonymity. As with cover designs, the standard of the programme note has varied from the extremely helpful to the bald, useless or downright misleading and incorrect. The record companies soon provided extra protection to supplement the cardboard cover since dust is an even greater enemy of the narrow grooves of the LP disc than it is of those on the coarser shellac. One company experimented with transparent cellophane covers that were slipped over the cardboard sleeves but these were quickly torn. Other experiments included various forms of rice paper inner envelopes but these, too, are easily crumpled as the record is returned to the sleeve. Practically all companies now provide either polythene covers that are comparatively tough and which offer good protection against dust when the record is stored, or else they use a stiff white paper envelope with a transparent polythene inset which allows the record label to be seen. As the envelope is placed inside the sleeve its open top edge fits snugly against the top of the sleeve, whose own opening is in the side, and so an efficient dustproof container results. D.G.G. use a different type sleeve to the other companies with a polythene envelope sewn into the inside of the sleeve, which opens like a book. The moral of these experiments should be plain—that record librarians should see that discs are as well protected as possible from dust.

In the U.S.A. the distributors of E.M.I. records (under the trade name "Angel", which was merged into the group's associate, "Capitol", at the end of 1957) offered new records in alternative packagings, as has been mentioned. The de luxe packages were of the highest quality with an appropriate cover of high artistic standard, extra protection in the form of telescoping jackets, elaborate notes with music illustrations and, in the case of vocal works, the complete text. "Thrift" editions offered a standard jacket design and omitted the notes though the text was still quoted for vocal works. Angel later introduced a middle level, suitably entitled the "library" series, which offers a relatively plain package but includes notes. Releases were confined to chamber music, so that such records were slightly cheaper to buy than music played by symphony orchestras. Another type of record unknown in Britain is the Westminster "laboratory" disc which is intended for the collector to whom the quality of the sound is of paramount importance. Only about half the amount of music found on an LP is provided so that the music grooves are limited to the outer part of the disc; it is the inner grooves towards the centre of the record that are most likely to suffer from distortion. The package is contained in a polythene bag with a zipp fastener, while programme notes stress details of the recording. The same performances are usually available on ordinary Westminster LP discs. Thus a work which occupies two normal discs will be sold by Westminster at $4.98 in a de luxe package and $3.98 in a thrift package. The same work will occupy four "laboratory" discs and cost $7.50 per disc (prices are those of 1957). It is interesting to note that most recordings in these alternative forms originate in London.

In the eyes of British manufacturers the 7-in. disc does not appear to warrant the same treatment as its larger brother. First releases of Decca 45s were contained in flimsy paper envelopes of a similar pattern to those used with SP discs and E.M.I. followed suit, except that the group used cardboard instead of paper. When Nixa, Philips and D.G.G. entered the 7-in. market they used a sleeve similar in design to those of 10- and 12-in. records without any programme notes on the back and it was not until late in 1956 that E.M.I. gave classical 7-in. records adequate treatment with sleeves of plastic finish and a programme note on the back cover. Polythene inners are, at the time of writing, provided only by D.G.G. and Decca, but there are many firms that make these protective covers in all three sizes so that libraries can ensure at fairly small cost that every record in the collection has the protection of both sleeve and polythene inner envelope.

The space required for housing records may be estimated on a basis of approximately six records to each inch of shelving for LPs and eight for SPs. While the latter are thicker and heavier (which may need to be remembered when drawing up the specification for shelves) the single paper envelopes allow for closer spacing of records.

Because of the potential damage to sleeves from constant withdrawal from the shelf and subsequent return, the open-access library will advisedly make different shelf provision from that needed where the collection is handled only by members of the staff. The potential user normally wants to see the sleeve, so that the best form of shelving is that which shows the cover face-on. Something based upon the "browsing boxes" of the gramophone shop is what is required and Coventry's shelving appears to be excellent. These are made in units either 5 ft. or 2 ft. 7 in. wide and are about 12 in. in depth. In the bottom of each case are filed SP discs which are kept in cardboard boxes, each duly labelled with the name of the composer and title of the work contained. Above this is a smaller shelf for filing miniature scores; all the library's stock of these is kept on these shelves and a score may be borrowed at the same time as a record or set of records. This liaison has increased the use of the scores and also the pleasure of many users. At the top of the case is the filing space for LP discs, arranged in three ascending tiers with the records facing the potential user. Nearly all discs are therefore immediately visible; Leeds' choice of flat filing is less attractive. It causes little difficulty to the patron who has definite ideas as to what he wishes to borrow, but the borrower who has no settled choice but who wishes to see what is immediately available before reaching a choice is less happily placed. For the library with no SP discs, or only a handful, the Coventry method may be regarded as uneconomical since it requires a fairly generous allowance of floor space in proportion to the number of records displayed, though this has the compensating advantage of allowing adequate elbow room for quite a number of browsers at any one time. Shelving in racks, particularly when used by members of the staff only, houses a much greater number of records in less space, since the height of the lowest shelf can be just above ground level and the top shelf can be some 5 ft. up. In short, shelving deserves careful consideration, but a fairly accurate price for the various types can be obtained before figures are presented to the Library Committee for consideration.

Where the public has no access to the records themselves, financial provision must be made and space found for some sort of indicator to show users which records are available at the times of their visits to the library. The cheapest form is probably one made from ordinary book-pockets; the records that are available are indicated by book cards filed in the pockets, and the borrower takes the book card to the staff counter in order to obtain a particular record. Such an indicator can be efficient but it does give an air of improvisation and parsimony that the collection may well not deserve. The most popular type with British librarians is the indicator based upon some form of "visible index" marketed by most suppliers of office equipment. Cards are suspended in a metal frame, each card nearly overlapping the one below it, so that only the bottom half-inch or thereabouts of a card is visible except for the top card in the frame. Full details of the record are typed upon the body of

Coventry's method of displaying LP gramophone records. Miniature scores & albums of SP discs are filed below

the card (and these details may be sufficient for the cards to act as accession register also), and brief particulars are typed again on the bottom edge that will be immediately visible. A reader will see the brief details of composer, title and (perhaps) artist, and can lift the cards above in order to see the fuller entry on the body of the card should that interest him; there he can find details of the orchestra, artists, allocation of movements or acts to sides, etc.

This type of indicator is efficient and attractive in appearance but it may be regarded as rather expensive. A typical example is a frame that holds seventy-two cards and which cost £2 12s. in 1957, plus Purchase Tax. A collection of 1,000 discs will therefore need fourteen such frames. The cards act as a catalogue to show the library's stock and they also act as an indicator by a simple device. The bottom of each card consists, in fact, of a folded edge (upon the front of which the brief entry is typed); this edge is cut off at one end or a small hole is punched in it. This allows the book card (a misnomer, but the term in general use) which must be of a different colour, to be seen. When the record is in the hands of a borrower no coloured dot or portion of book card is visible, so that the would-be listener knows that the record is not available. An alternative method is to make book card and catalogue card of the same colour and to print a coloured spot behind the punched hole; in this case the appearance of the coloured spot shows that the book card has been removed and that the particular record is "out". The former method would seem to be cheaper and is possibly psychologically better, but the point is not of major importance. When a record contains two major works by different composers, one on each side, the entry for the second side will show a spot of a different colour or the catalogue/accession card will be of a different colour to act as a permanent guide to the fact that information as to the availability of the record must be sought under the name of the other composer; details of this reverse side must be shown in the entry. Slips of paper of a third colour may be placed in the fold of a catalogue entry to show that the particular work is reserved by a reader; this may be regarded as an unnecessary refinement as the reservation of records can be made without the use of such a slip in the catalogue, but it does provide information to potential borrowers who will realize that they will have to wait some time before the record becomes available again. While it is best that the metal frames holding these entries be kept upright and spread along a wall or walls to permit as many patrons as possible to use it at once, the catalogue/index may be filed flat in a series of shallow metal drawers or may be filed on a revolving metal stand, with each frame attached by one edge to the centre. This allows some degree of movement so that adjoining frames may be pushed away and the particular one required inspected. With both of these methods the use of the index is limited to one person at a time and this can be an important defect except at the quietest periods of the day.

A compromise method between the cheapness of the "home-made" indicator and the somewhat expensive office equipment is used by Woolwich; there the cards for each record are filed in racks which are actually manufactured for use in factories and works where employees clock on and off duty to file their time cards. These racks are less attractive than the visible indexes but they are also very much cheaper and operation is even simpler. Woolwich prepares two cards for each record—a buff one which acts as a book card and a white one which contains accession details and which is filed behind the buff card. To borrow a record, the reader takes the buff card to the assistant who finds the appropriate disc. With the book card gone, the white card is now visible and this indicates that the record is "out"—a similar result to that achieved by the visible index. Whatever type of indicator is used, its cost can be worked out in advance once the size of the opening stock has been determined and quotations can be obtained accordingly. Provision should obviously be made for probable expansion of the collection.

Though the indicator also acts as a catalogue it does not permit added entries for performers, title entries and the like, and a good case can be argued for the additional provision of a normal sheaf or card catalogue in the gramophone library. This could give fuller entry than on the indicator entry which could then be limited to the basic information on that part of the card which is immediately seen. It would also allow adequate entries for the "fill-ups", those shorter pieces of music that are apparently included to give the purchaser good value in terms of quantity, if not always of quality, when the main recorded work alone is of a length that does not conveniently fit on to an exact side or number of sides. There are also the records that contain four overtures or a series of brief orchestral or instrumental pieces. A library may have two or three versions of an intermezzo or aria yet each version as the secondary item on a disc; the patron who wishes to borrow this short work may find it difficult to trace in the visible index type of catalogue but simple if a normal catalogue (with necessary analytical and other added entries provided) is maintained. The pros and cons of this extra provision are considered later in this chapter when discussing cataloguing. In addition to a fairly full catalogue at the library there is much to be said for the issue of a printed or duplicated catalogue of the collection supplemented by occasional lists of later additions. Such a catalogue would suffer the obvious defect of being quickly out of date if the collection is well used but it can be a useful form of publicity, it gives readers the opportunity to study the library's holdings at leisure and make their own lists of the records that they would like to borrow and it may provide some of those added entries which are lacking in the visible index. Most of the collections started in Britain up to 1952 or so seem to have issued catalogues of their gramophone record stocks but later starters appear to have dispensed with the adjunct to the service, except in isolated instances.

The most expensive item in the cost of each loan is probably staff time, but this is the last item upon which to economize since so much of the value of the service and its efficient running depends upon the human element. If there is already a music librarian included in the establishment of the system the addition of one or two junior assistants should be enough. When a gramophone library is started in a library that has no music librarian there is a strong case for creating the post unless the collection is open on a part-time basis only. The creation of a new senior post may prove extremely difficult in the small library and may well require much hard work by the librarian in a larger system, but in the medium-sized and large library the potential use of the collection should make such an appointment a necessity if members of the public are to receive the expert, informed attention that is so highly desirable. In the very large library it is likely that there will already be a music librarian on the staff and an assistant can be appointed in charge of the gramophone library to work under the general direction of the music librarian. One might again instance the example of Detroit where there are seven professional staff in the Music & Drama Department. Each member of the staff has both general and special duties and the supervision of the record collection and room is the special duty of one assistant. She is responsible for all ordering and selection, though other members of the department will make suggestions, supervises the catalogue in the record room and trains and oversees the two half-time clerks and the one half-time page allotted to the record room. All members of the professional staff spend approximately eight hours weekly at the record desk and another twelve hours weekly at the main desk where music and book materials are handled. This interchange of duties is doubly valuable; it assists the integration of the service and also provides all members of the professional staff with experience in the gramophone record section.

Except in the very large British libraries the gramophone record collection is likely to have but one professionally qualified assistant; while usually called "Gramophone librarian" it would be better in almost every way to make the appointment that of "Music Librarian" with responsibility for the stock of books and scores relating to music in addition to the gramophone library. The two collections should show co-ordination, particularly in the choice of miniature scores, and the ideal should always be held in view whereby the two collections are housed as closely together as possible, preferably in a separate department. The person appointed should be a Chartered Librarian and the arguments in favour can be found in Chapter I. Despite the specialist knowledge possessed by the good gramophone or music librarian the salary offered is likely to be low. As for the number of staff required, it may be repeated that for collections where the public have no access to the records except via an indicator, an average of 150 transactions daily is a reasonable figure for each assistant; for open access the average may rise to approximately 200. It may be extremely difficult to determine how many staff will be required when a gramophone library is opened but the qualified assistant should be appointed, hours of opening possibly limited (both to reduce the need for part-time assistance from other departments and to gauge public demand) and a regular understudy be appointed as soon as it is obvious that the service will be beyond the capabilities of a single person. This second member of the department will almost certainly be unqualified professionally but choice should be made (if at all possible) of an assistant who has an interest in and some knowledge of music and who is keen to develop both. The use of any assistant who can be spared from another department or service point to act as relief assistant is to be deprecated; where such relief is necessary attempts should be made to limit the number of assistants who may be called upon for the duty, perhaps to two or three. One reason for this is that the assistant on duty should invariably set a good example to patrons in the ways of handling gramophone records, and careless

or inexpert treatment will lower the service in the eyes of the knowledgeable borrowers and provide a bad example for the person who
has just begun to use a gramophone; another point is that the
relationship between the music-lover and librarian must be closer
than is customary because of the need to check each record individually on issue and return. Basic instruction in the technique of handling gramophone records should be given to as many assistants as
possible, under the supervision of the gramophone librarian and if it
can be arranged for each junior assistant to spend some time in the
department, again under supervision, it will provide useful training
and also help to indicate those assistants who may be usefully
seconded for duty with the collection when the need arises.

The final item to be considered in connection with maintenance
costs is that of record replacements. Figures vary widely between
libraries and this suggests a parallel with books; in some areas the
stock receives less careful use than in others, while librarians vary a
great deal in their judgement as to the deterioration that must be
accepted in a disc before it is considered unsuitable for further issue.
With SP records there seems to be fair agreement that a collection is
unlikely to exceed an average of some thirty loans per record, though
loud orchestral works and other heavily recorded items will wear
much more quickly than this. LPs last longer because of the different
material used in their manufacture (which is much less abrasive than
shellac) and because the lightweight pick-up necessary for playing
bears less heavily on the grooves. Estimates as to the average potential life vary from fifty to eighty loans per record. Questions to users
of the collection at Coventry indicated that the average user played a
disc between two and three times before returning it to the library; if
this figure is valid elsewhere then it suggests that a record will
achieve some 120 to 200 playings before withdrawal. This is low
compared with the figure that one would expect from records in a
personal collection, but less careful handling and use on a variety of
machines reduces the potential life of a library copy of a recording.
This average figure will prove utterly wrong when applied to records
used for assistance in learning a foreign language. Here, understandably enough, the borrower is likely to play the record as often
as possible while he has it, and the number of individual loans from
the library before withdrawal is not likely to average more than
twenty-five to thirty. Another point to be mentioned here is that long
works (operas particularly) which run to more than one LP disc are

more likely to last longer in manual than in automatic couplings when a company issues the same recording in both versions. When automatic couplings are used, one disc drops on top of the preceding one when used with an automatic record-changer and if the mechanism of the latter is at all out of adjustment damage to the grooves of the record is likely; with manual couplings the user normally removes each record after its two sides have been played. Leeds Public Library includes in its regulations one that prohibits the use of automatic record-changers and the rule may be a useful deterrent even though it is probably unenforceable. The combined causes of wear and deterioration are likely to result in an average withdrawal of some 20 per cent of the stock each year and this allowance for replacement should be made.

Two other useful, though not essential, items might be considered in this brief survey of cost; the first is a gramophone and the second the provision of record-carrying cases for the use of the borrowing public. The library's own reproducer can be used for trying over new records, for testing those returned by patrons when damage is suspected, for checking upon the general condition of a record when it has been borrowed enough times to make its withdrawal likely, and for use in the provision of gramophone record recitals within the library. A fairly cheap and compact machine may do for the first three tasks but if the last-mentioned possibility is carried out then a really good high-fidelity record reproducer is necessary since many of the potential listeners will be used to good-quality reproduction and the library should show the remainder of the audience, by example, what can be achieved by a good recording played on a high-class machine. Library recitals have a successful history in many places; the lunch-hour concerts given at Holborn are an outstanding example. Some American libraries have tried the experiment of relaying concerts throughout much of the building but too many non-musical people have objected for the experiment to be more than a qualified success. The possibility has been canvassed of a gramophone record recital running during the library's hours of opening, to be heard through earphones located at selected points in the building. This would allow music-lovers to have their fill of music without causing annoyance to others using the library. Many large American libraries provide first-class concerts of gramophone records; those given in New York[6] and Cincinnati are regarded as models of their kind. If concerts are given then, as has been suggested earlier in this paragraph, high-class equipment must be regarded as a necessity. A radio-gramophone is not likely to be satisfactory; librarians tempted by its apparent economy in performing two different though related tasks are referred to almost any textbook on high-fidelity sound reproduction for information upon this point. It is generally agreed that the loudspeaker should not be housed in the same cabinet as the amplifier.

A number of public libraries provide record-carrying cases for use by the borrowing public. Records may well receive damage during the journey from the library to the user's home or on the return trip; an unprotected sleeve will suffer badly in wet weather. The simplest and cheapest protection is a brown-paper carrier bag similar to those provided by gramophone record shops. The life of this protection is likely to be short, particularly in wet or windy weather. Although the first cost is much greater, a high degree of protection is given by the use of specially made boxes of cardboard or fibreboard with corrugated paper used as packing within the box to reduce possible movement. Some American libraries use canvas, cloth or plastic bags but the capital cost of an adequate supply is high. A polythene bag, with corrugated card sheets inserted on each side to cushion the record(s) might well be an inexpensive and long-lasting answer to this problem. Where records have to be sent through the post, as is common in county libraries, extra stoutness is required. West Sussex County Library, for instance, uses vulcanized fibre boxes with full-depth lids. Cross-pieces of fibre are inserted in both lid and box to act as springs and prevent damage. These are excellent containers but necessarily expensive. Prices in 1952 were 10s. 9d. for a box suitable for 12-in. records and 1½ in. deep, and 14s. 3d. for a similar box but 3 in. in height. Current prices are likely to be appreciably higher.

It has already been explained that few figures are quoted in this section because needs and conditions vary so much between one library and another. The size of the opening stock, the style of shelving provided, the type of catalogue or indicator—these and other factors cause immense variation in estimated initial outlay for libraries serving comparable areas and population. Helpful information can always be obtained from the Library Association's Librarian & Information Officer as well as from other librarians who provide this particular service for the public. The only general rules are to provide the best possible—in music, staff and furniture; to have as large an opening stock as can be achieved, since it can never be too large or varied, and third (perhaps most important of all) to defer or abandon any thought of providing this service in a library that has not got a good book fund or is not providing a better-than-average service to its readers, and to realize that a gramophone record library that is expected to run on the proverbial shoe-string is highly unlikely to become a source of pride and satisfaction to either the librarian or the local public.

Rental collections

The rental collection is a common feature of the American scene. Discs are loaned for a stated period upon payment of a fee, and the monies from such transactions are devoted to the purchase of more new records for the collection. In some cases the library also maintains a "free" section, and discs from the rental collection may be transferred after a certain period; in others, such as Minneapolis, rental collection records are available for playing in the library (if on the shelves) providing that they have been in stock for more than six months but none of these discs is ever made available for home listening without charge. When rental collections are maintained it is a frequent corollary that patrons shall be allowed to vote for future accessions to the collection, the items receiving most votes being bought with the funds available. With libraries that maintain both rental and free collections it is not surprising to learn that the latter receive more use ([2] p. 75), although "The length of time the collection has been established, the size of the collection, or the number of discs which may be charged out at one time appear to have little effect on the circulation the collection gets. Other features, such as the location of the collection, interest and ability of the department's staff, the effectiveness of the library's publicity, may be more important."

Theoretically, rental collections are of academic interest only to British librarians but in fact, as has been mentioned, at least two libraries run their gramophone record collections on these lines. In one, the fee is 6d. for each LP disc for a loan not exceeding one week, plus a fine of 2d. for each day beyond that period (unless the loan is renewed). SP discs are lent at 1d. each for a week (though only major works are included in the collection so that the minimum charge is 3d. and many works will cost more to borrow), while language-teaching records are rented at 1s. for a week's loan because of the greater use they receive during the average loan. Fines and fees for 1956–7 amounted to just over £1,500 from an issue of 38,750 records and all of this money, together with an annual allowance from the local Council, was spent on records. In the second library the rental fee is higher at 1s. per disc per week though users have the option of purchasing a "season ticket" for £2; this is valid for twelve months and allows its possessor to change a single disc or work as frequently as desired without extra charge. Non-residents are charged, in addition, a subscription of 15s. a year. These charges may be thought to be high but are still appreciably less than the sum required to borrow and return the same number of records from a commercial lending library. Both public libraries claim busy and successful gramophone record libraries with a clientèle that is apparently quite prepared to pay a fair sum for this particular pleasure. It could even be argued that since payment is made according to the use made of the collection by an individual this is the fairest method and that the service is the more appreciated because it is not provided entirely from the local rates. On the other hand, there are a number of British librarians who feel that to charge for records is a retrograde step and that this part of our service should be as freely available as book borrowing.

Selection

Selection of the basic stock presents a difficult task. The problems to be faced involve the musical level of the collection, the proportions of the different types of music and the choice between alternative versions of a selected work. The choice should be made by the Music Librarian though the chief officer must accept final responsibility and may well lay down certain general rules for the guidance of his subordinate. Suggestions may be received from local gramophone societies, music teachers, etc., but these (useful as they may be) should not be allowed to upset the general proportions of the collection. There is probably good sense in keeping a small proportion of the money allocated for records in reserve to strengthen representation where demand proves heavier than expected, or to buy particular recordings in response to requests. A typical analysis has already been given on page 221. Selection can be made within predetermined limits by popular appeal. One American library ran a series of ballots in the local newspaper, listing a total of eighty-two works and ordering the fifty that received most votes. This may well have been most effective publicity, but it may also be considered to be an expensive method of selecting fifty records, particularly as the selection was for the opening stock and the series of advertisements should have resulted in an initial enrolment of many more than fifty would-be users. Westminster made a somewhat similar experiment with a rather different purpose. Balloting was held for the two most-desired items in a list of some half-dozen rather recondite complete operas. This scheme was apparently aimed at those users for whom the normal repertory is insufficiently wide, and allowed the librarian to gain some idea of the potential demand for each work and to stimulate interest in the collection as a whole.

A study of the gramophone catalogues issued by some of our public libraries will show that standards of selection are fairly generally agreed at a high musical level. These lists will also provide the questing librarian with a check on the opening stocks of these libraries, while supplements (where issued) will indicate if particular attention has had to be paid to certain sections of the collection. Selection of the basic stock can be simplified by the use of two valuable aids. The first is *The record guide* (and its supplements) which indicates which version of a work is that recommended by its knowledgeable compilers and draws attention to outstanding performances and recordings by means of a starring system. The other is *Record ratings* where each record has appended brief details of where reviews can be found plus a symbol indicating whether the review was favourable or not, or whether it tended to be somewhat noncommittal. Fuller details of these most admirable guides will be found in Chapter II. It must be remembered, however, that neither of these works can hope to be really up to date so that files of *The gramophone* and similar reviews must be checked for later performances; supplements to *Record ratings* appear in each number of the periodical *Notes*. There are other guides; one well-known gramophone shop in London issues a handbook with its recommended selection of the best recordings; selection is limited to much the same range that a public library is likely to cover. One of the commercial lending libraries of gramophone records issues a similar list; the firm goes much beyond this in that it offers to supply the entire collection and in return to provide some basic training free of charge for the assistants who will be administering the library collection. It is highly unlikely that these various sources will agree upon the "best" recording of more than a handful of works but they may give useful warning, by implication, of versions to avoid.

Gramophone Record Libraries

Once the basic stock is chosen current releases present much less of a problem, since this is a matter of keeping abreast of the various reviews of new records. Some criticisms will be too brief or be published months after the librarian has made his decision upon a particular recording, but the periodicals listed in Chapter II deal adequately in most cases with gramophone records; some consider very few where others review nearly all new classical issues but all have their use. Record reviews have much in common with book reviews in that some are mutually contradictory; a few are much more interested in the technical aspects of the records at the expense of the music or the performance. This should be taken into account in selection for there is a minority of users in every library who are interested primarily in the frequency range demonstrated by a new issue, in the orchestral balance achieved by the recording engineers, in the fidelity with which a triangle or a trombone has been caught by the microphone, etc., and only secondarily in the work played or its interpretation. Though this type of user may be regarded on occasion as a minor nuisance it is only proper that, in cases where two recordings provide equally satisfactory versions of the same piece of music, preference should be given to the recording that is the more adequate from the technician's viewpoint.

Record "clubs", on the lines of book clubs, have been a familiar part of the American scene for some years and there are now at least three which operate in Britain. There are similarities between book and record clubs for both provide works likely to be in popular demand at a price appreciably below normal and in a sleeve that is adequate but not nearly as attractive as ordinary commercial issues. Both performances and recordings are usually acceptable but rarely equal to the best available. In a few cases the record clubs have produced works that are not otherwise available, so that librarians will find it useful to keep in touch with these clubs and buy some of the issues, both of rarities and popular works in heavy demand. A difficulty is that these issues are rarely reviewed in newspapers or periodicals and so have to be bought on trust. The growth of these clubs seems to have stimulated the Decca Record Company to initiate an "Ace of Clubs" series in the spring of 1958. These discs, at nearly half normal prices, are reissues of older recordings (some originally on SP discs) and are limited to popular classics. This represents the first British "cheap edition"; one hopes the habit spreads.

Music Librarianship

Accession

Records will be ordered in the normal manner, generally from a local dealer or dealers. It is useful, however, to include a specialist London firm among a library's suppliers since such dealers can often provide an urgently required record by return of post and can also obtain special or unusual discs with the minimum difficulty and delay. It is good practice to require that all discs supplied to the library shall be "factory fresh". Not only does this avoid the record that may have been in stock for weeks or months in the gramophone shop and may have been played over several times, but it also means that when a recording has been re-engineered and its quality improved (though the original tape is still used), the library will receive such a version.

On receipt of a disc, it should be carefully examined for flaws. It will not be possible to play through all accessions, but any with scratches or pinholes or other blemishes should certainly be tried. At least one British library has installed a "Parastat", a machine which frees the disc from static electricity (which attracts dust to the grooves) and gives it a reasonable degree of immunity through many playings.

Accessioning may be carried out as with books, though libraries using a combination of catalogue and indicator may use the part of the card not normally visible for the inclusion of accession details and so make one card serve three purposes. Many libraries do not use their own accession numbers but use the manufacturer's catalogue number instead, with the suffix "A", "B", etc., in cases of duplication of discs. Difficulties may arise when records are withdrawn by one manufacturer and later reissued by another as has happened with many records originally issued in Britain by Columbia, withdrawn and then subsequently reissued by Phillips with entirely different numbers.

Catalogue numbers used to be fairly simple in SP days since manufacturers normally used a single or double letter prefix and the numerical sequence started at the number "1" and worked its way upwards over the years to numbers such as DB 4420 and K 1771. With LP discs manufacturers apparently decided that a prefix of three or four letters was required plus a four, five or six figure number. New sequences rarely start at the number 1 but with a minimum of four figures, though there is no apparent reason for this. Perhaps as a precaution against mistakes when ordering discs, the companies often arrange that numbers do not overlap but that a different sequence is used for each size and price, so that an order with a slightly incorrect prefix but the right numerical suffix might well still produce the desired record. Makers are not always consistent on this point, however. One might instance the English issue of Decca: 12-in. classical discs were numbered from LXT 2500 onwards and the 10-in. equivalent from LX 3000 upwards. The cheaper red-label category began the 12-in. sequence at 4000 and the 10-in. from LM 4500. Records of overseas companies for whom Decca acted as British agents were allotted different numbers again. Capitol discs began their 12- and 10-in. sequences at CTL 7000 and CCL 7500, and the same method was continued with six-figure numbers for Telefunken and Ducretet-Thomson, etc. It will be noted that all 12-in. issues included the letters "L" and "T" in the prefix with the exception of the cheaper LM category. When the LXT series reached LXT 2999 a fresh sequence was started at LXT 5000. All of this is a consistent scheme, yet when the firm introduced its "medium-play" records they were given the prefix LW but numbered from 5000 upwards and thus duplicated the second LXT allotment.

Libraries that give their own accession numbers to records may find it a good policy to follow manufacturers and make different sequences for the different record sizes; this is useful for shelving purposes as it is best to put all 12-in. records together, all 10-in. and all 7-in. Such a plan also assists identification of a record by its number. The process may be carried a stage further with the accession number providing an approximate indication of the type of record by relating accession number to classification. Details of this method are given in the following section on classification.

When records arrive from the supplier they need to be checked against order and invoice and then examined carefully for possible flaws or damage. Even "factory-fresh" specimens may be imperfect. The library's possession of a record player is useful in this connection as doubtful sections can be played over, and if every disc has the first few grooves played the occasional "swinger" can be discovered at once. A "swinger" is a record that is incorrectly pressed so that the grooves do not centre on the spindle hole; the pick-up wavers from side to side as the record plays and the tone wavers with it. With a long-playing record even a very small error can produce distressing results. There must be a limit to the time spent on checking and it will be generally agreed that the American library that has the cataloguer play through each and every record, following the score to discover any cuts in performance and listening carefully for any imperfections in the record, is taking the matter much too seriously.

There are two general methods in use to indicate library ownership. The first is to paste a piece of paper with the library's name on the record and the second is to use an electric stylus. With SP records it was simple to have printed semicircular labels with the library's name and perhaps leaving room for accession number, etc. Because of the increased amount of music on an LP side it has been found necessary by some manufacturers to use much more of the label to give details of the contents of a side and of the performers and to reduce the space used for the trade name and design accordingly. In order to avoid covering any of this information libraries usually now have small gummed slips about an inch long and half as wide which will paste over the trade name on the record; this is not likely to cause any difficulty in identification. When an electric stylus is used the identification mark will be written in black or white according to the colour of the record label and the library's initials and possibly the accession number of the record can be easily marked. The information can be incised on any convenient part of the label; it will usually be somewhat less neat and uniform than an adhesive label though possibly less easy to remove. Library initials should be enough, partly as an economy and because ownership will also be shown, in all probability, somewhere on the record sleeve. A lost disc initialled "B.P.L." is likely to be returned to its owning library, be it Battersea, Bebington or Burnley and not sent to the wrong one.

Classification

Where the library is so organized that members of the public do not handle the records on the shelves there is little apparent need for classification of the stock; arrangement by the accession number or maker's catalogue number will be adequate for the assistant in charge to extract the correct disc on request. Shelf arrangement in sequences of manufacturers' numbers is the normal practice of shops that sell gramophone records and even the British Broadcasting Corporation with its immense collection finds this method the most satisfactory— so that smaller libraries should have no difficulty in making such a system work.

Neither of these numerical arrangements is likely to be satisfactory when the collection is open to users. Various methods of classification are possible. One may use the scheme already adopted for music, with a prefix such as "P" or "G" to indicate a disc. This method was advocated more than twenty years ago by Dorothy G. Amesbury (in the *Library Journal* for 1st June 1937) on the sensible grounds that a library user already familiar with the music library would quickly adjust himself to the problem of finding gramophone records of a particular type of music. A slightly earlier article in the same periodical (15th February 1937) by Ethel Louise Lyman recommended a form of alphabetico-class arrangement, mainly mnemonic. This scheme began with CS (Choral works, sacred), CSe (Choral works, secular), and so on through Flute (F), Masses (M), Organ (ORG), piano trios (P.3), string quartets (S.4), to Historical sets (X), Anonymous works (Z) and Folk songs (ZF). Such a scheme has obvious limitations (Masses, for example, are also sacred choral works) but should be easy both to apply and understand with most records in a collection. A third method of classification, used with a large collection, was the arrangement of material in broad groups by means of accession numbers. The numbers 10,000 to 19,999, for example, were allotted to single SP records (i.e. brief works that were accommodated on not more than one disc) and this block was sub-divided into different types: 10,000 to 11,999 for historical recordings; 15,000 to 15,999 for folk music; 18,000 to 18,999 for children's records, etc. Within each group the earlier numbers were given to 10-in. records and the later ones to 12-in. This scheme has its attractions but the difficulty was that some sequences were completed long before others, so that secondary sequences had to be used in some cases. A modification, which does not classify but separates sizes and speeds, is in use at Detroit. A 12-in. LP might be numbered 332–1234 (the prefix indicating first the speed and then the size, with the actual accession number after the dash), a 10-in. 330–5678 and a 7-in. disc 457–001.

A fourth method is that adopted at Coventry where a single sequence under composer is used for all 12-in. records with a second sequence for 10-in. discs and a third sequence for non-musical works. This brings the works of a composer, in most cases, into one of two places and the method is simple to grasp and administer. Where more than one composer's name is shown on the record sleeve (e.g. where a disc contains a work by Brahms on one side and a composition by Schumann on the other) the disc can be filed either under the name of the composer who appears first on the sleeve or else under the one whose name is first alphabetically. The former is perhaps the simpler, the latter the more consistent. The catalogue entry, however, must make it clear that the work by the second (or third) composer will not be found in its apparently correct place but instead is with the works of another composer. Such a method, rough and ready as it may appear, brings together nearly all the works of each composer, avoids any problems of classification (such as those between "grand" and "light" opera) and should be generally understood. With "recital records", arrangement will be under the name of the artist, conductor, person or group that has made the batch of recordings. If records are shelved so that only the fore-edge is showing it is good policy to stick a strip of coloured paper at a set distance from the top or bottom of the sleeve to indicate the genre of the disc—thus opera might have a red slip, symphonies a blue one, etc. Such a guide to the type of music would still be useful when the record was visible face on, where this type of shelving is in use.

Wohlford[1] mentions eight common methods of filing which have been adopted in various American libraries. The first is alphabetical arrangement by composer; the second is by record number; the third choice is by accession number allotted by the library; the fourth arrangement is by Cutter number for the composer; the fifth is also by Cutter number plus the Dewey class number to allow sub-division of the works of a single composer; sixth is classified arrangement by Dewey Decimal classification, and seventh a classified arrangement used by the Library of Congress music scheme. The eighth and last arrangement is that according to a classification scheme produced by Philip L. Miller of the New York Public Library, the man generally regarded as the doyen of American record librarians. The first, fourth and fifth arrangements are all basically by composer, the second and third methods by an arbitrary number and the last three by actual classification.

Cataloguing

On no single matter does British and American practice diverge so sharply as on this point; while a considerable amount of transatlantic method has been adopted in England the detailed entry with its many secondary cards for performers, analyticals, etc., has been ignored in favour of brief entries under composers only. The lengthy section that follows devotes considerable space to full cataloguing, even though a British librarian may decide, having read it through, that his own method is justified by its economies.

Gramophone records present many parallels with music scores but have a number of distinguishing features that necessitate special cataloguing rules. The entry may be divided into the usual four divisions of composer, title, imprint and collation. The title may be that shown upon the record itself or it may be one that the cataloguer has had to supply (a similar situation to that which is not infrequent with sheet music). Imprint, with books, consists of place of publication, name of publisher and the date. Place of publication presents no real difficulty with records but is not likely to be required except with obscure or oversea firms. The publisher is probably best shown by use of the name on the record label rather than the actual name of the firm, though the two may well coincide. The date of issue is never shown on the record, and though it can often be found with little difficulty it rarely has much value. It will, of course, give the reader an idea of how old the recording is, or perhaps one had better say, how new; the disc may have been issued in one country for months or years before it is released in another. In the latter place the date of issue will perhaps mislead. Some discs give the date of recording, particularly with a special occasion (though D.G.G. "Archive" discs always include this date on the information card presented with each record), and this may be worth adding in a note. Rather than quote the date of issue, the cataloguer is more likely to quote the manufacturer's catalogue number. Though there are many exceptions it is fairly general practice to issue records in fairly regular numerical sequences so that the catalogue number will often indicate a comparative date of issue so far as each particular record "brand" is concerned. Since collation describes the physical format of a book, it has a similar function with a record but instead of listing pagination, illustrations, etc., it includes such items as the diameter of the record, its playing speed, the number of sides allotted to the work and the fact as to whether it is microgroove.

The Music Library Association issued a *Code for cataloging phonograph records* in 1942. It was, according to the preface, "designed as an integral part of the larger 'Code for cataloging music' " and consisted of four introductory pages and twenty-eight pages of text. The work was divided into four parts. First was a section on cataloguing itself; second, comments on special types of phonograph (gramophone) records; third, suggestions for filing and shelving, while the last part quoted sample entries. This code appears to have been the starting point for the Library of Congress rule number 9a, "Phonorecords", which appeared in a preliminary edition in 1952 and which contains the L.C. rules for discs, cylinders, wire and tape-recordings, player-piano rolls, etc. This single, though much sub-divided rule, reappeared almost unaltered in the second edition of the A.L.A. and M.L.A. *Code for cataloging music and phonorecords* in 1958. Both the earlier and later versions are described in some detail below, the former because it allows for further comment upon some of the problems facing the gramophone record cataloguer while the latter gives a better arrangement of items and shows something of the value of a preliminary edition which is amended later in accordance with the ideas of people who have been putting the trial version to the test of everyday use.

The first section of the M.L.A. 1942 Code is divided into two parts: the first deals with sources of information and the second lists the items to be included in a catalogue entry. The three suggested sources are the record label, reviews of the record(s) and special record bibliographies. With SP discs the label identification was often fantastically vague—"Gavotte, by Bach" or some equally unhelpful title was quite commonplace. The situation has improved immensely with LP discs, possibly because the back of the covering sleeve is normally used to give details of the music. Even so, record companies are still far from perfect in this matter. Where a gramophone company omits information or even gives wrong details the mistake is often indicated by a record reviewer particularly when he is a specialist on that particular composer, period or instrument. If reviewers fail to notice the error it may well be corrected in *The world encyclopaedia of recorded music* where some minor miracles of identification have appeared. *W.E.R.M.*, however, can only be of value in this connection if the actual recording is of sufficient age to appear in one or other of its volumes.

The M.L.A. suggested order of entry under composer was as follows: (1) the conventional title, i.e. the form of title under which all versions and extracts of a work will be filed, whatever the language of the record label. The use of a "conventional title" has been discussed in the earlier chapter on cataloguing. (2) The actual title as it appears on the record label, the record sleeve or on the album in which the record is contained or on the title-page of any analytical notes which may be issued with the work. After the title is added (where necessary) a note as to the form of genus of the music, e.g. Symphony, Song for tenor, etc. (3) Imprint, which comprises the place of publication (useful mainly with imported discs in Britain, but of wider application in the U.S.A. where there are many minor recording companies in different parts of that vast country), the producer, i.e. the name on the label ("Parlophone" rather than "Electrical & Musical Industries"). British cataloguers would normally treat discs actually issued in Britain under the label name, which may be that of the original ("Supraphon", "Telefunken", etc.), or of the English agents ("Westminster" and "Bach Guild" issued in Britain with the "Nixa" label). Place of publication may be useful for records which have to be specially imported and which are not usually available from gramophone shops, e.g. the Chinese records imported into Britain by Collet's. The final items of the collation are date of issue and date of recording (though the code suggests that it is not worth taking too much trouble to discover either date), the catalogue number(s) of the record(s) allotted by the manufacturer and the matrix numbers. These last are the equivalent of an identity number and are quite independent of the catalogue number. The matrix number is engraved on the record in the space between the label and the inner grooves of the recording; this same number is usually repeated in small type somewhere on the record label itself. With SP discs the matrix number was often valuable. In many cases it indicated the country or place where the work was recorded (H.M.V. discs recorded in their London studios were numbered in a single sequence with the prefix "OEA" or "2EA"; the former was for 10-in. discs, the latter for 12-in. Recordings in Vienna by this company had the prefix "VH", in Scandinavia "CS" and so on) and usually the matrix number consisted of a prefix followed by a number, as in the examples quoted. In certain cases the matrix number was followed by the number of the "take", i.e. it indicated the number of attempts required before a satisfactory recording was achieved; this was usually once or twice, but I have found numbers as high as eight and even higher figures may well be in existence. As with the publishers' plate numbers on sheet music so the matrix number was an excellent method of finding a relative date for a recording. Incidentally, it sometimes made nonsense of a reviewer's comment that "Madame X was in much better voice than last month" when the matrix numbers would clearly indicate that the two discs were made at the same recording session.

This quite useful aid has lost most of its value since with LP discs the number is simply that of the completed side which may well contain items recorded at different times and even in different places; there is no indication of the number of attempts required before the side was recorded to the mutual satisfaction of both artist and manufacturer simply because the whole technique of recording has altered with LP discs. In the old days, a complete side of three to four minutes had to be made at a time; now much longer periods are possible since the recording is made on tape. Where a few bars are unsatisfactory, the defective portion can be performed afresh and re-recorded and the new piece spliced into the original tape to replace the excised section. For various reasons the conductor or artist may still prefer to record in brief spells, relying upon the technician and splicer to join the sections together into a coherent whole. Normally these tape joins are quite indistinguishable but occasionally a difference in recording level, of tape hum or (quite inexcusably) a slight variation in the actual pitch of the notes makes the join obvious. What the buyer often gets, in fact, is not a recording of a single performance but a synthesis of the best parts of two or three recordings. There is, therefore, little excuse today for a record that contains wrong notes or bad intonation.

The album or set number of a lengthy work may be regarded as the gramophone record equivalent of a series note and in Britain is peculiar to SP discs; thus Brahms's second piano concerto played by Artur Schnabel with the L.P.O. conducted by [Sir] Adrian Boult was contained in H.M.V. "Album 245" and bore this number in gold lettering at the base of the album's spine. Comparatively few LP works require albums—the need is usually restricted to complete operas—and the companies have not found any need to allot numbers to these, it would appear. After the set number the M.L.A. Code suggested that the number of sides and the size of the disc(s) should be quoted; this is a useful place in which to add the playing speed of the record. That item of information was not necessary in 1942 since all commercial discs were then of the 78 r.p.m. type. The next item, "Method of recording", is likely to require mention only for the items that are acoustically recorded, i.e. those made before the introduction of electric recording around 1924 or 1925. Some American libraries also have "instantaneous recordings", which are similar to tape-recordings in that they can be played back at once. "Medium of performance" quotes both the actual instrument(s) used in the recording and, if different, the instrumentation for which the work was originally written, e.g. "Fauré - Dolly, op. 56; for orchestra. Originally written for piano duet, and orchestrated by Henri Rabaud." This item is followed by the name or names of performer(s), the language of the text if a vocal work and the author of the words. The provision of an analytical booklet or album of descriptive notes is mentioned and this in turn is followed by a note of any cuts (i.e. omissions) in the recording. This information is usually obtained from a reviewer's criticism; it has already been suggested in this chapter that to listen to every new disc, following the performance with a score, is time consuming and expensive though it may provide considerable enjoyment to the members of the staff detailed for the task.

The Code's next item is "Complete identification" for such works as ballets compiled by one man from the music of another or for a work such as Tchaikovsky's *Swan Lake* ballet which is rarely recorded in full and in which different recordings select different excerpts. This information may be contained in reviews or, for older recordings, in *W.E.R.M.* Cataloguers should always check this source since a "new" recording may have appeared some time previously in another country. The M.L.A's specimen entry continued with a contents note together with a statement as to other works recorded on the same disc or employed as a "fill-up" on the last side of an album set. Where a work took, for example, seven sides to record it was common practice to use the eighth for a short work or excerpt, generally by the same composer and normally by the same artists; a blank side was apparently not popular with the manufacturers. With LP discs, the spare side on a similar recording may well be utilized for the recording of a major work. An obvious example is provided by recordings of Beethoven's ninth symphony which require three sides; the fourth may well contain the first or eighth symphony complete.

This completes the sequence of details listed in the M.L.A. Code, though the work also contained suggestions, based on Dr. Harold Spivacke's article, "The cataloging of folk-song records" in *Notes* for November, 1937, for dealing with this type of material.

The Library of Congress rule (and the 1958 M.L.A. revision) amends this somewhat erratic order. Briefly, the L.C. sequence is as follows: (1) Composer; (2) Conventional title, to which is added a descriptive word to show that the entry refers to a recording and not to a music score. For gramophone records the word added is "Phono-disc", and this allows entries for books, scores and records to be filed in a single sequence with the possibility of confusion between them reduced to a minimum. (3) The transcription of the title is taken from the record itself or the containing sleeve. (4) Imprint is limited to the trade name of the publisher, serial identification (i.e. record number plus album number, if any) and date of release of the record to the public by the manufacturer. The recording date is given only when provided on the disc or its sleeve. (5) Collation for records notes the number of albums (if more than one), the number of sides (including fractions of a side) and notes that a single-sided record is counted as one side. The diameter of the record and its playing speed are then quoted. (6) Notes include the name of the performer and the medium, the edition used in the recording (if easily discovered), details concerning performance, the duration of the work, contents and a reference to other works on the same disc that have received separate entry.

These meticulous rules raise the problem of how much detail is required in a gramophone record catalogue. Mary Wohlford[1] quotes what would appear to be an extreme case of full cataloguing. Fort Wayne, Indiana, has a population of about 140,000 people and required six extra staff—three full-time professional cataloguers, one sub-professional and two clerical employees for its gramophone record collection. The reasons can be found in an article in the *Library Journal* for 15th March 1949 (p. 428 et seq.). It is obvious that many American librarians are perturbed at the amount of detail involved in full cataloguing and the staff time expended. "Several people mentioned that the life of a record is fairly short, and that therefore detailed cataloguing is a waste of time and money in a heavily used collection."[5] This is emphatically the view of British librarians, since almost all have restricted cataloguing in their collections to a brief composer entry and ignored all added entries except for discs that contain two works by different composers. Though this may be regarded as being below the mini-mum that readers would expect, it seems in fact to have been found reasonably adequate for most enquiries providing that other guides, particularly the *Gramophone Long-playing classical record catalogue*, are at hand to answer enquiries for recordings by particular artists, etc.

However brief the main entry, it should always contain the opus number of the work recorded or the thematic catalogue number (which is its equivalent) in the case of Bach, Mozart, Domenico Scarlatti, Schubert, Vivaldi, etc. This is a most useful safeguard against the unintentional duplication of works with rather vague titles (Fugue in F, Sonata in C minor). Although some of the items listed in the M.L.A. and L.C. rules may be regarded as unnecessary, there is much to be said for making the main entry as full as possible, particularly if it is the only entry. Libraries using a visible index as a combined accession register, catalogue and indicator can usually find space on the card, above that strip which is immediately visible, for a fairly full entry which would supplement the "finding title" that is all that can be shown on the small space which is normally visible. If the card above is lifted, the interested user can then find fuller details of the record. If full cataloguing to a greater or lesser degree is to be carried out, there is much in favour of a card or sheaf catalogue which can include entries for artists, musical forms, etc., which cannot be shown on an indicator. There is also a fairly strong case for the production of a printed or duplicated catalogue in which fuller information could be provided than is normally visible on the index entry. Music-lovers would be able to decide at leisure which records they wish to borrow and would use the visible index purely as an indicator and ignore its secondary function as a catalogue; one patron consulting the detailed entry on the body of the card must automatically obstruct the use of many other cards while he is making his search.

Where all added entries are omitted information must be found, as suggested in a previous paragraph, from various other sources. The quarterly catalogue published by *The Gramophone* has already been suggested as an invaluable guide to discovering the recordings made by an individual artist (and will also show when a particular record was reviewed in *The Gramophone*) but omits any records which have been deleted from the manufacturers' catalogues, some of which may still be in the library's stock. Printed guides (the *One-spot guide* in the U.S.A., *The Gramophone's* quarterly catalogue and *The Record guide* and similar works in Britain) are often extremely useful in tracing a single work in a recorded anthology where the library has failed to make analytical entries. Limited cataloguing of this type provides very real economies but at the expense of the borrower who is primarily interested in recordings of piano concertos or of works conducted by Karajan, etc.

Added entries can be brief and simple and need consume little time in preparation. Form entries, in particular, can be very brief, e.g. under the general heading "Symphonies" all important information would be conveyed by "SCHUBERT—no. 2; Boston S.O. (Munch)" followed by the manufacturer's or library's catalogue number. If this is still thought to take too much time then the card or sheaf could bear the heading "SYMPHONIES" followed by the composer's name and a stereotyped form of entry, or even a rubber stamp, with such words as "For recorded works in this form, consult the composer's name in this [or the composer] catalogue". The enquirer interested in the history and development of the symphony or in symphonic recordings would then look under the composer's name to discover which of his symphonies were in stock and in which recordings, etc. Added entries for executants would appear to be justified on at least two grounds. First, two performances of the same work may vary considerably in tempi, dynamics and outlook. One has only to compare (on SP discs) the last movement of Mozart's popular *Eine kleine Nachtmusik* played by orchestras conducted by Sir Thomas Beecham and Bruno Walter to find two utterly different accounts of the same music. Secondly, there are many occasions when a work is recorded at the request of the artist rather than at the desire of the recording company to have what is possibly a second or third version of a work in their catalogue; this is one reason for the multiplicity of recordings of certain hackneyed works. Another major reason is apparently that many people will buy the latest recording irrespective of its merits, though that point is only partly relevant here. Thirdly, the name of the performer is often the simplest and most easily remembered method of differentiating between versions of the same work, particularly when issued by the same company. Title entries have obvious value for operas, cantatas and other vocal works, symphonic poems and nicknamed orchestral works and the like; this is particularly true since titles are not indexed in a separate sequence in *W.E.R.M.* or the other gramophone record guides.

Whether printed, duplicated, typewritten or in manuscript, entries in the catalogue should be so laid out that the performer's name is easily visible as in the Detroit examples quoted later in this section. The name should be followed by a word or abbreviation, preferably in brackets, to indicate the type of voice or instrument, e.g. (tenor), (flute) or standard abbreviations of such terms; the name of the instrument is generally preferable to the longer though perhaps more accurate form (flutist) or (flautist). To avoid possible confusion between the name of the soloist(s) and that of the conductor in works with orchestra it is suggested that individual performers be named before the orchestra and the conductor afterwards, and that the conductor's name should still be listed after that of the orchestra for music without soloists. Thus, to use the set quoted earlier of a numbered album, the Brahms concerto would be shown, in its shortest form, "Schnabel (pf), L.P.O. (Boult)". A symphony would simply require an entry as "Hallé O. (Barbirolli)". Main entries would normally expand to include Christian names though the standard abbreviations of orchestras could well be retained for all entries. There are two further points which arise from this method of entry. First, despite the precedence given in this form to the orchestra over the conductor, I would still prefer added entry to be made under the latter's name rather than that of the orchestra. While not, perhaps, usual practice, it can be justified on two grounds: (a) that it is almost invariably the conductor's reading of a work that constitutes the vital difference between versions and (b) because the orchestra's name does not always appear on records or may appear in pseudonymous form for reasons of contract. It would seem that conductors invariably record under their own names. The second point concerns abbreviations of orchestral names. Some are, musically speaking, common currency in this country, e.g. L.P.O., L.S.O., R.P.O., B.B.C.S.O. For overseas orchestras such initials as N.Y.P.S.O. or V.P.O. are equally acceptable but to use "Phil.O", "P.O." or "Phil.Orc." is bad, since the abbreviation might refer to either the Philadelphia or Philharmonia Orchestras; both have made many recordings.

A printed or duplicated catalogue is prepared for the library user to take home and browse through at leisure so that he can note those recordings that he would like to borrow. Though out of date as soon as it is issued, unless the collection is unhappily static, the catalogue's value can be high; if it is well produced it should be an excellent advertisement for the library in general and the gramophone record collection in particular. Most catalogues are sold at a low price which usually covers only part of the cost of production. Since it can be read at home without haste, the argument can be made that a fairly full entry under composer is all that is required, other entries being dispensed with in order to keep the bulk of the catalogue as small as possible. Another method of reducing the length of entries is to indulge in abbreviations but, except for orchestras, these are ideally kept to a minimum. The space saved by printing "Conc. vn. & o." rather than "Concerto for violin and orchestra" can only really be justified for a very large collection such as that maintained at Westminster or Hendon, but their double-column entry is not attractive though it saves considerable bulk in the catalogue. The smaller collection should not have the same compulsion for highly abbreviated entries and the librarian should be prepared to list entries in a single column and to limit the number on a single page rather than crowd in the maximum possible. No better example of attractive layout for a medium-sized collection is likely to be found than that issued jointly by Lambeth and Finsbury in 1949. Composers' names were printed in 24-point Bembo, ignoring Christian names with the single exception of Johann and Richard Strauss. There was no sense of constriction in the individual entries. If printing is not considered possible for any reason, then duplicated catalogues (particularly if produced on the multilith machine) can be clear and attractive, providing, once again, that sufficient space is allowed for entries. The limitations of a typewriter are admittedly very real compared with the variety of type faces used in *The record guide*, where different playing speeds and record sizes are clearly distinguished typographically (and much more successfully than in the *World's Encyclopaedia of Recorded Music*), but good typewriting can produce perfectly adequate and attractively laid-out entries as the Lewisham catalogue of 1952 showed.

There is no British code available for the cataloguing of gramophone records, though a sub-committee was set up by the Library Association in 1944 to consider this matter. It held a number of meetings over a period of some eighteen months but its findings have never been published. This seems particularly unfortunate since it is understood that considerable progress was made in reaching agreed solutions to many of the really difficult problems that face the record cataloguer and the sub-committee contained some distinguished names. In the U.S.A. the Code formulated by the M.L.A. and the Library of Congress rule 9a appeared long after many public libraries had instituted rules for their own collections. One of the best individual codes is that of Detroit Public Library which codified its rules in preliminary form in 1951; these require just over five quarto pages of single-space typewriting. The first two paragraphs deserve quotation in full:

Gramophone Record Libraries

"In so far as is possible general *principles* of book cataloging are followed in the cataloging of phonograph records. Variations in card forms and entries are described in the following code.

"The catalog card carries the following items of information: Accession number; main entry; conventional title; transcribed title; issuing firm; album number; disc number; date of issue; number of sides; size of disc; series note; performer and language of text; type of recording; descriptive notes and booklet; cuts; contents; contents of other parts of a side, of the other side, or of remaining sides of an album."

This clearly suggests very full cataloguing and the remainder of the Code amplifies these points with the addition of rules for subject and added entries. But Detroit, in common with many other American libraries, is constantly attempting to simplify its procedures and to omit entries that are of doubtful value or which contain information easily found elsewhere. By 1957 no mention was made of descriptive notes (since practically all LP records carry them) nor of the contents of a disc if it contained more than ten items. Cuts are no longer indicated and certain of the added entries such as analytical entries (with certain exceptions) and "history cards" (mentioned below) are no longer provided. Cataloguing is no longer centralized and branch libraries make their own catalogue entries for gramophone records in accordance with their own estimates of local needs and this method, though perhaps unorthodox, appears to work quite efficiently. Entries are made for certain arrangers of music (if thought to be of sufficient importance) while the history card was used to show such things as the personnel of a string quartet with dates and details of changes as individuals drop out and are replaced, or to give details of the movements of Handel's *Water music* selected by Sir Hamilton Harty for his popular suite. Useful as these cards were, it was felt that they absorbed too much valuable time to compile and that such questions can usually be answered by reference to books.

The following card samples, including tracings, should help to make much of this part of the chapter clear and indicate something of the detail necessary if full cataloguing is to be attempted. It may be remarked that Detroit follows the Library of Congress rules for Russian transliteration where a British library would probably follow the spelling found in *Grove*; it should also be noted that series and other added entries are not made automatically but only for specified items. For example, the arranger only warrants an added entry when he has made a definite contribution to the particular work; one might cite Vincenzo Tommasini's arrangement of Scarlatti sonatas and fugues which provide the basis of the ballet *The good humoured ladies*. In an example quoted, Robert Russell Bennett is given separate entry since he orchestrates many Broadway shows, especially those of Cole Porter and Richard Rodgers, and his orchestral arrangements are generally considered superior to those of other arrangers of the same music.

Examples

MAIN ENTRY 332–2253 Rimskii-Korsakov, Nikolai Andreevich, 1844–1908
[Grande Pâque Russe. Overture]
Russian Easter Overture, Op. 36. Mercury MG 50028. [1954]
1s. 12″
Detroit Symphony Orchestra: Paul Paray, conductor.
Reverse side: Symphony, no. 2. Op. 9. "Antar".
1. Overtures: I, Detroit Symphony Orchestra. II, Paray, Paul, 1886–
III, Rimskii-Korsakov, N. Symphony, no. 2. Op. 9. "Antar".
x T. x T: (Russian) x Rimskii-Korsakov, N. Russian Easter Overture.

SUBJECT CARDS 332–2253 Overtures:
Rimskii-Korsakov, Nikolai Andreevich, 1844–1908 [Grande Pâque Russe. Overture]
Russian Easter Overture, Op. 36. Mercury MG 50028. [1954]
1s. 12″
Detroit Symphony Orchestra: Paul Paray, conductor.
Reverse side: Symphony, no. 2. Op. 9. "Antar".

258

332–2752 Verdi, Giuseppe, 1813–1901
         [Operas. Selections]
         Arias. Capitol P 8279. 1954.
         Robert Weede, baritone; Concert Arts Or-
         chestra; Nicholas Rescigno, conductor.
         Contents: *s.1.* Un ballo in maschera.
         Eri tu.—Falstaff. Ford's monologue—
         Il trovatore. Il balen—Rigoletto. Pari
         siamo; Cortigliani. *s.2.* Otello. Iago's
         credo—La traviata. Di Provenza.
         Don Carlo. Death of Rodrigo.
     1, Opera—Recordings. I, Weede,
        Robert, 1903– . II, Resciagno,
        Nicholas. III, Concerts Arts Orchestra.

Until the middle nineteen-fifties analytical entries would have been made for all the above excerpts; now such entries are limited to records which contain four or less separate titles. This means that such entries are usually for lengthy excerpts and not for brief arias. At the same time it was realized that this economy would make it difficult to trace short items that are in popular demand and which often appear in record collections and anthologies—works such as Debussy's *Clair de lune*, Rimsky-Korsakov's *Flight of the bumble bee*, etc. These are not normally listed separately in the various record guides to current releases. Similarly it was considered helpful to note works featuring less usual instruments and certain composers whose names appear in musical histories but rarely in performance. Finally the need for a title index for such popular songs as were in the library's collection and which may be regarded as "evergreens", and for folk tunes was also appreciated. As a result of these diverse needs, a Record Analytics File has been created in the Music & Drama Department and is maintained by that department. This is independent of the main catalogue created by the Catalog Department.

Three examples of different types of card found in this file should help to make its functions clear:

Bassoon:
330–0418 Vivaldi. Concerto in D minor for bassoon, string orches-
        tra and harpsichord   London LS 591
332–1536 Phillips, Burrill. Concert piece for bassoon and string
        orchestra   Columbia ML 4629

Dufay, Guillaume:
332–3070 Gloria in History of Music in Sound, Vol. 3
—71 Victor LM 6016
332–3597 Motets of the 15th & 16th centuries with Easter themes
(Welch Chorale) Lyrichord LL 52

    In the still of the night (from Rosalie—1937)
        (Porter)
332–3218 Cole Porter songs (Carlyle & Shaver)
    Walden 301

In the last entry above Carlyle and Shaver are the names of the performers on the record. All three entries are part of a single alphabetical sequence which is kept primarily for staff use. The final example is of an entry for arranger and is taken from the main catalogue:

ADDED ENTRY: Bennett, Robert Russell, 1894–   , arr.
ARRANGER   35135   Porter, Cole, 1893–
      —36   [Kiss me, Kate. Selections; Arr. orchestra]
            Kiss me, Kate—Orchestral selection by Robert Russell Bennett. Columbia Album X336: 13073–74.
            [1950]
            3s. 12″
            Houston Symphony Orchestra: Efrem Kurtz, conductor.
            Descriptive notes printed on inside cover. s.4: Fauré. Pavane. Op. 50. F♯ minor.

These examples may be regarded as achieving a very high standard; though few libraries in Britain are likely to be half as thorough, it is as well that cataloguers should see what can be done and also remember the Detroit catalogue does not make exhaustive entries—some added entries are purposely omitted, as has been shown, and minor items such as playing time, matrix numbers, etc., are not included. These entries may well serve as a guide even with a simplified form of cataloguing. My own preferences, for limited cataloguing, would be a fairly full main entry under the composer plus brief added entries for performers and conductors, but omitting entry under the

Section of Music and Drama Department, Detroit Public Libraries

latter when entry has already been made under a soloist. Using once again the example quoted earlier in the chapter of the Brahms second piano concerto, the work should have a fairly full entry under the composer, brief entry under the name of the soloist (Schnabel), but no entry under Sir Adrian Boult or the orchestra. For orchestras all that is necessary is a simple *See* reference: London Philharmonic Orchestra. *See* under the following conductors: Beecham, *Sir* Thomas; Boult, *Sir* Adrian, etc. The main entry would satisfy those who wished to know which works the library had by a particular composer and the added entries would answer, by reference, questions on recordings by particular artists. Consideration might be given on the lines suggested earlier in this section to the inclusion of extremely brief form entries, such as "Symphonies", "Overtures", "String quartets" and the like. Title entries might be omitted, use being made of manufacturers' catalogues to answer enquiries for a work with a particular title; an index could be compiled, or references included in the catalogue listing names of pianists, sopranos, string quartets, etc., represented in the collection. This would answer the needs of the user whose greatest interest might be in tenor singers and who would enquire what examples of tenor arias are in the library. For details of such works, the enquirer would need to check under the name of each individual artist—but he would have been given the names of all tenors represented in the collection and so have the major part of his question answered.

Entries on the lines suggested would almost certainly answer the great majority of questions asked. This is not likely to alter the fact that, in general, British librarians prefer to make a single entry under the composer, trusting to answer other enquiries by a combination of good memory, catalogues and reference books and possibly a certain amount of good fortune. When one considers the expense and time involved in full cataloguing this attitude has something to commend it and many American libraries are having to simplify and reduce entries through economic necessity. Although printed cards for records have now been available for some years from the Library of Congress it would seem that only a fairly small minority of American libraries make use of this service. Only 17 per cent. of the sample libraries replying to the questionnaire sent out by the special committee on Bibliographic Control of Audio-Visual Materials[6] bought L.C. cards for the gramophone record collections. The major criticisms appeared to be that too few titles were available from this source (a difficult problem to solve in a country where there appear to be dozens of small manufacturers), that the time lag between the issue of a record and the availability of catalogue cards for it was too great and that the printed cards were too detailed and inflexible. The last complaint is one that cannot be answered in a system that prints cards for use in almost every type of library. It is for the library to amend and simplify the L.C. card if necessary rather than for L.C. to lower their standards and so create fresh problems for other libraries.

Detailed cataloguing is not confined to American libraries, for the American Memorial Library in Berlin takes an immense amount of trouble over its discs. Entries are duplicated on cards approximately 5¼ in. wide and 4 in. high, and a single LP disc may require two or three of these cards—a "recital" record even more. The exact dates of a composer's birth and death are given under his name. For symphonies, sonatas, etc., the tempi of the individual movements are shown. Details (the year and, if known, the place) of the composition of a work are given, the place and date of the first performance of the work and the actual playing time of the record are shown; the latter is usually to the nearest minute but is not infrequently to the exact second. With a jazz record, such as an LP by Duke Ellington and his Orchestra the playing time of each individual item is given. Analytical entries are duly made for all discs which contain more than one work. It may be doubted if all these items are of general interest but the Berlin collection is used primarily by students, and recitals are a regular part of the programme; these facts may possibly justify the immense amount of time and trouble that are required for cataloguing to this degree.

GRAMOPHONE AND SOUND-PROOF ROOM

The uses of a gramophone record reproducer have already received comment in this chapter as an aid to the staff; the machine can also be useful to patrons. In the U.S.A. the provision of listening rooms has been fairly common but these are now being superseded in many libraries by machines which have one (or possibly up to four) earphone attachments. Wohlford[1] reported on listening facilities in twenty-five libraries. Of these, seven made no provision at all, five had listening rooms and thirteen had earphone attachments. Andersen[2] states that out of fifty-two large municipal libraries, thirty-two allow borrowers to hear records before taking them from the building but says that this practice is not generally encouraged. In some places (Detroit and Minneapolis are examples) gramophones may be used for reference purposes and both records and a machine may be reserved at a given time on a specified date for the maximum of one hour. A disadvantage of the provision of listening facilities is that many users expect to be able to play over their own records on library equipment and are aggrieved when they find that this concession is not made.

The machine with earphone attachments has many advantages; the user can be in full view of the staff, two or more machines can be used in a very limited space and since no problems of sound-proofing arise, their proximity creates no rival areas of sound. Machines with more than a single pair of earphones attached may have their own difficulties—it is not always easy to decide, for instance, which of the people around the machine is nominally the borrower of the record and is in charge. The whole scheme of allowing people to listen to records in the library may create other problems when the system is wholly or mainly a rental one, though the consistent method would be to charge a hiring fee for the use of the machine. While it is useful to have the user of the machine under direct observation experience has shown that not infrequently it is the over-cautious user who has the worst accidents with records and it must be admitted with some regret that music-lovers, in general, are not mechanically minded. Certain libraries have the earphones or cubicles at a distance from the turntable which is in the staff enclosure or near by. An outstanding example of this is again provided by the American Memorial Library in Berlin where records are not issued at all for home use but can only be played in the library. The sound-proof cubicles in this building will hold three or four persons. Each cubicle contains a loudspeaker, a volume control and a telephone which is connected with the playing desk; on this last, listeners can report technical defects in the record, request repetition of a part of a disc, etc. With each playing, the date is added to a card which is kept with the record, so that the exact number of performances and general condition of the record are immediately available.

The question as to the best type of machine for public library use does not permit of a simple answer. Though it is more than ten years old, an article in the *Library Journal* for December, 1947, on "Some findings on sound equipment" still has much validity. The machine with earphone attachments has become increasingly popular in the larger gramophone shops in Britain together with the provision of small cubicles which have no doors, loudspeakers in the ceiling and a system of damping that absorbs nearly all of the sound and allows only a whisper to escape from the cubicle. These types may be regarded as self-policing. The provision of one or more machines of either type will obviously add to the capital cost of the record library as will the provision of any sort of sound-proof or sound-absorbing cubicle, but one cannot doubt that such a provision will receive excellent use and it should be regarded as highly desirable even if not absolutely necessary.

THE DEPARTMENT IN ACTION

This section of the chapter is divided into the following sub-headings: The issue desk; Rules and regulations; Period of loan: Fines; Damage and fragility; Issue methods.

The issue desk

Although the provision of shelving for the collection has been considered, no mention has been previously made of the desk or counter from which discs are issued to users and to which they are returned after borrowing. Within general limits the size of the desk will depend upon the amount of room that can be spared in the department, the possible adaptation of existing furniture, etc. The issue and return of records at the same enclosure used for book loans is not recommended. The two things are very dissimilar in format and it is much more difficult to discover damage to a gramophone record than to a book; this affects the time factor. For preference the gramophone desk, counter or enclosure should be constructed so that the assistant on duty can sit comfortably and not have to stand. Secondly, it is desirable to have both good natural and artificial lighting (and the latter is doubly important if the former is poor) to allow the careful examination of the surface of each record as it is borrowed and again when it is returned to the library. This separation of books and records should also mean that only trained staff handle the discs; if the general issue desk has to be used for both books and records, keen music-lovers may well be horrified by the inexpert handling the discs may receive from certain members of the staff.

Gramophone Record Libraries

This is one of the major points in which the library staff should attempt to educate by example. An aid, both practical and psychological, to checking the condition of each side of a disc is the provision of an inspection lamp of the type used by manufacturers; Hornsey has found this to be a valuable accessory. The third desirable feature of the desk, which again makes the general enclosure unsuitable, is sufficient space to allow the record to be taken out of its sleeve and examined without the assistant needing to be a contortionist or to be unduly cramped for space. A free space some 5 ft. in width and 3 ft. in depth would seem desirable.

Rules and regulations

Every library will need to make its own rules and regulations for users of the gramophone record library; these will probably be based upon those of other libraries and upon the specimen set prepared by the Library Association. The first rule may deal with eligibility, e.g. whether individuals may join, if provision is limited to those actually residing within the library's area, if there is a lower age limit. Use may be restricted to ratepayers, though this is difficult to enforce; societies and schools are usually allowed to borrow records through the Chairman and Secretary in the one case and the Headmaster and Music Master in the other. Societies may have to prove a certain minimum membership, for cases of "one-man" societies have not been unknown in areas where individuals were prohibited from making use of the collection. The privilege of free use of the collection may be extended to non-residents who are employed in the library area; on the other hand, all those who live outside this area may be asked to pay a subscription which may or may not be fixed to cover estimated use. The income from subscriptions of this nature varies considerably. Some London boroughs whose neighbours do not provide a gramophone record library find that many "outsiders" are prepared to join as subscribers and this experience may prove relevant in other urban areas where one authority provides a record library and an adjoining one does not. In many cases a deposit is required before any discs may be borrowed; this may vary from a few shillings to the cost of a single LP record. The sum is usually regarded as a useful deterrent to the casual enquirer who has no serious interest in the service, and the deposit also acts as some sort of safeguard against damage and default. To cover the possibility of non-return of a long operatic set in a single album a very high deposit would be required and this would undoubtedly prevent many honest residents from becoming members, so that £2 is the usual maximum sum that libraries demand. Whatever the deposit, it is refunded when the borrower ceases to use the library though any monies outstanding for loss of or damage to records is automatically deducted.

So far as is known all British libraries use a special application form for potential users of the gramophone record library and issue a special ticket which can be used for records only. In some cases the form asks for the name of the manufacturer of the motor and pick-up; it is useful to ask if the potential borrower has a sapphire or diamond needle fitted to his pick-up—if he does not know the answer, it is almost certain to be a sapphire. Certain libraries have reserved the right to visit users' homes and inspect the machines which it is proposed to use. This may perhaps be considered as somewhat high-handed until it is remembered that one user with an unsuitable gramophone can steadily and rapidly cause the condition of the stock to deteriorate, spoil the enjoyment of subsequent users of those discs which have been maltreated, and cause a higher proportion of the fund for records to be used upon replacements than would otherwise be necessary.

In general, only one ticket is issued and is coloured or otherwise printed so that it is immediately distinguishable from the library's ordinary tickets upon which books are borrowed. The one ticket usually allows a single LP disc, or a given number of SP discs, to be borrowed at the one time though it is customary to allow a complete work, such as an opera or symphony, which occupies more than a single disc to count as one disc. In the United States, particularly where mechanical methods of book charging are used, patrons have no special ticket for borrowing records. Conditions may be extremely generous. Detroit allows a maximum of ten LP discs at a time and even this limit was only introduced to reduce the risk of loss from new patrons who join, borrow records and promptly disappear.

Rules and regulations will always contain one concerning copyright. A typical one is that of Hornsey which reads: "Records will be issued to borrowers on the express understanding that the loan does not confer on the borrower any right or licence in respect of copyright or public performances." Leeds goes even further and requires the borrower to indemnify the Corporation against any infringement of copyright. Normally, copyright problems should not arise. Gramophone record societies are usually well informed upon this point and also about performing rights (which are not the same thing) and should certainly belong to the National Federation of Gramophone Societies since through this body they receive financial concessions from the Performing Right Society Ltd. The individual borrower who plays records for his own enjoyment in his own home should have no worries on these two points. The position is a little complicated but is well explained in W. W. Johnson's *The gramophone book* (Hinrichsen, 1954) under "Copyright" and related entries. American libraries have a rather different worry; their problems concern the many patrons who borrow discs from the public library and copy them on to tape recorders. Such people are often those who are most demanding for new "releases" with this idea in mind. Libraries with reference or archive collections may be asked permission by individuals to make tape-recordings in the library of some of the rarities; such permission is usually refused.

Loan period: Fines

There is no general agreement as to how long a user should be allowed to retain a disc or set without incurring a penalty; the majority allow a week's loan only but a large minority permit a fortnight's borrowing before fines are charged. The shorter period is probably sufficient for a work contained upon a single disc but for any longer composition this limitation may give the borrower musical indigestion. It is much easier to achieve Coventry's average of two-and-a-half playings in a week with a forty-minute symphony than with an opera that takes two hours or more to play through once. A loan period of seven days helps the collection to achieve a fairly high rate of turnover and this is useful when the collection is barely sufficient to meet demands; on the other hand it is not surprising to learn that when Hornsey, in response to public demand, altered its loan period from seven to fourteen days, the number of records borrowed in a month showed a decline but the number of records on loan at any one time remained steady. With rental collections a very different pattern may emerge. In Detroit, where payment is made for every disc taken from the library, it is usual for patrons to borrow two or three discs at a time and to return them within the same number of days. Reminder notices are sent to patrons after fifteen days.

Unless a record or set has been reserved by another reader it is usual to allow renewal, though some libraries permit this once only as a further means of ensuring that the collection is circulating as evenly and as rapidly as possible. Most British libraries will accept reservations and charge the same fee as that asked for book reservations; the practice is much less common in the U.S.A., possibly because photo-mechanical charging methods do not allow a charge to be "stopped" as is possible with Browne charging where a coloured signal can be inserted with the book card and ticket without difficulty. The income from reservation fees is likely to be very small; it may be supplemented in part by the sale of catalogues of the gramophone library stock and of supplements to this but the major income will come from fines charged for the retention of records beyond the time allowed under the rules and regulations. It is usual to make charges at a rate much in excess of that charged for books. This, again, should help to keep the stock circulating rapidly and at the same time help to offset some of the costs of the service. The rate of fine charges varies immensely. In London's Metropolitan Boroughs the minimum charge is 2d. per disc for a week overdue, or less; the maximum is 6d. per disc or per set for each day overdue. This latter figure is the maximum permitted under the London County Council (General Powers) Act, 1955. The average charge in Britain seems to be 3d. a week or part of a week; only one library is known that includes Sundays in its calculations of the time a record is overdue though the library itself is closed on that day.

Special conditions may be imposed in respect of records used in learning foreign languages and similar specialist-teaching material. It is usual to limit borrowers to a single record at a time and not lend the complete set, while many libraries make a schedule of dates by which a reader can hope and expect to collect his next record and so plan his course ahead. The success of such a scheme depends almost entirely upon the co-operation of those using the records; at least one library is withdrawing its sets of language records as they wear out simply because a high proportion of patrons flatly refused to return records when due, despite requests. Quite unfairly, though perhaps naturally, members of the staff were often blamed for this state of affairs by disappointed borrowers and since the gramophone record service was getting a completely undeserved bad name as a result, the Library Committee felt bound to curtail their activities so far as this particular type of disc was concerned.

Gramophone Record Libraries

Damage and fragility

Readers are normally asked to pay for any damage and a rule to this effect is usually inserted in the regulations. Many libraries also provide that the librarian may, at his discretion, charge the user with the entire cost of a record or, if the missing or damaged disc cannot be replaced without buying the complete set, the cost of the set. In such a case the culprit is allowed to retain the record or set of records. Hornsey tempers justice with mercy in that "the Council may reduce the sum to be paid for replacement by an appropriate amount in respect of wear and tear to the old set of records"; one would hope that any fair-minded librarian would act likewise. If a record is scratched but is still considered playable and fit to be lent to other borrowers it is customary to make a charge for the damage, note the defect and return the record to the shelves. Charges may be made at the discretion of the assistant in charge (and so can vary from the swingeing to the paltry), there may be a fixed sum for any damage, or a library may follow the example of Boston, Massachusetts, where it was found that damage to records declined considerably when a ruling was introduced under which the fine for a scratched record was graded according to the length of the scratch.

Although gramophone records are fragile only a very small percentage receive obvious damage, but too many suffer from unfair wear and tear through ignorance or carelessness. All users realize the possibility of damage and one presumes that they take precautions against dropping the disc or placing it where it can be sat on or otherwise maltreated. Fortunately, perhaps, the British climate does not provide many days on which a record, left in a parked car, is baked and warped by a very hot sun. This is a not-uncommon source of trouble in those parts of the United States and other countries where the summer temperature is appreciably higher than ours. Patrons apparently tend to regard an accident of this nature, by some form of specious logic and self-deception, as an "Act of God" rather than the natural result of their own thoughtlessness.

The SP disc, manufactured basically from shellac is brittle and easily broken, particularly from side pressure, and it rarely survives accidental dropping. Such records must be carefully stored in the library, and if shelved vertically should be in small batches so that too many records are not leaning in one direction thus causing strain on the end discs. Scratches on shellac discs need to be quite deep to be objectionable and even a long scratch will not last more than two

269

or three minutes. The LP disc of vinylite or geon is called "unbreakable" (though one is not advised to put this too drastically to the test) and is usually slightly flexible, though there is considerable variation in the thickness of the disc between different manufacturers. These are very real advantages but are more than compensated by a strong susceptibility to dust (the biggest problem with LP discs) and static electricity. The shallow grooves are much more easily scratched than an SP record, and a fairly long scratch may cause a regular click for ten minutes or longer; this can be most objectionable. Static electricity is usually overcome by wiping the record with a slightly damp cloth before and again after playing; it is static electricity that attracts much of the dust. Water will suffice for this wiping but one of the various proprietary makes of liquid on the market is usually more effective and helps to clean the record. Even with this precaution the record may suffer from unexpected "plops" and slight clicks—a fairly sure sign that dust is still in the grooves. Manufacturers usually provide an inner envelope as a precaution against dust settling in the grooves while the record is stored and any record not provided with this protection when bought should have a polythene cover fitted as standard practice in the library. This accent on dust may be considered over-emphatic but books on high-fidelity sound equipment and sound recording often include micro-photographs of the grooves of LP discs before and after playing; the effects of various destroying agents (particularly dust and a worn needle) are unhappily obvious.

As has been suggested in a previous section it is an admirable idea to issue to each new reader a leaflet giving details of the service, such as hours of opening, fine and reservation fees, and listing the rules and regulations applicable to the department. The leaflet might also contain notes upon the proper care of records. These can be prepared from advice in books and from the first-hand experience of record-lovers or the librarian can usually obtain suggestions from most of the larger manufacturing companies upon request. When incorporated in a leaflet the difficulty will be the old one of persuading users of the gramophone collection to read the notes. If one of the old heavyweight pick-ups or SP type of needle is used an LP disc can be ruined at once but potential users of the collection today are unlikely to make such elementary mistakes, even with a plug-in or turnover head, both of which allow the same pick-up arm to be used for either LP or SP records.

Gramophone Record Libraries

The greatest problem facing the librarian today with this particular service is probably that of wear and tear and the replacement of records. Many patrons expect that records borrowed from the library shall be in almost as good condition as those in their own personal collections, yet many users appear to be blissfully unaware of the limited life of both sapphire and diamond needles. The latter are good for at least 4,500 sides if correctly fitted but manufacturers of LP records consider that a sapphire stylus should be due for replacement after 100 12-in. sides have been played, i.e. the recommended life is only thirty-six or thirty-seven hours' playing time. After this the worn point of the needle may have a damaging and abrasive effect on the grooves of every disc played. The keen-eared listener will recognize a falling-off in quality particularly in the high and low frequencies and in an increase in surface noise. If new users are asked to state on the application form whether their machine is fitted with a sapphire or a diamond stylus it should be possible to take some action. If a stroke is made on the back of the ticket for every record borrowed (in rows of ten for ease of checking) it is reasonable to draw the borrower's attention to the fact that he had borrowed twenty records and assuming that each record had been played only twice and he had no discs of his own, his needle had reached the end of its estimated safe life and should be replaced. No further records should be loaned until this has been done. It would be reasonable to accept the assurance of most library users upon this point, but one library in the London area apparently insists upon seeing the receipted account if it has any doubts upon this score. Such a method may be regarded as somewhat high-handed but is well justified if the average library life of a disc is to be extended beyond the average figures quoted earlier.

Leeds includes in its regulations one concerning care of records which includes provisions that records will be handled by the edges and not finger-marked on the playing surfaces, that automatic record-changing apparatus will not be used for long-playing records and that no section of a complete work will be played more frequently than the remainder. While it may be quite impossible to enforce these prohibitions they are more likely to receive regard from users than if they were simply printed as advice to borrowers, though not all librarians will agree that this is the best method of approaching the problem. The ban on automatic record-changers may seem surprising; the reasons have already been stated. Some firms (Victor in the U.S.A. and H.M.V. in Britain are examples) now market discs that are thicker in the centre and at the rims so that the grooves cannot come into contact with those of a record above or below, but it is unlikely that all the library's collection will be of this type. It is an added safeguard for the library to add manual rather than automatic couplings whenever available as this increases the chances that each disc will be removed from the turntable before another is played even though the machine is equipped for automatic record-changing.

The apparent slowness with which discs are issued to borrowers and accepted from them on return is accounted for by the need to check each record individually for scratches and other marks. These are usually noted in Britain by the somewhat rough and ready method of making indications in chinagraph pencil within the margin between the playing surface and the record label. Arrows and other hieroglyphics are soon mutually understood by both staff and borrowers and the method is usually accepted as a reasonable one. A more accurate visual check can be achieved by the insertion of a piece of paper with the disc; on the paper are drawn or printed two circles to represent the two sides of the record. These can be the same size as the disc or a reduced representation. One circle is noted as side one and any scratches and marks noted on the sheet in approximately the correct position and to scale. Whatever method is used to indicate visible defects, care should be taken to see that the gramophone librarian and potential borrower agree that all scratches are marked before the record is taken from the library since any which are not already indicated are charged for when the record is returned. Librarians must realize, however, that these methods of indicating scratches can only be approximate and that an apparently badly-marked record may play excellently while a disc with little visible damage may prove to be almost worn out. Discs of the latter type are unusual but by no means exceptional. Visual checking can never be really satisfactory and a record should be tried over, probably only for a minute or two per side and at the points where the recording is obviously at its heaviest, every now and again in order to tell whether it should be discarded. Replacement will depend upon the popularity of the recording, whether it is still available and whether a superior version has been issued since the disc was added to the library stock.

Gramophone Record Libraries

Issue methods

The methods of issue for gramophone records vary in British libraries to a much greater extent than is the case with books. Some libraries use the simplest possible methods while others have a more complex system to allow better records to be kept; it may be valuable to know how many times a particular disc has been borrowed or which recordings have been taken from the library by a particular patron over a given period. The most common system is the normal Browne method in which the intending borrower takes the book card (though "record card" would be a more accurate description here) from the indicator and hands it to the assistant; the latter finds the requested disc, checks it for visible damage and gets the patron to do the same (adding a note of any scratches that have been overlooked in previous inspections) and then files the charge, which is the record card and user's ticket, in the day's issue. The problem of indicating to the borrower the date by which the disc is due for return causes some difficulty. The safest and most obvious method is to affix the date label to the front of the sleeve by means of a suitable adhesive or transparent cellulose tape but this practice obviously defaces the sleeve and may ruin an attractive design. The reverse of the sleeve is even more unsuitable since the presence of the date label here will obscure the analytical notes, etc., which are even more valuable than the photograph or design on the front of the cover. A modification is to stick the date label at the most convenient place on the sleeve, either front or back, in the position that obliterates least of the information or design. It is obviously advantageous to leave the name of the composer, title of the work and the performer unobscured if at all possible. The label is stamped with the date of return when the record is out of the sleeve for examination.

The second method is to use a date card which is pushed inside the sleeve when the record is issued to a borrower. Thin card is preferable to paper since it will be less likely to get creased. The disadvantage here is that the borrower may lose or mislay the card or get it mixed with another when more than one member of the family uses the gramophone record library; either type of accident will cause filing problems but of a type that should be simple to solve.

A third method is to have a manilla envelope into which both record and sleeve are inserted and the date label is stuck on this envelope. Once again the careless user can get records and envelopes mixed unless each of the latter is clearly marked with the catalogue

273

number of the record that is kept in it. When the collection is run without public access to the discs themselves the records can remain on the shelves in these envelopes which provide yet another protection against dust; with open-access the envelopes will need to be filed separately and "married" to the appropriate discs as they are borrowed. To assist in this the catalogue number of the record should be clearly marked along the fore-edge of the envelope. If, however, records are supplied in the first envelope to hand, the service is speeded up though a check upon the number of loans achieved by a particular disc is lost. American libraries using photographic systems of charging are in this position and so cannot usually provide statistics to check upon the average use a disc receives before withdrawal.

Should the library wish to keep a file of users who have borrowed each disc the simplest method is to note on the book card the ticket number of the patron or some similar method of identification—a method reminiscent of that commonly practised in British libraries before the First World War. As an alternative a patron may be required to fill in a card on each visit to the library and indicate on it the number(s) of the record(s) borrowed. This is done at Hornsey where the reverse of the card is used to indicate if a miniature score has been borrowed at the same time and if a carrying box has been issued. Thus each card gives a detailed record of the transaction but is obviously expensive both in time and stationery. If patrons complain that certain records are in a much worse condition than the number of loans would appear to warrant it is not difficult to check back and see the names of those who have previously borrowed these discs and if there is any common factor, i.e. one person has borrowed many of these particular works, then future borrowings by this individual would be scrutinized particularly carefully. The Hornsey method would also allow the librarian, should he so wish, to discover the listening tastes of various patrons, to see how many usually limit themselves to works of a particular type and how many are apparently catholic in their selections from the stock.

As has already been indicated it is difficult to estimate the average life of a record and different libraries provide widely varying figures —one librarian suggests only thirty loans for an LP disc, another's collection achieves eighty, while a third has surprisingly claimed a figure approaching two hundred. The only safe generalization is that the heavier and more congested recordings such as are found with many modern orchestral and operatic works are likely to need replacement much more quickly than discs containing instrumental, solo vocal and chamber music which are borrowed as frequently. Some of our patrons will point out, when they return a gramophone record, that its condition is poor and it can be put on one side for checking by a member of the staff at the first convenient opportunity; this is a most valuable use of a gramophone in a library. A simple and apparently effective scheme was devised at Lambeth where a slip was issued with every record after it had been loaned a certain number of times; the next borrower was asked to report upon it and state if, in his opinion, the disc should be withdrawn or if it was still in satisfactory condition for further loans. Patrons were generally only too pleased to help maintain the stock in good physical condition in this way. If the answer to the request was that the record ought to be withdrawn, then it could be checked by the staff (since some borrowers will naturally be rather more particular than others as to the amount of wear that is acceptable); if the record is reprieved, a second slip could be inserted after a set number of further loans and the process repeated until complaint was made.

TAPE-RECORDINGS

It was suggested fairly early in this chapter that a library might well compile a collection of recordings to illustrate certain aspects of its history. The tape recorder is now an accepted part of life for many people, and amateur recordings of a speech or ceremony can be quite adequate. If more than one copy is required or performance is likely to be frequent it is possibly advantageous to have the recording transcribed from tape, i.e. to have it copied and produced in the form of a gramophone record. Under normal circumstances, however, it will be sufficient to file a tape in the Local Collection for use as required. Providing a disc or tape is kept at a moderate temperature and under the same conditions as are recommended for the storage of books, the probable life is many years. There is little definite information available upon this point and the results of a two-year study project on this subject to be undertaken by the Library of Congress will be awaited with great interest. The investigation is due to start in 1958 and has been financed by a $65,000 grant from the Rockefeller Foundation.

If recordings and performances of tapes are to be made with any frequency then it is plain that the library should possess its own tape recorder; prices vary immensely but adequate models with two-speed motors (3¾ in. per second for speech and 7½ i.p.s. for music or for recordings with a wider acoustic range and better tone quality) that will reproduce both speech and music acceptably cost, at the time of writing, from about £50 upwards. There are many cheaper models available and a library may find one of these suitable for its purpose. The value of having local ceremonies on record, such as the Mayor's speech upon acceptance of office, the opening of a new branch library and similar public events, appears to be barely realized. Local worthies might be persuaded to talk and recall the past when it might be impossible for them to put their reminiscences on paper; even a faithful transcript of their talk by an excellent shorthand-typist does not convey the same flavour of accent and stress as does a recording.

In the summer of 1957 an article was published in the magazine *Time* in which it was predicted that the disc would be obsolete in five years when it would have been superseded by tape. It is highly doubtful if this will prove true in the U.S.A., and it seems quite impossible that it will happen in Britain, at least for very many years. Tape has been making an increased appeal for some time. In Britain the two major partners in the E.M.I. group—H.M.V. and Columbia—have issued pre-recorded tapes. The first small batch of releases was made late in 1954 and the slow rate of increase in the number of works available in this form suggests that the new medium is making but slow headway with music-lovers. One obvious reason is that a pre-recorded tape costs more than twice the price of its equivalent issue on disc. Similar tape-recordings in the U.S.A. were issued from about the same date as in Britain and the first steps in making these available to the public through the local library have been made in one or two places.

The advantages of this form are various, but the chief claim is that one link in the chain is eliminated by the fact that needle and pick-up are not needed—the items whose combined result is to cause maximum wear and tear on disc. Theoretically, tape should last indefinitely but the heads through which it passes can become magnetized and need attention fairly regularly if tone quality is to be retained. Other disadvantages of tape include its unhandiness, its susceptibility to damage and the ease with which a recording can be erased. It is much more difficult to put a tape on a machine for playing than it is to place a gramophone record upon its turntable and, if the "second side" is wanted, the first side (recorded on the top half of the tape) has to be run through the machine so that the tape can come through backwards, playing the second work, which is on the lower half of the tape. If tape becomes unwound from its reel the user may find himself struggling, Laocoon-like, to restore it to order. The plastic base of the tape is easily damaged and torn, though repair is simple and quick. On expensive machines it is possible to super-impose fresh material upon a recording so that comments or inter-polations could be made. The accidental erasure of a tape is a mishap that manufacturers have generally made almost impossible if the machine is used properly. The tone quality of a good tape recording is sometimes considered to be better than that of its equivalent disc though tape hum may well replace the needle hiss of the older form. Because of its simpler construction a good tape recorder is cheaper than a gramophone covering the same frequency range and with the same tone quality. This may result in an increased demand for the new reproducer, while the various manufacturers are producing some machines that will play recorded tapes but which will not record, so that these are reproducing machines only.

Stereophonic sound

The development of stereo tape during 1957 was seen by a num-ber of critics as another nail in the coffin of the disc recording. The top and bottom halves of the tape receive recordings from two matched microphones set in slightly different positions to simulate the binaural hearing of man. The tape needs a special reproducer and two loudspeakers so that the two halves of the tape are repro-duced separately but simultaneously. The results would seem to depend to a great degree upon the correct positioning of the loud-speakers and the listener between them; when accurately done the results are amazing. An orchestra can be heard deployed across a platform; in opera it is possible to "hear" the singer moving from one side of the stage to the other. Disc has replied to this threat with stereophonic recordings also; the two sides of each groove are at right-angles to each other and the top of each groove is at 45 degrees to the record surface, so that each groove is in the form of a 90-degree "V" in the record. Once again, the reproducing system has to be duplicated to allow the two separate channels to be played separately. The first commercial recordings were issued during 1958 and it is much too early, as these words are written, to forecast their future. This depends entirely upon public response which is certainly being encouraged by the comparatively low price of suitable machines and components for adapting existing monaural machines. If stereo discs become the accepted standard, only slight modifications should be necessary to public library practice as outlined in the previous pages.

The pressure is again on the manufacturers of tape-recordings (though these same firms are producing stereophonic discs) to bring their prices down before tape can develop as a really serious rival to disc; eventually, of course, the newer medium may achieve not only parity but supremacy. Until that time comes, however, few libraries are likely to make pre-recorded tapes generally available for public loan.

CONCLUSION

Though the time may still be some years ahead that the public library will normally reckon to include tape-recordings for home lending, the day of the gramophone record library is very much of the present, particularly in the U.S.A. and to a lesser degree in Britain. This chapter should have shown something of the difficulties to be faced in starting and maintaining a service of this nature, and it has also tried to indicate both the range of material available and the fact that a gramophone record library can and should be one of the most rewarding activities in a public library service. It should enrich the lives of those who use the service and though such patrons may be a small proportion of the local community it is generally the very section to which many of our efforts are directed and whose satisfaction may be regarded as proof that the library is playing its part in the cultural activities of its area in addition to providing recreation for a larger body of users.

Where the gramophone record library is already in being it may well need a transfusion to give it greater life, by the provision of a better supply of new records, perhaps more staff to give better service and possibly more space to allow the service to keep abreast of both actual and potential demand. If the collection is proving unattractive to local residents some of the reasons may have been suggested in the previous sentence. Extra space may be impossible to provide, added staff almost as difficult to acquire but the addition of a larger number of new records should not be beyond the wit of a good

Gramophone Record Libraries

librarian. The day has yet to come when recordings, on disc and/or tape, will be regarded as part of the normal library service in every town but it may well be nearer achievement than we think.

REFERENCES

1. WOHLFORD, Mary Kathryn. *A study of record collections in Public Libraries of the U.S. and Canada: a thesis submitted to the Graduate Council of Kent State University.* . . . 1950. (Typescript)
2. ANDERSEN, Elizabeth Louisa. *A study of recordings in 60 municipal Public Libraries serving populations of 75,000 and over as of 1948.* . . . 1950. (University of Chicago.) (Typescript)

These two unpublished theses overlap in part but are extremely useful in providing facts and figures relating to the American scene up to the late nineteen-forties. A microfilm copy of each is included in the Library Association library.

3. LUENING, Otto. *Music materials in the public library.* . . . 1952. (New York; Columbia University.)
4. MUSIC LIBRARY ASSOCIATION. *Code for cataloging phonograph records.* 1942.
5. HAMMAN, Frances, *ed. Bibliographic control of Audio-visual materials: Report of a Special Committee.* 1957. (*Library resources and technical services*, vol. 1, no. 4, pp. 180–97.)
6. e.g. SHANK, William. *Bryant Park concerts of recorded music* (New York Public Library Bulletin, Nov., 1951), pp. 527–30.

SUGGESTIONS FOR FURTHER READING

DEAN-SMITH, Margaret. *Proposals towards the cataloguing of gramophone records in a library of national scope.* ("Journal of Documentation", vol. 8, no. 3, September, 1952.)

The article is based upon experience gained in the gramophone record collection of the British Broadcasting Corporation. The author recommends that the fullest information should be provided on the card filed under the title of the work; only brief details are given on the composer entry. A third file, for artists, is also recommended. There is unlikely to be general agreement upon the methods suggested but they are certainly worth serious consideration. It is worth recalling here that (according to *The Radio Times* for 9th May 1958) the gramophone record accessions to the library for 1957 was 8,372 and that these necessitated no less than 68,265 entries in the catalogue.

Music Librarianship

HART, Richard, *and* BURNETTE, Frances. *Non-musical collections.* ("Library Journal", vol. 83, no. 4, 15th February 1958, pp. 536–43.)

This article, written by the Head of the Literature and Language Department of the Enoch Pratt Free Library in Baltimore and his Administrative Assistant provides a most useful summing-up of the various types of discs, other than music, now available. It should certainly encourage any who feel doubtful that these can provide a useful extension to records of music. The same issue of the *Library Journal* also contains an interesting article on "Tapes in the library".

JOHNSON, William W., *compiler. The gramophone book: a complete guide for all lovers of recorded music.* 1954. (Hinrichsen, for the National Federation of Gramophone Societies.)

This is a quick-reference work arranged on the dictionary principle and it contains several items useful to music librarians and to those in charge of gramophone record libraries. The sections that should be read include: "Books on the Gramophone", which is divided into three parts: (a) Available books, (b) Out-of-print books, (c) A selection of American and continental books; "Journals devoted to the gramophone", "Record numbers and prefixes" (a useful guide to discs issued in Britain between 1931 and 1952) and "Societies" which lists the names of all known societies in Britain, arranged under counties.

The Library Association Record, vol. 51, no. 7, July, 1949.

This issue, devoted to "Recorded music collections" has been mentioned during the preceding chapter. It contains articles by the librarians of Burnley, Holborn and Lambeth and by the Assistant-in-Charge of Music at Westminster; each writer deals with his or her respective collection and the methods on which it is administered. Though some years old, the issue is still valuable. Mr. Callander describes in some detail the methods of lending records which he introduced at Lambeth, while Miss Hickling contributes valuable information about the Westminster collection which had the largest opening stock and has remained the biggest gramophone record library in this country.

LOVELL, L. G. *Gramophone record provision in public libraries* ("The Library Association Record", vol. 56, no. 7, July, 1954).

This gives an interesting and informative analysis of answers to a series of questions answered by the majority of British librarians with gramophone collections under their control. The article gives excellent reasons to justify the provision of the service but is rightly insistent upon the need for adequate financial resources.

COWAN, Jean C. *The care and treatment of long-playing records in public libraries* ("The Librarian and Book World", April-May, 1958). pp. 76-9.

Miss Cowan is in charge of the Hendon gramophone record library, one of the largest in Britain. This article deals, in part, with the education of both staff and library users; it is a useful complement to the same writer's appendix to Donald Mason's *Primer of non-book materials* . . . (Association of Assistant Librarians, 1958) which deals more with practical problems of accessioning, cataloguing and administration.

Postscript (1962)

Two corrections must be noted. Chingford was not the first British library to issue records to individual borrowers (p. 185); Herefordshire County Library began its service at the end of 1940. The investigation begun in 1958 (end of p. 275) was completed and the results published as *Preservation and Storage of Sound Recordings*, by A. G. Pickett and M. M. Lemcoe. The book was published in 1959 by the Library of Cogress at 45c.; it is available in Britain through H.M.S.O. This report, *inter alia*, is strongly in favour of vertical storage for gramophone records in tightly-packed racks. This expert recommendation must override my comment in the last paragraph of p. 226.

One major development since 1959 has been the great increase in the number of cheap releases and re-issues, now marketed by all the major companies. Many such records are excellent value and can make an appreciable difference in the cost of a collection, particularly for libraries that are starting a record section. *A Guide to the Bargain Classics* (by Edward Greenfield, etc., published in 1962 by the Long Playing Record Library, Blackpool, 15s.) provides expert advice. Some of the American discs mentioned in the chapter (such as "Caedmon", "Camden" and "Folkways") have now appeared in Britain. The last-named series are expensive, but "Camden" provides some wonderful bargains for librarians.

Stereophonic discs, though up to four years old, are still provided by few British libraries. Those that do include such recordings find them popular and the potential life seems likely to be but little less than that of their monophonic equivalents. Collectors are slowly changing over to stereo equipment, but there has been nothing of the immediate widespread rush to convert to twin-channel reproduction which seems to have occurred in the U.S.A. New records are still issued in both mono and stereo versions and, while the majority of our borrowers retain their monophonic-only equipment, there is little justification in buying too high a proportion of stereo discs. Purchases of the latter might be concentrated on works in which stereophony has most to offer—those for large orchestra, opera, and similar complex scores.

Tape recordings have grown in popularity, particularly as prices have been noticeably reduced during the last three years and also because good quality musical recordings can now be reproduced from tape playing at a speed of $3\frac{3}{4}$ inches per second, compared with the previous acceptable minimum of $7\frac{1}{2}$ i.p.s. This new speed doubles the playing time for the same amount of tape. In the U.S.A. the faster speed is apparently the norm for stereo though $3\frac{3}{4}$ i.p.s. tapes have a growing share of the market. However, disc is far from obsolete (see para. 2, p. 276) and tape continues to present problems in checking, etc., that make its use for public loan too much of a risk in the eyes of British librarians.

My own experience in administering a gramophone record library and in comparing notes with other librarians has led me to the firm conclusion that careful examination of every record on its return from each loan is necessary if discs are to have the length of life that should be expected and if we are not to lose our keen and conscientious members. Such checking is difficult at busy times yet limited or inadequate examination is almost certain to result in a shortened life for many records. What is saved in staff time by cursory checking is more than counterbalanced by the necessarily increased expenditure on replacement of worn-out discs. With proper checking there should normally be no need to replace a record until at least 50 issues have been achieved; even after 100 borrowings some records should still be in good playing condition. Libraries that make no check, or a purely superficial one, may need to withdraw discs before they have achieved twenty loans.

Appendix I

MUSIC CATALOGUE: SUBJECT HEADINGS

BOOKS ON MUSIC
- AMATEUR OPERATICS
- BALLET MUSIC
- BANDS
- CAROLS
- CASTRATI
- CHAMBER MUSIC
- CHOIRS AND CHOIR TRAINING
- CLARINET PLAYING
- CLARINETS
- CONCERTOS
- CONCERTS
- COUNTY MUSIC COMMITTEES
- FLUTE PLAYING
- GRAMOPHONE RECORDS
- GRAMOPHONES
- HARMONY AND COUNTERPOINT
- HYMNS
- JAZZ
- KEYBOARD INSTRUMENTS
- MUSIC
    - Analytical notes
    - Appreciation
    - Church
    - Collective Biography
    - Composition
    - Editing
    - History (sub-divide by country)
    - Study and teaching
    - Thematic catalogues
    - Theory
- MUSIC FOR THE THEATRE
- MUSICAL BOXES
- MUSICAL FORM
- MUSICAL INSTRUMENTS
- MUSICAL PLAYS
    - Libretti

282

Appendix I

MUSIC SCORES

283

CHAMBER MUSIC			Septets
			Sextets
			Trios
CHAMBER MUSIC	S	A	PIANOFORTE
			ORCHESTRAL
			VIOLIN AND PIANOFORTE
			VIOLONCELLO AND PIANOFORTE
CHORAL MUSIC	S	A	ANTHEMS
			CANTATAS
			HYMNS
			MADRIGALS
			MASSES
			ORATORIOS
			VESPERS
CLARINET			
COMIC OPERA		S	OPERA—Light and comic
CONCERTOS			For miniature scores, *see* ORCHESTRAL—Concertos

For arrangements of pianoforte concertos, *see* PIANOFORTE—Concertos

For other instrumental concertos with orchestral score arranged for the pianoforte, *see* under name of instrument, e.g. OBOE, VIOLIN

CORNET			
COUNTRY DANCES		S	DANCES
DANCES			
DRAMATIC MUSIC	S	A	OPERA
			MUSICAL PLAYS
DRUM			
FILMS—Pianoforte selections	S	A	PIANOFORTE
—Vocal selections	S	A	MUSICAL PLAYS
FLUTE			
FOLK SONGS		S	SONGS—Folk and traditional
GRAND OPERA		S	OPERA—Grand
GUITAR			
HARP			
HORN			
HYMNS			
INSTRUMENTAL			*See* under name of instrument, e.g. PIANOFORTE
LIGHT OPERA		S	OPERA—Light and comic
LUTE			
MADRIGALS			
MANDOLINE			
MASSES	S	A	VESPERS
MUSICAL PLAYS	S	A	OPERA—Light and comic
			Pianoforte selections S A PIANOFORTE
NATIONAL ANTHEMS		S	SONGS—Folk and traditional

Appendix I

NONETS	S		CHAMBER MUSIC—Nonets
NEGRO SPIRITUALS			
OBOE			
OCTETS	S		CHAMBER MUSIC—Octets
OPERA—GRAND			
LIGHT AND COMIC	S	A	MUSICAL plays
ORATORIOS	S	A	CANTATAS

ORCHESTRAL—Concertos
    —Overtures
   —Study and teaching
   —Symphonies

ORGAN

OVERTURES   For miniature scores, *see* ORCHESTRAL—Overtures
For overtures for pianoforte solo or duet, *see* PIANOFORTE and PIANOFORTE—Duets, respectively

PIANO ACCORDION

PIANOFORTE—Concertos
       For miniature scores, *see* ORCHESTRAL—Concertos
For other works written or arranged for two pianists, *see* PIANOFORTE—Duets—One piano and PIANOFORTE—Duets—Two pianos
   —Duets—One piano
      —Two pianos

PLAINSONG			
QUARTETS	S		CHAMBER MUSIC—Quartets
QUINTETS	S		CHAMBER MUSIC—Quintets
RECORDER			
REQUIEMS	S		MASSES
SEPTETS	S		CHAMBER MUSIC—Septets
SEXTETS	S		CHAMBER MUSIC—Sextets

SONGS—Choral
   —Folk and traditional S A NEGRO spirituals
   —Student

STUDENT SONGS	S		SONGS—Student

SYMPHONIES   For miniature scores, *see* ORCHESTRAL—Symphonies
For symphonies arranged for piano solo or duet, *see* PIANOFORTE and PIANOFORTE—Duets, respectively

TRUMPET			
VIOLA	S	A	CHAMBER music
VIOLIN	S	A	CHAMBER music
VIOLONCELLO	S	A	CHAMBER music

PART II

INTRODUCTION

This half of the book comprises a series of lists of recommended musical scores. It must be stressed that an attempt has been made to give a representative but not a comprehensive stock; the last would be an almost impossible achievement. Such recommendations of works that ought to be found in the stock of a public library have been made before, but the sections that follow vary from previous ones in two important respects. First, recommendation is usually made in five stages and, secondly, many of the items are annotated. A minimum basic stock list for a small music collection is of limited use to the librarian who wishes to make more adequate representation, and in an attempt to make the lists of use to music collections from the start to a size that may well require the services of a full-time music librarian, a system of grading is included. The bare bones —the stock that should be found in the smallest independent library—is indicated by the prefix (a); the second choice which will increase representation to some degree is shown as (b), and so on to the fifth and last choice, marked (e). Items in this last class are often of equal musical merit to those recommended for previous purchase but they are likely to be in less demand, usually because they are less known—and too many music-lovers tend to like what they know and be unwilling to extend their musical horizons. Where the demand for music for a particular instrument is likely to be very limited indeed, then the grading of choices is not made while, for reasons explained at the beginning of chapter VIII, miniature scores are divided into seven categories, from (a) to (g).

My first article in our professional press was entitled *Organ music in the public library* (in *The Library Association Record* for July, 1938) and gave annotated recommendations. The works there were divided into two classes, "Indispensables" and "Highly recommended"; the same works suggested then are to be found later in this book but the

289

two categories have been extended to five. As then, the annotations are intended to give brief information about the composer and/or the music and it is hoped that these will help librarians to reach decision when considering the purchase of a work. In several cases the lists of books for further reading at the end of a chapter will include specialist works that are annotated and these books should be bought, even in the very small library, as important aids to good selection.

The actual content of the recommendations is obviously personal, and no other librarian is likely to agree with it *in toto*, but I hope that music librarians will find little at which to cavil. I have attempted to cover a fairly wide field and to include a proportion of less-known works without straying into the perverse. It is always difficult if not impossible to forecast which pieces of modern music will find their way into the accepted standard repertory in due course and any selection of contemporary works may well look odd within a very few years—but that is no excuse for omitting recent publications.

The sections that follow may be regarded as self-contained, but are not intended for continuous reading. The librarian who increased his selection of solo piano music to include all items listed as (a) and (b) need not feel that he must dutifully buy all the (a) and (b) recommendations in the section on piano duets. If he has revised his stock to include all the primary recommendations in one field and has met with no response from library users, he may be justified in spending less money on that part of the collection providing that he remembers that the supply very often creates the demand in the library. On the other hand, my own suggestion would be that all the items marked (a) should be bought in all categories so that the music section covers all the major categories usually included in the small library; this may take the smallest library two or three years to do if no special funds can be applied for adding scores. When this is done further accessions can be made from the (b) category, and so on. Except with the first five categories of miniature scores none of the sections is of equal size; there are over thirty works recommended for the violoncello of which a sixth are recommended for first purchase (a), a tenth at (b) and one-third of the list at (e). This is simply the result of trying to judge each work separately and not to recommend the scores in neat and tidy parcels with the same number of works in each.

There seems to be no useful purpose in making graded selections for music that is not normally stocked in the smaller music section, such as works for the French horn; instead, the item or items most likely to be useful have been marked with an asterisk. If there is local demand for music written for one of the less-common instruments, the recommendations can be found and decision made for purchase. Where there is no apparent demand, then the asterisk might be regarded as the equivalent of a category (f). Another point that must be stressed is that these selections are made by an English librarian in terms of British public libraries. It is hoped that the lists will be of value to librarians elsewhere but they may justifiably feel that there is too great an emphasis on English music and insufficient on their native composers. For these reasons they may decide to reduce the English representation but the graded selection may still be a useful guide as to which English works ought to be bought first.

If the charge is made that the selected music is "highbrow", it is admitted. The public librarian does not usually expect to find colleagues recommending mass produced fiction for serious attention and I see no reason for including the musical equivalent. I hope that the scores recommended will have permanent value.

At the end of each chapter is a list of books, limited for general convenience to those written in English. There are, of course, many important books of a similar nature written in foreign languages and these can be traced fairly simply in the normal music encyclopaedias and bibliographies. The works quoted at the end of a chapter give further information and suggestion on the repertory of particular instruments, etc. Where reference is made to one of these books in the course of an annotation, the author's name only is quoted, e.g. under Chopin's piano works, "Hutcheson recommends the Peters edition . . .". Particulars of the book by Hutcheson will be found at the end of the chapter together with an appraisal of it. These authoritative works will allow the librarian to take a second opinion upon some of the works listed in the preceding chapter and will also help in choosing a wider selection than that covered by this work should further selections be desired.

Finally, a word on editions and titles. With composers whose works are still protected by copyright there is normally no choice of edition. In other cases there may be a superfluity, and five or six different editions of popular classics are not uncommon. Only occasionally is preference for a particular edition shown, mainly because there is usually little to choose between them, but also because there are often only one or two editions available at the time the work is ordered. The librarian can sometimes afford to wait for a particular edition but speed may well be an important factor, particularly when a work is bought in response to a reader's request. In certain cases one edition has a definite advantage over its rivals (I would instance the new Peters edition of Haydn's *Piano sonatas*); when this is so, that edition is clearly recommended. While the original publisher is usually given, cases will be found where the English agent's name is quoted instead; this is usually because the name of the original publisher is not given on the title-page, or else is an oversight on my part. A list of British agents for overseas publishers is given at the end of this part of the book, together with abbreviations used for certain publishers.

Checking editions, etc., during the recent years has proved a wearisome and often puzzling task though here, as in other parts of the book, I have received considerable generous assistance. Despite this, it is obvious that every available edition of a particular work is not always included; an omitted edition may be the equal of the one listed. The British librarian, at least, can usually rely upon a good specialist supplier to trace and order any work wanted, and the bibliographical position should become progressively better as the files of *The British Catalogue of Music* lengthen.

I have attempted to follow my own cataloguing suggestions for titles. Symphonies, sonatas, etc., are given in English, but descriptive works such as operas, tone poems and song cycles are usually entered under the original title unless better known in English. While this may not be consistent it should aid finding and checking. The same principle has been used for the index to works listed in this half of the book. The index includes, in many cases, the individual titles of works which form part of a suite, song cycle or the like, when requests may be made for one item from the complete set. This sometimes results in apparent contradictions—it would appear at first sight that Debussy is much better represented than Chopin, until one realizes that "Complete piano works" of the latter covers more individual items than the many lines of entries for Debussy. In addition to providing a quick means of reference, the index serves a second purpose in indicating the range of works of individual composers.

Prices are not quoted. I discussed the matter with a number of colleagues and by a large majority they felt that the trouble involved in getting and listing current prices was not worth while, since costs fluctuate so rapidly today. The librarian should try and keep abreast with current catalogues of the major publishers. The final point is that reference is not infrequently made to the fact that a work has been recorded. This can be an important factor, since music-lovers owning or borrowing a recording of a work will often want to follow the performance with the score, and this will increase the potential demand for a rarely performed work considerably.

Chapter VI

INSTRUMENTAL MUSIC

THE PIANO

The section of the music stock devoted to solo piano music is usually the most popular, and is the one by which the collection as a whole is often judged. It is frequently alleged that the number of people learning to play the piano is rapidly declining; this may be true but there are still many players coming to the public libraries and an encouraging proportion of this public is willing to borrow some less familiar music if the opportunity is offered. What is far from encouraging is that the selection provided in many libraries that otherwise have a high standard of both fiction and non-fiction provision will include "film selections" and similar ephemeral music of no real value and, at the same time, fail to stock many works that are classics.

It is not as though the field of good piano music is small. The knowledgeable musician realizes that there is a tremendous amount of important music that he is never likely to know well and rarely be able to hear unless he has access to gramophone records of it. The selection that follows is but a minute proportion of that which has some genuine claim, for one reason or another, to inclusion in the library stock. In order to keep the list within bounds, all arrangements (such as symphonies, orchestral suites, ballets, etc.) have been excluded though piano transcriptions by Busoni and Liszt do find a place since these two composers re-wrote rather than arranged certain works by other composers. I do not suggest in any way that the inclusion of arrangements is wrong—far from it—but would recommend that stress should be laid on music that has been written specifically for the piano. The same argument applies, in fact, to all sections of music scores.

Light music provides even more controversial ground. Popular music of the Eric Coates and Coleridge-Taylor types is omitted from the lists that follow though some lighter pieces are included. The

Instrumental Music

representation of such popular works is left entirely to the discretion of the individual librarian.

Because of the regular demand for piano music and because almost every library will almost certainly have at least a small collection in this field, the lists that follow cover a fairly wide range from the hackneyed to the unusual; the grading scheme has been explained in the introduction to this part of the book. When a good representative stock has been accumulated the librarian with very limited musical knowledge should be able to add new works to stock with growing confidence since reissues as well as new works are often reviewed in musical periodicals (*see* Chapter II) and a brief check in Grove, Scholes, Thompson, etc., should reveal the musical standing of any composer whose name may be unfamiliar.

ALBENIZ   (d) *Iberia*, 4v. (Union Musical Española)

              (e) *Suite española, op. 47* (Union Musical Española)

Many more people will recognize the *Tango* (op. 165, no. 2) of Albeniz than will know the name of the composer. The twelve pieces that make up the four volumes of the first work recommended are inspired by different parts of Spain. The score is difficult to play and marred in parts by too lavish decoration of the music, yet for all that these pieces hold their place in the piano repertory and should be borrowed with reasonable frequency. If desired the four volumes could be bound into one or two. The *Suite* contains eight pieces of a similar nature to those in *Iberia*.

ARNE   (d) *8 sonatas* (Augener)

T. A. Arne (1710–1778) is best remembered as the composer of *Rule, Britannia*. These sonatas were intended as harpsichord lessons and have some importance in the history of music. Despite their pedagogical intent they are still enjoyable to play.

AURIC   (e) *Petite suite* (Heugel)

Georges Auric (b. 1899) is a French composer who was at one time one of the group known as "Les Six". His works show what might be regarded as typical French refinement and delicacy tinged with a certain acidity.

BACH, C. P. E.   (d) *Piano works*, 2v. (Universal)

The second (and most talented) son of J. S. Bach; his musical stature has been sadly overshadowed by that of his father but these works display a fresh and vigorous personality that deserves to be heard in its own right.

BACH, J. C.   (e) *10 sonatas*, 2v. (Peters)

Johann Christian was the youngest son of Johann Sebastian Bach and is sometimes known as the "English" Bach through his long residence in this country. His Italian style of writing was popular and he had considerable influence

295

upon the young Mozart. These sonatas are generally attractive and should be within the technical ability of the competent amateur pianist.

BACH, J. S.

(c) *Anna Magdalena's notebook* (Associated Board; Peters)

(b) *English suites*, 2v. (Augener; Breitkopf; Universal)

(a) *French suites* (Augener; Breitkopf; Universal)

(e) *Goldberg variations* (Breitkopf; Peters; Schirmer)

(b) *Inventions in two and three parts* (Augener; Breitkopf, 2v.)

(c) *Italian concerto: Chromatic fantasia and fugue* (Augener; Breitkopf; Schirmer)

(d) *Partitas*, 2v. (Augener; Schirmer; Universal)

(d) *18 little preludes and fugues* (Augener; Schirmer)

(c) *24 short preludes and fugues* (Peters)

(a) *Das Wohltemperirte Klavier* (*the "48" preludes and fugues*) (Assoc. Board; Augener; Breitkopf; Peters; Schirmer; Universal, etc.)

Although not written for the modern pianoforte nearly all of Bach's keyboard pieces can be played satisfactorily on it, and the smallest collection of scores should contain some representation of this composer.

Whatever title one may use, the "48" comprise one of the most important sets of works in the entire piano repertory. These preludes and fugues are sometimes known as the pianist's "Old Testament" (the "New Testament" being Beethoven's piano sonatas) and are a first choice for any music section. As indicated above there are many different editions, most of them good; for the student, in particular, the best and most useful edition is likely to be that published by the Associated Board (of the Royal Academy and Royal College of Music, London) edited by Sir Donald Tovey and Harold Samuel.

If, as is sometimes alleged, Shakespeare is spoiled for many during their schooldays, so is Bach for those who had to learn some of his easier works in their early piano lessons. Nevertheless, even in those works whose purpose is primarily educational (such as the *Inventions* and the *Anna Magdalena* pieces) the music is enjoyable in itself. The *Inventions* are a useful training ground for the technical difficulties met with in the "48". Only the *Goldberg variations* are difficult to manage on a modern pianoforte and the Schirmer edition is particularly recommended here. It is edited by Ralph Kirkpatrick and has a very full and informative introduction.

BACH–BUSONI

(c) *Chaconne in D minor* (Breitkopf)

(c) *Organ prelude and fugue in E♭ major* ("St. Anne") (Lengnick)

(d) *Organ toccata and fugue in D minor* (Breitkopf)

(b) *6 organ choral preludes* (Breitkopf)

Instrumental Music

These wonderful works need, in most cases, a better-than-average technique to be played at all well. The transcriptions show Busoni's genius for the piano to the full. In some works the piece is transformed yet the spirit of Bach remains strongly in evidence. The *Chaconne*, written by Bach for unaccompanied violin (and part of the work known either as *Violin sonata no. 4* or *Partita no. 2*) is the most striking example of Busoni's methods of free adaptation. His use of the lower half of the piano's register is often noteworthy. The first three works recommended make a convenient single volume for libraries that prefer made-up volumes to thin pieces of sheet music. It may be mentioned that the Breitkopf edition of Bach's piano works is edited by Busoni with the exception of the *French suites*, where the editor is Busoni's pupil, Egon Petri.

The large music collection might also usefully add the *6 preludes and fugues* (Peters, 2v.) transcribed from organ works by Liszt.

BACH, W. F.   (e) *8 fugues and 12 polonaises* (Peters)

                  (e) *6 sonatas*, 2v. (Nagel)

Wilhelm Friedemann was, in his father's eyes, the son with the greatest share of the Bach talent for music-making; he was also the "black sheep" of the family. The fugues indicate his abilities as a composer; the polonaises are of considerable variety with those in the minor keys the more successful. As a sonata composer W. F. Bach made no innovations but the works should give pleasure.

BALAKIREV   (d) *Islamey: oriental fantasy* (Schauer)

                  (e) *Piano sonata* (Zimmermann)

Islamey is a fiendishly difficult piece to play but is included in these lists for two reasons. It has an important place in the repertory of the piano and has been recorded several times as well as receiving occasional broadcasts, so that it may well be borrowed to follow another's performance rather than for a personal assault on the music by one of our own patrons. The sonata is considerably less well-known though it is less difficult than the fantasy and deserves to be equally popular. The two works would conveniently bind together.

BARBER   (c) *Excursions, op. 20* (Schirmer)

              (e) *Sonata, op. 26* (Schirmer)

Samuel Barber is best known in Britain for his *Adagio for strings*, op. 11, which was originally written for string quartet. The *Excursions* are (according to the composer's own prefatory note) in "small classical forms into regional American idioms", and are both amusing and effective—it is not every serious composer who has written music in boogie-woogie style! These pieces make a useful introduction to an important contemporary American composer whose *Sonata* (dating from 1949) is of much more serious intent and considerably more demanding in technical standards.

BARTÓK   (c) *Album* (Chester)

             (d) *14 bagatelles, op. 6* (Zerboni)

             (d) *10 easy pieces* (Liber-Southern)

             (c) *For children: 32 selected pieces* (Boosey)

             (b) *Mikrokosmos: 153 progressive piano pieces*, 6v.

                  (Boosey)

(e) *Sonata* (Universal)

(e) *Suite, op. 14* (Universal)

The library that excludes purely teaching material may well omit the first three volumes of *Mikrokosmos* which is a work designed to provide a graduated series of piano studies particularly in modern harmonies and rhythms, etc. The last three books (classed as "Moderate" and "Difficult") have musical interest to entertain the performer in addition to the technical problems which he has to solve. A number of these short pieces have been recorded. The *Album* contains fourteen pieces, including five of the *Bagatelles* and would bind with the *Easy pieces* which provide an ideal starting point for those who wish to know more of Bartók's music. The *Sonata* dates from 1926 and is the composer's biggest single work for piano; it is difficult to play both technically and interpretatively.

BAX

(c) *Burlesque* (Chappell)

(c) *Country tune* (Chappell)

(c) *A hill tune* (Chappell)

(c) *In a vodka shop* (Augener)

(c) *Lullaby* (Chappell)

(c) *Mediterranean* (Chappell)

(c) *A mountain mood* (Chester)

(c) *Serpent dance* (Chappell)

(c) *Winter waters* (Chester)

Bax's major piano works, the four sonatas, are sadly neglected. The first two are written in a single continuous movement, the third and fourth in more conventional form though the third is written in the unusual key of G♯ minor. The smaller pieces are much more popular and one or two albums could be made up of these. *In a vodka shop* derives from a visit made by the composer to Russia; *Lullaby* and *A mountain mood* are both written in variation form, and *Winter waters* (sub-titled *Tragic landscape*) is a highly effective passacaglia. These four pieces, together with *A hill tune*, are the recommended pieces if nine are considered too many. An album of Bax pieces, sold by Cramer, contains seven of the listed items.

BEETHOVEN

(b) *Ecossaises and German dances* (Augener, 2v; Peters)

(a) *Piano sonatas* (Assoc. Bd, 3v; Augener, 2v; Breitkopf, 2v; Peters, 2v; Ricordi, 2v; Schirmer, 2v, etc.)

(b) *Other original piano works* (Henle, 2v; Peters, 1 or 2v, etc.)

(a) *Variations*, 2v (Augener; Peters; Schirmer, etc.)

It is surprisingly difficult to get a nearly complete coverage of Beethoven's piano works. Most British users will be happy with the Associated Board edition of the sonatas, edited by Harold Craxton and Sir Donald Tovey, and these works are a prime necessity in every collection. The Henle (Urtext) edition is recommended for the lesser works.

Instrumental Music

BERG   (e) *Piano sonata, op. 1* (Universal)

A passionate work requiring excellent technique; it shows something of the influence of Schoenberg. The sonata has been recorded.

BERKELEY   (e) *3 Mazurkas (Hommage à Chopin)* (Chester)
     (e) *6 Preludes* (Chester)
     (e) *5 short pieces* (Chester)
     (d) *Sonata* (Chester)

Lennox Berkeley (b. 1903) is an English composer who has written in many forms. His piano music is modern (in the best sense), well written and usually difficult. The fifth *Prelude* is written in $\frac{7}{8}$ time—a most unusual rhythm.

BLISS   (d) *Sonata* (Novello)

An important but difficult modern British work.

BLOCH   (e) *5 sketches in sepia* (Schirmer)

BOWEN   (e) *24 preludes, op. 102*, 4v. (Chester)

York Bowen (b. 1884) is a British musician whose merits as a composer, particularly for the piano, appear to be constantly underrated. These *Preludes* are in all major and minor keys.

BRAHMS   (a) *Piano works*, 2v. (Augener; Peters)

     (a) *Variations on a theme of Paganini, op. 35*, 2v. (Augener; Peters)

These works are popular with both professional and amateur pianists. There might well be more than one copy stocked of those works in constant demand, such as the *Rhapsodies*. It should be noted that the *Waltzes* were originally written for piano duet and later arranged by the composer for piano solo in two different versions, the second entitled "easy". Neither version is included in the volumes listed above.

BRITTEN   (c) *Holiday diary: suite for piano, op. 5* (Boosey)

The suite dates from 1934 when the composer was twenty. Though an early work it is by no means a negligible one and is written in a light-hearted mood.

BULL   (c) *Selected pieces* (Augener)

Dr. John Bull (1563–1628) was, at different times, organist at the Chapel Royal and at Antwerp Cathedral. According to Scholes, "he ranks as one of the founders of the modern pianoforte repertory" and these pieces for virginals can still interest modern pianists. The volume is edited by Sir Granville Bantock.

BUSONI   (c) *Indianisches Tagebuch (Indian diary)* (Breitkopf)

Busoni was one of the greatest pianists in the history of music, though he considered himself primarily as a composer and therefore bitterly begrudged the time spent on travelling and concert performances. His works are far from popular as many musicians find them too impersonal despite the excellent craftsmanship in the writing. They are certainly not negligible and this suite, based on genuine Red Indian themes, is a very good starting point for anyone interested in this German-Italian composer. The recommended work is, strictly speaking, only Book 1 of the *Indian diary*; the second book, opus 47, is for small orchestra. The enterprising librarian who may wish to buy other works is advised to get the *Elegies* which comprise seven pieces and the *Sonatinas* numbers 2 to 6, also published by Breitkopf. The first sonatina (with a different publisher) has long been out of print. The sonatinas vary considerably both in length and difficulty. The fifth, *Sonatina brevis*, is a free transcription of the Bach "little" *Fantasia and fugue in D minor*; the sixth, *Sonatina super Carmen*, is based on tunes from Bizet's opera and may well be intended as a character study of Carmen herself.

BYRD   (b) *Selected pieces* (Augener)

William Byrd was one of the greatest Elizabethan composers and he excelled in almost every branch of music. These short pieces give some indication of his genius. The large library should possess his keyboard works (edited by Edmund H. Fellowes) which comprise volumes 18–20 of the complete works (Stainer & Bell).

CASELLA   (e) *Sonatina in tre tempi* (Ricordi)

CHABRIER   (d) *Pièces pittoresques* (Enoch)

Chabrier is an underrated composer and these brilliant pieces deserve to be better known than they are.

CHOPIN   (a) *Complete piano works* (Augener, 3v; Durand, 12v; Frederyk Chopin Institute, Warsaw, 14v; O.U.P., 3v; Peters, 10v; Schirmer, 13v; etc.)

In the opinion of many pianists Chopin is the greatest composer of all for the piano and nothing less than the complete works will suffice. Not only this but fairly heavy duplication (possibly in different editions) will probably be needed to keep abreast of constant demand. Hutcheson recommends the Peters edition with the Durand edition (edited by Debussy) as second choice. Schirmer issue two different editions of which that edited by Mikuli is recommended. Other publishers who issue some but not all of the piano works are Novello (8 vols.) and Universal (7 vols.). The best current edition is that published in Warsaw; this edition will eventually include Chopin's complete works in 26 volumes. Prices and standard of production increase the attractiveness of this presumably most authentic version.

CIMAROSA   (e) *32 sonatas*, 3v. (Eschig)

Early sonatas in one-movement form and fairly simple to play.

CLEMENTI   (e) *Gradus ad Parnassum: 29 selected studies, arr. Tausig* (Augener; Ricordi; Universal)
                  (e) *12 sonatas*, 2v. (Schirmer)
                  (d) *Sonatinas, op. 36, 37, 38* (Assoc. Board; Augener; Schirmer)

In the view of many pianists Clementi is a name for the history books rather than a composer whose music still lives. This is to do scant justice to the many pieces that can be played and thoroughly enjoyed today. The *Gradus ad Parnassum*

Instrumental Music

is one of the earliest sets of graded piano exercises and the complete set comprises 100 studies. The fact that the selection made by Carl Tausig is available in more than one edition indicates how well it has retained its value and these were recommended many years ago by Paderewski, in an article published in the *Strand Magazine*. The *Sonatinas* are delightful and are generally within the scope of the average amateur; the *Sonatas* are more difficult and less attractive but still have interest. The Schirmer edition includes the best from the sixty written by the composer.

COPLAND   (c) *Four piano blues* (Boosey)

                       (b) *Piano sonata* (Boosey)

Aaron Copland (pronounced "Copeland") is one of the most important contemporary American composers. The *Piano blues* cover a period of twenty-two years (though not in chronological order) and these are quite accessible to the good amateur pianist, as is the *Sonata*, and are quieter and much less jazz-like than the title suggests.

COUPERIN   (b) *Pièces de clavecin*, 4v. (Augener)   *OR*

                       Harpsichord pieces (Schirmer)   *OR*

                       Selected keyboard pieces (Peters)

François Couperin (often known as "Couperin le Grand" in order to distinguish him from a number of related composers) wrote these pieces for the Court of Louis XIV. The music reflects the elegance of the period and the composer was renowned both as performer and as a composer for the harpsichord. His influence was great as can be seen (to quote but a single example) in the *French suites* of Bach. The Augener edition, edited by Brahms and Chrysander, contains a very good selection of the shorter pieces, should provide considerable enjoyment for the pianist of today and is the recommended version. The two smaller selections are obviously more suited to the need of the small library or a mobile stock collection.

CRAMER   (e) *Etudes: 84 studies*, ed. Rheinhold, 4v. (Augener)

                                OR

                       60 studies, ed. Bülow (Ricordi; Universal)   *OR*

                       50 studies, ed. Bülow (Augener, 2v; Schirmer)

It is often forgotten that the founder of the famous music firm was both pianist and composer before he added publishing to his other musical activities. These studies are primarily of technical interest but they also have a distinct musical value. For all but the largest libraries, one of the Bülow selections is recommended.

CUI   (e) *Album* (Augener)

Eleven pieces of moderate difficulty by the nineteenth-century Russian composer.

CZERNY   (e) *The art of finger dexterity, op. 740* (Augener; Schirmer)

(e) *Daily studies, op. 337* (Augener; Schirmer)

(e) *101 exercises, op. 261* (Augener; Schirmer)

(e) *School of velocity, op. 299* (Augener; Schirmer)

Czerny is a composer whose opus numbers nearly reach the thousand mark and many of the individual works are of considerable length. His exercises were tremendously popular in Victorian times but less so today. The works recommended are those that have withstood the winnowing of time and changing fashion, and they appear likely to be played as technical exercises for many years to come even though their musical value is small. Only the large library will need all four volumes. For the librarian who considers one volume adequate for his library, opus 740 should be the choice; this, with the Clementi *Gradus ad Parnassum* was particularly recommended by Paderewski years ago as ideal practice material for the budding pianist.

DEBUSSY

(c) *Arabesques* (Durand)

(a) *Children's Corner suite* (Durand)

(e) *Estampes* (Durand)

(b) *Images*, 2v. (Durand)

(d) *Four le piano* (Jobert)

(a) *Préludes*, v. 1 (Durand)

(d) *Préludes*, v. 2 (Durand)

(a) *Suite bergamasque* (Jobert)

The piano music of Debussy is a landmark in the history of the repertory for the composer exploited harmonies and effects that had not previously been discovered and his influence on later composers is immense. He was primarily a miniaturist and nearly all his works are intended to conjure up a picture in sound. Even the strongest opponents of impressionism admit his genius in this. Most of his works should be included in the stock of the small library even though the cost is comparatively high. Those shown for first choice are the ones most likely to be requested. The second book of *Préludes* is considerably less popular than the first and many critics feel that Debussy's powers had waned during the intervening three years. The two sets that make least technical demands upon the pianist's technique are probably the delightful *Children's corner* (where, despite friends' assurances that an elephant is called "Jumbo", Debussy obstinately retained *Jimbo's lullaby*) and the early *Suite bergamasque* which is usually required for its third movement, the popular *Clair de lune*. The large collection may also add the *12 Etudes* (Durand) which concentrate upon technical problems.

DOHNANYI

(d) *4 Rhapsodies, op. 11* (Arcadia)

The influence of Brahms upon these works is fairly apparent, but the *Rhapsodies* are deservedly popular in their own right and have an attractive Hungarian flavour.

DVOŘÁK

(a) *Humoreskes*, 2v. (Simrock)

For many people there is but one *Humoreske*—the seventh in the set of eight. This is to underrate the others which also contain much engaging music. The remaining piano works of Dvorak are of limited interest; the famous *Slavonic Dances* are much more successful in their original form for piano duet.

Instrumental Music

FALLA   (e) *4 Spanish pieces* (Durand)
         (e) *Fantasia baetica* (Chester)

The *Spanish pieces* are somewhat after the style of a refined Albeniz; the *Fantasia* is the most extended of Falla's piano works and is difficult to play.

FAURÉ   (b) *Barcarolles, Impromptus, Nocturnes* (Heugel)
         (b) *6 Barcarolles and 5 Impromptus* (Hamelle)
         (b) *Barcarolles nos. 10–13*, 4v. (Durand)
         (b) *8 Nocturnes* (Hamelle)
         (c) *Nocturnes nos. 11–13*, 3v. (Durand)
         (c) *10 Préludes* (Hamelle)
         (d) *5 Valses and Mazurka* (Hamelle)

Gabriel Fauré is undeservedly neglected outside his own country, and pianists should be encouraged to discover his works; a generous selection in the library stock is an obvious pointer. The *Barcarolles* and *Nocturnes* are probably the best and most fascinating pieces but publishing arrangements make it impossible to provide a single volume with the complete works of either type. The Heugel album listed first contains *Barcarolles*, nos. 7–9, the fourth and fifth *Impromptus* and the ninth and tenth *Nocturnes*. Thus three volumes are needed to complete the *13 Barcarolles*, three for the *Nocturnes*, or five for the two complete sets. To the complete *Préludes*, op. 103 the publishers have added a tenth—a piano arrangement of the prelude to the lyric drama *Pénélope*. A *Piano album* published by Hamelle contains *Barcarolle no. 6*, *Romance no. 3*, *Impromptu no. 2*, *Sicilienne*, op. 78, *Improvisation*, op. 84, *no. 5*, and an arrangement of the *Berceuse* from the suite *Dolly*, op. 56.

FIELD   (d) *Nocturnes* (Peters; Schirmer; Ricordi)

These pieces are attractive and not too difficult. Their historical importance as forerunners of the similarly named pieces by Chopin is well known.

FRANCK   (b) *Prélude, aria et finale* (Ashdown; Hamelle; Ricordi)
         (a) *Prélude, chorale et fugue* (Ashdown; Hamelle; Peters; Schirmer)

Franck's works are spoiled for many musicians because of excessively chromatic writing and an organ-loft approach to piano writing. These two works, though, are popular with both amateur and professional pianists and the second work is extremely impressive when well played. These two items would conveniently bind together.

GADE   (e) *Aquarellen, op. 19* (Schirmer)

Though somewhat faded, these fairly simple and tuneful pieces will still prove attractive to many patrons.

GERSHWIN (d) *Three preludes* (Chappell)

These original piano solos are obviously derived from Gershwin's knowledge of jazz. He was himself an excellent pianist and these works may well be over-

303

looked though they are to be preferred to piano arrangements of the *Rhapsody in Blue* and *An American in Paris*.

GIBBONS   (d) *Selected pieces* (Augener)

Orlando Gibbons was a virginals player at the court of King James I of England, and later organist of Westminster Abbey. He is a most important keyboard composer of the early seventeenth century.

GRAINGER   (b) *Country gardens* (Schott)
                (b) *Irish tune from County Derry* (Schott)
                (b) *Shepherd's hey* (Schott)

These well-written and popular pieces are certain of frequent use. They are noteworthy for the fact that the directions as to speed, dynamics, etc., are expressed in colloquial English instead of the more normal Italian and the music has various tit-bits of information spread around and enclosed in "boxes". *Molly on the shore, Mock Morris* and *Handel in the Strand* are three short orchestral pieces that have been successfully "dished up" (to use the composer's own expression) as piano solos and could well be bound with the three recommended pieces.

GRANADOS   (b) *Goyescas*, 2v. (Union Musicale Franco-Espagnole)
                (d) *Spanish dances*, 4v. (Union Musicale Franco-Espagnole)

Goyescas are pieces based upon the pictures and tapestries of the famous Spanish artist Goya. As with so many sets of piano solos one item in particular has proved incomparably more popular than the rest (in this case it is no. 4, *La maja y el ruiseñor, The lover and the nightingale*) but the whole suite is well written for piano in an attractive Spanish idiom. It is not easy to play, however. The four volumes of *Spanish dances* are probably more immediately pleasing but are of lesser musical value.

GRIEG   (a) *Complete piano works*, 3v. (Peters)

Few amateur pianists have failed to play or enjoy some of Grieg's piano works, particularly the *Lyric pieces* (which comprise volume 1 of the collected piano works). These brief sketches, often with poetic titles, are generally within the scope of the performer whose pianistic attainments are quite modest. Some duplication may be required particularly in the larger system. At the time of writing the three volumes are not obtainable but the individual books which make up the complete set of *Lyric pieces* are.

HANDEL   (a) *Suites*, 2v. (Augener; Peters)

Written for the harpsichord, but thoroughly enjoyable on the modern pianoforte. The works will stand comparison with Bach's compositions in the same form. The popular theme and variations on *The harmonious blacksmith* is to be found as part of the fifth suite. The Peters edition is the better.

HARRIS   (e) *Little suite* (Schirmer)

Instrumental Music

HAYDN (a) *Piano sonatas*, 4v. (Peters)

There are many fine works as well as a few poor ones in these sonatas, which are slowly regaining popularity with pianists after a period of comparative neglect. It should be noted that there are various methods of numbering the sonatas, none of them chronological; the normal standard adopted is that of Breitkopf & Härtel. A comparative table of the Augener, Joseph Williams and old Peters (now Novello) editions is to be found in Stewart Macpherson's *Form in music*; this list deals with 17 sonatas. The recommended volume contains 43 sonatas and second choice would be the Breitkopf set, also in four volumes, which contains 42 sonatas. Peters adds an extra sonata as "no. 11" so that all subsequent numbers are one higher than the equivalent Breitkopf number. The Augener edition, in 2 volumes, contains 23 sonatas; the Novello is a reprint of the pre-World War II edition published by Peters and its 4 volumes contain 34 sonatas. Ricordi and Schirmer both publish 20 sonatas in 2 volumes. From these figures it will be seen that the two recommended versions are by far the most complete though there are, in all, over 50 piano sonatas.

HELLER (e) *Art of phrasing, op. 16* (Augener; Schirmer)

(d) *Preludes in all keys, op. 81* (Augener)

(e) *[Studies] 25 melodious studies, op. 45* ⌈ Augener;

(e) *30 progressive studies, op. 46* ⎹ Ricordi;

(e) *25 studies in rhythm, op. 47* ⎸ Schirmer;

⌊ Universal

Stephen Heller (1813–1888) was Hungarian by birth but spent most of his life in Paris. The recommended *Studies* are somewhat out of favour these days but they are well written and not too difficult for many amateurs. The smaller library may find one or two of the four choices marked (e) sufficient, but the large collection should have all in stock. The *Preludes* are both later and maturer works.

HINDEMITH (e) *Ludus tonalis* (Schott)

(d) *3 sonatas*, 3v. (Schott)

Ludus tonalis is described as "Studies in counterpoint, tonal organization and piano playing" and consists primarily of twelve linked fugues in different keys. The work is impressive but very difficult. The piano sonatas all date from 1936 and can be played as a sequence. Antony Hopkins described these, in a B.B.C. broadcast, as "the finest modern sonatas". The second is the least difficult.

IBERT (c) *Histoires* (Leduc)

Ten light and attractive pieces, of which the most popular is *Le petit ane blanc* (*The little white donkey*).

D'INDY (d) *Pour les enfants de tous les ages, op. 74*, 3v. (Rouart, Lerolle)

There are twenty-four of these pieces for children of all ages and the short works are written in the style of different composers.

305

IRELAND

(d) *Decorations* (Augener)

(b) *London pieces* (Augener)

(c) *Sarnia* (Boosey)

(c) *Sonata* (Augener)

(c) *The towing path* (Augener)

(d) *Two pieces* (*For remembrance; Amberley wild brooks*) (Augener)

(d) *Two pieces* (*April; Bergomask*) (Augener)

John Ireland has written many piano pieces; though not unpleasantly "modern" to the conservative ear they are written in a distinctive and pleasing idiom. Ralph Hill considered the piano sonata to be "the greatest written by a British composer" (in the Penguin *British music of our time*, p. 203) but the composer's most popular work is one of his slightest—*The holy Boy* (from *Preludes for piano*, published by Boosey). If desired, most of the works listed above could be bound together in one or two volumes, though the Sonata should be kept separate.

JACOB

(e) *Sonata* (Williams)

JANÁČEK

(e) *In the mist* (Artia)

(e) *On the overgrown path* (Artia)

Two examples of the work of a Czech composer whose true stature is only being discovered some thirty years after his death, which took place in 1926.

KABALEVSKY

(e) *Sonata no. 1, op. 6* (Anglo-Soviet)

(e) *Sonata no. 2, op. 45* (Anglo-Soviet)

(d) *Sonata no. 3, op. 46* (Anglo-Soviet)

(d) *Sonatinas, op. 13*

(c) *5 sets of variations (for students), op. 51* (Leeds Music)

The three sonatas are important modern works, and are comparatively difficult to play well; the second is the most demanding. All three would conveniently bind together in a single volume. The two opus 13 sonatinas are slighter and present fewer technical problems to the pianist. The variations are very suitable for children and pianists of very limited abilities; the composer has written a number of other works of a similar nature (*Children's pieces, op. 27, Variations, op. 40*, etc.) which would be suitable for use in the junior library.

KODALY

(e) *Gyermektancok* (Boosey)

This is a set of twelve dances, all on the black keys.

KOECHLIN

(e) *12 Esquisses, op. 41 (Sets 1 & 2)* (Salabert)

(e) *12 petites pièces, op. 41b* (Salabert)

These three dozen pieces are all brief and in a variety of musical styles. Clean and fastidious writing marks most of these works, and Koechlin is not known to many pianists, who would enjoy these pieces if they could be persuaded to try them.

Instrumental Music

KRENEK   (d) *12 short piano pieces, op. 83* (Schirmer)

The pieces are written in the twelve-tone technique on the same basic row. They are not difficult to play and supply an excellent introduction to this type of music.

KUHLAU   (d) *Sonatinas, op. 20, op. 55, op. 59* (Augener)

KUHNAU   (d) *6 Biblical sonatas* (Broude)

An early example of programme music and of considerable intrinsic interest. Kuhnau was a predecessor of J. S. Bach at the church of St. Thomas in Leipzig.

LARSEN   (e) *3 Norwegian dances, op. 2* (Norsk Musikforlag)
                       (e) *3 piano pieces, op. 3* (Norsk Musikforlag)

LISZT   (a) *Années de pèlerinage* (Durand, 4v; Schirmer, 2v.)

                   (a) *Consolations; and, Liebesträume* (Augener, 2v; Schirmer; Universal, 2v.)

                   (b) *Etudes d'exécution transcendante* [*Concert studies*] (Augener)

                   (a) *Hungarian rhapsodies, 1–16*, 2v. (Augener; Ricordi; Schirmer)

                   (b) *Hungarian rhapsodies, 16–19* (Paragon)

                   (c) *Paganini studies* [*Etudes d'exécution transcendante d'après Paganini*] (Augener, 2v; Schirmer)

                   (d) *Sonata in B minor* (Augener; Schirmer)

                   (d) *Liszt Society publications* [In progress] (Schott)

Liszt is too often regarded as a composer of shallow, showy and generally vulgar music and for these reasons his importance as a composer (and innovator) for the piano is often insufficiently realized. His exploitation of the resources of the piano has affected almost every subsequent composer for the instrument. Only few of his works can be played by those of modest attainments but the well-equipped amateur pianist will find a mine of interest. Liszt's piano works normally show careful workmanship, are extremely pianistic and lie well under the hands though players with a large span are at a considerable advantage here. Many Liszt works have been excellently recorded on disc and this fact may increase the use of the scores provided.

The Schirmer edition of the *Années de pélerinage* contains the first and second years (or series) and the supplement; the Durand edition contains all these together with the third year which comprises seven pieces of much lesser stature than their predecessors. Published volumes of the *Hungarian rhapsodies* usually contain the first fifteen of these plus the *Rhapsodie espagnole* but the last four (nos. 16 to 19) are virtually unknown. Liszt's biggest work in every sense is perhaps the *Sonata*, but its technical difficulties (like those of the concert studies) are likely to limit borrowings to listeners rather than performers.

In addition to the works recommended, the large library will find it worth while to add some of the many volumes of Liszt's piano transcriptions, of which the Bach organ works, Schubert songs and Wagner album are particularly noteworthy. The Liszt Society volumes contain many works not found in any other edition; at the time of writing four volumes have been published: v. 1, *Late piano, works*; v. 2, *Early and late piano works*; v. 3, *Hungarian and late piano works*; v. 4, *Dances*.

MACDOWELL   (c) *New England idyls, op. 62* (Elkin)

                        (a) *Sea pieces, op. 55* (Elkin; Chappell)

                        (b) *Woodland sketches, op. 51* (Elkin; Chappell)

MacDowell is generally regarded, in Britain at least, as the first of a growing line of American composers though his works clearly show his European training. Possibly overrated in the U.S.A., he is certainly underrated outside that country. Generally speaking, MacDowell's miniatures are delightful and many can be played by the least talented pianist. *To a wild rose* and *A.D. 1620* are perhaps over-familiar but there are many other (and several better) pieces that are too rarely heard.

MARTIN   (e) *8 Préludes* (Universal)

"Modern" and difficult works by the contemporary Swiss composer. They date from 1949.

MEDTNER   (c) *4 fairy tales [contes], op. 26* (Boosey; Novello)

                        (e) *Sonata idylle, op. 56* (Edition Russe)

There are a number of pieces bearing the general title "Contes", op. 13, op. 20, op. 26, etc. They vary in difficulty and effectiveness but are pleasant and pianistic. The major works are less immediately attractive. To regard Medtner as an inferior Rachmaninov (as some appear to do) is to underrate a distinct and individual style.

MENDELSSOHN   (a) *Complete piano works*, 5v. (Augener)

Mendelssohn still suffers from the reaction to his over-popularity in Victorian times. Copies of his *Lieder ohne Worte* (*Songs without words*) (which comprise volume 1 of the edition listed above) are to be found in the majority of batches of older music given to the library and the modern performer tends to overlook Mendelssohn's craftsmanship. No one could express better the magic of the fairy world. The Augener edition is a good one and the works themselves are almost guaranteed to provide considerable enjoyment for many others in addition to the now elderly ladies who learned his pieces in their girlhood days. The Peters edition (also in 5 volumes) is at present o.p. The other four volumes of the Augener edition contain miscellaneous pieces (vols. 2, 3 and 5) while volume 4 includes 2-piano arrangements of the two piano concertos and three concert pieces.

MILHAUD   (e) *L'automne: suite* (Salabert)

                      (c) *Une journée: 5 pieces* (Mercury)

                      (b) *Saudades do Brazil*, 2v. (Schott)

Milhaud is probably the most important member of the French group of the nineteen-twenties known as "Les Six" and his works are worth the attention of the amateur pianist. The Brazilian dances date from 1920 and were the result of a visit to that country. *L'automne* dates from 1932 and *Une journée* from 1946, so the three works give a fairly representative picture of his development as a writer for piano.

MOMPOU   (b) *Canciones y danzas*, 8v. (Salabert)
      (d) *Scènes d'enfants* (Salabert)
      (e) *Suburbis* (Salabert)

Federico Mompou (b. 1893) is a Spanish composer who tends to dispense with bar lines to his music though the melodies usually fall into generally accepted rhythmic patterns. The eight brief *Songs and dances* are founded on popular Spanish airs and arranged with great artistry, deserving to be much better known than they are.

MOSZKOWSKI   (d) *3 concert studies, op. 24* (Augener)

Moszkowski, a Polish composer of attractive light music, is today under something of a cloud and is a much less popular writer than thirty years or more ago. His works, according to Hutcheson, "always succeed in creating a maximum of effect with a minimum of difficulty" but Lockwood suggests that "The player of Moszkowski's music needs well-developed fingers capable of executing spidery passage work and wide skips with delicacy and accuracy".

Here is a composer who has suffered much from editors, arrangers and simplifiers and the original should always be bought if possible. Unfortunately, it is often difficult to discover with many of his works which was or is the original. The larger collection, for example, might well add *From foreign parts, op. 23, 5 waltzes, op. 8, 6 pieces, op. 83* and the *Spanish dances, op. 21* (all Augener) but at least two of these sets were originally written for piano duet, though the solo piano arrangement appears to be most successful in nearly all cases.

MOZART   (a) *Miscellaneous piano pieces* (Assoc. Board; Henle, 2v; Peters, 2v.)
      (a) *Sonatas*, 2v. (Assoc. Board; Augener; Breitkopf; Ricordi; Schirmer; Universal)

Mozart's limited solo piano output is often neglected by public libraries in favour of arrangements of symphonies, overtures, etc. The sonatas should be in the smallest collection and the volume(s) of miscellaneous pieces is only slightly less important. The various editions of the sonatas use different systems of numbering and a key to seven editions is provided by Hutcheson who recommends the Breitkopf edition as the best. The Associated Board edition (edited by York Bowen and Abyn Raymer) can be confidently recommended. It contains twenty sonatas of which the first seventeen are in the same order as the Urtext (Breitkopf) edition, listed by Hutcheson. It may be mentioned that both Breitkopf and Henle claim to publish the Urtext (definitive) edition.

MUSSORGSKY   (b) *Pictures at an Exhibition* (Augener; International Music; Schott; Schirmer)

This piano suite is much better known in orchestral guise (the arrangement by Ravel being the most popular) but it is well worth purchase in its original form even though much of it is well beyond the scope of the average amateur.

As in almost all his works, the composer shows an original and unconventional mind. The suite has been recorded in both piano and orchestral versions and the Hawkes pocket score (which uses the Ravel orchestration) quotes the original piano score under the orchestral parts. The recommended edition is the I.M.C. one since it contains good-sized monochrome illustrations of some of the pictures, etc., by Victor Hartmann that inspired the work.

NIELSEN (d) *Chaconne, op. 32* (Hansen)

(d) *Theme and variations, op. 40* (Hansen)

Though Nielsen may be regarded primarily as an orchestral composer, his piano works are important and well written. In both of these works the variations are excellently developed from the opening theme. Smaller libraries may prefer to buy the *Album of ten pieces* which contains some earlier and much slighter works (from opus 3, etc.) and some arrangements of items from Nielsen's opera *Maskerade*.

PADEREWSKI (e) *Chants du voyageur, op. 8* (Ashdown)

(d) *Variations and fugue in B♭ minor, op. 23* (Ashdown)

Paderewski is often regarded, on account of his famous *Minuet in G, op. 14, no. 1* (Ashdown), as a composer of salon music but his other works are of much greater depth. Some of his music, it is freely admitted, has already faded and is unlikely to be revived but the two works mentioned are worthy of their places in a library stock. At the time of writing the *Variations* are out of print.

PARRY (e) *Shulbrede tunes* (Augener)

Contains ten fairly brief and well-written pieces.

POULENC (a) *Mouvements perpetuels* (Chester)

(d) *Napoli: suite* (U.M.P.)

(c) *Pastourelle* (Heugel)

(e) *Promenades* (Chester)

Poulenc was another member of "Les Six" and his music is attractive, witty and unpretentious. The first of the *Mouvements perpetuels* is very popular. A wider range of his piano music could well be bought in the larger collection.

PROKOFIEV (e) *10 pieces, op. 12,* 10v. (Schauer)

(d) *Sarcasms, op. 17* (Boosey)

(b) *Sonata no. 6, op. 82* (Boosey)

(c) *Visions fugitives, op. 22* (Boosey)

This Russian composer who died in 1953 is best known for his *Peter and the wolf* and his *Classical symphony*, but he also wrote a considerable amount of piano music of extremely variable quality. Prokoviev himself was an excellent pianist and many of his works are beyond the scope of the average amateur. The items listed above are of some importance and are likely to remain in demand after many of the composer's other works have ceased to arouse interest.

Instrumental Music

PURCELL   (b) *Suites: Toccata, Lessons and Pieces*, 4v.
              (Chester)   *OR*
              Suites (Augener; Novello; Schirmer)

Purcell's keyboard music is probably more strongly represented in British libraries than those elsewhere, which is natural, for he was one of Britain's finest composers. The eight suites are of considerable interest to any pianist with an affection for seventeenth-century music. The Chester edition is recommended, but for the library that does not wish to buy four volumes the Augener edition is suggested since it contains all the Suites as well as some miscellaneous pieces. The publisher's title is *Select pieces*. The Schirmer edition includes an *Alman* with the Suites, while the Novello edition contains six Suites only.

RACHMANINOV   (a) *Prelude, op. 3, no. 2* (Augener; Boosey; Cramer;
                  Ricordi; Schott, etc.)
                  (a) *Preludes, op. 23* (Boosey)
                  (a) *Preludes, op. 32* (Boosey)

Rachmaninov is an outstanding example of the small band of musicians who were outstanding as composers, executants and conductors. Because he was not a musical innovator (a fault that is also alleged in Brahms) Rachmaninov's works are often given insufficient recognition. In addition to *the* Prelude (the opus 3, no. 2, in C♯ minor) the others are barely known, but they are skilfully written and well worthy of study by the amateur pianist.

RAMEAU   (e) *Pièces de clavecin* (Durand)

An important French composer of the eighteenth century. The volume recommended is edited by Saint-Saens and contains over fifty pieces. Smaller libraries may prefer to buy *Select pieces*, published by Augener.

RAVEL   (a) *Gaspard de la nuit* (Durand)
              (c) *Jeux d'eau* (Schott)
              (d) *Miroirs* (Schott)
              (e) *Sonatine* (Durand)
              (b) *Le tombeau de Couperin* (Durand)

Ravel is one of the most important modern composers for piano and his influence, together with that of Debussy, has affected a tremendous amount of subsequent piano composition. Ravel's pieces need both an assured technique and a good sense of style if they are to be performed successfully. The composer was a great perfectionist, constantly rewriting and polishing and this partly accounts for his small output. Many of the piano works were orchestrated by the composer himself, four of the six movements of *Le tombeau de Couperin* providing an example. The three movements of *Gaspard de la nuit* (*Ondine, Le gibet, Scarbo*) are often played singly rather than in sequence.

RAWSTHORNE   (e) *Bagatelles* (O.U.P.)
                  (e) *Four romantic pieces* (O.U.P.)
                  (e) *Sonatina for piano* (O.U.P.)

These works are worth including in the larger stock as examples of contem-

311

porary music that is well written and which should be of interest to those pianists who like to try their skill on modern music as well as on the established classics.

REGER   (c) *6 Burlesken, op. 58* (British & Continental)
        (d) *Characterstücke, op. 32*, 2v. (Universal)
        (e) *Improvisationen, op. 18* (Augener)
        (d) *Sonatinas, op. 89*, 4v. (Bote & Bock)
        (e) *4 studies for the left hand alone* (Universal)

"Reger's enormous output for the piano is not well known in this country" write Friskin and Freundlich, and that remark is equally true of British pianists. Even the long-playing gramophone record which has caused an immense widening of the available musical repertory has hardly touched Reger though many lesser composers have received generous treatment on disc. The *Burlesques* are in the styles of other composers. The large collection might add the *6 Preludes and fugues, op. 99* (Bote & Bock) and Reger's two major piano works, both long and technically demanding, *The variations and double fugue on a theme of Bach, op. 81* (Hinrichsen) and the *Variations and fugue on a theme of Telemann, op. 134* (Peters).

REIZENSTEIN   (e) *12 Preludes and fugues*, 2v. (Lengnick)
              (e) *Sonata in B major* (Lengnick)

Franz Reizenstein (b. 1911) is a naturalized British composer whose works are assuming a growing importance. His style is not easily assimilated and these works require a good technique.

SAINT-SAENS   (e) *Etudes for the left hand, op. 135* (Durand)
              (e) *6 Waltzes* (Durand)

While the main intention is technical development, these six Studies are musicianly and are much more enjoyable listening than their title might suggest. The composer's major work for two hands is the *Caprice on airs from "Alceste"* (Schirmer) which is difficult but extremely effective.

SATIE   (e) *Gymnopédies* (Rouart, Lerolle)

A French composer noted for his satirical and beautifully clear music. He wrote comparatively little, but a large proportion of his works is for solo piano. The *3 Gymnopédies* (an untranslatable word of the composer's own devising) are probably the best-known solo pieces.

SCARLATTI, D.   (a) *Selected sonatas* (Augener, 2v; Francis, Day & Hunter; Peters; Ricordi; Schirmer, 2v.)

These sonatas, which are really sonatinas, are nearly all brief single-movement works and only a handful have become well known. For many years it was the custom to play Scarlatti in arrangements by Tausig and others whose editions nearly always tended to over-elaboration. Modern concert pianists have usually reverted to the original scores, with a considerable gain in clarity and charm. The works can sound delightful on a modern pianoforte provided that the performer remembers that they were originally written for harpsichord and scales down his tone accordingly.

For many years the standard edition has been that of Alessandro Longo,

Instrumental Music

published in ten volumes of 50 sonatas each and with a supplementary volume of 45 sonatas, published by Ricordi. The selection at the head of this entry published by this firm contains 25 of the works edited by Longo. His system of numbering the sonatas has been the standard one so that the famous *Pastorale* in D minor is identified as L. 413, and the *Cat's fugue* as L. 499.

The position has now been complicated by the American, Ralph Kirkpatrick. Not only has he written the standard life of the composer but he has re-edited a number of the sonatas and it seems likely that a complete new edition of Scarlatti sonatas will appear; musicians will then have to cope with both K. and L. identification numbers since the two sequences are quite dissimilar. Kirkpatrick's editing is much more to modern taste and the Schirmer edition must be the recommended one; the two volumes contain 60 sonatas in all. The much smaller volume published by Francis, Day & Hunter would make a useful addition as it contains an unhackneyed selection of 12 sonatas edited by Manchester's music librarian, Leonard Duck. The Augener edition, edited by Thomas F. Dunhill, contains 29 sonatas and the Peters edition 25.

Domenico Scarlatti was born in 1685, the same year as both Bach and Handel, and his father, Alessandro Scarlatti, has an important place in the history of the development of opera.

SCHOENBERG   (e) *3 piano pieces, op. 11* (Universal)

                      (d) *6 piano pieces, op. 19* (Universal)

                      (d) *5 piano pieces, op. 23* (Universal)

Schoenberg is famous as founder of the "twelve-tone" school of atonality—music without key and in which any one note in the scale is regarded as equal in importance to any other, so that this music lacks the tonic (or key-note) to which our ears have long been accustomed. To many people, in fact, Schoenberg's music is not music at all. The opus 11 works are not easy to grasp but there are some remnants of normal tonality; the opus 19 pieces are brief and are the most approachable of Schoenberg's piano music. The last of the opus 23 pieces, the *Waltz, op. 23, no, 5*, has won fame as the first piece of music composed to a "tone-row". Large collections could complete the composer's piano works by the addition of the *Suite, op. 25* and *Two pieces, op. 33* (both Universal). None of these works is likely to be popular but their importance is undeniable.

SCHUBERT   (a) *Fantasias, Impromptus and Moments musicaux* (Augener, 3v; Schirmer; Universal)

                      (b) *Piano sonatas*, 2v. (Augener; Peters; Schirmer; Universal)

                      (c) *Dances (complete)* 2v, (Henle)

The smaller pieces such as the *Moments musicaux* are of sufficient popularity to warrant duplication, perhaps in different editions. If, however, only one copy of each of the first two recommendations is to be stocked then both should be in the same edition since the contents tend to vary between the editions. Augener publish the two *Fantasias* (*The Wanderer, op. 15* and opus 78) separately, with the *Impromptus* and *Moments musicaux* in a single volume. The *Fantasia, op. 78* is also known as a *Sonata* with the result that Augener and Schirmer include 10 sonatas in their volumes but Peters show 11, including the op. 78. There are, in fact, no less than 21 sonatas by Schubert but several are incomplete. These unfinished works (with one exception) were completed by W. Rehberg and were at

313

one time available in the Steingräber edition but are at present o.p. The Universal edition, edited by E. Ratz, contains 14 sonatas.

The remaining volumes of *German dances* and similar works are of light-weight pieces that are often very brief but which are popular with amateur pianists. There are 435 of these pieces in two volumes.

SCHUMANN   (a) *Complete piano works*, 4v. (Augener)

There is no need to stress the value of this composer's piano works. *Album for the young* still provides excellent fare for many who need elementary works that are both tuneful and of musical value, while *Scenes of childhood* (especially the movement *Träumerei [Dreaming]*) are almost equally popular. Schumann's other works provide further pleasure for pianists of varying abilities. Alternatives to the Augener edition are (i) the fourteen volumes of Universal which omit the *Sonatas, Forest scenes*, etc. and (ii) the Clara Schumann edition in thirteen volumes published by Breitkopf. American librarians have Peters and Kalmus editions easily available; both are good.

SCOTT   (c) *Danse nègre, op. 56, no. 5* (Elkin)

         (c) *Lotus land, op. 47, no. 1* (Elkin)

Cyril Scott has written a number of small, attractive pieces for piano. They are well suited to the instrument for the composer himself was an excellent performer. The two examples given, together perhaps with other works such as *Water wagtail, op. 71, no. 3, Vesperale, op. 40, no. 2* and *Allegro poco scherzando* (which is no. 1 of *Three little waltzes*) might well be bound together to form a single album; this would be particularly useful to those libraries that do not normally provide short single works. Elkin publish three albums (of which the third is o.p.) of Cyril Scott's piano works but these do not contain any of the well-known pieces.

SCRIABIN   (b) *Prelude and nocturne for the left hand, op. 9* (Belaieff)

         (c) *24 Preludes, op. 11* (Belaieff)

         (d) *12 studies, op. 8* (Belaieff)

         (e) *Studies, op. 42* (Belaieff)

Scriabin's reputation has waned considerably since his death in 1915; his "mystic" chord no longer mystifies and his philosophy is dead. Yet his piano works, whose difficulty varies enormously even in sets sharing the same opus number (as in the *Studies, op. 8*, listed above), deserve to be better known than they are and are rewarding to the persevering pianist. In addition to the works listed the large collection could usefully consider adding some, if not all, of the ten piano sonatas. The fourth, which is of considerable technical difficulty, is perhaps the best. American librarians can buy all ten sonatas in a single volume (Leeds Music).

SHOSTAKOVICH   (d) *3 fantastic dances, op. 1* (Boosey)

         (e) *24 preludes, op. 34* (Boosey)

         (c) *24 preludes and fugues, op. 87*. 2v. (Leeds Music)

         (e) *Sonata no. 2, op. 64* (Boosey)

The latest of the recommended works, op. 87, shows Shostakovich's natural

Instrumental Music

genius for writing fugues, a gift which can be seen in some of his other works. As with some other composers, the set comprises an example in each major and minor key. These two volumes must be considered as important contemporary writing. The other recommended works, in comparison, are much slighter but are still worth having; they provide examples of his style that is sometimes witty and often angular.

STRAVINSKY   (e) *Etudes, op. 7*, 4v. (Schauer)

Stravinsky is primarily an orchestral composer but has written a limited amount of music for the pianist. The four studies are of sufficient importance to be included in the larger collection.

SZYMANOWSKI   (c) *Etudes, op. 4* (Universal)

(d) *Métopes, op. 29* (Universal)

(e) *9 preludes, op. 1* (Universal)

Karol Szymanowski (1883–1937) is the most important Polish composer since Chopin but his works are unlikely to achieve anything like the popularity of those by his compatriot for they are difficult both for performer and listener. Although Szymanowski's type of modernity may not be too easily assimilated the music bears constant repetition and should provide a steadily increasing interest with continued performance.

TCHAIKOVSKY   (d) *Album for the young, op. 39* (Augener; Ricordi; Schirmer)

(c) *The months of the year, op. 37* (Augener; Schirmer)

Most of Tchaikovsky's solo piano work is of inferior quality but the twelve pieces (one for each month of the year) that make up opus 37 are well written and attractive, especially *Troika* (November). The other work comprises simple pieces useful to children and adults with very limited technique.

TIPPETT   (e) *Sonata in G major* (Schott)

An important modern British work that needs an excellent technique.

TURINA   (e) *Cuentos de España (Contes d'Espagne), op. 20 and op. 40*, 2v. (Rouart, Lerolle)

These pieces have the colourful writing and attractive Spanish rhythms of Albeniz and Granados, but the music is of a lesser calibre. The large collection might also add the *Danzas Gitanas*, also in two volumes (op. 55 and op. 84) published by Salabert, and one or other of the shorter suites of pieces such as *Jardins d'Andalousie, op. 31* (Rouart) and *Femmes d'Espagne* (Rouart).

VILLA-LOBOS   (e) *Choros no. 5—Alma Brasileira* (Schott)

(d) *A Prolè do Bébé, series I*, 8v. (Schott)

(d) *A Prolè do Bébé, series II*, 9v. (Schott)

(e) *10 pieces on popular Brazilian children's songs*, 2v. (Schott)

Heitor Villa-Lobos is probably the best-known of a growing band of Latin-

American composers and his output is amazingly large and varied. It is also very confusing, partly because he does not use opus numbers. *A Prolé do Bébé* consist of short pieces of widely varying technical difficulty; the first set is devoted to "the baby's dolls" and the second to "the baby's animals", and the music is as colourful as the individual titles suggest. The *Cirandas*, sixteen fairly simple pieces based on children's songs would be recommended, but only nine are at present available in Britain and the prices are prohibitive.

WEBER   (c) *Piano pieces* (Augener; Schirmer)

                     (d) *Piano sonatas* (Augener)

The four piano sonatas (edited by Liszt in the edition available) are difficult and little known, except for the *Perpetuum mobile* that forms the last movement of the first sonata, op. 24. This work, like the others, has good movements but is uneven in inspiration. The five miscellaneous piano pieces have been much more popular, particularly the *Invitation to the dance, op. 65.*

EARLY KEYBOARD MUSIC

In general, composers of the pre-Bach era have received scant attention in the previous section. There are two reasons for this; much of this music does not sound well on the modern pianoforte, and many of the composers are today available only in anthologies. The pieces themselves are often extremely brief, the titles are sometimes attractively naïve and the sense of key much less developed than in subsequent centuries. The music is historically important and much of it is intrinsically delightful so that at least one of the collections listed below should be added to stock. It need hardly be added that there are many other similar collections not necessarily inferior to those listed.

KASTNER, *ed.*   *Old Portuguese keyboard music*, 2v. (Schott)

OESTERLE, *ed.*   *Early keyboard music*, 2v. (Schirmer)

This comprises a selection of music written for virginals, spinet, harpsichord and clavichord. Book I is sub-titled "Byrde to A. Scarlatti" (the final "e" on the English composer's name is unusual but admissible), and Book II "Couperin to Rameau". There are 122 pieces in all.

REDLICH, *ed.*   *Elizabethan virginal music* (Universal)

These twenty-four pieces are all by English composers (Bull, Gibbons, Farnaby, etc.) and are selected from the *Fitzwilliam Virginal book* and *My Ladye Nevell's books*, two of the four most important sources of this type of music.

GLYN, *ed.*   *Fitzwilliam Virginal mss: a selection* (British & Continental)

Instrumental Music

FULLER MAITLAND &
BARCLAY SQUIRE,
eds.   *Fitzwilliam Virginal book: selected pieces* (British &
Continental)

In his *Oxford Companion to Music*, Dr. Percy Scholes declares that "The English virginal is of the highest importance in the history of music . . .", while a great authority in this field, Van den Borren, shows in considerable detail (in his *Sources of keyboard music in England*) the debt that later keyboard writers owe to the English virginalists. The original manuscript from which the above selections are taken is probably the most important of all in this field. It is in the Fitzwilliam Museum at Cambridge (England) and has provided the only known copy of many early English pieces. The book contained the repertory of an early seventeenth-century amateur virginal player and the complete manuscript (edited by Maitland and Squire) was published in two volumes by Breitkopf and is now available in both Breitkopf and Broude editions. It should be noted that the two selections given above do not overlap.

PIANO DUETS

Music in this form is of no great antiquity for with one or two exceptions it dates back only to the latter half of the eighteenth century when Mozart and J. C. Bach, then living in London, introduced it. During the nineteenth century the piano duet flourished and many of the greatest composers wrote music for four hands, one piano. In addition a tremendous amount of orchestral music was arranged for this same combination. Many a symphony is too complex to be reduced adequately to the compass of two hands but a much more satisfactory arrangement is possible with two performers.

The art of duet playing has declined considerably during this century and although there has still been a certain amount of first-class music written in this form contemporary composers would appear to find it much more attractive to write music for two pianos. As for arrangements, the growth of opportunity to hear orchestral works in their original form at concerts, by radio and gramophone record, etc., has lessened the attraction of the overture and symphony arranged for piano duet, although there are still a number of pianists who will borrow and enjoy them.

To some extent librarians have themselves to blame for the decline of interest in this section since all too frequently the selection is overweighted with arrangements while so much attractive music, originally written for piano duet, is not provided. It is also a section in which a certain amount of "spring cleaning" is often needed by the relegation of old and unattractive scores and their replacement by modern editions and by newer works.

The lists that follow are divided into two sections: first the original works, then the arrangements. The library that has very few original works in stock could, with great advantage, add more— possibly a number of those listed here.

BEETHOVEN (b) *Complete piano duets* (Augener; Peters; Universal)

While these works do not reveal Beethoven at his greatest, they still have interest for most pianists. The two sets of variations (on an air of Count Waldstein and upon a German song) are the most important items.

BIZET (c) *Jeux d'enfants, op. 22* (Durand)

This suite is better known in its orchestral form but the original setting provides great entertainment for both duettists and, if well played, for audience also. There are twelve short pieces with titles of children's games.

BOWEN (e) *4 pieces, op. 90* (O.U.P.)

York Bowen is a contemporary (b. 1884) British composer who has written some excellent music both for piano solo and duet, but his works are neither well known nor often performed. Two of these four pieces (no. 1, Prelude and no 3, Serenade) are at present in print, and with two *Suites* are good examples of modern works for piano duet.

BRAHMS (a) *Hungarian dances*, 2v. (Augener; Schirmer)

(a) *Waltzes* (Augener; Peters)

It is often forgotten that Brahms's famous waltzes were originally written for piano duet. All the works are well written for the medium and extremely attractive to play.

BUSONI (e) *Finnish folk-tunes, op. 27* (Breitkopf)

Busoni's only work for duet, written at the age of 22. These dances have remained almost completely unknown and are not included in either Rowley or Friskin & Freundlich.

DEBUSSY (c) *Petite suite* (Durand)

(e) *6 épigraphes antiques* (Durand)

The suite is another set of pieces better known in the orchestral version than in the original. The *Epigraphes* are late works based upon earlier, discarded sketches. There is controversy as to their value yet when well played their effectiveness cannot be denied. In addition to these two sets, Debussy also wrote a Scottish march for piano duet, published by Jobert.

DVOŘÁK (a) *Slavonic dances, op. 46* (Lengnick)

(a) *New Slavonic dances, op. 72* (Lengnick)

(c) *Legends, op. 59* (Lengnick)

Instrumental Music

The two sets of *Slavonic dances* (there are eight in each) and some of Schubert's are essential in the smallest collection. Dvořák himself arranged the dances for orchestra and also for piano solo. The duet form is, however, the original form and a most attractive one. The *Legends* are but little inferior; Dvořák was, generally speaking, a poor writer for solo piano but a great one for duettists.

FAURE   (c) *Dolly: suite, op. 56* (Hamelle)

This suite appears to be known to few duettists but should give a great amount of pleasure to those who borrow and try it. There is an orchestral version of the suite, arranged by Henri Rabaud.

GRIEG   (d) *Two symphonic dances, op. 14* (Peters)
            (d) *Norwegian dances, op. 35* (Novello; Peters)

The *Symphonic dances* were originally planned as a symphony but eventually emerged in their present form. The other work is also an original one for this medium. The writing is not as effective as Grieg's for piano solo but both works are likely to be in reasonable demand from pianists.

HINDEMITH   (e) *Sonata* (Schott)

MOSZKOWSKI   (c) *Polish dances, op. 55* (Peters)
            (b) *Spanish dances, op. 12* (Peters)

Moszkowski was a Pole and his "Spanish" music is patently spurious yet these duets (like his others) are cheerful, grand fun to play and pleasant for the listener. Some further works (such as the *New Spanish dances, op. 65*) are worthy of consideration if the two recommended works prove as popular as they should.

MOZART   (c) *Piano duets* (Augener; Peters; Schirmer; Universal)

As mentioned in the introduction to this section, these works are among the earliest written for piano duet but they continue to retain their place in the repertory, though they are not perhaps representative of Mozart at his greatest.

POULENC   (e) *Sonata* (Chester)

A typical example of the composer's brilliant and amusing style.

RAVEL   (d) *Ma mère l'Oye* (Durand)

This *Mother Goose* suite is better known in its orchestral version but sets interesting problems for keyboard players who need to be above average if this work is to be performed satisfactorily.

SCHMITT   (d) *Feuillets de voyage, op. 26* (Durand)
            (c) *Humoresques, op. 43* (Chapelier)
            (b) *Pièces romantiques, op. 42* (Chapelier)
            (e) *Reflets d'Allemagne, op. 28* (Mathet)
            (a) *Sur cinq notes, op. 34* (U.M.P.)

Alec Rowley declares this composer's four-hand works as "probably the finest in the whole modern repertoire" and the enterprising librarian will make some attempt to obtain at least one of the sets listed above. In the opus 34 pieces, one pianist confines himself to a five-finger group while the other produces enchanting sounds about this simplicity. The *Reflets* are the most difficult. These five works and recommended order of choice were kindly selected by the late Alec Rowley.

SCHUBERT   *Complete piano duets*, 4v. (Peters) [v. 1, (a); v. 2–4(c)]

Schubert probably wrote more music for piano duet than any other composer and a selection of his works should be the first choice for any collection. The small collection may content itself with the first volume but the other three should be bought as this section grows. Volume 1 provides the best start since it contains the most popular pieces, including the one that has far outstripped the others in general popularity, the D major *Marche militaire* from opus 51. Duettists will know that this particular march is no better than most of the other sixteen written by the composer. Duets are rarely played on the concert platform nowadays; Artur Schnabel and his son, Karl-Ulrich Schnabel, gave performances and made some quickly-deleted recordings in the nineteen-thirties, and the tradition has been maintained by the younger Schnabel and his wife as well as by the Viennese team of Paul Badura-Skoda and Georg Demus—but these duets are for playing rather than for listening.

SCHUMANN   (c) *Complete piano duets* (Peters)

There are four sets—the *Oriental pictures* [*Bilder aus Osten*], op. 66, subtitled "Six impromptus" with very innocuous eastern touches; *12 duets* (*for little and big children*) *op. 85*, which live up to their title by being attractive to both adults and children; *Ball scenes*, op. 109 (9 pieces) and *Children's ball*, op. 130 (6 pieces). The last two sets are not up to the standard of their predecessors, though they are still attractive. Schirmer publish a separate edition of the op. 85 duets and Augener the op. 66 set.

TCHAIKOVSKY   (d) *36 Russian folk songs* (Peters)

These duets reverse normal procedure, for here the primo part is less difficult than that written for the bass player.

WEBER   (e) *Piano duets* (Peters)

There are three sets—opus 3, opus 10 and opus 60. All are lightweight works that provide pleasant relaxation for duettists who enjoy music that is not too difficult. Breitkopf publish the eight pieces that form op. 60 in a separate album, at present out of print. The opus 3 pieces are entitled *6 petites pièces faciles*, and opus 10 consists of eight separate items.

DUET ARRANGEMENTS

BEETHOVEN   (b) *Symphonies*, 2v. (Augener; Schirmer)

An ever-popular set with duettists. The first volume is likely to be used more frequently than the second. The *Overtures* may also be considered as a useful addition.

BIZET   (d) *L'Arlésienne suite* (Schirmer)

BRAHMS   (c) *Symphonies* (Schirmer)

GRIEG   (b) *Peer Gynt: suites nos. 1 and 2, op. 46 and op. 55* (Peters)

Not too difficult for amateurs (which may account for the great pleasure it gave me many years ago). As in most duet arrangements, the bass part is generally distinctly easier than the treble.

HAYDN   (b) *Symphonies*, 2v. (Augener; Schirmer)

These are the twelve "Salomon" symphonies and are the last that Haydn wrote. Such well-known examples as the *Surprise, Oxford* and *London* are included in these volumes, but the symphonies are not in numerical order.

MOZART   (c) *12 Symphonies*, 2v. (Augener; Schirmer)

A misleading title, for the first volume contains symphonies 41, 40, 39, 38, 35 and 36 in that order; the second volume includes the *Posthorn serenade, K. 320,* the *Haffner Serenade, K. 250,* Symphonies 31, 34 and 33 and a symphony now known to be by Leopold Mozart, and numbered by Einstein as K.Anh. 293.

SCHUMANN   (e) *Symphonies* (Augener; Schirmer)

WALTON   (d) *Façade: two suites*, 2v. (O.U.P.)

WARLOCK   (c) *Capriol* (Curwen)

This is a most attractive suite with some grand discords at the end to awaken any dozing listeners. The work is well known in its original form for string orchestra; the arranger of the piano duet is not indicated so is presumably the composer.

A FURTHER SELECTION

In the early part of 1953 the Sunday morning programme of the B.B.C., "Music Magazine", included two programmes on piano duet music. They were given by two people who were long renowned as performers of music at two pianos—Ethel Bartlett and Rae Robertson. Speaking in antiphon with occasional examples on the studio piano, they recommended a host of works. Many of them are already included in the previous section but others are given below with a minimum of comment. The addition of these duets would naturally strengthen the section greatly, particularly in contemporary and near-contemporary works. The speakers dealt with the works in chronological order but for convenience they are listed below alphabetically.

BERNERS   *Valses bourgeoises* (Chester)

CASELLA	*Pupazetti* (Ricordi)
CLEMENTI	*4 sonatas* (Peters)
GRIEG	*Waltz caprices, op. 37* (Peters)
KOECHLIN	*4 Sonatines françaises*, 4v. (O.U.P.)
LAMBERT	*3 Pièces nègres* (O.U.P.)

Played on the white keys, and in Latin-American rhythms.

MENDELSSOHN	*Andante and variations, op. 83a; Allegro brillante, op. 92* (Augener; Schirmer)
MOSCHELES	*Familienleben, op. 140*, 2v. (Kistner)
	Sonata in E, op. 121 (Kistner)

These duets were apparently enjoyed by Chopin.

RAWSTHORNE	*Creel suite* (O.U.P.)
RESPIGHI	*6 short pieces* (Rahter)
SATIE	*3 pièces en forme de poire* (U.M.P.)

Mentioned as being particularly amusing to play.

STRAVINSKY	*Trois pièces faciles* (Chester)
	Cinq pièces faciles (Chester)

FOUR HANDS—TWO PIANOS

Music written for two pianos is naturally limited in appeal for few patrons are fortunate enough to have either the space or the money to possess two pianofortes except in certain areas. On the other hand, contemporary composers appear to find it much more attractive to write for two pianos rather than for piano duet; this is understandable, and is underlined by the fact that although there is a public for two-piano recitals, duets are apparently limited to amateur performance.

Even if one admits that two-piano works are of limited use to most of our borrowers the attraction of the piano concerto with orchestral score arranged for a second piano is undoubted. It is obvious that only one out of every ten who borrow such a score will be able to play it with a second pianist providing the accompaniment; for the rest, their interest is in the solo part. This might suggest that the library could content itself with the provision of a single copy of each work but this is not recommended. Despite the possibility of restricted use, I feel that two copies are much better. The librarian can either have both copies bound in a single cover, with the second copy in a pocket at the front or rear of the binding or else treat the two copies as independent and bind them separately. In the latter case, the musician who can arrange a two-piano session will need to get both copies of the work but two people interested primarily in the solo part can both borrow the work at one time. This also has the advantage that both copies are likely to receive approximately equal wear and tear.

ARENSKY   (b) *Suite, op. 15* (Schirmer)

Arensky is not one of the world's greatest composers but his piano music still appears occasionally in concert programmes. This suite is enjoyable to play and provides interesting listening that does not make too heavy demands upon the concentration of the audience.

BRAHMS   (a) *Variations on a theme of Haydn, op. 56b* (Breit-
                kopf; Lengnick; Peters; Schirmer)

This work is unusual in that the composer wrote this two-piano version and the better-known orchestral version at the same time. He often played one of the piano parts himself in this arrangement, which is almost as fine as the orchestral one. There is also a *Sonata in F minor* which is a two-piano arrangement of the *Piano quintet, op. 34*, but this is not recommended as the work is much less effective for two pianos than for piano and string quartet.

DEBUSSY   (e) *En blanc et noir* (Durand)

Three pieces, one of Debussy's last compositions. Like most of his very late works this has been viewed very differently by critics but current opinion in general is that the works are both important and effective.

MILHAUD   (e) *Le bal Martiniquais* (Salabert)
                (e) *Scaramouche* (Salabert)

Light and undemanding music that is popular with two-piano teams.

MOZART   (d) *Sonata in D major, K.448* (Augener; Peters;
                Schirmer)

This is probably one of the earliest two-piano works ever written but is still worthy of its place in the repertory. There are other Mozart two-piano works, mainly arrangements by the composer himself of compositions originally written for a mechanical organ; these are less successful.

RACHMANINOV   (c) *Suite, op. 17* (Boosey)

An engaging work, beautifully written, that appears with some frequency in concerts of two-piano music.

SCHUMANN (e) *Andante and variations, op. 46* (Augener; Schirmer)

A work generally within the scope of competent amateur pianists.

This section is completed with a short list of piano concertos recommended for stock. There are numerous other works of this genre that appear with some regularity in concert and radio programmes and the librarian should have little difficulty in further selection. It may be suggested that any piano concerto, etc., that appears in the lists of recommended miniature scores is well worth consideration for a place in the two-piano section also.

BACH (c) *Piano concerto in D minor* (Peters; Schirmer)

BEETHOVEN (d) *Piano concerto no. 4, in G major, op. 58* (Augener; Novello; Peters; Schirmer)

(c) *Piano concerto no. 5, in E♭ major ("Emperor"), op. 73* (Augener; Novello; Peters; Schirmer)

BRAHMS (d) *Piano concerto no. 2, in B♭ major, op. 83* (Augener; Peters; Schirmer)

DOHNANYI (e) *Variations on a nursery tune, op. 25* (Lengnick)

FRANCK (b) *Variations symphoniques* (Peters; Schirmer)

GRIEG (a) *Piano concerto in A minor, op. 16* (Peters)

MOZART (c) *Piano concerto in D minor, K.466* (Augener; Peters; Schirmer)

(b) *Piano concerto in C major, K.467* (Augener; Peters; Schirmer)

(d) *Piano concerto in A major, K.488* (Augener; Peters; Schirmer)

RACHMANINOV (a) *Piano concerto no. 2, in C minor, op. 18* (Boosey)

SCHUMANN (b) *Piano concerto in A minor, op. 54* (Augener; Peters; Schirmer)

TCHAIKOVSKY (a) *Piano concerto no. 1, in B♭ minor, op. 23* (Augener; Peters; Schirmer)

ORGAN MUSIC

There should always be some demand in a public library for organ music, since every town will have its amateur and semiprofessional organists. If there is a lack of interest in this section of the stock by those qualified to use it then the reason is likely to be the lack of variety in the collection and perhaps the standard of selection also. A poor stock will only interest the potential user for one or two visits. The librarian has a very wide repertoire from which to choose but, regrettably, much of it is musically worthless. Selection is not made easier by the fact that no really well-known composer, with the solitary exception of Bach, ever composed regularly for the instrument. Some excellent composers of organ music have been much less successful in other fields of composition and so perhaps get overlooked. Another factor that tends to obscure the best organ music is that too many organists still include in their programmes third-rate music and orchestral works arranged for organ, on the apparent assumption that good organ music is too "heavy" for recital purposes. This attitude is fortunately waning and one only rarely meets such works as *The storm* (by one of several composers, but all calculated to require every stop at the organist's command in the middle of the work) written to display Victorian organs and to prove the organ's claim to be "the king of instruments".

The works listed below are all, with two exceptions, original works, i.e. they are not arrangements of works written for any other instrument or instruments. They are also, in my opinion, compositions of permanent value. Selections are graded as in other sections, but it is worth mention that the librarian wishing to make further additions to stock can choose wisely from the works listed for playing tests each year by the Royal College of Organists. These are published in the appropriate section of *The Musical Times* and are also listed, with a note of editions and suggestions for playing, in *Musical Opinion*. The R.C.O. makes its announcements of selected works fairly early in the year.

BACH   (a) *Complete organ works* (Augener, 10v; Bornemann, 12v; Breitkopf, 9v; Peters, 12v; Schirmer, 12v.)

These are the prime essential for any collection of organ music as Bach is still the pre-eminent composer for the instrument. There are a number of editions available and all of those listed above can be recommended to a greater or lesser degree. The Augener and Novello editions originate in Britain, Breitkopf and Peters in Germany, Bornemann in France and Schirmer in the U.S.A. The Augener edition, published in ten volumes tends to be rather fussy with its overzealous suggestions for the registration (i.e. choice of stops) for each work. The Peters edition is published in nine volumes plus three for the choral preludes. It is thoroughly reliable but suffers from the opposite fault, for here the tempi and phrasing marks are limited to those given by Bach himself, and these are very few. The notes are in German only and the same drawback (so far as English users are concerned) affects the Breitkopf edition.

The Schirmer edition, edited by Widor and Schweitzer, is very good. Each volume has a long introductory note with suggestions for playing. The Bornemann (U.M.P.) edition has another Bach player of the first rank in Marcel Dupré as its editor, and the introductory notes are in French, German and English.

The Novello edition is, at the time of writing, changing in part from one editorial edition to another. The original set comprised twelve books, edited by Sir Frederick Bridge and James Higgs, and was issued between 1881 and 1895. Two books of selected choral preludes (Books 13 and 14) were later withdrawn when the complete choral preludes were issued as Books 15 to 20; these were edited by Sir Ivor Atkins. This edition comprises, therefore, eighteen books (1–12; 15–20). Novello's are now issuing a new edition of the material contained in the original books 1–12 and this new version is edited by John Dykes Bower (organist of St. Paul's Cathedral) and Walter Emery, and these will eventually be published as Books 1–14, thus filling the gap of the two missing numbers. It can be understood then, that the contents of each individual book do not tally with those of an earlier edition so that the two versions will not mix. This new edition, together with Books 15–20 which are likely to need no more than slight revision, appears to be the best edition for British public libraries. The library that lacks Bach's organ works is therefore advised to buy Books 15–20 together with such books of the new edition as are available and to complete the set as the remaining books are issued. Both old and new sets (for the Bridge-Higgs edition will remain current until the newer version is complete) will conveniently bind into three, four or five volumes if desired.

BOELLMANN   (c) *Suite Gothique, op, 25* (U.M.P.)

This suite is well known for its last two movements (the third and fourth). These are the rather sickly *Prière à Notre Dame* and the exciting *Toccata;* both are often played separately.

BONNET   (b) *12 pieces, op. 5* (Leduc)
              (c) *12 pieces, op. 7* (Leduc)
              (d) *12 pieces, op. 10* (Leduc)

Joseph Bonnet died in 1944 and was a French composer and organist known internationally as a virtuoso for he toured the United Kingdom, Canada and the United States giving recitals. The three volumes of varied pieces are popular with organists.

BOSSI   (e) *Organ works,* 2v. (Peters)

Enrico Bossi (1861–1915) is another player, in this case an Italian, still remembered as a touring virtuoso of the instrument. His compositions are perhaps too showy for some tastes but they are written with expert technique.

BRAHMS   (a) *Choral preludes, op. 122,* 2v. (Novello)
              (b) *Fugue in A♭ minor* (Augener; Lengnick)

The *Choral preludes* are the last work of Brahms and were published post-

Instrumental Music

humously. The fugue is the composer's only other important organ work, and it is perhaps the only one written in this most unusual key. It has no opus number and was published in 1864. The suggested works are available as part of the complete organ works (Breitkopf) but this edition is not recommended as it introduces the less-familiar C-clef in certain passages and the text is in German only. The Novello edition has both German text and English translation.

BUXTEHUDE   (b) *Organ works* (Peters, 2v; Hansen, 5v.)

Buxtehude was the most famous organist of his day in Germany and the story of the 200-mile walk by the young Bach in order to hear the older composer is well known. It is only comparatively recently that organists have realized that there is a large amount of excellent organ music written before the time of Bach and the two Peters volumes are worth adding to stock as examples of this. The first one contains the large-scale works—the *Preludes and fugues*, etc., and the second the *Choral preludes*.

DUPRÉ   (d) *3 Preludes and fugues* (U.M.P.)

During the last half-century the French nation has produced a number of first-class organists who have also been composers for the instrument. These works are often noisy and difficult but with very real merits and some of them appear fairly regularly in organ music recitals. Of the three related works recommended here, the last is the most popular; the subject of the fugue (i.e. the opening theme that is developed throughout the work) is a jaunty tune that is easily recognized and remembered.

ELGAR   (e) *Organ sonata no. 1, op. 28* (Breitkopf)

Elgar had a fair amount of experience as a church organist in his younger days, and this (surprisingly enough his only organ work) receives an occasional performance. The so-called *Sonata no. 2* is an arrangement by Sir Ivor Atkins of the *Severn Suite* written by the composer for brass band.

FRANCK   (a) *3 Chorales* (Durand; Peters; Schirmer)
         (b) *10 pieces* (Schirmer)   *OR*
             6 pieces (Durand; Peters, 2v.)   *AND*
             3 pieces (Durand; Peters)

Franck is usually considered to be the founder of the large and flourishing school of modern French organ composers. His own works for the instrument are among his best compositions and have not suffered the same diminution in popularity that has affected other works. The *Chorales* are excellent, particularly the most popular (no. 3, in A minor) and the other works are likely to receive fairly regular use by organists borrowing from the library. The Schirmer edition is recommended here; the other editions could well have the two volumes bound together.

FRESCOBALDI   (d) *Organ works*, 2v. (Peters)

Girolamo Frescobaldi (1583–1643) is another composer in the pre-Bach line whose works are becoming of increasing interest to organists. He was, for two separate periods, organist of St. Peter's, Rome. The edition recommended is edited by Hermann Keller and the first of the two volumes contains the complete *Fiori Musicale*. The publishers suggest that these short, severely contrapuntal pieces are ideal for use in the Roman liturgy. Two volumes of selected works are available published by Breitkopf.

GIGOUT   (b) *10 pièces* (Leduc)
                 (e) *12 pièces* (Leduc)

Like so many members of the modern French school of organists and composers, Gigout lived well beyond the age of eighty and was well known as a teacher and performer, as well as a composer. The *Toccata* in the first volume of recommended pieces has been an established favourite for many years with organists.

GUILMANT   (b) *Sonatas*, 8v. (Schott)

Guilmant is another of the large and important school of composers, teachers and performers. His music is well written and in general is more conventional and less reliant upon virtuosity than that of many of his successors. The eight sonatas may be considered too expensive to purchase at once, in which case the first and fourth (op. 42 and op. 61) are the recommended choice. There is also a number of other pieces that deserve inclusion in the large collection, including the composer's most popular work, the *March on a theme by Handel, op. 15* (Schott) based on "Lift up your heads" from *Messiah*.

HANDEL   (c) *Organ concertos* (Bornemann, 3v.)

These works have been arranged for solo organ by Marcel Dupré. Any editor of the concertos has to face the problems of making a satisfying whole of organ solo sections in the original in which the orchestra is playing alone and others in which both organ and orchestra are playing together, and also of making due allowance for the fact that Handel's own notation of the solo part was often simpler than that actually performed. The editor has to consider, therefore, the need for embellishing the organ part in correct contemporary style. These Dupré arrangements are probably the finest but others are available, e.g. the Peters edition of opus 4, edited by S. de Lange, and the Paxton edition of op. 4 and op. 7. Volume 1 of the Bornemann edition contains the six concertos, op. 4; volume 2, numbers 7 to 12 (opus 7), and volume 3, numbers 13 to 16.

HARWOOD   (e) *Organ sonata no. 1, op. 5* (Schott)

Basil Harwood is one of the many English composer-organists whose names are hardly known except to other organists. This sonata is a fine work, well written and effective, but Harwood's name usually appears in recital programmes as the composer of the brief, difficult but very attractive *Dithyramb, op. 7* (Novello) or the *Paean, op. 15, no. 3* (Novello).

HINDEMITH   (e) *Sonatas*, 3v (Schott)

The three sonatas are well laid out for the organ but seem rather dry, so that they need good performance to maintain the listener's interest. The first two both date from 1937.

HOWELLS   (c) *3 Psalm preludes: sets 1 & 2* (Novello)
                 (e) *Sonata* (Novello)

This contemporary British composer has written music for many different instruments and combinations of them and has had considerable experience as an organist. The *Psalm preludes* are excellent examples of a type of music which British composers appear to find particularly congenial. The organ sonata is a somewhat elaborate work but is in the best modern tradition.

KARG-ELERT   (a) *14 choral preludes, from op. 65* (British & Continental)

(c) *12 choral preludes, from op. 65* (British & Continental)

Karg-Elert never really fulfilled the promise of his early days when he seemed to have the potentialities of another Bach. The *Choral preludes* that comprise opus 65 total over sixty, in six books; these two volumes selected from this large collection have been edited by Laurence Swinyard who has translated the directions to the organist from the German and arranged the two volumes in ascending order of difficulty.

KREBS   (e) *Organ works* (Peters)

This German composer was Bach's most famous pupil. He wrote in many different forms but, except for his organ music, his compositions are very rarely heard and he suffers from a neglect that is not really justified.

LISZT   (b) *Complete organ works*, 2v. (Peters)

Liszt's organ works show his admiration for J. S. Bach; the *Prelude and fugue on B-A-C-H* is some indication of this. The English terminology of B♭, A, C, B natural, spoils the rebus. Liszt's works are extremely effective when well played although they are usually difficult virtuoso pieces. The two most popular works are the one already mentioned and the *Fantasy and fugue on "Ad nos ad salutarem"*. Both items are in the second volume which should have preference if only one is bought. The *B-A-C-H* work is published separately by Augener and Novello.

MENDELSSOHN   (a) *Organ works* (Augener, 2v; Novello, 2v; Peters; Schirmer)

The composer was himself a fine organist and did much to introduce and make popular in this country the organ music of Bach. Mendelssohn's own compositions for organ are well written and their popularity shows little sign of waning, particularly with less talented organists. The works comprise *3 Preludes and fugues, op. 37* and *6 sonatas, op. 65*. The Novello edition is well printed and arranged and is the one most likely to satisfy British organists.

MOZART   (a) *Fantasia in F minor, K.608* (Augener; Bornemann; Peters)

This work is the second exception in this section in that it was not written for a pipe organ but for another instrument—in this case, a mechanical organ. The *Fantasia* is a fine and powerful work of Mozart's last period and the Bornemann edition, arranged by Dupré, is recommended. Two other works for mechanical organ have been arranged for the modern instrument by Herbert Ellingford and published by Augener; these are the *Adagio and allegro in F minor, K. 594* and the *Andante in F major, K. 616.*

NIELSEN (e) *Commotio, op. 58* (Hansen)

This was Carl Nielsen's last major work; its importance is only equalled by its difficulty. The work is in four movements—Fantasia; Fugue I; Andante sostenuto and Fugue II.

PARRY (d) *Choral preludes*, 2v. (Novello)

These are now Parry's only organ works that remain in the modern repertory, probably because the hymn tunes themselves are generally well known to English listeners, and also because the standard of writing is high.

PEETERS (e) *Chorale preludes, op. 68, 69, 70*, 3v. (Peters)

These works comprise ten items in each opus number, making a total of thirty preludes. Flor Peeters is a contemporary Dutch composer and organist (b. 1903) and these works are slowly achieving some popularity in Britain. They are not too difficult and many of the tunes are known to English audiences.

REGER (d) *12 organ pieces, op. 59* (Peters)

  (e) *30 short choral preludes, op. 135a* (Peters)

Max Reger, though popular in his native Germany, has not been regarded very highly outside that country for his style has been considered too heavy, turgid and lacking in light and shade. Despite these criticisms it is generally admitted that his organ music is technically extremely well written. He himself was a first-class performer on the instrument.

Although they are uneven in inspiration there is some excellent music in the pieces that make up opus 59 while the *Choral preludes* are short and fairly simple; they could prove useful to many organists who often require something of this nature to fill a brief interval during the course of a service. The publishers refer to the opus 59 volume as "Set I" and the two subsequent volumes (both of which also contain twelve *Choral preludes*) as Set II (op. 65) and Set III (op. 80).

REUBKE (b) *Sonata on the 94th Psalm* (O.U.P.)

Julius Reubke (1834–1858) was a favourite pupil of Liszt, who thought highly of his work. This fine composition indicates what a great potential organ composer was lost by his early death. The sonata is extremely difficult in many places and has been excellently edited by Herbert Ellingford.

RHEINBERGER (a) *Organ sonatas*, 20v. (Novello)

  (c) *Meditations* (Novello)

  (d) *Trios* (Novello)

In most musical fields, Josef Rheinberger (1839–1901) was a third-rate composer who has been completely forgotten but his organ music is probably second only in quality to that of Bach. The twenty organ sonatas are all important though not all of equal value. During the nineteen-thirties these works were edited by Harvey Grace (who was organist of Chichester Cathedral and editor of *The Musical Times*) and many of the problems and difficulties that had previously faced the performer in an earlier edition (and which had reduced the popularity of the works) were overcome. Although issued separately, the sonatas will bind conveniently into four or five volumes if desired. For the small library that cannot buy all twenty works at once I would recommend numbers 2, 7, 12 and 14 as being among the best as well as providing some idea of Rheinberger's development as an organ composer. The *Meditations* and *Trios* are much simpler and will provide useful material for the organist who cannot cope with the technical demands of the *Sonatas*.

As an alternative to the recommended edition, Sonatas 1 and 2 are available from Augener, and 3, 4 and 5 (edited by Lemare) in the Schirmer edition.

ROWLEY   (c) *Choral preludes based on famous hymn tunes*, 5v. (Ashdown)

Short, not too difficult, and ideal material for many an amateur organist.

SCHUMANN   (d) *6 fugues on the name "Bach", op. 60* (Novello, 2v; Peters)

Schumann, like Liszt, was a great admirer of Bach and these six studies show the nineteenth-century composer in an unusual light—as a writer of strict counterpoint. The works were written for organ or pedal-piano. Despite the fact that the same subject is common to all the works the fugues are well varied and musically interesting.

STANFORD   (d) *Sonata no. 1, in F major, op. 149* (Augener)

Stanford, with Parry, did much for the renaissance of English music in the early years of this century but his own music is now infrequently heard. This Irish composer wrote his five organ sonatas comparatively late in life and the first is probably the best. Augener's publish the fifth, the intermediate ones being issued by Stainer & Bell.

VIERNE   (d) *24 pièces en style libre*, 2v. (Durand)

Vierne was a blind organist and composer and much of his music is often noisy, dissonant and extremely difficult to play. These two volumes, however, contain simple and attractive pieces that can be played effectively on a very small organ; the pedal parts are optional.

WESLEY, S. S.   (d) *Introduction and fugue in C♯ minor* (Novello)

Samuel Sebastian Wesley was a grandson of the Methodist leader Charles Wesley, and lived from 1810 to 1876. He was one of the finest performers of his day and was organist at no less than four different cathedrals during his life. His anthems are still sung in the Church of England and this *Introduction and fugue* is probably his best organ work. A shorter piece that still retains much of its popularity is the *Holsworthy church bells* (Novello).

WHITLOCK   (c) *5 short pieces for organ* (O.U.P.)
                       (c) *4 extemporizations* (O.U.P.)
                       (d) *Plymouth suite* (O.U.P.)

Percy Whitlock was an English organist who wrote music that was at once both musicianly and popular and his early death at the age of 43 (in 1946) was regrettable. The clear registration and effective layout of the music make his works thoroughly playable by the competent organist. If desired these three sets of pieces would conveniently bind together.

WIDOR   (a) *Symphony no. 5, op. 42, no. 1* (Hamelle)

Widor was yet another of the long-lived French player-teacher-composer school and he actually recorded the *Toccata* from this recommended *Symphony* when he was over eighty—no mean feat for the work calls for considerable agility in both hands and feet. Both Vierne and Widor wrote organ "symphonies" (six and eight of them, respectively) that are, for all practical purposes, organ sonatas. The title occasionally misleads some people into thinking that the works are arrangements of orchestral music. The large collection could include others of the two sets (four in op. 13 and the rest in op. 42) with advantage. All are published by Hamelle who also publish the Vierne *Symphonies*.

WILLAN   (e) *5 preludes on plainchant melodies* (O.U.P.)

Well-written works by an English-Canadian organist and composer.

In addition to the works listed above, mention should be made of a series of organ pieces issued under the general title "Library of organ music by British composers", with editorial supervision by Martin Shaw and published by Cramer. A number of the works are arrangements and not original organ pieces and, as with almost all series, the quality of writing varies. There are, however, some attractive, brief pieces by eighteenth-century composers such as John Stanley and William Boyce. These could usefully be bought and, if desired, made into one or two volumes, with similar works in the series.

The section on organ music may be considered long and the selection large, yet there are still many other excellent composers for the instrument whose names have been omitted in order to keep recommendation within bounds. Pachelbel, Scheidt and Sweelinck are three important composers of the pre-Bach era. Contemporary composers omitted include Jongen (Belgium), Messiaen (France) and Yon (Italy). There are a host of American composers whose names seem entirely unknown beyond their own continent. British omissions are also numerous—a whole library of choral preludes by native composers could be built without difficulty. Finally, attention might be drawn to an article in *Musical Opinion* for April, 1952, in which a correspondent has collated the organ recital programmes listed in that periodical over a period of three years. The librarian who wished to assure himself of a proved demand might find this information very useful.

STRING MUSIC

Library provision in this field is usually limited to music for the

Instrumental Music

violin and violoncello with possible selection for the viola. Solo music for the double-bass, the largest member of this family, is rarely required although it may be recalled that the great conductor Koussevitzky first made his name as a virtuoso on this instrument. A nearby school or amateur orchestra may completely upset the normal pattern of local demand. Provision will generally be of works with pianoforte accompaniment although there should be un-accompanied works also in stock. It is necessary to include concertos and similar works with the orchestral accompaniment arranged from the orchestral score. Finally, it must be understood that the section that follows is limited to music for solo instruments; chamber music is dealt with later in this chapter.

Violin

BACH
(a) [*Unaccompanied*] *sonatas* (Augener; Breitkopf; Novello; Schirmer; Universal)

(b) *Violin and clavier sonatas* (Augener, 2v; Schirmer, 6v; Universal, 6v.)

(a) *Concerto in A minor* (Augener; Breitkopf; Schirmer)

(a) *Concerto in E major* (Augener; Breitkopf; Schirmer)

(c) *Double concerto in D minor* (Augener; Schirmer)

The *Violin sonatas* present a minor problem in nomenclature in that the second, fourth and sixth are alternatively known as the first, second and third *Partitas*, which is a better descriptive title. Fortunately all six works are in different keys so that confusion should be easily avoided. The works make considerable demands both upon soloist and audience but are among the greatest ever written for the violin. The favourite is no. 4 (*Partita no. 2*), in D minor; this contains the famous *Chaconne*. The *Sonatas for violin and clavier* are much simpler, both to play and to hear, but are also of lesser stature. The *Double concerto* is written for two violins with string orchestra accompaniment and continuo; the arrangement here is for two violins with piano accompaniment.

BARTÓK
(e) *Sonata no. 2* (Boosey)

(e) *44 duos for two violins* (Boosey)

The *Sonata* dates from 1922; like the great majority of Bartok's works it is difficult music to play and to comprehend but is well worth the necessary effort. The *Duos* (1931) are primarily teaching material and are written in similar fashion to the composer's *Mikrokosmos*, for solo piano. Many of the brief pieces are based upon folk-tunes. A further suggestion is the *Romanian folk-dances from Hungary* which were written for piano solo but which have been excellently transcribed for violin and piano by Bartók's friend, Zoltán Székely.

333

BEETHOVEN (a) *Concerto in D major, op. 61* (Augener; Peters; Ricordi; Universal, etc.)

(c) *2 Romances, op. 40 and op. 50* (Augener; Peters; Ricordi; Universal, etc.)

(a) *Sonatas* (Augener; Peters; Ricordi; Universal, etc.)

The ten *Sonatas for violin and piano* are a basic requirement for the smallest collection. It may be mentioned that the Augener edition is edited by Fritz Kreisler whose playing of the works was unsurpassed. The concerto is one of the most popular in the repertory and the two brief *Romances* (with orchestral accompaniment in the original) have gained in popularity with the appearance of excellent modern gramophone recordings.

BRAHMS (a) *Concerto in D major, op. 77* (Augener; Schirmer)

(a) *Sonatas, op. 78, 100, 108,* 3v. (Augener; Schirmer)

All three sonatas contain something of Brahms's genius but the second is the least difficult to play. The concerto is a great favourite with both violinists and audiences. The composer also made an arrangement of the op. 120 clarinet sonatas, but this violin and piano version is not really satisfactory.

BRUCH (c) *Concerto no. 1, in G minor, op. 26* (Peters)

CASELLA (e) *Concerto* (Universal)

CHAUSSON (e) *Poème, for violin and orchestra, op. 25* (Breitkopf; Peters)

CORELLI (c) *12 sonatas, op. 5* (Augener, 2v.)

The last of these sonatas, known as *La Folia*, consists of a set of variations, and is easily the most popular of the set.

DEBUSSY (e) *Sonata*

One of Debussy's last works and one upon which critical opinion is still sharply divided. Some say that it is the writing of a sick and dying man, with inspiration sadly lacking; others claim it to be a masterpiece of compression and a work of considerable importance.

DELIUS (e) *Concerto*

(d) *Sonata no. 3* (Boosey)

The third (and last) of the violin sonatas is the only one that is performed with any regularity. The concerto has received several good recordings and is in the form of a single rhapsodic movement.

DVOŘÁK (c) *Concerto in A minor, op. 53* (Lengnick)

(e) *Sonatina, op. 100* (Lengnick)

(e) *Sonata in E major, op. 57* (Lengnick)

The concerto cannot be counted as one of Dvořák's best works but it still achieves occasional performance. Alec Robertson (in his life of the composer) says that the sonatina is "little more than chips" from Dvořák's workshop, but admits the charm of the work. The sonata is a bigger work and is also one that appears to be neglected by British violinists.

ELGAR   (b) *Concerto in E minor, op. 61* (Novello)

     (c) *Sonata in E minor, op. 82* (Novello)

The concerto is a long work written by the composer when in his prime and it needs an accomplished soloist for a successful performance. The sonata is one of Elgar's last compositions (it was written in 1918) and it provides considerably greater enjoyment for the violinist than for the pianist.

FAURE   (d) *Sonata no. 2, in E minor, op. 108* (Durand)

FRANCK   (b) *Sonata in A major* (Boosey; Novello; Shirmer; U.M.P.)

GLAZUNOV   (e) *Concerto in A minor, op. 82* (Belaieff)

GRIEG   (c) *Sonata no. 3, in C minor, op. 45* (Peters)

The last and best of the sonatas, and well suited to amateur talents.

HANDEL   (a) *6 sonatas* (Augener; Breitkopf; Novello; Peters; Schirmer; Schott)

These sonatas form part of Handel's opus 1, which comprises *Fifteen solos for a German flute, hoboy or violin, with a thorough bass for the harpsichord.* From this title it might appear that any of the three instruments could play any sonata, but in fact each work was written for one only of these three and this is indicated in the manuscript at the beginning of each sonata. The six for violin are numbers 3, 10, 12, 13, 14 and 15. Others in the series will be found in the section dealing with flute music.

A word must be added concerning the accompaniment. As the original title indicates, Handel provided a ground bass only (i.e. the bass line plus a note of the appropriate chord structure when the harmonies changed) and from this the contemporary harpsichord player would extemporize a suitable accompaniment. For this reason the modern accompaniments in the different editions vary considerably and are not necessarily in eighteenth-century style. The Schott edition is recommended since in addition to the usual "realized" accompaniment it also shows the original figured harmony, so that the performer can revert to eighteenth-century practice if sufficiently skilful; this edition also includes a part for violoncello which would be wanted to reinforce the bass-line if a harpsichord was used to accompany the violin. Second choice of edition would be the Novello where the realization of the accompaniment is by Arnold Dolmetsch.

HAYDN   (c) *Concerto in C major* (Breitkopf; Peters)

While there are a number of concertos attributed to Haydn only three are indisputably his, including this one in C major. It has its attractions but cannot be rated as one of the master's greatest works. Haydn's *Violin sonatas* are not recommended for stock since they are mainly works for piano solo with violin accompaniment; on the other hand, the large collection would do well to include the little-known *6 duo-sonatas* for violin and viola.

HINDEMITH   (c) *Sonata in D major, op. 11, no. 2* (Schott)

                  (e) *[Unaccompanied] sonata in E major* (Schott)

Hindemith's opus 11 consists of six works—two sonatas for violin and piano, one for violoncello and piano, one for viola and piano, and one each for unaccompanied viola and violin respectively. The recommended work is the most frequently performed; it dates from 1920, some fifteen years earlier than the unaccompanied sonata, which has no opus number.

IRELAND   (c) *Sonata no. 1, in D minor* (Augener)

                  (c) *Sonata no. 2, in A minor* (Boosey)

The earlier work won Cobbett's International Competition for a violin sonata in 1909 and has since been revised. Though the second sonata won no prize it is generally considered to be an even finer work.

KREISLER   (a) *[Violin pieces]* (Schott)

This famous violinist published a number of light pieces in the Viennese style under his own name, and was also responsible for many "transcriptions" of the works of minor eighteenth-century composers, and it was years before it was discovered that these were fraudulent, in that Kreisler had written them also. Later editions of the pieces substituted "in the style of . . ." to clarify the position. In both fields the composer shows delightful craftsmanship and a real melodic gift and the works are perennially popular with both professional and amateur violinists. Schott's publish eleven works as "original compositions" and a series of "classical manuscripts", etc. A number of works such as the *Caprice Viennois*, *Liebesfreud*, etc., would conveniently bind into a single volume. At least two public-library suppliers sell bound albums of this type.

LALO   (d) *Symphonie espagnole op. 21* (Schirmer; U.M.P.)

Although the work is of limited popularity it remains in the standard repertory because of its fine technical writing which gives the virtuoso an excellent vehicle to demonstrate his or her accomplishments.

LEKEU   (d) *Sonata* (Rouart, Lerolle)

Guillaume Lekeu (1870–1894) was a pupil of Franck and d'Indy. Unfortunately he died of typhoid fever before he was able to fulfil the immense promise he had already shown as a composer. This sonata is probably his best work.

MENDELSSOHN   (a) *Concerto in E minor, op. 64* (Augener; Peters; Ricordi; Schirmer; Universal)

MOZART   (b) *Concerto in G major, K.216* (Breitkopf; Peters; Schirmer)

                  (a) *Concerto in D major, K.218* (Augener; Peters; Schirmer)

                  (a) *Concerto in A major, K.219* (Augener; Breitkopf; Peters; Ricordi; Schirmer)

Instrumental Music

> (a) *Sonatas*, 2v. (Augener; Breitkopf; Peters; Ricordi; Schirmer)
>
> (c) *2 duos for violin and viola, K.423, 424* (Peters)

The violin sonatas cover almost the whole of Mozart's brief life and contain some of his finest music. The duos are little known but (like the Haydn examples) are well worth recommending to both violinists and violists. The concertos are comparatively early works but are Mozart's best known pieces for violin; they are extremely popular. The above three concertos are often known as numbers, 3, 4 and 5 respectively, and the large collection could usefully add the remaining three.

NIELSEN (d) *Sonata no. 1, in A major, op. 9* (Hansen)

(d) *Sonata no. 2, in G minor, op. 35* (Hansen)

(e) *Concerto in C and D major, op. 33* (Hansen)

All three recommendations are important works by this Danish composer in whom interest has recently grown. His style is a very personal one and may not be acquired at once.

PAGANINI (b) *24 [unaccompanied] caprices, op. 1* (Augener; Peters; Schirmer)

During his lifetime it was considered impossible for any other violinist except the composer himself to play them. Even today, with the great advances in technical standards that have taken place since Paganini's death in 1840, the *Caprices* are still considered extremely difficult to play well. Other composers (Brahms, Liszt, Rachmaninov, etc.) have used themes from one or other of the *Caprices* for works of their own.

POULENC (e) *Sonata (to the memory of Garcia Lorca)* (Schott)

PROKOFIEV (d) *Sonata no. 1, in F minor, op. 80* (Boosey)

(e) *Concerto in D, op. 19* (Boosey)

RAVEL (b) *Pièce en forme de Habanera* (U.M.P.)

Though originally written for voice and piano this work is much better known and is much more popular in this present arrangement which was made by the composer.

RUBBRA (c) *Sonata no. 2, op. 31* (O.U.P.)

This work dates from 1931 and should prove enjoyable both to performers and listeners. Two good recordings of the sonata have been made.

SAINT-SAENS (b) *Introduction and Rondo capriccioso, op. 28* (Durand)

A very popular favourite with violinists and audiences. Though the music may lack profundity its tunefulness and technical mastery may be regarded as almost adequate substitutes.

SARASATE (b) *Spanish dances*, 4v. (Lengnick)

Sarasate, like Kreisler and some others listed in this section, was an out-

337

standing violinist who showed very great technical skill in transcribing works for the violin. The music is rarely of the first quality but violinists of every calibre usually include some of these dances in their repertoires.

SCHUBERT (d) *3 sonatinas, op. 137* (Augener; Schirmer)

Not vintage Schubert but still calculated to give pleasure to most violinists.

SCHUMANN (c) *Sonata in A minor, op. 105* (Augener; Schirmer)
(d) *Sonata in D minor, op. 121* (Augener; Schirmer)

Both sonatas date from 1851 and are among the best of Schumann's later compositions, showing no signs of that deterioration that affected many of his works towards the end of his composing life. The Augener edition provides both works in a single volume.

SIBELIUS (b) *Concerto in D minor, op. 47* (O.U.P.)

This warm and romantic work is appreciably different from the other major compositions of Sibelius and is popular with many who find the composer's symphonies much less enjoyable.

STRAUSS, R. (c) *Sonata in E♭ major, op. 18* (Universal)

A comparatively early work (as the opus number indicates) but one in which the composer's personal style is apparent and in which the writing is very effective.

SUK (b) *4 pieces, op. 17* (Simrock, 2v.)

These pieces by Dvořák's son-in-law deserve to be much better known. Each lasts about four minutes and all are well written for both performers. An excellent recording was made by the ill-fated Ginette Neveu and her brother.

SZYMANOWSKI (e) *The fountains of Arethusa, op. 30, no. 1* (Universal)

A technically difficult showpiece for expert violinists and equally expert pianists.

TARTINI (b) *Sonatas* (Augener, 3v; Schirmer, 2v.)

Though Tartini wrote dozens of sonatas, he is almost universally known by one of them—that in G minor known as *The Devil's trill* (derived from a dream that the composer is alleged to have had). The Augener volumes contain sonatas in G major and G minor (in one volume), the *Devil's trill*, and a third volume with a sonata in C major and another (*Giga*) in D major. Schirmer publish two sonatas (in E minor and G major) in one volume and the *Devil's trill* in a second; this last work is available in a number of other editions, including two from Ricordi, one of which is edited by Kreisler. Other works by this popular eighteenth-century composer include a *Concerto in E major* (Peters) and a *Concerto in G minor* (Novello).

TCHAIKOVSKY (a) *Concerto in D major, op. 35* (Augener; Peters; Schirmer)

Instrumental Music

VAUGHAN
WILLIAMS   (c) *Concerto in D minor* (O.U.P.)
        (b) *The lark ascending* (O.U.P.)

The concerto was originally entitled *Concerto accademico*; the amended title is probably better since the work is not nearly as forbidding as the original might suggest. The other work was inspired by Meredith's poem of the same title and, in the original, the soloist is accompanied by a string orchestra.

VIEUXTEMPS   (d) *Concerto no. 5, in A minor, op. 37* (Schirmer)

Henri Vieuxtemps (1820–1881) was a Belgian virtuoso and this concerto is typical of his works. It has little musical value but is popular with audiences because of its technical brilliance, though this limits performance to good players.

WALTON   (d) *Concerto* (O.U.P.)

A long work, written specially for Jascha Heifetz, and outside the scope of all but the most accomplished violinists.

WIENIAWSKI   (b) *Legende, op. 17* (Augener; Schirmer)
        (c) *Polonaises brillantes, nos. 1 (op. 4) and 2 (op. 21)*
          (Schirmer)
        (b) *Scherzo tarantelle, op. 16* (Augener; Schirmer)

This composer was a Polish virtuoso who wrote music to display his own outstanding technique. As with other composers of this type his music has no great value but is excellently set out for its instrument and makes little demand upon the intellect of the audience. The recommended works would bind in one volume.

Viola

It is only in fairly recent years that the viola has emerged from the "poor relation" category. Its enhanced standing is almost entirely due to the efforts of Lionel Tertis whose technique and interpretative ability showed how much more could be done with the viola than was generally recognized. This skill, combined with determined persuasion, resulted in many new works being added to the viola repertory especially by British composers. Despite this, the average player is still dependent on transcriptions and chamber music for a large proportion of his music-making.

ARNOLD   (d) *Sonata* (Lengnick)

BACH   (e) *3 sonatas* (Peters; Ricordi)

These works were written for the viola da gamba and clavier, but sound well played by viola and modern pianoforte.

BAX   (b) *Sonata* (Chappell)

This contemplative work was composed in 1921 and is a product of the composer's maturity. It is reckoned to be one of his finest works.

BENJAMIN   (b) *Sonata* (Boosey)

Arthur Benjamin is an Australian, born in 1893, whose most popular work to date has been *Jamaican rumba*. However, this sonata shows him in more serious vein. The three movements are unconventional for a sonata, being an Elegy, a Waltz and a Toccata.

BERLIOZ   (a) *Harold in Italy, op. 16* (Jobert)

This is a symphony with viola obbligato rather than a viola concerto. The work is based upon Byron's *Childe Harold* but the connection is barely recognizable. The solo part was written for Paganini (who was almost as great a virtuoso on this larger instrument as he was on the violin). He paid for the work but refused to play it. Good recordings on gramophone records in recent years have helped to make the work more popular, but the score is at present o.p.

BLISS   (e) *Sonata* (O.U.P.)

BRAHMS   (c) *Clarinet sonatas, op. 120* (Augener)

These two works may be played, on the composer's own authority, by viola and piano and so can fill a useful dual-purpose role. An alternative edition, published by Breitkopf, has the first sonata only available.

BURKHARD   (d) *Sonata, op. 59* (Bärenreiter)

Willy Burkhard (b. 1900) is a contemporary Swiss composer whose works are receiving some notice in Britain, particularly on the radio.

DITTERSDORF   (e) *Sonata in E♭ major* (Novello)

Dittersdorf was a contemporary of Haydn and Mozart and is barely remembered today despite a large musical output. This sonata is a pleasant piece of music, typical of its period but showing little sign of musical personality.

HANDEL   (d) *Sonata for viola da gamba and cembalo*
                         (Augener)

HINDEMITH   (b) *Kleine Sonate, op. 25, no. 2* (Schott)
                         (b) *Sonata in F major, op. 11, no. 4* (Schott)

Hindemith is a viola player himself and has played the instrument in a professional quartet (the Amar Quartet); he writes, therefore, with a first-hand knowledge of the instrument's capabilities, and these are two excellent examples of twentieth-century music for the viola.

D'INDY   (e) *Sonata* (Salabert)

An arrangement for viola and piano of the violoncello sonata, op. 84.

JACOB   (e) *Concerto* (O.U.P.)

Though Gordon Jacob is perhaps best known as a teacher, his skill as a composer is also appreciated by performers. The pianoforte accompaniment hides the skilful orchestration of the original. At the moment this arrangement is o.p.

MILHAUD   (d) *Sonatas nos. 1 and 2* (U.M.P.)
             (e) *Concerto* (Universal)

RAWSTHORNE   (e) *Sonata* (O.U.P.)

REGER   (d) *3 suites for unaccompanied viola, op. 131d* (Peters)

Reger is often accounted a dull composer and unaccompanied viola may hardly be regarded as providing sprightly music—yet these works are most enjoyable when well played. If added to stock some persuasion may be required with local players before they will consent to try this music with the somewhat unusual opus number.

RUBBRA   (e) *Concerto* (Lengnick)

SCHUMANN   (a) *Märchen Bilder, op. 113* (Augener; Schirmer)

These *Pictures from Fairyland* consist of four pieces, pleasantly varied.

WALTON   (a) *Concerto* (O.U.P.)

Probably the best known of all modern viola concertos and rated by Sir Donald Tovey as "one of the most important modern concertos for any instrument". It dates from 1929 and needs a first-class violist and an equally accomplished pianist to produce a satisfactory performance.

As mentioned in the introduction to this particular section, there is still a paucity of suitable works for viola so that a library is advised to buy, as first or second choice, some of the excellent arrangements made by Watson Forbes and Alan Richardson and published by O.U.P. The two editors have chosen mainly seventeenth- and eighteenth-century works, often written for obsolete instruments such as the viola da gamba, etc. Several of these pieces, bound together, would make a suitable album.

Violoncello

This instrument is second to the violin in popularity among string instruments and selection should show awareness of the fact. There is a very large repertory of varied quality both original works and transcriptions.

BACH   (a) *6 sonatas (suites) for unaccompanied 'cello* (Augener; Peters; Ricordi; Schirmer)
             (e) *3 sonatas for viola da gamba and clavier* (Peters)

The unaccompanied works are never likely to be popular but violoncellists

Z   341

know them as some of the finest in their whole repertory. The technical difficulties are tremendous in some sections though one might not think so when listening to the recorded performance of a Casals or a Starker. The titles "sonata" and "suite" are used indiscriminately.

The viola da gamba (or bass viol) was the lowest in pitch in the normal chest of viols and the violoncello is its modern successor. These same sonatas, transposed up, have been recommended in the viola section.

BEETHOVEN (a) *Sonatas* (Augener; Peters; Ricordi; Schirmer)

These five sonatas cover most of Beethoven's creative life, for there are two sonatas that make up opus 5, two more for opus 102, and in the middle is the single sonata opus 69, the most popular of the five. Riezler, in his great critical biography of the composer, declares that the last two sonatas "cannot be called favourites for they are ungrateful for the instrument and problematic in construction". Despite that they are standard works in the 'cellist's repertory.

BOCCHERINI (c) *Concerto in B♭ major* (Breitkopf)

The problems of balancing the low-pitched tones of an instrument that lacks penetrating power against an orchestra seems to have deterred all but a handful of composers. One result has been that this not-very-distinguished work which, in modern performance, owes rather more to its editor (Friedrich Grützmacher) than to its alleged composer, appears with some regularity in concert programmes. For most people Boccherini remains the composer of a single work—the famous *Minuet*.

BRAHMS (d) *Sonata no. 1, in E minor, op. 38* (Augener; Henle; Schirmer)

(b) *Sonata no. 2, in F major, op. 99* (Augener; Henle)

Both works are important, but the second shows the increased maturity that one would expect when comparing the opus numbers.

DEBUSSY (e) *Sonata in D minor* (Durand)

One of the composer's last works (written in 1915) it shares the varied opinions that these late compositions receive. A majority of critics appear to regard the work as inferior (for Debussy) and not particularly representative.

DELIUS (d) *Sonata* (Boosey)

DVOŘÁK (a) *Concerto in B minor, op. 104* (Lengnick)

Excellent performances recorded for the gramophone have helped to increase the popularity of what is probably the finest 'cello concerto of all.

ELGAR (b) *Concerto in E minor, op. 85* (Novello)

Elgar's last major work, dating from 1919. After a cool reception when first performed it has grown steadily in public estimation and is now played with some frequency. The concerto is much more restrained than Elgar's other important orchestral works.

FAURE (e) *Sonata no. 1, in D minor, op. 109* (Durand)

(e) *Sonata no. 2, in G minor, op. 117* (Durand)

Instrumental Music

GRIEG   (c) *Sonata in A minor, op. 36* (Peters)

An interesting work deserving of more frequent performance.

HAYDN   (a) *Concerto in D major* (Breitkopf; Peters; Schirmer)

This pleasant and unaffected work was originally attributed to Haydn, later to his pupil Anton Kraft, and now once more to Haydn. Whoever wrote it, the work is very popular with 'cellists and audiences.

HINDEMITH   (e) *Concerto (Kammermusik no. 3), op. 36, no. 2* (Schott)

HONEGGER   (e) *Sonata* (Sirène)

IRELAND   (c) *Sonata in G minor* (Augener)

A typically mature work (dating from 1923); it is unduly neglected.

MARCELLO   (b) *Sonatas* (Schott, 4v.; Ricordi, 5v.)

Benedetto Marcello (1686–1739) is one of a number of eighteenth-century composers who wrote violoncello music within the compass of the average amateur. The Schott edition includes 7 sonatas in all with three books containing two works (A minor and E minor; C major and G major; F major and G minor) and a Sonata in D major. The E minor sonata published separately (no. 63 in Schott's "Classical violoncello music" series) is the same as that contained in the first of the other volumes. The five Ricordi sonatas duplicate four of those published by Schott (D major, E minor, G major and G minor), but the fifth in G (Ricordi catalogue no. 405) major is not duplicated.

MENDELSSOHN   (a) *Violoncello works* (Augener; Peters)

There are four works—*Variations concertantes, op. 17, Sonata in B♭ major, op. 46, Sonata in D major, op. 58* and a *Song without words, op. 109.* All are pleasant, well-mannered and written with considerable technical skill, as is customary with this composer. The sonatas are the most frequently performed of the four works.

POPPER   (d) *Higher 'cello school,* 4v. (Novello)

               (e) *Suite, op. 69* (Peters)

David Popper (a German Czech despite his English-sounding name) is remembered chiefly as a performer on and a great teacher of the 'cello. The *Higher 'cello school* is still considered one of the best sets of technical training pieces.

RACHMANINOV   (c) *Sonata, op. 19* (Boosey)

A fairly effective work in which the piano writing is much better than that for the 'cello; the latter is treated as a junior partner rather than an equal.

REGER   (e) *3 unaccompanied suites, op. 131c* (Peters)

A companion set to the suites listed in the section for Viola music.

RUBBRA   (e) *Sonata, op. 60* (Lengnick)

SAINT-SAENS   (e) *Concerto no. 1, op. 33* (Durand)

                       (d) *Concerto no. 2, op. 119* (Durand)

SAMMARTINI   (c) *Suite in C major* (Schott)

SCHUBERT   (b) *Arpeggione sonata, D.821* (Breitkopf; Peters)

This is the only work still known that was written specifically for the arpeggione, an instrument that was something of a combination of guitar and 'cello, played with a bow; invented by Stauffer in 1823 it was deservedly short-lived. The work plays perfectly well in its arrangement for violoncello and is well worth attention by the amateur 'cellist even though the sonata is not vintage Schubert.

SCHUMANN   (e) *Adagio and allegro, op. 70* (Durand)

                       (c) *5 Stücke im Volkston, op. 102* (Durand)

                       (e) *Concerto in A minor, op. 129* (Durand)

                       (d) *Fantasiestücke, op. 73*

The concerto and the *5 pieces in popular style* are both original works for the instrument and both show some signs of that mental ill-health that affected so much of Schumann's later music. The composer made an arrangement for violin and piano of the opus 102 pieces and the other two items are also arrangements of music written for another instrument. The *Adagio and allegro* was originally written for French horn and Schumann made alternative versions for violin and 'cello. The *Fantasy pieces* were for clarinet, but again Schumann made versions for violin or 'cello. The *3 romances, op. 94* (Augener), written for oboe and piano, with an arrangement for violin and another for clarinet have also been published for 'cello and piano and once again provide tuneful, enjoyable and not-too-difficult works for the amateur player.

An out-of-print volume published by Peters contained the op. 70, 73 and 102 items.

TCHAIKOVSKY   (c) *Variations on a rococo theme, op. 33* (Augener; Peters)

A work for violoncello and orchestra notable for its excellent writing for the soloist. The music is tuneful and easily assimilated.

Double Bass

In the opening remarks on the provision of string music it was suggested that double-bass players are comparatively rare. There are a number who play the instrument in dance bands but in the great majority of cases these performers do not appear to be users of the public library music stock. If, however, music is required for this instrument, the following pieces are suggested.

DRAGONETTI   *Studies for the double bass* (Carisch)

The composer was a young contemporary of Haydn and his prowess on the unwieldy instrument is almost as legendary as that of Paganini on the violin. Dragonetti used, for instance, to play the 'cello part of a string quartet on his double-bass with apparent ease and in perfect balance with the other members of the team. These studies are useful for players who wish to improve their technique.

HINDEMITH   *Sonata* (Schott)

The name of Hindemith appears in almost every section of these lists for he has apparently written a sonata for every instrument of the orchestra. There should be no need to stress his importance as a composer but it should be mentioned that he has shown willingness to write music for any instrument or combination if commissioned to do so. Even if every work is not a masterpiece none falls below a highly competent standard.

LECLERCQ   *Concertino* (Leduc)

MORBIDUCCI   *Concerto in D minor* (Peters)

SCHMITT   *Morceau de concours* (U.M.P.)

Guitar

This instrument has gained respectability and caste through the efforts of Andres Segovia. Until the middle nineteen-fifties it would have been adequate in small- and medium-sized libraries to provide one or two pieces at most. The arrival of "skiffle" and the ensuing upsurge of interest in the guitar has altered the position and libraries may now usefully stock a somewhat larger selection, though many of the players of the instrument will have no interest beyond jazz and folk music and will be unable to read printed music.

In addition to the pieces listed below it should be noted that some foreign guitar music is imported into Britain by Clifford Essex, and these pieces include some transcriptions of lute music. They could form a useful addition to the collection, as would some of the transcriptions by Segovia (Schott).

CASTELNUOVO-
  TEDESCO   *Sonata for solo guitar* (Schott)

DIABELLI   *Sonatina for guitar and piano* (Oesterreichischer
                Bundesverlag)

HANDEL   *8 Aylesford pieces* [arr. Segovia, for solo guitar]
                (Schott)

SOR   *Easy pieces, op. 35* (Oesterreichischer Bundesverlag)
                12 easy pieces from op. 60 (Universal)

Fernando Sor (whose dates of birth and death vary in different musical dictionaries but are approximately 1780–1839) was a Spaniard who has been called "the Beethoven of the guitar". He is probably the best-known composer for the instrument and his works deserve fuller representation if the number of scores in the guitar section are increased.

WEBER   *Divertimento for guitar and piano, op. 38*
                 (Schlesinger)

Weber played the guitar himself and left this pleasant lightweight piece to remind posterity of the fact.

[See pp. 290–1 for explanation of asterisks in following sections.]

MUSIC FOR WIND INSTRUMENTS

Recorder

This instrument was the forerunner of the flute and fell out of use as the transverse flute became more popular. During the nineteen-thirties, however, interest in the recorder was revived after a gap of some two centuries, and it is now a comparatively popular instrument with amateur musicians mainly because a fair amount of skill can be acquired in a short time. Much of the credit for this revival must go to the Dolmetsch family who made a special study of several old instruments that had fallen into disuse. For modern consort purposes (a "consort" of recorders being a small group playing music in parts) there are usually four different instruments—the descant, treble, tenor and bass recorders. The smallest and highest-pitched of the family, the sopranino, is occasionally seen or heard and its lowest note, "F", is the top note of the treble stave. The descant recorder is pitched a fourth lower, and the treble a fourth lower again which makes the pitch of the latter an octave below that of the sopranino. Similar intervals separate the other two members of the family. The normal range is a seventeenth, i.e. two octaves and a tone, so that the top note of the descant recorder is shown as D^{iv}, but expert players can achieve notes above the nominal range. The instrument tends to sound an octave lower than its actual pitch so that the shrillness that one might expect is absent. For solo work the treble recorder is the favoured instrument and it has a wide repertoire of seventeenth-, eighteenth- and twentieth-century music. Librarians wanting more works for recorders will find many suitable works in the Schott catalogue.

ARNOLD   *Sonatina for recorder and piano, op. 41* (Paterson)

Malcolm Arnold is a composer with a growing reputation and this is a good modern work with the added attraction for the librarian that either flute or oboe may be used as alternative solo instruments.

Instrumental Music

HANDEL   *Fitzwilliam sonatas for treble recorder* (Schott)

The manuscript for this set of sonatas is in the Fitzwilliam Museum at Cambridge and the accompaniment has been arranged from the figured bass by Thurston Dart. The original accompaniment would be by harpsichord and viola da gamba but the present realization may also be played by pianoforte and violencello or by piano alone.

HINDEMITH   *Trio for recorders in C and F* (Schott)

MURRILL   *Sonata for treble recorder (or flute) and harpsichord (or piano)* (O.U.P.)

Herbert Murrill was Head of the Music Department of the British Broadcasting Corporation at the time of his death in 1952. As suggested by the title, the work should appeal to flute players as well as those of the recorder, but it includes some notes outside the ordinary range of the latter instrument and is technically difficult.

PURCELL, D.   *Sonata in F* (O.U.P.; Ricordi)

Daniel Purcell was a younger brother of the famous Henry. The Ricordi edition is arranged by Fleury and the O.U.P. by Joseph Slater; both were famous flautists. The Italian edition is to be recommended as the O.U.P. version omits the first movement of the work which is recommended for beginners.

SHAW, M.   *Sonata for recorder (or flute) and harpsichord (or piano)* (Cramer)

Another contemporary British work that has, for the librarian, a double usefulness.

TELEMANN   *Sonata in F* (Schott)

Flute

Unless there is a local professional or amateur orchestra, flautists (or flutists) are infrequently met as library borrowers. Where dual-purpose works (i.e. those that can be played with an alternative instrument as soloist) are bought the cataloguer should ensure that the necessary added entries are made under the alternative instruments. Three of the modern British works in the section immediately preceding provide examples of works of this nature.

BACH   *Sonata in A minor* (Durand; Peters)
                6 sonatas (Breitkopf; Peters)

The sonata in A minor is for unaccompanied flute. The other six comprise two sets of three sonatas each; one set is for clavier and flute and the other for flute with continuo. This last means that the accompanying instrument is not specified but that the composer has provided the bass line together with necessary indications of the harmonies to be used. The result is that modern editions require a worked-out accompaniment and that different editions will vary in the piano part as with the Handel violin sonatas previously recommended. On the composer's authority, these six works may be performed with violin as solo instrument.

BAX *Four pieces* (Chappell)

CHAMINADE *Concertino* (Enoch)

DEBUSSY *Syrinx for unaccompanied flute* (Jobert)

Originally entitled *Flûte de Pan*, and intended for performance as incidental music to a play.

FAURE *Fantasie* (Leduc)

HANDEL **9 sonatas, op. 1* (Boosey; Peters; Schott)

The sonatas for German (i.e. transverse) flute, oboe or violin and continuo can be issued to three different sets of musicians and so are very useful additions to stock. The problems of solo instrument and of accompaniment to Handel's opus 1 are discussed under the composer's name in the section on violin music. In Hunt and Donington's *Practical method for recorder* are mentioned "12 sonatas, op. 1", and it is stated that four of the sonatas were originally intended for performance by recorder. These were numbers 2, 4, 7 and 11 which are shown as 2, 7, 4 and 5 respectively in the Peters edition, and 1, 2, 3 and 5 in Breitkopf. In the *Practical method* it is also stated that many passages in the later editions have been written an octave higher than the original. The Breitkopf edition, containing all 9 sonatas, is o.p.; the Boosey edition includes 8 sonatas and Peters and Schott 7 each.

In addition to the sonatas recommended Handel wrote three sonatas (to which no opus number was added by the publisher) for flute and cembalo; these merit inclusion in the larger collection of flute works.

MOZART **Concerto in G major, K.313* (Boosey; Breitkopf)
*Concerto in D major, K.314 (Boosey; Breitkopf)

These are two of the most popular works with flautists and they are equally popular with audiences. It may be appropriate here to mention that Mozart also wrote three quartets for flute and strings (K. 285, K. 298 and K. a. 271).

QUANTZ *7 sonatas* (Forberg)

Johann Quantz (1697–1773) was the teacher of Frederick the Great for a period of over thirty years and composed hundreds of works for his royal pupil. His book on flute playing is still of value and these sonatas (edited by Fischer and Wittenberger) give a fair sample of his quality as a composer.

Oboe

This instrument presents the third example of one whose current popularity is due, in the main, to a single executant. Léon Goossens, like Tertis and Segovia in their respective fields, has persuaded composers to write new works and to arrange old works for the oboe. The repertory of original works is still extremely small and it should be noted that several of the oboe "concertos" are, in fact, based upon sonata movements, etc., of various eighteenth-century composers.

BRITTEN   *6 metamorphoses after Ovid, op. 49* (Boosey)

Written for unaccompanied oboe, these works do not provide easy listening.

CIMAROSA   **Concerto* (Boosey)

This popular work is an arrangement by Arthur Benjamin of movements from various piano sonatas, rewritten for oboe and strings. An excellent recording has helped to make the work well known to many people who have never heard it in the concert hall.

CORELLI   **Concerto* (Boosey)

Sir John Barbirolli has followed Arthur Benjamin's example and has fashioned a most attractive work from keyboard pieces by Corelli.

DUNHILL   *Friendship's garland, op. 95* (Boosey)

Five miniature pieces which are tastefully written.

HANDEL   **3 concertos* (Boosey)

HINDEMITH   *Sonata for oboe and pianoforte* (Schott)

One of the later examples of Hindemith's works for individual instruments; this sonata dates from 1938.

MOZART   *Concerto* (Boosey)
            Sonata (Boosey; Chester)

The sonata is an arrangement of the oboe quartet, K. 370, which is a rarely played though thoroughly enjoyable piece of work. A splendid recording was made many years ago by Léon Goossens and members of the Léner String Quartet.

NIELSEN   *Fantasiestücke, for oboe and piano, op. 2* (Hansen)

This is a very early work of Nielsen's as is indicated by the opus number. The pieces are lightweight but are well written for both performers and are attractive.

PERGOLESI   *Concerto in C major* (O.U.P.)

Another Barbirolli arrangement of movements from various works of the eighteenth-century composer. Like the Corelli "concerto", it is scored for oboe and strings.

REGER   *Romance in G* (Breitkopf)

SAINT-SAENS   *Sonata, op. 166* (Durand)

SCHUMANN   *3 romances, op. 94* (Augener; Schirmer)

Three pleasant and unpretentious works; the composer wrote these pieces with clarinet or violin as alternative solo instruments and there is an arrangement (included in the appropriate section) for violoncello and piano.

SINIGAGLIA   *Variations on Schubert's "Heidenroslein", op. 19* (Breitkopf)

STRAUSS, R.   *Concerto* (Boosey)

VAUGHAN
  WILLIAMS   *Concerto* (O.U.P.)

Cor Anglais

This is an alto oboe with little solo music in its repertory. Oboe players often "double" on the cor anglais, whose dark and somewhat plaintive tone can be heard in the opening theme of the slow movement of Dvořák's *New World symphony* and in the pastoral section of Rossini's *William Tell overture*. If a full-sized work is required, one can recommend the ubiquitous Hindemith who has written a *Sonata for cor anglais and piano* (Schott).

Clarinet

This is the most popular of orchestral wind instruments and much first-class music has been written for it. Both Mozart and Brahms numbered a great clarinet player among their personal friends and wrote immortal works for the instrument as a result.

BRAHMS   *Sonatas, op. 120* (Augener; Boosey)

These two works have already been recommended in the section on viola; they were actually written for clarinet but may be played (on the composer's authority) on either instrument. Brahms's great works for the clarinet are the *Clarinet trio* and (more particularly) the wonderful *Clarinet quintet*.

BUSONI   *Elegie* (Breitkopf)

DEBUSSY   *Petite pièce* (Durand)
           Rapsodie: for clarinet and piano (Durand)

Although written as test pieces these works do not carry obvious signs of their pedagogic origin and are well suited to the instrument.

DUNHILL   *Phantasy suite, op. 91* (Boosey)

IRELAND   *Fantasy sonata* (Boosey)

A brilliant work, first performed in 1943. The title is somewhat contradictory

Instrumental Music

and the rhapsodic side of the fantasy is more in evidence than the formal design associated with a sonata.

MOZART *Concerto in A minor, K.622* (Boosey; Breitkopf; Ricordi)

This is probably the greatest work written for the clarinet and is one of the composer's last. Clarinet players have also a great affection for the *Clarinet quintet, K. 581.*

NIELSEN *Concerto* (edition Dania)

One of Nielsen's last works, it is somewhat enigmatic and bad-tempered and requires an expert technique.

SCHUMANN *Fantasiestücke, op. 73* (Schirmer)

These three pieces were originally called *Soiréestücke* (a reminder that musicians have often committed shocking atrocities upon foreign languages) and are pleasant and attractive pieces. They are rarely performed as a group since all three are in the key of A (two in the major key, one in the minor) and this limits the contrast between the works. The composer made alternative arrangements of these pieces with violin or 'cello as the solo instrument.

STANFORD *Sonata for clarinet and piano, op. 129* (Stainer & Bell)

The slow movement of this work is entitled *Caoine*, a form of Irish lament. It was recorded years ago by Frederick Thurston, with an interesting and amusing *Suite for two clarinets* by Alan Frank on the reverse. The Stanford work is typical of its composer in being well written; the solo part may be played by a viola but sounds less successful in this form.

WEBER *Concertino in E♭ major, op. 26* (Boosey; Breitkopf)

The work is in the form of a single movement and is a great favourite with clarinettists since it allows full scope for a display of virtuosity.

Bassoon

Because of the instrument's comic possibilities, with its difference in tone between top and bottom registers, the bassoon is often regarded as a musical buffoon. Yet the instrument can produce pleasant tones (though a British performer will sound very different from a French or German player) and plays serious music in an enjoyable way. Should any works be required, the following brief list is offered for consideration.

FOGG *Concerto* (Elkin)

Eric Fogg (1903–1939) was a Manchester man of considerable promise as a composer. This concerto was played several times during the nineteen-thirties at Henry Wood Promenade Concerts with Archie Camden as the soloist. The second half of the concert on these occasions was normally enlivened by Balfour Gardiner's piece for three bassoons, the *Witches' dance from "Macbeth"*.

JACOB   *Concerto* (Williams)

MOZART   *Concerto, K.191* (Boosey; Breitkopf)

An early work of Mozart's but probably the best-known concerto for this instrument.

SAINT-SAENS   *Sonata, op. 168* (Durand)

Saint-Saens' last three works were sonatas for oboe, clarinet and bassoon, all written in 1921. They show both his usual fastidious skill as a composer and his lack of profound musical feeling.

WEBER   *Concerto* (Breitkopf)

BRASS INSTRUMENTS

There is usually little demand for works written for members of the brass family but brief recommendations for the French horn, trumpet and trombone are given below.

French Horn

BEETHOVEN   *Sonata for horn in piano, in F major, op. 17* (Boosey)

HAYDN   *Horn concerto no. 2, in D major* (Breitkopf)

A pleasant work though of doubtful authenticity.

MOZART   *Horn concerto no. 2, in E♭ major, K.417* (Breitkopf)
                       Horn concerto no. 4, in E♭ major, K.495 (Breitkopf)

There are four of these concertos of which the last three are all written in the same key. There is little to choose between the four, all of which have remained in the repertory, but the last is probably the most popular.

SCHUMANN   *Adagio and allegro, op. 70* (Breitkopf)

A minor piece but written with a good understanding of the instrument's capabilities. Rather surprisingly, the solo part may be played by violin or 'cello and separate editions are available from the same publisher.

STRAUSS, R.   *Concerto no. 1, in E♭ major, op. 11* (Universal)

Strauss' two horn concertos were written at the two ends of his composing life. While the early one may be regarded as little better than a student work, it still shows the promise of the composer and is written with a very real understanding of the instrument's capabilities, since Richard's father was a horn player himself.

Trumpet

HAYDN   *Concerto* (Boosey)

This is easily the most famous concerto for the instrument, and its current popularity in Britain dates from the recording of the second and third movements made on a single Columbia disc in the middle nineteen-thirties with George Eskdale as the soloist.

Instrumental Music

HINDEMITH   *Sonata for trumpet and piano* (Schott)

RIISAGER   *Concertino* (Novello)

An attractive work by a contemporary Danish composer. It consists of three short movements; the second is played with the solo instrument muted and the third includes variations upon a tune extremely reminiscent of *Three blind mice.*

Trombone

MARTIN   *Ballad for trombone and piano* (Universal)

CHAMBER MUSIC

This field of music has always been a minority interest though that minority is usually the keenest and most knowledgeable section of the music library's public. The long series of midday concerts in London's National Gallery and the B.B.C. "Music in miniature" programmes both helped to increase interest in chamber music, though this is more likely to be reflected in a greater demand for miniature scores of chamber works than in requests for parts for actual performance. Many members of professional orchestras are keen performers of chamber music for their private relaxation and most communities of any size have at least a handful of players (often all of them amateur) who would like to find some suitable music in their local public library.

Music-lovers whose interests are bounded by orchestral, solo instrumental, operatic music, etc., are often completely unaware or ignorant of the amount of really first-class chamber music that has been written. Limited demand for this type of music, the expense of buying the several parts and the further costs involved in binding them suitably—these and other factors tend to restrict provision to a minimum or to exclude it altogether. Yet the smallest independent library should provide one or two works at least, and this type of music would seem to be ideal for a scheme of local co-operation. If one library buys Mozart's piano quartets, for example, a neighbour could purchase those of Brahms, while a third could buy Dvořák's second piano quartet, etc. Co-operation between libraries is always admirable and is doubly so when it increases the chances of use of a work that may be borrowed from its own library but once in two or three years. This may sound uneconomic but it must be remembered

353

that this same work's potential life is limited only by the physical deterioration of the score providing that choice is limited to works of permanent musical value.

I would suggest that the librarian of the small library should provide some music for piano trio and string quartet as these two types of musical combination are the most popular. The larger library should naturally provide a wider selection of chamber music of these types and also add one or two examples of quintets, etc. Arrangements for piano trio of the type of music usually played as accompaniment to people eating and drinking tea and cakes in a restaurant do not deserve purchase. In passing, library assistants (particularly cataloguers) should know that a "string quartet" is always understood to be a combination of two violins, viola and violoncello; any other combination of four stringed instruments would always have the instruments designated. A "string trio" consists of violin, viola and 'cello (i.e. a string quartet minus the second violin), so that Boccherini's *Trios for two violins and violoncello* would be shown in that manner, in contrast to Beethoven's *String trios, op. 9*. A "piano trio" comprises piano, violin and violoncello. By the same system of nomenclature, a "clarinet quintet" is not, as one might have thought previously, a piece of music written for five clarinets but music for one clarinet plus a string quartet; an "oboe quartet" is written for oboe with string trio, etc.

It has been recommended in the previous paragraph that every library should provide at least a token selection of chamber music; the lists below give suggestions for a medium-sized basic stock, with a minimum number of (a) and (b) selections. Annotations are infrequent because expert guidance from two members of an amateur string quartet of long standing is available to help both librarian and performer. This very practical help is contained in Aulich and Heimaran [*see* "Further reading"].

Trios

BEETHOVEN   *Piano trios* (Augener, 8v; Breitkopf, 7v; Peters)

These works span the whole of Beethoven's working life, from opus 1, no. 1 (1792) to the variations, op. 121a. If a single trio is bought it must be opus 97, the *Archduke trio*, one of the finest examples of music for this medium.

The Peters edition is particularly recommended with 11 trios, including the *Clarinet trio, op. 11*. Augener publish 9 trios in 8 volumes and Breitkopf 7 trios in their "Kammermusik" edition. Both latter editions include the op. 97 trio.

Instrumental Music

BERKELEY   *Horn trio, op. 44* (Chester)

Written for horn, violin and piano. This most attractive modern chamber work dates from 1952.

BRAHMS   *Piano trios* (Peters)

Brahms wrote five piano trios, ranging from the early op. 8 to the late op. 114 —though the opus 8 work was, in fact, revised at the same time that the last trio was written. The latter and its predecessor, op. 101, are the two most frequently performed. The opus 40 trio allows French horn, viola or violoncello to join the piano and violin.

All five trios are available separately in the Peters edition (so that it is possible to stock only the last two, or to add all five over a period of years); Augeners publish three only, op. 40, 87 and 101, but they are markedly cheaper than the equivalent trios in the Peters edition.

DVOŘÁK   **Piano trio in E minor* ("*Dumky*"), *op. 90* (Lengnick)

A "Dumka" (plural "Dumky") is a lament with alternating sections of slow, sad music and quick, bright ones. The trio of this Dvořák work has six such sections.

HAYDN   *Piano trios* (Peters, etc.)

There are no less than thirty-one of these trios of which numbers 29–31 are written for piano, flute and 'cello, though the flute part can be played by a violin. Generally speaking, the pianist is the most important member of a Haydn trio and the violoncellist counts for least, for he is rarely allowed to stray away from the bass line of the piano part. The numbering of the trios is usually that adopted by Peters which bears no relation to chronology. The publishers' numbers 1 to 6, for example, were written some five years after those known as numbers 29–31. The best-known trio is number 1, with its famous *Gipsy rondo*.

The current Peters edition contains twelve of the trios; an alternative edition published by Breitkopf offers ten separately published numbers, while Augener publish 12 trios in 6 volumes.

MOZART   *Piano trios* (Augener, 7v; Schirmer, 8v.)
        Sinfonia concertante, K.364 (Peters; Schirmer)

The K. 498 trio was originally written for clarinet, viola and pianoforte and sounds much more effective in that form than when the clarinet is replaced by a violin. The two best trios, recommended for buying when the complete set is too expensive, are K. 502 and K. 542; these are listed by the publishers as numbers 2 and 3. Both editions (and one by Breitkopf) contain the same works, but Schirmer also publish the trio, K. 442, in D (called no. 8 by the publishers) which was not finished by Mozart but was completed by Stadler who performed the same function for several works that Mozart left incomplete at his death.

The *Sinfonia concertante* is a double concerto with violin and viola as the solo instruments. The orchestral accompaniment has been arranged for piano.

SCHUBERT   *Piano trios, op. 99 and 100* (Augener, 2v; Peters; Schirmer, 2v.)

The trio in B♭ major, op. 99 (D. 898) is one of the loveliest pieces in the whole field of chamber music and the one most likely to influence favourably those who declare that they have neither time nor liking for this sector of musical composition. The second trio (Deutsch number 929) is hardly less attractive.

String Quartets

BARTÓK (e) *6 string quartets* (no. 1, Zerboni; nos. 2–5, Universal; no. 6, Boosey)

These six works are probably the most important in the field of twentieth-century chamber music; yet they are never likely to achieve popularity since they are far beyond the scope of the non-professional quartet and require sustained, concentrated listening by the audience. The last two quartets pose the fewest problems for the listener and are those recommended for first purchase.

BAX (d) *String quartet no. 1, in G major* (Chappell)

In this work Sir Arnold Bax answered those critics who declared that he could only write music that was complex and highly coloured. The quartet is attractive, tuneful and straightforward. During World War II it was played to many audiences of Service personnel by the Griller String Quartet.

BEETHOVEN (a) *String quartets nos. 1–6, op. 18, nos. 1–6* (Augener, 2v; Peters)

  (b) *String quartets nos. 7–9 ("Rasoumovsky"), op. 59, nos. 1–3* (Augener; Peters)

  (b) *String quartets nos. 10–11, op. 74 and op. 95* (Peters)

  (d) *String quartets nos. 12–16, op. 127, 130, 131, 132, 135; Die Grosse Fuge, op. 133* (Peters; Schirmer, 5v.)

These string quartets are often divided into three groups—the opus 18 works are "early", the opus 59, 74 and 95 quartets are "middle" and from opus 127 onwards are the "late" quartets. The Peters edition of the quartets is published in three volumes divided in this fashion, and a similar edition by Breitkopf is o.p. The small library will probably be content with the first six quartets, and the medium library should certainly include also the middle period quartets for these are still within the scope of the good amateur team. All three of the opus 59 works are known as the "Rasoumovsky" quartets, while the opus 74 is known as the "Harp" quartet and the opus 95 work, called by Beethoven "Quartetto serioso", is sometimes known as the "Serious" quartet.

The large library most certainly should include all the quartets despite the difficulties they pose both to performers and listeners, for they are perhaps the greatest utterances ever given to four players. The Schirmer edition published op. 130 and 133 together since the latter work (*The great fugue*) was originally intended as the finale for the former; Beethoven, however, realized that it was too weighty for its purpose and eventually completed the op. 130 quartet with a shorter and simpler last movement.

BOCCHERINI (e) *Selected string quartets* (Barenreiter)

Instrumental Music

BORODIN   (d) *String quartet no. 2, in D major* (Boosey)

Famous for the *Nocturne* which forms the second movement of the work.

BRAHMS   (c) *String quartets* (Peters)

There are three quartets, the first two forming opus 51 and the third opus 67. Augener publish op. 51, nos. 1 and 2, in two volumes; Breitkopf issue the three works in a single volume that is at present out of print.

BRIDGE   (d) *3 Idylls* (Augener)

                (e) *3 Novelettes* (Augener)

Frank Bridge (1879–1941) was a British composer and teacher and a fine viola player. These are attractive small works.

BRITTEN   (c) *String quartet no. 2, in C minor, op. 36* (Boosey)

One of Britten's major works, and composed as a homage to Henry Purcell.

DEBUSSY   (d) *String quartet, in G minor* (Durand)

DVOŘÁK   (c) *String quartet, in F major, op. 96* (Lengnick)

This is the sixth of Dvorak's eight published quartets and is by far the most popular, though it took the composer but a fortnight to write. For many years the work has been known in Britain as the *Nigger quartet*—an appellation that is now found distasteful by many people, and which is being superseded by the better title of the *American quartet.*

HAYDN   (a) *30 string quartets* (Peters, 2v.)

There are over eighty string quartets by Haydn. This puts a complete collection beyond the reach of any but the largest public libraries, but the recommended selection should be within the scope of all but the smallest libraries. For them, Augener publish fifteen of the best-known quartets in separate volumes. Taken as a whole, the Haydn quartets are among the finest in the whole chamber music repertory.

HINDEMITH   (e) *8 pieces, op. 44, no. 3* (Schott)

MENDELSSOHN   (d) *String quartets* (Peters)

This volume contains the complete works in this form—op. 12, 13, 44, 80 and 81.

MOZART   (a) *String quartets* (Peters, 2v.)

The Peters edition contains the complete set of 27 quartets; the Breitkopf edition, at present o.p., only 23. The earlier quartets are infrequently played but the last ten are extremely popular with both amateur and professional quartets. These works (entitled by the publisher *10 celebrated quartets*) form the first of the two volumes recommended; the same ten examples (from K. 387 to K. 590) are also available singly from Augener, and this firm also issues the K. 172 quartet and the string quartet version of *Eine Kleine Nachtmusik, K. 525.* Whichever edition is preferred these ten quartets should be regarded as basic stock in any public library.

RAVEL (d) *String quartet* (Durand)

SCHUBERT (b) *4 string quartets* (Augener; Peters)

The two best known and most popular of Schubert's quartets are those usually known as nos. 13 and 14, the opus 29 (D. 804) and the *Death and the maiden quartet* (op. posth., D. 810); the latter gets its name from the song with the same title which is used by Schubert in the second movement of the quartet. These two works, together with the two quartets forming opus 125 (in E♭ and E respectively) comprise the recommended volume. In the Peters edition this is the first volume of the "complete" quartets, in two volumes. The second volume contains five other quartets and should be bought for the large collection. Schubert left a number of unfinished quartets; this accounts for apparent discrepancies in numbering.

SIBELIUS (d) *String quartet in D minor ("Voces intimae"), op. 56* (O.U.P.)

Though an important work in the string quartet repertory it is difficult to play and comprehend. Perhaps this is why it is surprisingly omitted from the recommendations in Aulich and Heimeran.

SMETANA (d) *String quartet no. 1 ("From my life")* (Peters)

TCHAIKOVSKY (b) *String quartet no. 1, in D major, op. 11* (Augener; Peters)

This is the quartet in which the famous *Andante cantabile* appears. The third quartet, op. 30, is also worth adding to stock but both Augener and Peters editions are at present out of print.

VERDI (d) *String quartet* (Peters; Ricordi)

WOLF (c) *Italian serenade* (Novello)

There is an alternative version of this work for small orchestra but it is often felt that the quartet is the more successful medium. The work itself is strongly rhythmic and very attractive.

Piano Quartets

BEETHOVEN (d) *Piano quartet in E♭ major, op. 16* (Augener; Schirmer)

BRAHMS (a) *Piano quartet no. 1, in G minor, op. 25* (Breitkopf; Peters; Schirmer)

(a) *Piano quartet no. 2, in A minor, op. 26* (Breitkopf; Peters; Schirmer)

(a) *Piano quartet no. 3, in C minor, op. 60* (Breitkopf; Peters; Schirmer)

DVOŘÁK (d) *Piano quartet no. 2, in E♭ major, op. 87* (Lengnick)

Instrumental Music

FAURE (e) *Piano quartet no. 1, in C minor, op. 15* (Hamelle)
       (d) *Piano quartet no. 2, in G minor, op. 45* (Hamelle)

Both works are omitted from Aulich and Heimeran, possibly because French chamber music has, in general, little appeal for German musicians.

MOZART (a) *Piano quartets, K.478 and K.493* (Augener, 2v; Peters)

PURCELL (c) *"Golden" sonata* (Augener)

This is the ninth of *10 sonatas in iv parts*, originally published in 1697. Written for two violins, bass and continuo, this version is for violins, 'cello and piano.

SCHUMANN (e) *Piano quartet in E♭ major, op. 47* (Augener; Peters; Schirmer)

Quintets

BEETHOVEN *Quintet for piano and four wind instruments, op. 16* (Peters)
           String quintet in C major, op. 29 (Schott)

The delightful opus 16 quintet is written for piano, oboe, clarinet, French horn and bassoon; it is to some extent indebted to a Mozart quintet (K. 452) written some twelve years earlier for the same combination of instruments. Beethoven himself made an arrangement of this work for piano quartet in which form it is better known though less successful. The string quintet is a later but little-performed work.

BLOCH *Piano quintet* (Schirmer)

This work dates from 1924 and is one of the most important modern examples. Though there is some writing in quarter-tones the work is far from forbidding.

BRAHMS **Clarinet quintet, in B minor, op. 115* (Boosey; Lengnick; Peters)
DVOŘÁK *Piano quintet, op. 81* (Lengnick)
ELGAR *Piano quintet in A minor, op. 84* (Novello)
FRANCK *Piano quintet in F minor* (Hamelle)

An attractive work, probably the finest piece of chamber music that Franck wrote. Omitted from Aulich and Heimeran.

MOZART **Clarinet quintet, in A major, K.581* (Boosey; Breitkopf)
        String quintets (Peters, 2v.)

The string quintet in G minor, K. 516 is particularly recommended for the library that wishes to buy only one of the composer's ten works in this form.

359

SCHUBERT   *Quintet for piano, violin, viola, 'cello and double-
              bass, in A major ("The trout"), op. 114, D.667*
              (Breitkopf; Peters)
            *Quintet in C major, for 2 violins, viola and 2 'cellos,
              op. 163, D.956* (Peters)

These are two of the loveliest of all chamber music works and deserve inclusion in the medium-sized collection.

SCHUMANN   *Piano quintet in E♭ major, op. 44* (Augener; Peters; Schirmer)

SHOSTAKOVITCH *Piano quintet, op. 57* (Leeds Music Corporation)

One of the most consistently attractive works of this somewhat erratic Russian composer. The quintet dates from 1941.

Larger Groups

The demand for sextets, septets, octets and nonets is likely to be very small indeed and only the largest library will normally stock such works. Chamber music, by definition, is understood to have a single instrument to each part, and the parts themselves are of more or less equal importance. As soon as there are two or more instruments playing the same part, then the music is not chamber music but for small orchestra. Because of this "one instrument, one part" rule, chamber music is usually limited to nonets and smaller combinations but there are borderline cases such as Mozart's Serenade for *13 wind instruments, K.361*, etc. For recommended works, Aulich and Heimeran is again the suggested guide.

FURTHER AIDS TO SELECTION

Piano

FRISKIN, James, *and* FREUNDLICH, Irwin. *Music for the piano: a handbook of concert and teaching material from 1580 to 1952.* 1954. (New York: Rinehart.)

This is the fifth volume of that invaluable series "The Field of music" with Ernest Hutcheson as its series editor and whose own work (see below) is a useful complement to this one. *Music for the piano* is divided into five parts: The earliest keyboard music; Pianoforte music from Haydn to the earliest twentieth century; Pianoforte music of the twentieth century; Original works for four hands; Music for piano and orchestra. Generally speaking, Freundlich is responsible for the first, third and fourth sections and Friskin for the other two. The arrangement appears to have worked excellently though it has resulted in some inconsistencies. For instance, John Ireland and Nicholas Medtner were both born in 1879, but the latter is listed with composers "From Haydn to the twentieth century" and the former with "Pianoforte music of the twentieth century".

Within each section composers are treated alphabetically, and their works are usually arranged by opus number or, when there is none, chronologically. With major composers arrangement by form is often adopted to bring together all sonatas, all variations, etc., and in such cases there is often a short list of easier compositions immediately following the composer's name. This helps the amateur of limited technical ability to select works by the greatest composers that are within his capacity. In certain cases the works of a composer are listed in arbitrary fashion. The individual works are listed on the left-hand margin of each page and the annotation to the right of it. Works in several movements (such as sonatas) and others which comprise several pieces (such as *Iberia* by Albeniz, Debussy's *Children's corner*, etc.) usually receive annotation for each movement or piece. Works of lesser importance may have a single annotation which draws attention to the more attractive or better-known items. The publisher's name is quoted at the end of each annotation; an exception is made when one publisher handles the entire output of a single composer (and this is indicated at the beginning of the entry) or when there are a number of available editions. In the latter case, a frank note on the available editions follows the composer's name. A particular edition may be recommended or (more rarely) a suggestion as to an edition to avoid may be met with.

Part I, The early keyboard music, is divided into seven sections. The first two deal with English music (from *c.* 1580 to 1650; and the seventeenth and eighteenth centuries respectively), the remainder with French, Italian, Spanish, Portuguese and German composers. Part II consists of a single sequence of 104 pages (out of the book's total of some 430). Part III, The 20th century, has three sub-divisions—Composers in Europe (including Israel and Russia), Composers in the U.S.A. (including foreign-born residents such as Bloch, Martinu and Stravinsky) and Composers in Latin-America (with foreign-born residents again included). The value of these last two sections, in particular, is immense to the British librarian, for many

361

of the names and the great majority of the works listed are completely unknown in this country. Part IV deals, in two sequences, with piano duets and works for two pianos. The former is not as comprehensive as Alec Rowley's book (see below) but includes a number of works that are not found in the English publication. Part V is also divided into two parts; one is for solo piano and orchestra and the other lists music for two or more pianos and orchestra. The work is completed by an Appendix which lists anthologies of early keyboard music and "Some further reference editions of early keyboard music", and by an index of composers. The work must be regarded as a most important bibliographic aid to music librarians.

HUTCHESON, Ernest. *The literature of the piano: a guide for amateur and student.* [1951.] Hutchinson.

The author, Australian by birth and American by residence, was a concert pianist for many years. In this book he covers a wide field with separate chapters devoted to the more important composers of piano music. The general arrangement is chronological, while major works are considered individually with hints on interpretation. There is some evaluation of editions in the case of a few composers such as Beethoven, Brahms, Chopin, etc., and these comments are of practical value; British librarians, however, must remember that Hutcheson lists American editions which may only be available in Britain through other publishers.

Some chamber music is included (piano quartets and quintets, etc.) and a bibliography and a good index complete a book that should be consulted before buying any unfamiliar piano music. As in the previous work recommended, the chapter on modern American composers has obvious value. Contemporary British composers are quite well represented though generally without annotation. There is one odd error; Howard Ferguson's piano sonata is specifically recommended, but is listed on page 331 as by "George Fergusson".

LIVERPOOL PUBLIC LIBRARIES. *Catalogue of the Music Library: the piano, its music and literature.* 1949. (Liverpool P.L.)

This list was compiled by Liverpool's music librarian, Mr. K. H. Anderson. Liverpool's collection of scores dates back to 1859 and this catalogue gives some indication of the development that has taken place over ninety years. The complete catalogue to this large collection, published in 1954, rounds out the picture but is less handy for those interested solely in piano music. The later catalogue is arranged on dictionary principles, the earlier volume in classified order by modified Dewey, with books on technique, collections of piano works (general and national), solos by individual composers, duets, two-piano music, and such works as trios for one piano, six hands, etc., arranged in that order. There is a separate section for children's music and books on the piano, pianists, etc., are also included. The catalogue contains over a hundred pages, is a useful check and finding list, and can provide suggestions for the expansion of almost any library's piano music section. The catalogue itself is noteworthy for its cover for the keyboard design along the inner edge makes the subject obvious at a glance.

LOCKWOOD, Albert. *Notes on the literature of the piano.* 1940. (Chicago: University of Michigan Press.)

This book considers works for piano duet and for two pianos in addition to solo piano compositions; chamber music is excluded but piano concertos are listed. In general, the arrangement is alphabetical under composers' names but musicians considered of lesser importance are found under headings such as "Miscellaneous American composers", "The Clavecinists", etc., and these headings are inserted in the general sequence. Under each composer (whose Christian names are given first) the following information is given: Date of birth and death, his piano works (usually arranged in order of opus number or alphabetically where opus numbers are not used) and the publisher or publishers of each work. There is also a general survey of the composer's achievements which is often personal and unorthodox without being eccentric. In the preface, Lockwood writes: "The remarks appended to the lists of compositions may seem sketchy, but I have purposely left them as they are, since the book is intended as a stimulus rather than an encyclopedia." An asterisk is used to denote the best works of a composer or a work which is extremely popular but this sign is omitted as being meaningless in the case of the great composers. Except for Bach, the relative merits of different editions is not discussed; items here are arranged in the sequence of the Peters catalogue, and the Busoni (Breitkopf) edition of Bach's keyboard works is particularly recommended for students. Minor composers have their works listed without comment, while the entry for Beethoven includes a list of composers who have written cadenzas for any or all of the first four piano concertos. The section devoted to the Clavecinists is divided into two parts—those composers to whom individual volumes have been devoted, and the second part to albums, anthologies, etc. In an appendix are listed Compositions for piano and orchestra, Sonatas, Pieces for two pianos, Concert études, and Pieces for children and young people.

Thus, the librarian who wishes has the choice of three volumes of critical and expert opinion upon the very wide field of piano music. It is a chastening thought that all are of American origin.

Piano Duets

ROWLEY, Alec. *4 hands—1 piano: a list of works for duet players.* 1940. (O.U.P.)

This invaluable work has already been recommended in the appropriate section earlier in this chapter; it is most regrettable that it is out of print with no apparent prospect of reprinting. The work considers duets under eight headings: The classics; General; The French school; French educational; English composers; Educational; Etudes; Graded pieces. There is a good index to assist easy reference. For educational duets (i.e. those in which one part is played by the teacher and the other by the pupil) the relative difficulty of the two parts is indicated by the usual mnemonics, e.g. "Secondo MD—Primo M." Easy, Moderate, Moderately difficult and Difficult are the four stages. Dates of birth and death are given for some composers and not for others, but entries are usually arranged in order of opus number, quoting publisher(s). A number of works have annotations; these vary in length from three words to five lines.

Attention should also be drawn to Friskin and Freundlich's *Music for the piano*, which has an important section on piano duets.

Organ

ROBSON, R. Walker. *The repertoire of the modern organist.* [?1925.] (Musical Opinion.)

The list of recommended works is in a single alphabetical sequence of composers. It includes a number of arrangements and some very inferior original works. There are brief annotations with useful comments indicating the degree of difficulty and a brief description of the work itself. The book is o.p.

Instrumental Music

WESTERBY, Herbert. *The complete organ recitalist: international repertoire-guide (historical, educational and descriptive) to Foreign, British and American works*. [?1933] (Musical Opinion)

The book includes plates of famous organists and organs. There is a general introduction followed by chapters on organ music, divided by nationality. Many works are listed but annotations are extremely brief, often limited to two or three words. The book is out of print.

Violin and viola

LETZ, Hans. *Music for violin and viola*. 1948. (New York: Rinehart.)

This is the second in "The Field of music" series. The major part deals with violin music, only eleven of the 107 pages of text being devoted to the viola. Works for solo instrument and those with piano accompaniment (either original or an orchestral accompaniment arranged for piano) are all listed in a single sequence under composers. For each individual musician the actual arrangement of single items appears to be quite arbitrary, and this makes reference difficult for those composers who have written more than one or two pieces for the instrument. Each page is divided into four columns: Composer; Title; key and opus number; Grading and remarks. The indication of grading is limited entirely to the technical difficulties of a work and excludes those of interpretation. First, second and third positions (which deal with the position of the left hand on the instrument's fingerboard, and which become progressively more difficult) are shown as A, B and C respectively and each group is sub-divided into three so that A1 is the indication of minimum difficulty and C3 a work calling for very high technical skill.

When concertos and similar works are listed each movement is shown separately in the "Remarks" column and a suggested tempo is given in cases where the composer has omitted any metronome marking or other precise indication. Max Bruch's *Scotch* [*sic*.] *fantasy, op. 46* may be quoted as an example. The composer's name is in the first column, the title and opus number in the second. The grading is shown as C3 and the first movement, *Grave* has a recommended speed of fifty-four crotchets (or quarter-notes) per minute, with the comment, "Somber, like a funeral march". The author recommends that the *Adagio cantabile* of the second movement should be taken at a speed of eighty-eight quavers (eighth-notes) per minute, and remarks "Full and rich". The third movement is noted as "Joyful and rhythmically alive" and the last as "A folk song of great simplicity building up to great emotional warmth".

It can be seen that this information is likely to be of far greater use to the performer than to the librarian who would have appreciated a note as to the status of the music and details of the publisher or publishers.

At the end of the section for violin music is "A graded course of teaching material for the violin (schools) and methods of technic" which is arranged from the first to the ninth year. A similar section follows the list of viola music but is limited to advanced method, on the assumption that the violist will have started as a violinist and so will not require elementary material.

The section for viola music is arranged on similar lines to that for violin. Coverage in the work is variable; standard works and a good selection of out-of-the-way pieces can be found, but there are notable omissions, e.g. Bartók is not included in the section on violin music—a bad gap in a work that makes any pretence to comprehensiveness. The *4 pieces, op. 17* by Suk are only half represented. The third and fourth pieces receive entry and comment, but the first volume which contains op. 17, no. 1 and op. 17, no. 2 is omitted for no apparent reason. Despite these and other drawbacks, however, the work is a valuable one for librarians since it provides a useful indication of technical difficulty and a reasonable coverage of the repertory for the two instruments.

Harp

RENSCH, Roslyn. *The Harp: from Tara's Halls to the American schools*. 1950. (New York: Philosophical Library.)

The three sections of this book deal with the history of the harp, fundamentals and suggested music. This last, the only part relevant here, is divided into six chapters. The first is entitled "Harp methods for the beginning student" and each book listed is given four or five lines of annotation. The second chapter on "Albums for the beginning student" includes under each recommended work its title, composer, publisher and place of publication, with date, pagination and a contents note where necessary. The third chapter, "Ensemble music of easy to medium grade for the harp with school music groups" gives title and composer only, with a note of the particular ensemble for which the work is written.

The fourth chapter of this section is the major one for librarians: "Selected composers, compositions and recordings." This lists composers in alphabetical order; where the work is a transcription for harp the name of the arranger or arrangers is given; where there is more than one arrangement available then the transcribers are shown in alphabetical order. The list includes works (and recordings) in which the harp has a prominent part though not necessarily as a solo instrument. Publishers' names are not shown in this list. The final chapter, on "Selected harp solos for school assemblies, plays and programs" grades the music in four degrees of difficulty and gives suitable music for different seasons of the year. It also includes solo harp music for theatrical productions (Fantasy music; Incidental music; Dance music, etc.).

For the librarian who needs to trace music for the harp this work would seem to be a most valuable aid.

Recorder

HUNT, Edgar H., *and* DONINGTON, Robert. *A practical method for the recorder*. 2v. 1935. (O.U.P.)

The first volume is divided into two parts, the first of which gives instructions for playing the instrument and also includes a brief bibliography, while the second part gives some simple pieces for recorder. The second volume is devoted entirely to music.

The list of recorder music is still useful, and there is a separate list of arias for solo voice with recorder obbligato. The book is out of print, and a much wider selection of suitable music has become available during the subsequent years. An excellent current work is the *School recorder book*, by E. Priestley and F. Fowler, valuable to adults as well as to younger learners.

Flute

CHAPMAN, F. B. *Flute technique*, 2nd edn., 1951. (O.U.P.)

This book includes, in an appendix, a list of music for the flute but there is neither annotation nor recommendation. The list is divided into four sections: Flute and pianoforte; Flute or flutes only; Voice and flute, etc.; Flute and other combinations. Each section is arranged alphabetically by composer giving year of birth and death (when known), title of work, opus number (if there is one) and publisher.

Oboe and cor anglais [*English horn*]

ROTHWELL, Evelyn. *Oboe technique*. 1953. (O.U.P.)

This work is in the same series as *Flute technique* mentioned above and the layout of the individual entries follows the same pattern. This list is divided into three sections: Oboe and piano (including works originally written for oboe and orchestra, but not other transcriptions) and works for unaccompanied oboe; Oboe and orchestra, which includes concertante works with orchestra; Chamber music. This last head is split into five sub-sections: (i) Oboe with strings; (ii) Oboes and cor anglais; (iii) oboe and voice or voices; (iv) duets, trios and quartets with various instruments, and (v) quintets and works for larger combinations. Throughout the lists the works for cor anglais are arranged within the one sequence and indicated by an asterisk. No individual works are recommended and the author specifically disclaims any guarantee as to the musical quality of the works listed.

Clarinet

RENDALL, F. Geoffrey. *The clarinet: some notes upon its history and construction*. 1954. (Williams & Norgate)

The book contains an appendix of "A list of music" which normally provides composer, title of work, publisher and date. Three bibliographies of clarinet music are listed, followed by Tutors, Studies, Concertos, Sonatas, Suites and occasional music, Duets (sub-divided into Music for two clarinets, Clarinet and violin, Clarinet and flute, etc.), Trios (similarly sub-divided) and increasing groups to Nonets with a final section on Larger groups. A second list of bibliographies contains books and articles dealing with the clarinet.

Bagpipe

ASKEW, Gilbert. *A bibliography of the bagpipe*. 1932. (Published for the Northumbrian Pipers' Society by Northumberland Press, Newcastle-on-Tyne.)

This is a pamphlet of twenty-seven pages and it includes a list of recommended works published between the years 1511 and 1932. For librarians who wish to purchase music for the bagpipe, the following four publishers are among those who issue music for the instrument:

J. & R. Glen, 497 Lawnmarket, Edinburgh.

Peter Henderson Ltd., 24 Renfrew Street, Glasgow, C.2.

Paterson, Sons & Co. Ltd., 52 Buchanan Street, Glasgow, C.2.

Patersons Publications Ltd., 36–40 Wigmore Street, London, W.1.

Woodwind and Brass

CAMDEN, Archie, *and* KERRISON, Jan. *Woodwind and brass.* 1953. (Fountain Press)

This small book, from the series "How to choose an instrument", includes under each individual instrument a note listing suggested tutors, studies, concertos and other works. There is also a list of "Woodwind chamber music" which contains some thirty recommended works, with the publisher shown in nearly all cases.

Chamber Music

AULICH, Bruno, *and* HEIMERAN, Ernst. *The well-tempered string quartet: a book of counsel and entertainment for all lovers of music in the home.* 1938. Novello.

Originally published in Germany in 1936 under the title *Das stillvergugnügte Streichquartett*, the excellent English translation of D. Millar Craig was issued two years later. There are chapters on quartet playing, a useful list of five "Helpful books" (with long annotations) and an Appendix, which comprises more than half the book, listing recommended works, A number of English compositions have been added by the translator and they are easily distinguished by the symbol ("T") after a composer's name. Naturally enough, the bulk of the recommendations are of string quartets. Composers are listed in alphabetical order, with dates. Individual works are arranged in opus number or chronological order. In addition to long and practical annotations, small marginal notes are included for selected works. For instance, a note in the margin opposite the entry for Haydn's string quartet op. 1, no. 6 (no. 57) is "Christened *André Hofer* quartet", while lower down the same page, against op. 2, no. 3 (no. 60) is the comment "Very enjoyable to play". The annotations deal both with the music and with difficulties of performance. Thus Dvořák's opus 61 quartet is described as "Even finer in its musical ingredients than the one discussed above . . .", while the final sentence reads: "Some passages are very difficult."

The sections dealing with other chamber works are divided into two categories: "Emergencies" and "Windfalls". The former lists music that can be played when one member of the quartet fails to appear, while the latter starts with "An extra viola!" and "Two 'cellists". Other "windfalls" considered are "The Sextet" and, under the heading "Unlikely to happen", the double quartet. "Occasions worth trying for" are "String quartet with clarinet" and two sections added by the translator, "String quartet with oboe" and "String quartet with harp"—the latter recommending the Bax quintet. Two longer sections cover pianoforte quartets and quintets (though Heimeran appears to harbour grave doubts as to the wisdom of including a pianist in a chamber music group) with a final note about chamber music works that include a part for the double bass.

The work is written with wit, wisdom and affection and is invaluable both to the amateur quartet player and music librarian.

Chapter VII

VOCAL MUSIC

OPERA

Operas are usually provided in public libraries in the form of vocal scores, i.e. the parts for different voices are shown on separate staves but the orchestral accompaniment is reduced to a double-stave arrangement for pianoforte. In addition to the vocal scores, libraries may also provide miniature scores, piano scores and opera libretti. In the first, the orchestral score is shown in detail with a separate line for each individual part and the whole score is printed in small type—a miniature copy of the conductor's score. It resembles the miniature score of a symphony, etc., with the addition of the vocal lines and words and because of its length is usually very much thicker than the normal orchestral score. The piano score is an attempt to compress all the music, vocal and orchestral, into the compass of the two hands of a pianist. The words are often shown above or between the staves. This once-popular form of arrangement is now in much less demand, possibly because of the influence of radio and gramophone, and also because the proportion of music-lovers who cannot play an instrument is steadily increasing; for these reasons, the piano score is not a very good purchase today. It should be understood that this type of score should be classified with piano music and not with the vocal scores. Libretti, since they show no music, will be shelved apart from the scores but might be placed as nearby as convenient. As has been stressed in an earlier chapter, the catalogue entry should be quite unambiguous and show quite clearly when the entry is for libretto only, in order to avoid disappointing an enquirier who actually requires a score. Many patrons will only give a superficial glance at the catalogue entry so that clarity is highly desirable. A note at the end of the entry stating that the library has (or has not) a vocal and/or miniature score of the opera may well draw attention to the fact that the libretto does not give the music. Such a note would perhaps not be necessary for any entries made under the name of the librettist, for one assumes that the reader who looked under Hugo von Hofmannsthal for *Der Rosenkavalier* would primarily be interested in the words. This long paragraph can be summed up, therefore, with the suggestion that the small and medium-sized library will normally limit its accessions of operas to vocal scores unless there is expressed demand for miniature scores or libretti also. It should be added that the inclusion of a gramophone record lending library may well stimulate interest in miniature scores; libretti are usually provided by the issuing companies with the discs.

Since opera is generally one of the most expensive types of music to buy, the wise librarian will try to ensure that every purchase is likely to meet with occasional demand, at least, during the lifetime of the copy. Some general factors that should influence choice may be briefly considered here. First, the opera should have current or historical importance. In other words, it should be performed with some regularity today or at least qualify for an occasional revival. If one or two arias from an otherwise forgotten opera are to be found appearing in concert programmes or in gramophone record catalogues then there is almost certainly some potential demand for the score. For the smaller library the temptation to buy the vocal score of a new opera, whatever the nationality of the composer should be resisted unless the work shows signs of finding a place in the regular repertory and this is a tremendous hurdle for any new work. This may sound heretical, unadventurous and even retrograde as a policy, yet can save the library many pounds. Operas such as Albert Coates's *Pickwick*, Eugene Goossens' *Judith* and even Vaughan Williams's *Sir John in love* may be cited as examples. All have received Covent Garden performances, all are by eminent musicians and were favourably received and reviewed—but the British public has shown an almost complete lack of interest in these works and overseas performances have been almost nil. Of the post-1940 operas only *Peter Grimes* has managed to make what appears likely to be a permanent impression on the musical world and Britten's other operas have yet to prove nearly as successful. In short, in this particular field the conservative librarian may spend his money to better advantage than his more enterprising colleague. It must be emphasized again, however, that this is the policy recommended for the smaller collection only; the larger library should expect to be more venturesome and the gramophone record library once again will have its effect. The library that possesses no recordings may well manage without any Menotti scores; the library that includes any of his operas on disc will surely receive enquiries for the score.

Another point to be considered is that of language. Where an opera is written in a language other than English it is advisable to get a score that includes the original words (unless in an unfamiliar alphabet) if possible. Should an English translation be included so much the better. It must be remembered, however, that many of the older English translations are horrible distortions of both the original libretto and the English language. Most recorded performances and many of those broadcast are given in the original tongue, while translations are usually less grateful to sing; for instance, an open vowel on a high note in the original may have to be sung to an "ee" or other constricted vowel in translation, to the singer's disadvantage. Alternatively, the translator has to depart from a close translation of the original in order to provide a word with an open vowel for the crucial note or in order to make certain words rhyme. Thus it can be seen that opera scores in the original tongue have much to commend them, particularly if that language is French, German or Italian. Even a performance in Czech can be followed from a score, though Czech and Russian works may be sung more frequently in translation than in the original. It is particularly unfortunate that many of the pre-1939 editions with words in two or three languages have not reappeared since 1945, so that the choice of edition today is much more limited than it was twenty years ago.

Duplication is usually needed only for operas in constant demand, such as *Faust, La Bohème,* etc. In branch libraries with small music collections only a token selection of vocal scores is usually required, provided that this is backed up by an adequate service to answer readers' queries and requests and perhaps by the addition of music "Units" as suggested in Chapter I. Such limited provision will allow more money to be spent on widening the range of the collection as a whole or on duplicating instrumental music that is in more regular demand. Where operas have become part of the public domain then it is often possible to buy editions in different languages, in different translations into the same language, and at different prices. Where alternatives are available it is worth discovering the price of each before ordering unless one edition is outstanding.

The selection that follows is a conservative one; one reader has written that "the approach is too historical for a public library circulating collection". The reasons for this conservative attitude have been given earlier and the total is limited to about one hundred operas of which some thirty-five are listed as (a), and the second and subsequent choices number about a score each. Let it be reiterated that this selection will be inadequate for the library with a gramophone record collection—the addition of a recording of an opera such as *Simon Boccanegra* should be regarded as adequate cause for the accession of the vocal score also. The selection may also prove too narrow for the librarian serving a highly intelligent public that listens to the many unusual operas broadcast on the Third Programme of the B.B.C.; certainly many American librarians will have other ideas, with regular Saturday afternoon broadcasts from the Metropolitan Opera House in New York covering most of the country and with the spread of the "opera workshop" movement with some professionals and a larger number of advanced amateurs studying and singing together whole works or excerpts. This movement has renewed the demand for one-act operas and has produced a crop of classical and near-classical works by native composers, many of whom (such as Alec Wilder, Carlisle Floyd, Vittorio Giannini) are almost completely unknown in Britain.

The American librarian may also dispute the credentials of German and Sullivan in this section or argue that an equally good case can be made out for Irving Berlin, Leonard Bernstein, Cole Porter, etc. Opera, in short, is a case somewhat apart, for one can argue the merits of many composers and works that are successful in one or two countries but which fail elsewhere. These may still fail to reach the opera house abroad but the interchange of recordings between different companies in various countries has meant that the limited number of keen enthusiasts for certain works can now hear their favourite operas on disc and this fact must have some effect on many public libraries. In short, the following lists may well need considerable expansion in many libraries in order to meet local demand.

The letter(s) after the name of a publisher indicate the language(s) of the words—E, English; F, French; G, German; I, Italian, and so on. Where no identifying letter is given the words are in English only. In most cases the language of the original libretto should be guessed easily enough from the title of the work or the nationality of the composer. Where it seems some doubt might exist a clarifying note is included in the annotation.

Vocal Music

The recommended works are all vocal scores (or in the parlance of the M.L.A./A.L.A. Code, "piano-vocal scores"), i.e. the voice parts in full with the orchestral accompaniment arranged for piano. This is the normal version required, but many librarians who should know better continue to ask music suppliers for "full scores". It is perhaps as well that they are rarely taken at their word, since they would probably find the size of the full score and its price equally alarming and embarrassing.

BEETHOVEN
(a) *Fidelio, op. 72* (Boosey, E. G.; Novello, E. G.; Universal, G.)

Beethoven's only opera and one of the finest in the entire repertory. It is performed fairly regularly by the leading companies and one or two of the individual arias reinforce the complete recordings to be found in the gramophone catalogues.

BELLINI
(c) *Norma* (Ricordi, I.; Universal, G.I.)

(e) *I Puritani* (Novello, I.E.; Ricordi, I.)

(d) *La sonnambula* (Ricordi, I.)

All three works are still part of the regular repertory in Italy and receive occasional revivals elsewhere. Complete recordings are to be found in the gramophone catalogues, and individual arias sometimes appear in concert programmes, though the types of voices for which Bellini wrote are rarely found today. Many libraries may well possess old scores of one or other of these operas and if the physical condition is satisfactory, they should certainly be retained in stock.

BERG
(e) *Wozzeck* (Universal, G.)

This opera was for long regarded as an unsuccessful experiment in the "twelve-tone system" but performances at Covent Garden in 1952 proved extremely impressive and aroused considerable interest in Britain. A complete recording has been issued in the U.S.A. and although the opera is never likely to achieve more than a very limited popularity with a small minority of music-lovers, it is still a minor landmark in the history of opera.

BIZET
(a) *Carmen* (Cramer)

(c) *Les pecheurs des perles* (Choudens, F.)

Carmen needs no introduction, but a score giving the original words as well as an English translation is sadly needed. The *Pearl fishers* is hardly ever staged outside France and Italy yet it contains some lovely music and two or three items from it are often performed. Novello publish a concert version of *Carmen*.

BOITO
(e) *Mefistofele* (Ricordi, I.)

Arrigo Boito (1842–1918) is best known as the librettist for Verdi's *Otello* and *Falstaff*. His own version of the Faust legend has been fairly successful in Italy, after a discouraging first night, but has apparently failed to export well, so that demand for the score is likely to come primarily from those who can listen to complete recordings or excerpts from the opera.

BORODIN   (b) *Prince Igor* (Belaieff, R.F.G.)

BRITTEN   (e) *Albert Herring* (Boosey)
                          (d) *Billy Budd* (Boosey)
                          (a) *Peter Grimes* (Boosey)
                          (c) *Rape of Lucretia* (Boosey, E.G.)
                          (d) *Turn of the screw* (Boosey)

Peter Grimes is easily the most successful opera produced since the Second World War, for it has been performed all over the civilized world. Britten's other operas have been less successful and the librarian of the small library may consider them too expensive to add except in response to definite demand. Complete recordings have been made of both *Peter Grimes* and *The turn of the screw*.

CHARPENTIER   (e) *Louise* (Heugel, F.E.)

The opera is set in Paris at the turn of the present century. The work maintains a precarious footing in the general repertory and is best known to most people for the soprano aria *Depuis le jour*.

DEBUSSY   (c) *Pelléas et Mélisande* (Durand, F.E.)

One of Debussy's greatest works but its atmosphere, style and untranslatable libretto require (it would seem) a French cast for successful performance. It is certainly much longer than average, but at least three complete gramophone recordings have been made; this indicates some potential demand for the score.

DELIUS   (e) *A village Romeo and Juliet* (Universal, G.E.)

This is the opera that contains the ever-popular *Walk to the Paradise garden*, and, like Delius's other operas—*Fennimore and Gerda*, *Irmelin* and *Koanga*—is alleged to be practically unstageable. All are out of print, but are certainly worth adding to stock if discovered second-hand or are reprinted since broadcasts and recordings of excerpts should provide some demand. There is also the incidental music to James Elroy Flecker's *Hassan* (Boosey, G. E.).

DONIZETTI   (b) *Don Pasquale* (Ricordi, I; Boosey, I. E.)
                          (d) *L'elisir d'amore* (Ricordi, I.)
                          (e) *La fille du régiment* (Universal, G.; [concert version, Novello, E.I.])
                          (d) *Lucia di Lammermoor* (Ricordi, I.; Schirmer, I.E.)

Donizetti wrote more than sixty operas but these four are the only ones known to most opera-lovers. It is often forgotten that *La figlia del regimento* (*The daughter of the regiment*) was originally written to a French libretto though neither available version provides the French words. Vocal scores of Donizetti's operas can often be bought second-hand very cheaply. His works were very popular with the Victorians, suffered a sad decline and now appear to be returning to public favour.

FALLA   (e) *La vida breve* (Chester, F.S.)

Demand for this opera is likely to come from those people who have access to the wonderful complete recording of the work.

FLOTOW   (e) *Martha* (Novello, E.G.)

Probably better known in its Italian translation though originally written to a German text. Act II contains *The last rose of summer* and Act III the tenor aria *M'appari* (*Ach, so fromm*) which are still great favourites.

GAY   (a) *Beggar's opera* (Boosey)

This work is available in two different versions, the one edited and arranged by Alfred Austin and the other by Benjamin Britten. The former has been a popular favourite since the production at Hammersmith in 1920, and many people still prefer this version to its newer rival which is sometimes accused of being too sophisticated for the music. If the work is duplicated, the obvious course is to stock both versions for patrons to make their own choice. *Polly*, the sequel (also Boosey) is very much less popular. A third version (O.U.P.), edited by E. J. Dent, is at present o.p.

GERMAN   (a) *Merrie England* (Chappell)
            (a) *Tom Jones* (Chappell)

GERSHWIN   (c) *Porgy and Bess* (Gershwin Publishing Co.)

This is probably Gershwin's most successful attempt to fuse classical and popular music. Repeated performances in the U.S.A. and Britain, complete recordings and discs containing excerpts, several of which have received critical approval, suggest that the work may yet become part of the standard repertory.

GIORDANO   (e) *Andrea Chénier* (Heugel, I.; Ricordi, I.; Sonzogno, I.G.)

The opera is rarely performed outside its native Italy, but is well represented on gramophone records.

GLUCK   (b) *Alceste* (Ricordi, I.; U.M.P., F.)
            (e) *Iphigénie en Aulide* (Peters, G.)
            (e) *Iphigénie en Tauride* (Peters, G.)
            (c) *Orphée et Eurydice* (Peters, G.F. *or* G.I.; Novello, I.E.; Ricordi, I.)

Gluck's operas are now the oldest in the normal repertory though performances are now limited mainly to France. *Orphée* is a revised French version of the Italian *Orfeo ed Euridice* but it is the earlier Italian version that is the more frequently performed and recorded so that a version with Italian words is desirable.

GOUNOD   (a) *Faust* (Chappell, E.F.)
            (d) *Roméo et Juliette* (Schirmer, E.F.; Choudens, F.)

HANDEL   (c) *Serse* (Peters, G.)

Efforts to revive any of Handel's multitude of operas seem doomed to failure but individual arias will always be popular. *Serse* (or *Xerxes*) contains the immortal Largo, *Ombra mai fu*. Copies of Handel operas already in stock should certainly not be discarded though they may be better retained in reserve stock.

HOLST (d) *The perfect fool, op. 39* (Novello)

This is a one-act opera that parodies both Wagner and the conventional Italian operatic tenor. The ballet music has become popular during the last few years and the opera itself seems ripe for revival and could hope to meet with far greater success than in its original production. *At the Boar's Head* is another one-act opera by this composer founded on the Falstaff scenes in Shakespeare's *Henry IV*, while earlier still is the effective *Savitri*, an opera di camera, with three soloists, a small orchestra and a small off-stage chorus, with an Indian story as its background.

HUMPERDINCK (b) *Hänsel und Gretel* (Schott)

LEONCAVALLO (a) *Pagliacci* (Ascherberg, I.E.)

MASCAGNI (a) *Cavalleria rusticana* (Ascherberg, I.E.)

MASSENET (d) *Manon* (Heugel, F.)

This is another score that is much better known to British opera-lovers through gramophone records than from live performances.

MENOTTI (e) *Amahl and the night visitors* (Schirmer)
  (e) *The consul* (Schirmer)
  (e) *The medium* (Schirmer)
  (d) *The telephone* (Schirmer)

Gian-Carlo Menotti (b. 1911) is an American of Italian descent who writes his own libretti and chooses contemporary settings for the action of these one-act operas, all of which have been written since World War II. They have been most successful in the U.S.A. but have received a much cooler reception in Britain; their future popularity must be regarded as problematical.

MEYERBEER (e) *Les Huguenots* (Heugel, F.)

Meyerbeer's many operas are worth retaining in reserve stock; demand is almost sure to come from those who wish to follow recorded or broadcast performances of an excerpt or two. It is amazing to contrast Meyerbeer's long run of success as an operatic composer with the subsequent total eclipse of his popularity.

MOZART (b) *Cosi fan tutte* (Novello, E.I.; Boosey, E.I.; Peters, I.G.)
  (a) *Don Giovanni* (Boosey, E.I.; Breitkopf, G.I.; Novello, E.I.; Ricordi, I.)
  (b) *Die Entführung aus dem Serail* [*Il Seraglio*] (Novello, G.E.; Peters, G.)
  (a) *Le Nozze di Figaro* (Boosey, E.I.; Novello, E.I.; Ricordi, I.)
  (a) *Die Zauberflöte* [*Il flauto magico*] (Boosey, E.G.; Novello, E.G.; Ricordi, I.; Universal, G.I.)

Vocal Music

The above titles indicate the original language of the text set by Mozart; the operas are also the most popular by this composer but the large library will doubtless complete the collection of vocal scores, particularly since all the operas are available in recorded form. There are seven of these works, of varying length and merit: *Bastien und Bastienne, La finta giardiniera, Il re pastore, Zaïde, Idomeneo, Der Schauspieldirektor* and *La clemenza di Tito*. The excellent English translations of E. J. Dent are used in the Boosey editions of *Don Giovanni, Figaro* and the *Magic Flute*.

MUSSORGSKY (b) *Boris Godunov* (Boosey, E.G.)

The above edition is in the Rimsky-Korsakov revision of the score; it is particularly unfortunate that the original version (O.U.P., with French and English words) is at present out of print. Performances may be in either version and there is still much controversy over the "improvements" made by Rimsky-Korsakov, though this is still the recension most frequently used. This great work's history is well worth investigation by the reader—it is a curious and at times almost unbelievable tale of an opera that was never completed by its composer.

OFFENBACH (c) *Les contes d'Hoffmann* (Cramer, E.F.)

Although remembered almost solely for its lovely *Barcarolle*, the opera has received successful recordings on LP discs and may be remembered as the subject of an excellent British film with Sir Thomas Beecham conducting the music. Some of Offenbach's buffa operas have been adapted successfully for the musical comedy stage.

PUCCINI (a) *La Bohème* (Ricordi, I.E.)

(b) *Gianni Schicchi* (Ricordi, I.E.)

(a) *Madama Butterfly* (Ricordi, I.E.)

(c) *Manon Lescaut* (Ricordi, I.)

(a) *Tosca* (Ricordi, I.E.)

(b) *Turandot* (Ricordi, I.E.)

With the possible exception of *Gianni Schicchi*, the comedy in a triptych of one-act operas, these works are too well known to require comment. The other two one-act works are *Suor Angelica* and *Il tabarro* (both Ricordi, I.). *Gianni Schicchi* is considered by some to be Puccini's finest achievement. It is not related in theme or characters to either *Sister Angelica* or *The cloak*; all three are entirely self-contained and the other two are as tragic as *Schicchi* is humorous. Ricordi also publish *The cloak*, an English language version of *Il tabarro*.

PURCELL (a) *Dido and Aeneas* (Novello; O.U.P.)

(b) *The fairy Queen* (Novello)

(c) *King Arthur* (Boosey; Novello [concert version])

These three works are hardly operas in the conventional sense but all are sure of occasional broadcasts and performances in Britain. *Dido* is the most coherent and successful of the three—and is by far the most popular and frequently performed.

RAVEL   (e) *L'enfant et les sortilèges* (Durand, E.F.)

          (e) *L'heure espagnole* (Durand, E.F.)

Two one-act operas contain some of Ravel's most delightful music; each has received at least one excellent recording with a French cast.

RIMSKY-

    KORSAKOV   (d) *Sadko* (Boosey, R.F.G.)

          (c) *Snow maiden* (*Snegorochka*) (Boosey)

Together with *Le coq d'or* (Schirmer, R. E.; unobtainable in Britain), these two operas are those by which the composer is best known. Concert audiences are reasonably familiar with the orchestral suite from the *Golden cockerel*, while the *Dance of the tumblers* and the *Song of the Indian guest* (*Chanson Hindoue*) from *Snow-maiden* and *Sadko* respectively are known to thousands who could not name the sources of the two popular excerpts.

ROSSINI   (a) *Il barbiere di Siviglia* (Novello, E.I.; Ricordi, I.)

          (d) *La cenerentola* [*Cinderella*] (Ricordi, I.)

          (e) *Le comte d'Ory* (Ricordi, I.)

          (e) *L'Italiana in Algeri* (Ricordi, I.)

The barber of Seville is one of the most popular of all operas; *Cinderella* maintains a somewhat precarious footing in the repertory and the *Comte d'Ory* has recently reappeared after a long period of almost complete oblivion. All these operas, and the *Italian girl* have received excellent recordings which use the same casts that presented highly-successful stage performances.

SAINT-SAENS   (a) *Samson et Dalila* (Durand)

SMETANA   (b) *The bartered bride* (*Prodana Nevesta*) (Boosey, E.; Peters, G.)

Critics rate *Dalibor* as Smetana's most successful opera—and once again gramophone records may help to increase the demand for that score. In the interim, the *Bartered bride* remains the great popular favourite outside its native country.

STRAUSS, J., jr.   (a) *Die Fledermaus* (*The bat*) (Weinberger-Cranz, G.E.; Schirmer)

An operetta, but one that has made its way into the repertory of the majority of the world's great opera houses because of its gay and irresistible melodies. Consideration might also be given to *Der Zigeunerbaron* (*Gipsy baron*) (Weinberger-Cranz, G.); an English adaptation for amateur production is available.

STRAUSS, R.   (e) *Ariadne auf Naxos* (Boosey, G.)

          (d) *Elektra* (Boosey, G.E.)

          (b) *Der Rosenkavalier* (Boosey, G.E.)

          (e) *Salome* (Boosey, G.E.)

None of the operas by Strauss has achieved the popular success of the *Rose cavalier* but the other recommended works receive sufficient performances to make provision of the scores justifiable.

Vocal Music

STRAVINSKY   (e) *The rake's progress* (Boosey, E.G.)

Stravinsky's only full-length opera, first produced in 1951; a highly-successful gramophone recording should help to stimulate demand, though the work is never likely to be a favourite. The opera was written to an English libretto.

SULLIVAN   (a) *The Gondoliers* (Chappell)

                (a) *H.M.S. Pinafore* (Cramer)

                (a) *Iolanthe* (Chappell)

                (a) *The Mikado* (Chappell)

                (a) *The pirates of Penzance* (Chappell)

                (c) *Ruddigore* (Chappell)

                (b) *Trial by jury* (Chappell)

                (a) *The Yeomen of the Guard* (Chappell)

"G. & S." need no annotation; their works are in steady demand in all British libraries. Not only should the works above be included in quite small collections, but duplication may be required in certain cases. Amateur operatic societies occasionally venture outside the selection given and the other comic operas such as *Princess Ida*, *Patience* and *The sorcerer* could well be added as additional choices.

TCHAIKOVSKY   (c) *Eugen Onegin* (Schirmer, G.E.)

                   (b) *Queen of Spades* [*Pique Dame*] (Schirmer, E.)

Both operas are known chiefly in extracts which form part of the repertory of many sopranos and tenors, but complete performances are occasionally staged. Tchaikovsky's other operas are almost completely unknown.

VERDI   (a) *Aida* (Ricordi, I.E.)

         (c) *Un ballo in maschera* (Ricordi, I.)

         (d) *Don Carlo* (Ricordi, I.)

         (e) *Ernani* (Ricordi, I.)

         (b) *Falstaff* (Ricordi, I.)

         (b) *La forza del destino* (Ricordi, I.)

         (c) *Macbeth* (Ricordi, I.)

         (a) *Otello* (Ricordi, I.E.)

         (a) *Rigoletto* (Boosey, I.E.; Novello, I.E.; Ricordi, I.)

         (a) *La traviata* (Novello, E.I.; Ricordi, I.)

         (a) *Il trovatore* (Boosey, I.E.; Novello, I.E.; Ricordi, I.E.)

Verdi composed many fine Italian operas and his popularity has been rising steadily during the past twenty years. For proof, one might cite the fact that nearly all his operas (including two or three omitted from the list above) are available in the U.S.A. on LP discs and most of the better-known tragedies are available in alternative recorded versions. There should be good Verdi representation in the smallest stock and the large collection would benefit from the inclusion of the operas omitted from the above list, e.g. *Nabucco* and *I Lombardi*. This is a very different position from 1893, when J. D. Brown recommended three operas only—*Il trovatore* (2 stars), *Rigoletto* (1 star) and *La Traviata*. *Don Carlo* is available in both the original five-act version of 1867 and the revised four-act form of 1884. While the latter is probably preferable, modern performances often add the first act of the 1867 version, omitted in the later revision.

WAGNER   (b) *Der fliegende Holländer* (Novello, E.G.; Peters, G.)

                  (c) *Lohengrin* (Schott, G.E.)

                  (a) *Die Meistersinger von Nürnberg* (Peters, G.; Schott, G.E.)

                  (e) *Parsifal* (Boosey, G.E.; Schott, G.E.)

                  (e) *Rienzi* (Schott, G.)

                  (a) *Der Ring des Nibelungen*

                      (i) *Das Rheingold* (Peters, G.; Schott, G.E.)

                      (ii) *Die Walküre* (Schott, G.E.)

                      (iii) *Siegfried* (Schott, G.E.)

                      (iv) *Götterdämmerung* (Peters, G.; Schott, G.E.)

                  (d) *Tannhäuser* (Novello, G.E.; Peters, G.)

                  (b) *Tristan und Isolde* (Schott, G.E.)

Wagner's popularity as an opera composer has declined as that of others, notably Verdi, has increased. Monday has long since ceased to be "Wagner night" at the Henry Wood Promenade concerts in London but the time is never likely to come when libraries will be able to dispense with the *Mastersingers* or *The Ring* from their collections; the genius of Wagner ensures that his works will remain in the repertory and, as musical fashions change, he is likely to regain popularity in due course.

WEBER   (c) *Der Freischütz* (Novello, E.G.; Universal, G.)

                  (e) *Oberon* (Novello, E.G.; Universal, G.)

Der Freischütz (an untranslatable title) is often considered to be the first truly "national" opera and is the only one to retain a precarious place in the repertory, mainly in its native Germany. Weber, like so many gifted musicians, was unfortunate in his choice of librettists; for this reason *Oberon* (first performed at Covent Garden) is known only by its lovely overture and the great soprano aria, *Ozean, du Ungeheuer* (*Ocean, thou mighty monster*).

WOLF-FERRARI   (b) *I gioielli della Madonna* [*Jewels of the Madonna*] (Weinberger, I.E.)

                  (c) *I quattro rusteghi* [*School for fathers*] (Weinberger, G.E.)

                  (d) *Il segreto di Susanna* [*Susanna's secret*] (Weinberger, I.E.)

None of these operas has any great profundity but all are tuneful and attractive, and are becoming better known in the English-speaking world. As his name suggests, the composer (1876–1948) was of mixed German-Italian ancestry.

Vocal Music

MUSICAL PLAYS

As with opera, so the provision of vocal scores of new musical comedies, etc., is a considerable gamble. The proportion that briefly flower and die is as high as in the operatic field. In Britain only three or four works were staged in the ten years after the end of World War II that seem likely to remain in public affection—*Oklahoma!*, *Annie get your gun*, *Bless the bride* and, perhaps *South Pacific*. Only *Bless the bride* is English, the others are all of American origin and suggest that the "musicals" there have far greater vitality than the home-grown specimens. *The King and I* and *My fair lady* are more recent examples of American successes (though with some British collaboration) that have triumphantly crossed the Atlantic, and others may well come to mind. Where the local amateur operatic and dramatic societies in Britain are content (and sometimes insistent) to limit their performances to Gilbert and Sullivan, with other old favourites such as *The Arcadians* and *The chocolate soldier* and modernity represented by Ivor Novello's works, there are many American performances of post-war works, done by both amateurs and professionals, and our pre-war favourites are very rarely revived in the U.S.A.

Many libraries with well-established music sections will have a number of vocal scores of the older musical plays, mostly ignored by today's borrowers. These works may well be discarded or, when one or two tunes have remained in popular favour, relegated to reserve stock and retained for the occasional enquiry.

Though no specific recommendations are included, mention should be made of *The musical production* by Cosser Turfery and King Palmer (Pitman, 1954) which lists, in an appendix, over 200 light operas and musical plays in alphabetical title order. It gives the name of the composer and also the name of the owner of the copyright of the work; the former is invaluable to the librarian, and the latter to the secretary of the local amateur operatic society.

MASSES, REQUIEMS, ORATORIOS, CANTATAS

Demand for this type of music is generally on the decline, though in some areas the interest in good choral music is still vigorous enough. The north of England and the whole of Wales provide examples of flourishing choral societies, male voice choruses, etc., but in many other places these bodies appear to be fighting rearguard actions against the attractions of other forms of amusement and a wider spread of interests; when the older singers retire their places are not being filled by younger people. It is noteworthy that those societies which continue to be most active are frequently those that are prepared to mix new and unfamiliar works with older, tried favourites; the society that lacks initiative and keeps to the same familiar and limited round that has sufficed for years is often moribund. Choirs are normally conservative in their tastes and the onus is on the conductor or committee to introduce new music, to overcome prejudices and to persuade the membership at large to give new pieces a fair trial however unfavourable first reactions may be.

Provision in the library of Masses, Cantatas and the like is normally in the form of vocal scores and this is invariably the arrangement of those works listed below. As in other sections of the music stock, the increasing interest in the gramophone record has had its effect upon demands on the library stock and will also make it reasonable to consider the provision of certain popular works in this particular section of the stock in the form of miniature scores. As has been stressed in so many places, the growth of the collection of discs and that of scores should be parallel when possible since the use of the former will often stimulate requests for the appropriate score with which to follow the performance.

A defunct choral society may well result in the receipt by the library of copies of works held by the society or its individual members. If the copies are received in bulk they may well be kept together for use by other societies in the library's area or outside. On the other hand, individual gifts are likely to be over a period and in smaller numbers; in this case the extra copies may be filed to act as replacements as those already in stock wear out.

BACH   (e) *Birthday cantata* [*no. 208*] (Breitkopf, G.)
     (c) *Christmas oratorio* (Breitkopf, G.; Novello, E.; Peters, G.)
     (a) *Mass in B minor* (Breitkopf, L.; Novello, L.; Peters, L.)
     (e) *Phoebus and Pan* [*no. 201*] (Novello, E.)
     (d) *St. John Passion* (Breitkopf, G.; Novello, E.; Peters, G.)

Vocal Music

(a) *St. Matthew Passion* (Breitkopf, G.; Novello, E.; Peters, G.)

The strong sense of religious belief allied with the wide practical experience of the composer make Bach's sacred music among the finest ever written. The style of the vocal writing, with its long runs and scale passages, often set to a single vowel, is quite different from that of composers today but is still completely effective when performed in proper style.

Bach was a choirmaster most of his life and knew exactly what would "come off" in performance. The *B minor Mass* and the *St. Matthew Passion* receive regular performance and must be included in any selection of the world's greatest choral music. A complete contrast in mood is provided by *Phoebus and Pan*, a secular cantata that gives the lie to those who feel that Bach is always sobersided and dull. The numbers in brackets are those of the Bach Society edition.

BEETHOVEN
: (d) *Mass in C major, op. 86* (Novello, L. *or* E.)
(a) *Mass in D major* [*Missa Solemnis*], *op. 123* (Breitkopf, L.; Novello, L.; Peters, L.)

The *Missa Solemnis* is an outstanding work that should be in every collection. The other recommended work was written ten years earlier and, though not outstanding, is worth inclusion in this section as the stock grows.

BERLIOZ
: (b) *L'enfance du Christ, op. 25* (Forsyth, E.; Novello, E.; U.M.P., F.)

It is only in recent years that this work has become well known outside France but the power and imagination shown by Berlioz is being increasingly recognized, and Christmas performances are becoming more frequent. The Forsyth edition is edited by Hallé.

BLISS
: (e) *Pastoral* (Novello)

This work is sub-titled *Lie strewn the white flocks* and sets 8 poems by five different authors; it is written for mezzo-soprano soloist, flute, tympani, choir and string orchestra. The cantata was composed in 1928 and is unexpectedly conventional for Bliss. The large collection could usefully add *Morning heroes* (Novello), a work often performed on Remembrance Day.

BRAHMS
: (a) *Requiem* [*Ein Deutsches Requiem*], *op. 45* (Breitkopf, G.; Novello, E.; Peters, G. *or* E.)
(c) *Liebeslieder waltzes, op. 52* (Lengnick, G.E.)
(e) *Neue Liebeslieder, op. 65* (O.U.P.)

The *German Requiem* has long been a favourite and two or three of the individual items are often sung as anthems. The *Liebeslieder waltzes* are perhaps strange companions, but are difficult to classify elsewhere. Both sets (with the exception of the very last item in the second set) consist of a chain of Viennese-style waltzes written for four voices (soprano, contralto, tenor and bass) with a highly important accompaniment for piano duet. These works reveal Brahms at his gayest.

BRITTEN   (e) *A ceremony of carols, op. 25* (Boosey, E. *or* G.)

(e) *Saint Nicholas, op. 42* (Boosey)

The earlier work dates from 1942 and is written for treble voices with harp (or piano) accompaniment. The later work is also primarily for boys' voices but adds a tenor soloist who has a technically difficult part and the accompaniment is for organ, piano duet, strings and percussion. The cantata outlines the life of Saint Nicholas within the very limited information we have today.

BYRD   (d) *Mass for 3 voices* (Stainer & Bell, L. *or* E.)

(d) *Mass for 4 voices* (Stainer & Bell, L. *or* E.)

(d) *Mass for 5 voices* (Stainer & Bell, L. *or* E.)

William Byrd is one of the great pioneer figures of English music. He is a most important figure both as a writer of vocal and of instrumental music. The three Masses can each be supplied with the original Latin words or with English words adapted for use in the Anglican church. The same publishers issue Byrd's collected works and the first volume contains the Masses and *Cantiones Sacrae* (1575). The Masses are much briefer than those written by eighteenth- and nineteenth-century composers.

COLERIDGE-
TAYLOR   (b) *Scenes from the song of Hiawatha, op. 30* (Novello)

DELIUS   (c) *A Mass of life* (Boosey, E.G.)

(d) *Sea drift* (Boosey, E.G.)

Sea drift is set for baritone solo and chorus to words by Walt Whitman and is performed with some regularity. Though a greater work, *A Mass of life* (to words by Nietzsche) is less frequently heard because of its length (about ninety minutes without intervals) and its technical difficulties. Both works have received superb recordings with Sir Thomas Beecham conducting.

DVOŘÁK   (e) *Requiem, op. 89* (Novello, L.; Artia, L.)

(c) *Stabat Mater, op. 58* (Artia, L.; Novello, L.)

Though it is infrequently performed, some critics rate the *Stabat Mater* as Dvořák's best choral piece; others maintain that the *Requiem* is even finer. These are opinions, but it is a fact that both works are rarely sung. Donations to the library may well include copies of *The spectre's bride*, written to an English text, at one time immensely popular, now almost completely unknown.

DYSON   (e) *The Canterbury Pilgrims* (O.U.P.)

A setting of the Prologue to Chaucer's work. The music is rather conservative in idiom for 1932, but is written with excellent craftsmanship and has proved popular with British choirs. The work calls for soprano, tenor and baritone soli in addition to the chorus.

ELGAR   (a) *The Apostles, op. 49* (Novello)

(e) *Caractacus, op. 35* (Novello)

(a) *The dream of Gerontius, op. 38* (Novello)

(b) *The Kingdom, op. 51* (Novello)

(e) *Scenes from the Bavarian highlands, op. 27* (Williams)

(d) *Scenes from the Saga of King Olaf, op. 30* (Novello)

Elgar's choral music should need no recommendation to British librarians. Its dramatic power suggests that the composer would have been extremely successful as an operatic writer and it is regrettable that Elgar's solitary essay in this form was at the end of his life, and did not progress beyond rough preliminary sketches.

FAURE   (a) *Requiem, op. 48* (Hamelle, L.)

This lovely work has increased rapidly in popularity during the last twenty or thirty years and has been recorded several times; this has helped to attract a wider audience.

HANDEL   (c) *Acis and Galatea* (Novello, E.)

(d) *Chandos Te Deum* (Novello, E.)

(d) *Dettingen Te Deum* (Novello, E.)

(e) *Judas Maccabaeus* (Novello, E.)

(a) *Messiah* (Novello, E.; Universal, G.E.)

(c) *Samson* (Novello, E.; Peters, G.)

(b) *Semele* (Novello, E. [abridged])

Many English choral societies automatically produce *Messiah* every year but often neglect Handel's other choral works, which is to underrate a wonderful writer for both soloists and chorus. Provision of the recommended works, and any others by the composer, may help to stimulate local interest.

HAYDN   (a) *The Creation (Die Schöpfung)* (Breitkopf, E.F.G.; Novello, E.; Peters, E.G.)

(c) *The Seasons (Die Jahreszeiten)* (Breitkopf, E.F.G.; Novello, E.; Peters, E.G.)

Haydn wrote many choral works; these two are by far the most popular though his *Masses* are slowly winning recognition and deserve representation in the large collection. The composer himself appears to have considered the *Creation* as his finest choral work. *The Seasons*, written to a very free German adaptation of Thomson's poem, gave Haydn less pleasure to write, but it remains a great work despite the fact that the level of inspiration drops a little in places.

HOLST   (b) *The hymn of Jesus, op. 37* (Stainer & Bell)

The text is taken from the Apocryphal Acts of St. John, and was translated into English by the composer himself, as was his custom. There is a strong element of plainsong in the work whose growing popularity is due mainly to the famous Huddersfield choir who have broadcast and recorded the work with immense success.

HONEGGER   (c) *Le roi David* (Chester)

The text of this drama is based on a drama by René Morax and tells the story of King David's life. Much of the work is allotted to a narrator, the chorus representing a frenzied crowd of Israelites. Despite the technical difficulties and the lack of a consistent style throughout the work (which has led to much critical comment), *King David* is becoming better known in Britain and appears in the repertory of a few enterprising choral societies. The Chester edition provides an English translation only and not the original words.

IRELAND   (c) *These things shall be* (Boosey)

The words are taken from *A vista*, by John Addington Symonds, and are set for tenor solo, chorus and orchestra. The work dates from 1937, and because it is a strong plea against war, it is often performed at Remembrance Day services. Ralph Hill, in *British music of our time* (Penguin, 1946), called this "one of the composer's most inspired works".

JACOB   (e) *The nun's priest's tale* (Novello)

KODÁLY   (e) *Psalmus Hungaricus, op. 13* (Universal, G.E.)

This is a setting for tenor, chorus and orchestra of a paraphrase of the 35th Psalm. The chorus is used in the modern manner of Walton's *Belshazzar's feast* rather than the more traditional Handelian style. The work is undoubtedly effective when well performed.

LAMBERT   (e) *The Rio Grande* (O.U.P., G.E.)

Set to a poem by Sacheverell Sitwell, this work is a product of the late nineteen-twenties. Its use of jazz idioms was considered rather startling at the time though these same idioms now tend to "date" the work. However, it remains popular with audiences and performers, probably on account of its cheerful exuberance.

MENDELSSOHN   (a) *Elijah, op. 70* (Novello, E.)

    (b) *Hear my prayer* (Novello)

    (d) *Lobgesang* [*Hymn of praise*], *op. 52* (Novello)

    (c) *St. Paul, op. 36* (Novello; Peters, E.G.)

MOZART   (d) *Mass in C minor* ("*Grosse Messe*"), *K.427* (Breitkopf, L.; O.U.P., L.)

    (c) *Requiem in D minor, K.626* (Breitkopf, L.; Novello, E. *or* L.; O.U.P.)

At the time of writing, the O.U.P. editions of both Masses are out of print. The Requiem was Mozart's last work, incomplete at his death, and finished by his pupil Süssmayer.

ORFF   (e) *Carmina Burana* (Schott, G.)

    (e) *Catulli Carmina* (Schott, G.)

    (e) *Die Kluge* (Schott, G.)

    (e) *Der Mond* (Schott, G.)

A separate English libretto is available for *Carmina Burana* which is set to

388

thirteenth-century poems. The three works are scenic cantatas, very successful in their native Germany and this success is now spreading to Britain and America, first through recorded and later from "live" performances. The repetitive rhythm can be most effective, especially in the concert hall, but these do not seem to be works that repay more than occasional repetition. *Carmina Burana* is first choice. *Der Mond* is based upon a Grimm fairy tale.

PALESTRINA   (e) *Missa brevis* (Novello, L.)

                 (e) *Missa Papae Marcelli* (Novello, L.; Peters, L.)

                 (d) *Stabat Mater* (Novello, L.)

Palestrina (*c.* 1525–1594) took his name from his birthplace just outside Rome, and was one of the greatest composers of liturgical music. The *Missa brevis* is comparatively well known, but the other Mass is probably the best written by the composer. Its name derives from the principles laid down by Pope Marcellus—it is clear, simple and the words are easily intelligible. The *Stabat Mater*, written for double choir (eight voices), was performed by the Papal choir on every Good Friday and is sometimes sung in Britain on this day; it is to be regretted that many less worthy works receive more frequent performance upon that occasion. All the three works are for unaccompanied choir and have no solo parts.

PARRY   (e) *Blest pair of Sirens, op. 101* (Novello)

This is probably Parry's most popular work with British choirs and dates from 1887. The words are by Milton.

PERGOLESI   (e) *Stabat Mater* (Novello, L.)

Written for soprano and contralto soli, women's chorus and orchestra.

PROKOFIEV   (e) *Alexander Nevsky, op. 78* (Boosey, E.R.)

This cantata is an arrangement of music originally written for a Russian film of the same name.

PURCELL   (c) *Ode on St. Cecilia's Day* (*Hail, bright Cecilia*) (Novello)

Purcell composed music for four odes in honour of St. Cecilia; she is the patron saint of musicians and music. The recommended work dates from 1692 and is the last and greatest of the four. It is still regularly performed in London on November 22nd each year.

ROSSINI   (d) *Petite Messe solenelle* (Ricordi, L.)

                (b) *Stabat Mater* (Novello, L.E.; Ricordi, L.)

The Mass may be "solenelle"—"petite" it is certainly not, for it lasts over ninety minutes if performed without cuts. Ignoring this joke of Rossini's, the music is effective and impressive, but the vocal score is very expensive (75s. in 1958).

SCHUBERT   (d) *Mass in A♭ major* (Breitkopf, L.; Novello, L. or E.)

                (c) *Mass in E♭ major* (Breitkopf, L.; Peters, L.)

The A♭ Mass was written between 1819 and 1822, the E-flat work in 1828.

The two works are among the most important of Schubert's choral compositions but the earlier work has suffered in popularity because of its unconventional key for a work of this type.

SPOHR (e) *Last judgment* [*Die lezten Dinge*] (Novello)

An old favourite that still occasionally receives performance. Many church choirs retain in their repertory two extracts—*Blest are the departed* and *Lord God of Heaven and earth.*

STAINER (a) *Crucifixion* (Novello)

STANFORD (e) *The Revenge, op. 24* (Novello)
(c) *Stabat Mater, op. 96* (Boosey)

The Revenge is a cantata and an early work, while the *Stabat Mater* is probably the composer's greatest choral work. Stanford (1852–1924) and Parry were perhaps the two greatest figures in the English musical renaissance in the early years of this century and have immensely influenced subsequent British composers.

TIPPETT (e) *A child of our time* (Schott)

A modern oratorio which uses negro spirituals as a contemporary equivalent of the chorales in Bach cantatas. The work has received an excellent recording.

VAUGHAN
WILLIAMS (b) *Flos campi* (O.U.P.)
(d) *Mass in G minor* (Curwen, L.)
(c) *Symphony no. 1* (*A Sea symphony*) (Stainer & Bell)
(e) *Toward the unknown region* (Stainer & Bell)
(d) *5 Tudor portraits* (O.U.P.)

Flos campi (*Flower of the field*) is a continuous suite in six sections scored for solo viola, small orchestra and chorus. The viola part is a difficult one and the chorus is wordless. The *Sea symphony* is a choral one, with words by Walt Whitman, and dates from 1910. Vaughan Williams went to Whitman again for the words of *Toward the unknown region*. The *Tudor portraits* is a choral suite set to words by the English poet John Skelton (1460–1529).

VERDI (b) *Requiem* (Ricordi, E.L.)
(d) *4 sacred pieces* [*Quattro pezzi sacri*] (Ricordi, L.)

For many years the Requiem was considered too operatic for its liturgical content but its genius has slowly won over critical opinion. The *4 sacred pieces* are an *Ave Maria*, a *Stabat Mater*, *Laudi alla Vergine* (from Dante's *Paradiso*) and a *Te Deum*, an incredible piece of music from a man well into his eighties.

WALTON (b) *Belshazzar's feast* (O.U.P., E.G.)

This tremendous work dates from 1931, and is set to words selected from Isaiah by Sir Osbert Sitwell. The scoring is for baritone solo, chorus, orchestra and brass band. The chorus is used in a barbaric and electrifying fashion and the music represents as difficult a test as a choral society is likely to meet. Much of the work's fame and popularity is due to the Huddersfield Choral Society whose superb performances in broadcasts and recording can be regarded as models.

ANTHEMS

The single anthem, because of its brevity, cheapness and problems of filing is generally considered outside the scope of the public library stock. Sets of anthems for use by local choirs are on a different basis and have been considered in Chapter I. Two collections of anthems, at least, give a good selection in a form that is both handy and convenient and may be useful to local choirmasters. They are mentioned below. Should recommendation for further anthems be required, reference may be made to the anthologies of English Church music recorded and issued on [English] Columbia gramophone records. These discs offer an excellent choice of some of the best (and occasionally some inferior) of our Cathedral music.

DAVIES, *Sir* Walford, *and* LEY, Henry G., *editors*. The Church anthem book: 100 anthems. (O.U.P.)

The Novello anthem book. (Novello)

The preface to the Novello collection says that it is "A selection of anthems within the power of average choirs covering all regular occasions". Both Sir Walford Davies and Henry Ley have been noted for their excellent work as choir trainers and the volume of anthems edited by them is equally suitable as a guide to music in which the quality of the selected works has been seriously considered.

SONGS BY INDIVIDUAL COMPOSERS

Introduction

The selection that follows is arranged on the same general principles as the remainder of the recommended scores. Songs, however, present added difficulty in listing, for different editions may contain the words in different languages, may use different translations of the original and in many cases both albums and single songs are available for different ranges of voice. The first two problems are also encountered with opera, but the last one is peculiar to songs; a soprano will find a song-cycle for contralto almost as useless as an arrangement of the same work for a violin or some other instrument.

As in the earlier sections of this chapter the initials after the publisher's name show the language(s) of the text of that particular edition; no initial indicates that the words are in English only. The letters "H", "M" and "L" in square brackets show that the work is available in settings for High, Medium and Low voice though occasionally a publisher has made things a trifle more difficult by offering a setting for High-Medium or Low-Medium voice. Where no indication of this type is given it may be assumed that only one setting (usually in the original key used by the composer) is available. With all these possibilities of variation, errors are more likely in this section than in most others.

If additional copies of a work are bought, either because of immediate demand or for stock in a branch library, etc., it is strongly recommended that a different voice range be represented if the work is available in more than one key. If, for example, the library already has a copy of selected songs by Brahms, for high voice, then the second copy might be a different selection (which would almost certainly overlap) for low voice. In cases where choice is available, it should not be automatically assumed that the first copy must be for medium voice; this will suit the majority but is unfair to the real sopranos, contraltos, tenors and basses. The advantages of a second edition for an extra copy are twofold: it may provide the particular translation favoured by a singer, and will satisfy the user who has a preference for the edition of one editor or publisher compared with another.

Songs are not likely to be as popular as piano music, in terms of the numbers borrowed, nor of vocal scores of operas, but they represent a valuable and important side of the work of many composers while singers deserve the encouragement of a well-chosen and adequate selection. Works have been selected in the hope that they will be of use and interest for years ahead as well as for today; if their purchase is regarded as a long-term investment then comparatively infrequent use is not discouraging.

The accompaniments of all the songs listed are either written or arranged for piano. The accompanist is still usually undervalued and the standard of pianistic ability required in the works that follow varies as widely as the demands made upon the singer by different composers.

ARNE (b) *20 songs* (Novello)

Dr. Thomas Augustine Arne (1710–1778) wrote numerous operas and the incidental music to many plays. His songs (generally from the incidental music) are possibly his best-known works, particularly those set to Shakespearian words such as *Where the bee sucks*. They still retain both freshness and popularity. Arne's most famous vocal setting is that of *Rule, Britannia*. At the time of writing the recommended volume is unfortunately out of print.

BACH   (a) *Songs and airs* (ed. Prout), 8v. (Augener, G.E.)

Bach wrote over 200 church and 23 secular cantatas and the greater part of this music is completely unknown to the average music-lover. The eight volumes recommended contain items selected mainly from these works and represents Bach at his best. Soprano, Contralto, Tenor and Bass have each two volumes allotted, containing 22, 18, 18 and 22 excerpts for each voice respectively. There are numerous alternative editions containing different selections.

BANTOCK   (e) *Songs from the Chinese poets*, 2v. (Chester)

Bantock chose to write many of his songs to words from foreign, particularly Oriental, lands; the two recommended volumes are representative. They are difficult to sing and need an extremely skilful pianist but are most effective when well performed. Bantock's two most popular songs are probably *A feast of lanterns* (from the third of the four sets, *Songs from the Chinese*) and *The lament of Isis* (which is the fifth of the *Songs of Egypt*). Both works are contained in a bound album issued by Cramer's, which also includes the two *Songs of the Western Isles, Praise ye the Lord, Great is the Lord*, and *By the waters of Babylon* (the first three items of *Six sacred songs*).

BAX   (e) *Cradle song* (Chappell)
               (e) *Green grow the rashes o* (Chappell)
               (e) *I heard a piper piping* (Chappell)
               (e) *5 Irish songs* (Chappell)
               (e) *The market girl* (Chappell)
               (e) *Rann of exile* (Chappell)
               (e) *The white peace* (Chester)

The usual view of Bax is as a symphonist and perhaps as a composer of piano music also, but his songs are often completely overlooked. This is to ignore some of his loveliest music. The recommended items would bind conveniently into one or two volumes if desired.

BEETHOVEN   (b) *Songs* (Augener, E.G.; Novello, 3v., E.G.; Peters, G.)
               (b) *An die ferne Geliebte, op. 98* (Augener, E.G. [H.L.]; Schirmer, E.G. [H.L.])

Generally speaking, Beethoven's songs are not an important part of his output and he appears to have had difficulty in writing for the voice and in reaching a satisfactory compromise between the rival demands of words and music. There are other editions than those listed above, e.g. the Boosey and Universal albums which are both out of print. At present only the second volume of the Novello edition is available while the Peters edition contains only 30 songs compared with the 67 in the Augener edition, which is therefore the one recommended. All editions contain the most frequeutly performed song—*Adelaide, op. 46.*

The song cycle *An die ferne Geliebte* (*To the distant beloved*) is the first set of its kind and represents the composer's highest attainments in this field of composition. The original setting is that for high voice.

BERLIOZ   (d) *Les nuits d'été, op. 7* (Augener, F.)

Berlioz wrote some two dozen songs; six of these comprise the above set, to words by Gautier. The composer later orchestrated the accompaniments. These works are a minor part of the composer's output but should be better known. The large collection might also include *La captive, op. 12.*

BOYCE   (e) *5 songs* (Augener)

For baritone voice.

BRAHMS   (a) *Complete songs*, 4v. (Peters, G. [H.M.L.]) *or*
                (a) *50 selected songs* (Schirmer, E.G. [H.L.])

Brahms was not unduly worried about the poetic quality of the words he set to music since he appears to have felt that the latter was paramount and the words of secondary importance. This is a minor flaw and Brahms is recognized as one of the finest song writers and examples of these works must appear in the smallest collection of vocal music. The songs are beautifully written both for vocalist and pianist, and it is extremely unfortunate that there is no available version of the complete songs with an adequate English translation. Simrock publish sixty songs (three volumes each containing twenty songs) but only the first of these is in print. This version contains both English and German words.

BRIDGE   (e) *Adoration* (Boosey)
                (e) *Come to me in my dreams* (Boosey)
                (c) *Fair daffodils* (Boosey)
                (b) *Love went a-riding* (Boosey)
                (e) *O that it were so* (Chappell)
                (e) *Thy hand in mine* (Boosey)

Frank Bridge (1879–1941) is known to singers almost exclusively for his highly effective *Love went a-riding* (with a difficult piano accompaniment) but a number of his other songs deserve to be equally well known. The recommended works would bind into a single album if desired.

BRITTEN   (c) *The holy sonnets of John Donne, op. 35* (Boosey)
                (d) *Les Illuminations, op. 18* (Boosey, F.)
                (b) *Serenade for tenor, horn and strings, op. 31* (Boosey)
                (c) *7 sonnets of Michaelangelo, op. 22* (Boosey, I.)
                (d) *Winter words, op. 52* (Boosey)

Nearly all of Benjamin Britten's songs appear to have been written for his friend Peter Pears. Generally speaking both voice part and accompaniment are very difficult so that this taxing music is likely to be borrowed more frequently by the listener than by the would-be performer. The cycles of songs comprising opus 18 and opus 31 were originally written with string-orchestra accompaniment.

Vocal Music

BUTTERWORTH   (c) *6 songs from "A Shropshire lad"* (Augener)

Housman's poems have attracted many composers; this set is one of the most successful. Butterworth was killed on the Somme in 1916 at the age of 31, thus cutting short what appeared to be a career of very great promise. The orchestral rhapsody *A Shropshire lad* is based mainly on one song of the cycle— *Loveliest of trees.*

CARPENTER   (e) *Gitanjaly* (Schirmer)

"The songs of John Alden Carpenter are too well known to need any introduction." Thus Kagen—yet this important American composer is almost entirely unknown in Britain. The cycle of six songs listed above should prove a useful introduction. The words are by Tagore.

CHABRIER   (e) *Mélodies* (Enoch)

An album of fifteen songs by this nineteenth-century composer.

CHAUSSON   (e) *20 songs* (Rouart, Lerolle)

Chausson was a highly accomplished song writer but one whose works are barely known outside the frontiers of his own country. Kagen particularly recommends nine of Chausson's songs and four of them are in the volume listed above—*La Chanson bien douce, op. 34, no. 1; Chanson perpétuelle, op. 17; Les heures, op. 27, no. 1,* and *Le temps de lilas* (from *Poème de l'amour et de la mer, op. 19*). The second and fourth of these songs were originally written with orchestral accompaniment.

CHOPIN   (e) *17 Polish songs, op. 74* (Schirmer, G.E. [H.L.])

CORNELIUS   (d) *Weihnachtslieder* [*Christmas songs*], *op. 8* (Hinrichsen, E.G. [H.M.L.])

Peter Cornelius (1824–1874) is a composer who ill deserves his present neglect. His songs are musicianly and attractive to sing and the six *Christmas songs* are written to his own words, for Cornelius possessed considerable poetic as well as musical ability.

DEBUSSY   (d) *Ariettes oubliées* (Jobert, E.F.)

(e) *Trois ballades de François Villon* (Durand, F.E.)

(c) *Chansons de Bilitis* (Jobert, F.)

(e) *Fêtes galantes* (Jobert, E.F.)

(e) *5 poèmes de Baudelaire* (Durand, F.)

To Debussy (in contrast to the attitude of Brahms) the words he set were quite as important as the music written to them. These French songs need a skilled interpreter and are never likely to become generally popular. The *Ariettes oubliées*, set to words by Verlaine, were dedicated to the famous American singer, Mary Garden. *Chansons de Bilitis* is probably Debussy's most successful set of songs.

DELIUS   (e) *Nietzsche songs* (Boosey)

(e) *5 songs from the Danish* (Boosey, E.G.)

(e) *7 songs from the Norwegian,* 7v. (O.U.P.)

Delius had a poor ear for words, his vocal line is often difficult and apparently unrewarding—yet the songs are most effective when well sung. Kagen suggests that Delius's use of French and German texts (together with German translations from the Norwegian) in preference to English words (to which he set a very small number of songs) may have militated against greater popularity. This is probably true both in Britain and the U.S.A.

DOWLAND   (c) *50 selected songs*, 2v. (Stainer & Bell)

During his lifetime Dowland was probably better known on the Continent than in his native England; for some years he held the position of Court Lutenist in Denmark. He was a first-class performer on that instrument, which is related to the modern guitar and most of his solo songs were written with lute accompaniment. He is one of the great Elizabethan and Jacobean song writers. A number of his songs have been recorded with lute or guitar accompaniment but most singers will be content with the arrangement for pianoforte of the lute tablature.

DUPARC   (d) *Songs* (Rouart, Lerolle, F.)

Few composers have been as self-critical as Duparc who destroyed the great majority of his compositions. Only thirteen songs satisfied his own standards and these are among the finest written in Europe during the last century, so deserve inclusion in the larger collection. This may seem paradoxical unless it is realized that the songs are not likely to be generally popular, for they demand a very high degree of interpretative skill and their atmosphere is not easily captured by a non-French singer. For the librarian who would like Duparc represented in his collection (as is right) but feels that the complete songs are too expensive, I would recommend *Chanson triste, L'invitation au voyage* and *Lamento*.

DVOŘÁK   (d) *Biblical songs, op. 99*, 2v. (Simrock, E.G. [H.L.])
              (a) *Gipsy songs, op. 55*, 2v. (Simrock, E.G. [H.L.])

The *Gipsy songs* contain seven excellent songs of well-varied moods, yet most singers know only one of them—*Songs my mother taught me*. The *Biblical songs* are infrequently sung today, though these, too, contain some lovely music. If desired, the two works would conveniently bind into a single volume.

ELGAR   (e) *Fringes of the Fleet* (Ashdown)
              (d) *7 Lieder* (Ascherberg)
              (b) *Sea pictures, op. 37* (Boosey)

Fringes of the Fleet (which is one of the comparatively few works of Elgar without opus number) is a set of four songs to words by Rudyard Kipling. They were first performed, with scenery and action, at the London Coliseum in 1917. Later, a fifth song (*Inside the bar*, to words by Gilbert Parker) was added to the set which cannot be considered vintage Elgar.

Sea pictures were written for Clara Butt to sing at the Norwich Festival of 1899. All five songs have words by different writers (including Elgar's wife) and the cycle has remained popular with contraltos since it was written. Elgar's other songs, the *7 Lieder*, have faded badly but are still in some demand.

FALLA   (e) *7 canciones populares Españolas* (Chester, F.Sp.)

That these songs are so well known outside their native country is due mainly to the agency of the gramophone record. There have been at least two first-class performances (with very different interpretations) by Conchita Supervia and Victoria de los Angeles and either set will guide the singer who wishes to sing these works in authentic style. An edition with English words only is published in the U.S.A. by Associated Music Publishers, but this may not be sold in the United Kingdom.

FAURÉ   (c) *La bonne chanson* (Hamelle, F.)

             (e) *Songs*, 3v. (Hamelle, F.)

The songs, like the remainder of Fauré's output, are tasteful and well written but insufficiently known outside his native France. *La bonne chanson* is a cycle of nine songs to words by Verlaine.

FINZI   (e) *Before and after summer* (Boosey)

A set of ten songs for baritone to words by Thomas Hardy. A second set, for the same voice range and from the same poet, is entitled *Earth and air and rain*.

FOSTER   (b) *Album of songs* (Schirmer)

A collection of the most popular songs of this short-lived American composer, who was almost entirely self-taught. *My old Kentucky home, The old folks at home* and others of his songs are likely to be in steady popular demand.

FRANZ   (c) *30 songs* (Novello, E.) *or*

             (c) *62 songs* (Schirmer, G.E. [H.L.])

Robert Franz (1830–1892) was the composer of over 300 songs, and is one of the most important German composers in this field. His songs are generally of a fairly simple type and are particularly suited to mezzo-soprano voices. With its wider selection, choice of range and inclusion of the original words as well as a translation, the Schirmer edition is strongly recommended.

GERSHWIN   (c) *The George Gershwin Song book* (Gershwin)

This album may seem rather frivolous in company with the classics but it is sure to be popular with many singers. It is of interest to pianists also; each song including a chorus for piano solo. This solo is written in the fashion that Gershwin himself played that particular melody, and indicates his own talents as a pianist.

GIBBS   (e) *By a bier-side* (Curwen)

             (e) *The fields are full* (Boosey)

             (e) *Five eyes* (Boosey)

             (e) *The mad Prince* (Curwen)

             (e) *Silver* (Boosey)

             (e) *To Anise* (Boosey)

C. Armstrong Gibbs (1889–) is a British composer who has most successfully set many of the poems of Walter De La Mare to music. The six songs listed were selected by the composer himself as a representative selection from over a hundred; they could be bound in a single volume if required.

GOUNOD   (e) *Mélodies*, v.1 (Choudens, F.)

There are three volumes of songs, and all three should be included in the large collection but the smaller music section will be content with the first volume since it contains the majority of Gounod's best-known songs, e.g. *Venise, Chanson de printemps, Ave Maria* and *O ma belle rebelle.*

GRANADOS — (d) *Coleción de Tonadillas* (Unión Musical Española, Sp.)

The tonadilla was introduced to the Spanish stage in the eighteenth century and was an interlude song. These twelve songs by Granados are written in the old style. As with the Falla songs, recorded performances by two outstanding Spanish singers have made the set accessible and given the non-Spaniard an opportunity to hear distinctive and attractive music that is rarely encountered in concert or broadcast performances.

GRECHANINOV — (e) *Flocons de neige (10 chants du monde enfantin), op. 47,* 10v. (Gutheil, R.F.G.E.)

(e) *Les fleurs du mal; 5 poésies de Ch. Baudelaire, op. 48,* 5v. (Gutheil, R.F.)

(e) *Quatre mélodies, op. 5* (Balaieff, R.F.G.)

Alexander Grechaninov (1864–1956) wrote a considerable amount of music; his songs are probably the best known part of his output. Very few indeed will be able to sing them in Russian, outside their native country, so that the first listed set which includes an English translation has a definite appeal. Kagen lists a host of songs by this composer, published in the U.S.A. by Ditson, but this edition cannot be imported into Britain. The best-known song of all, *Triste est le steppe* (known in English as *Over the steppe* or *The dreary steppe*) is the first song in the opus 5 set. The second song is entitled *La nuit,* but it is the work with the same title, but the third item in opus 20 (Belaieff), that is likely to be the version required.

GRIEG — (a) *Songs,* 4v. (Peters, G. [H.L.]) *or*

(a) *Selected songs,* 2v. (Enoch, Nor. E.) *or*

(a) *Selected Lieder,* 2v. (Peters, G. [H.M.L.])

Grieg's songs are usually brief and simple but extremely effective and characteristic of his best writing. Most singers include a few of the most popular songs in their repertoire but few are likely to emulate Miss Astra Desmond who learned Norwegian for the express purpose of gaining a better insight into the composer's intentions. Her five gramophone records (made for English Decca during the Second World War) are collector's pieces and are sung "in beautifully authentic style", to quote *The record guide.* Other songs by Kirsten Flagstad show how well the music is fitted to the Norwegian text and it is apparently affectation that makes many singers use a German translation. A few of the songs are actually written to German words.

Even the fairly small collection should have the complete songs despite the unfortunate lack of the original words in the Peters edition. For the very small collection, or as a useful duplicate, the two Enoch volumes with twenty and eighteen songs respectively are excellent. These quote the original Norwegian words together with an English translation by R. H. Elkin.

GRIFFES — (e) *By a lonely forest pathway* (Schirmer)

(e) *The lament of Ian the Proud* (Schirmer)

Vocal Music

Charles T. Griffes (1884–1920) is an outstanding American composer yet one whose name is almost completely unknown to British musicians. There are twenty-eight songs in all, some of them to German texts, and the two recommended above are those by which the composer is best known. Others (all from the same publisher) could be bought if it was desired to make up a volume of selected songs.

GURNEY   (d) *Songs*, 3v. (O.U.P.)

During World War I, Ivor Gurney (1890–1937) was wounded and shell-shocked; after the war he suffered poverty and neglect. As a result he had an almost complete mental breakdown. Only at the end of his life did recognition come to him and distinguished critics praised his talent and (more important) arranged for his best songs to be published. These songs are still known to too few singers.

HAHN   (d) *Mélodies*, v.11. (U.M.P., F.)

Although he was born in Venezuela, Reynaldo Hahn (1874–1947) is generally regarded as a French composer. He had a varied musical talent but is now remembered almost entirely as a composer of pleasantly melodious songs. The recommended album contains twenty songs. Two other volumes of songs are available.

HANDEL   (a) *Opera songs* (Boosey, I.E.)
                (b) *Oratorio songs* (Boosey; Novello, 5v.)
                (c) *Songs* (Boosey, 7v.)

Handel's operas are never likely to be staged again with the exception of occasional special performances. Similarly, many of the oratorios will be heard very rarely. The collections listed above are fairly representative, though there are a number of excellent alternatives, particularly in albums published by American and German composers. First choice should be a collection of opera songs since the smaller collection may well have no single example of a Handel opera in stock. Augener publishes a nine-volume edition (edited by Visetti) of songs from the operas and oratorios and these give a wide selection. The Novello edition of oratorio songs comprises two volumes for soprano and one each for contralto, tenor and baritone or bass. The seven-volume Boosey edition of songs is edited by Walter Ford and R. Erlebach. For American libraries, in particular, an attractive alternative is a two-volume edition in the "Musician's Library" published by Ditson. The first volume contains songs for high voice, the second volume for low.

HAYDN   (c) *Canzonettas and songs* (Peters, E.G.)

These songs represent one of the minor aspects of a great composer, but they are none the less attractive for that. *My mother bids me bind my hair* is probably the best-known work in the recommended volume which contains thirty-five works; fourteen of these are settings to English words.

HEAD   (e) *Over the rim of the moon* (Boosey, [H.L.])
              (e) *Six sea songs*, 6v. (Boosey [M])

Michael Head (1900–   ) is a British composer whose songs are often sung by British singers. His best-known songs include *Sweet chance that led my steps*,

399

Music Librarianship

Foxgloves (from *Short songs of the countryside*), *Little road to Bethlehem* and *The ships of Arcady* (the first song in *Over the rim of the moon*, which comprises four items), while *Sweethearts and wives* (the last of the *Six sea songs*) is an excellent example of the humorous type of song that delights so many baritones.

HOLST   (d) *Songs, op. 48*, 12v. (Augener)

These twelve songs, published separately, are to words by Humbert Wolfe and are among Holst's last compositions. Like all his later works they are extremely austere though listeners and performers today appear to come to terms with this phase of Holst without much difficulty—a contrast to the nineteen-twenties when each new work by this composer appeared to be less approachable than the last. The *Hymns from the Rig Veda, op. 24* (Chester, 3 v.) were originally written for women's choir and orchestra, but in an arrangement for solo voice with piano accompaniment make a useful second choice.

HUGHES   (d) *9 songs from Connacht* (Boosey)

                       (d) *Rhymes*, 2v. (Boosey)

                       (d) *Parodies*, 2v. (Boosey)

The songs of Herbert Hughes deserve more frequent performance for they are rewarding to sing and pleasant for the listener. The *Parodies* and *Rhymes* (sub-titled *Studies in imitation*) are amusing songs in the styles of the great composers and show Hughes's own skill. At present, only *Rhymes* is in print.

IRELAND   (c) *The land of lost content* (Augener)

                       (d) *Songs sacred and profane* (Schott)

Sea fever (Augener) is John Ireland's best-known song and his others are unduly neglected in comparison. *The land of lost content* is a cycle of six songs to words by A. E. Housman, while the *Songs sacred and profane* also number six; in this case three of the poems are by Sylvia Townsend Warner, two by Alice Meynell and one by W. B. Yeats.

IVES   (e) *(Selected songs)*

Charles Ives (1874–1954) is an extremely important and highly individual American composer whose songs are difficult (both for singer and audience)—but they well repay efforts to come to terms with them. Most of the 114 songs are available in collected volumes. Southern Music Publishers Inc. have issued *10 songs (1888–1902)*, *12 songs (1894–1921)* and *14 songs*. Any of these volumes is worth adding to a large British collection, and none costs more than 15s.; an American library might well consider these works as category (a) rather than (e).

KILPINEN   (e) *Lieder der Liebe, op. 60, 61*, 2v. (Bote & Bock, G.)

                       (e) *Lieder um den Tod, op. 62* (Bote & Bock, G.)

                       (e) *Spielmannslieder, op. 77* (Bote & Bock, G.)

Yrjö Kilpinen (1892–1959) is a Finn whose songs are still barely known despite the efforts of a small band of enthusiasts to propagate his fame. A volume of records, sung by the famous German baritone Gerhard Husch with piano accompaniment played by the composer's wife, was released as a limited "Society" issue in Britain by H.M.V. in the middle nineteen-thirties. The major works were the three sets listed above. Kilpinen has written songs to Finnish, Swedish and

German texts. Only the large collection is likely to need more than one of the cycles listed above unless experience suggests that wider coverage would be appreciated.

LEHMANN   (b) *In a Persian garden* (Cramer)

This song cycle, set to poems from the *Rubaiyat*, is for four soloists (soprano, contralto, tenor and bass) with orchestral or piano accompaniment. The work still retains much of its former popularity though it is rarely sung complete; rather single excerpts, such as the bass song *Myself when young*, are given.

LISZT   (d) *12 songs* (Schirmer, G.E. [H.L.])

Perhaps because the piano accompaniments are often extremely difficult, the songs of Liszt are not often sung today. They certainly do not deserve this neglect. Many of the seventy (or thereabouts) songs are unlikely to be revived, but the best have very real merits. The most popular is *Die Loreley* and critical opinion appears to favour *Oh! quand je dors* (to words by Victor Hugo) as his best song.

LOEWE   (d) *Album* (Schirmer, G.E.)

Carl Loewe (1796–1869) is famous for his ballads, which include German translations of *Archibald Douglas* and *Edward*; these, like his other songs, are usually sung by baritones or basses. Loewe's version of *Der Erlkönig* (*The Erl King*) is considered by some writers to equal Schubert's setting of the same poem.

MAHLER   (b) *Kindertotenlieder* [*Songs on the death of infants*] (Kahnt, G.E.)

                (c) *Des knaben Wunderhorn* [*Youth's magic horn*] (Universal, G.E.)

                (e) *7 last songs* (Kahnt, G.E.)

                (b) *Das Lied von der Erde* [*Song of the earth*] (Universal, G.E.)

                (d) *Lieder und Gesange aus der Jugendzeit* [*Songs of the days of youth*], 3v. (Universal, G.)

                (c) *Lieder eines fahrenden Gesellen* [*Songs of a wayfarer*] (Weinberger, E.G.)

Much of the interest evident in Mahler's vocal works since World War II can be traced to the performances and recordings of Kathleen Ferrier with Bruno Walter as accompanist or conductor. The fact that most of the cycles listed above are available on gramophone records is likely to stimulate demand. Only the *Songs of youth* were originally written with piano accompaniment; the others all had orchestral accompaniment. *Das Lied von der Erde* is, strictly, a symphony in six movements for orchestra with contralto and tenor soloists. This is the most famous of the vocal works and is set to German translations of Chinese poems. The orchestral score has proved difficult to adapt adequately for piano.

MARTIN, E.   (a) *Four songs of the Fair* (Enoch)

                (a) *Three more songs of the Fair* (Enoch)

Easthope Martin is a lightweight composer in this company but *Come to the Fair* appears to retain a tremendous hold on the affections of British audiences, and to be in the repertoire of every singer at popular concerts. The two sets would bind conveniently into a single volume if desired.

MARX (e) *Album*, 4v. (Universal, G.)

Joseph Marx has written many songs and his works in this field appear to be barely known outside his native Austria. Kagen recommends *Hat dich die Liebe berührt, Der Ton, Marienlied, Selige Nacht* and *Nocturne*; these five songs could be bound together to give a small representative selection.

MENDELSSOHN (d) *52 songs* (Augener, E. G. [L.]) *or*
20 songs (Hinrichsen, G. [H.M.]) *or*
16 songs (Schirmer, G.E. [H.L.])

Mendelssohn's songs, like his other works, are under something of a cloud today. They are well laid out for the voice and have effective piano accompaniments, and may well regain a little of their lost popularity as time goes on. Because of the wider selection, the Augener edition is recommended.

MOZART (c) *Concert arias* (Schirmer, E.G.)
(b) *Songs* (Augener, E.G.; Boosey, E.G.; Hinrichsen, G. [M.L]); Universal, G.E.

The songs are mainly small and unpretentious works and many of them are within the scope of the average amateur. The concert arias, on the other hand, are major pieces that demand a wide range and accomplished technique for adequate performance.

MUSSORGSKY (d) *Songs and dances of death* (International Music Co., E.R.)
(e) *Enfantines* [*Songs of the nursery*] (Augener, F.E.; Chester, F.E.)

Most people appear to think of Mussorgsky solely in terms of his operas (with *Night on the bare mountain* and *Pictures at an exhibition* as major exceptions), and to overlook all but one of his output of over sixty songs, which are both dramatic and highly effective. The famous solo is *The song of the flea*, almost his last song. It is unfortunate that nearly all his works in this form lack good English translations, since they would make these effective pieces much more accessible.

POULENC (d) *Airs chantés* (Rouart, Lerolle, F.)
(e) *Banalités* (Rouart, Lerolle, F.)
(c) *Le bestiaire* (Rouart, Lerolle, F.)

These songs are not easily interpreted. *Airs chantés* comprises four varied pieces, while *Le bestiaire* is a set of six brief and amusing songs on zoological subjects—the camel, carp, dolphin, etc. The words of *Banalités* are by Apollinaire.

PURCELL (a) *20 favourite songs* (Augener) *or*
Songs and airs, 2v. (Novello)

Purcell's songs should need no recommendation to British singers, even though too many appear to know only *Dido's lament* (from *Dido and Aeneas*), *The Blessed Virgin's expostulation* (to words by Nahum Tate, beginning *Tell me*,

402

some pitying angel; this is published separately by Schirmer) and *Nymphs and shepherds*. The songs are both dramatic and effective. The Novello edition is to be preferred since it contains 30 songs (15 in each volume) compared with 20 in the Augener edition. Purcell wrote well over one hundred songs as well as many in the operas.

QUILTER   (b) *7 Elizabethan lyrics* (Boosey)

              (a) *Shakespearian songs*, 3v. (Boosey)

Roger Quilter may be regarded as a minor composer but his songs are musicianly, attractive and effectively written. The three Shakespeare sets are opus 6, 23 and 30 respectively and would bind into a single volume. It might also be good policy to make up a volume of single works that do not appear in a set but which are very popular—songs such as *Love's philosophy*, *Music when soft voices die*, *Go, lovely rose*, *Now sleeps the crimson petal*, etc.

RACHMANINOV   (b) *Selected songs* (Boosey, R.F.E.G. [H.M.])

Like all works written by this composer, the songs are effective and well laid out for both soloist and piano. The Boosey selection consists of three songs each from opus 4, 14 and 26, two songs from opus 21 and one from opus 34. The large library could usefully widen its selection by the addition of all of these sets. The six songs which comprise opus 4 are for medium or high voice, except for the second which is for low voice. Similarly, the six songs of opus 8 are published with numbers 2, 4 and 5 available for medium or high voice, number 1 for medium voice only and no. 6 for high voice only. There are no alternative settings for the *12 songs, op. 21, 15 songs, op. 26, 14 songs, op. 34* and *6 songs, op. 38*. All of these are published in Britain by Boosey & Hawkes and have words in Russian, French, German and English.

An excellent two-volume selection of songs published by Breitkopf & Härtel is not available in Britain.

RAVEL   (c) *Chants populaires* (U.M.P., F.)

            (d) *Histoires naturelles* (U.M.P., F.)

            (c) *Cinq mélodies populaires Grecques* (U.M.P., F.)

            (e) *3 poèmes de Stéphane Mallarmé* (U.M.P., F.)

            (d) *Shéhérazade* (U.M.P., F.)

Ravel's songs are among the most outstanding produced by a French composer but they are difficult for effective performance and this undoubtedly limits their appeal. Many of the songs require an expert pianist. *Shéhérazade* (to words by Tristan Klingsor) is a cycle of three songs originally written with accompaniment by small orchestra, while the Mallarmé songs were written with piano, flute, string quartet, 2 flutes and 2 clarinets as accompanying instruments.

REGER   (c) *Schlichte Weisen [Simple melodies], op. 76, nos. 1–15* (Bote & Bock, G.E.)

            (d) *6 songs, op. 4* (Augener, G.E. [M])

            (d) *5 songs for high voice, op. 8* (Augener, G.E.)

            (e) *5 songs, op. 12* (Augener, E.G.)

            (d) *10 songs for medium voice, op. 15* (Augener, G.)

This German composer wrote a large number of songs, many of them with the attractively simple vocal line reminiscent of a folk song, and with straightforward piano accompaniments. Opus 76 contain Reger's best-known songs, so far as British singers are concerned, but only the first volume is available at the time of writing. There are sixty songs in all, in four volumes. Five of the songs are available separately and would form an attractive volume to many singers: *Two cradle songs (Mariä Wiegenlied [The Virgin's slumber song], op. 76, no. 52, and Zum Schlafen [The golden bird], op. 76, no. 59); Waldensamkeit [Quiet of the woods], op. 76, no. 3; Mein Schätzelein [My little sweetheart], op. 76, no. 14, and Des Kindes Gebet [Children's prayer], op. 76, no. 22.* All five songs include an English translation as well as the original German words.

SCHOENBERG   (e) *4 songs from "Gurre Lieder"* (Universal, G.)

Gurre Lieder is a song cycle for soli, chorus and a massive orchestra. The work is an early one and is somewhat overlarge for its musical content; it is not characteristic of the mature Schoenberg. The four songs should be of some interest, and while Schoenberg's later twelve-tone works are likely to have very limited appeal indeed, the songs of opus 3 and opus 6 may also be given a qualified recommendation.

SCHUBERT   (a) *Songs,* 8v. (Peters, G. *[See note below]*) *or*

    (a) *Selected songs,* 2v. (Schirmer, G.E. [H.L.])

    (b) *24 favourite songs* (Augener, G.E. [Original; L.])

The smallest collection should have at least one of the many available albums of Schubert songs, for their importance should need no stressing. For small and medium collections, the Schirmer volumes are recommended; each contains eighty-two songs and the well-known song cycles are included. The Augener edition is mentioned among smaller selections because of the excellent English translations of Richard Capell, and equally felicitous translations are to be found in single songs and two of the song cycles (*Die Schöne Müllerin* and *Winterreise*) issued by the Oxford U.P., though both cycles are o.p. in this edition at the time of writing.

The larger library should provide the complete songs even though the original German words only are given. The first Peters volume contains 92 songs, mainly those of the song cycles, and is available for high, medium or low voices. The second and third volumes contain 75 and 45 songs respectively and are available for high or medium-low voices. Volumes 4 to 7 contain 62, 52, 69 and 51 songs and offer no alternative ranges; all are given in the original keys. At the time of writing the eighth volume has still to achieve publication.

SCHUMANN   (a) *Songs,* 3v. (Peters, G. [v.1, H.M.L.; v.2 & 3, H.]) *or*

    (a) *77 songs* (Universal, G.E. [H.]) *or*

    (a) *55 songs* (Schirmer, G.E. [H.L.]) *and*

    (a) *Frauenliebe und Leben* (Schirmer, G.E. [H.L.])

Like Schubert, Schumann was a song writer of the very first rank and his works in this field may be considered basic stock. For small and medium libraries the two Schirmer volumes or the Universal selection would be sufficient; large libraries should stock the complete songs. There are many other editions with selections from the songs.

Vocal Music

SHAW   (d) *Seven selected songs* (Cramer)

Martin Shaw is a contemporary British composer whose songs are well written for both voice and piano. One or other of them often appear as test pieces in competitive festivals. His best-known song is probably *I know a bank* which appears in the bound selection recommended above. The other songs included are: *At Columbine's grave; The cuckoo; Glad hearts adventuring; Ships of Yule; Song of the palanuin bearers* and *Wood magic.*

SIBELIUS   (e) *Black roses* (Breitkopf; E.F.)

                    (e) *First kiss* (Breitkopf; E. F.)

                    (e) *The tryst* (Breitkopf; E. F.)

The songs of Sibelius are not an important part of his compositions but still deserve representation in the large music collection. The three songs listed above are the only ones available in Britain at the time of writing with the exception of a song arrangement of the famous theme from *Finlandia*, with English words only, entitled "Be still my soul". This last is not recommended.

STANFORD   (d) *The fairy lough, op. 77, no. 2* (Boosey)

                    (d) *A soft day, op. 140, no. 3* (Stainer & Bell)

                    (b) *Songs of the Fleet, op. 117* (Stainer & Bell)

                    (c) *Songs of the sea, op. 91* (Boosey)

The two sets of songs are for baritone, chorus and orchestra, and have a verve that has kept them popular favourites for over fifty years. Only a handful of the many songs that Stanford wrote have remained in the repertory but some are really lovely, particularly the two recommended. The best-known song attributed to Stanford is *Trottin' to the fair* which is actually an arrangement of a traditional Irish melody.

STRAUSS   (c) *Lieder album*, 4v. (Universal, G.E. [H.M.L.])

The songs of Richard Strauss are well written and effective and he is probably underrated in this sphere of activity in Britain. Understandably enough, a handful of songs have become much better known than the remainder, e.g. *Ständchen* [*Serenade*], *op. 17, no. 2*, and *Morgen* [*Morning*], *op. 27, no. 4*. The four volumes listed contain forty-four songs in all and all the best-known Lieder are included.

TCHAIKOVSKY   (b) *12 songs* (Schirmer, G.E. [H.L.])

Although they represent but a minor part of his output, Tchaikovsky's songs are typically written with assured craftsmanship. The two songs most frequently sung and recorded are (to give them the English titles by which they are generally known) *None but the weary heart, op. 6, no. 6*, and *At the ball, op. 38, no. 3.* Kagen complains of the inadequacy of the majority of translations into English of Tchaikovsky's songs.

VAUGHAN
WILLIAMS   (d) *On Wenlock edge* (Boosey)

                    (c) *Songs of travel* (Boosey)

Vaughan Williams wrote excellently for the voice. *On Wenlock edge* is one of the many song cycles set to poems selected from Housman's *A Shropshire lad*, and is written for tenor, piano and string quartet. *Songs of travel*, to words by Robert Louis Stevenson, for voice and piano, contains the popular songs *Bright is the ring of words* and *The vagabond*; most library users, however, are likely to look for *Linden Lea* (Boosey), *Orpheus with his lute* (Keith Prowse) and *Silent noon* (Ashdown) which could be bound together, if desired.

VERDI   (d) *Operatic excerpts*, 6v. (Peters, G.I.)

These are not songs at all, of course, but a series of operatic arias that provide handy material for solo singers interested in Italian opera. Two of the six volumes are for soprano (30 arias), and there is one each for mezzo (7 arias), tenor (23), baritone (20) and bass (13 arias).

WAGNER   (d) *5 Gedichte für eine Frauenstimme* (Schirmer, E.G. [H.L.])

The five songs, to words by Mathilde Wesendonck, are a product of Wagner's maturity and two of them (*Im Treibhaus* [*In the hothouse*] and *Träume* [*Dreams*]) were studies for *Tristan und Isolde*. There have been at least two excellent gramophone recordings to increase interest in the set. Wagner's earlier songs are much less typical (and also much less important), but might well be included in the stock of the large music collection.

WARLOCK   (b) *Album of songs* (O.U.P.)
                       (d) *Peterisms* (v. 1, Chester; v. 2, O.U.P.)

Peter Warlock, the pseudonym of Philip Heseltine, was one of our finest song writers. The biography by Cecil Gray is fascinating but shows an unhappy man apparently unable to come to terms either with the world or himself. Warlock's ambivalent nature (the "Warlock" and "Heseltine" aspects) is reflected in his songs. The one side is represented by the simple song, often with an ornate accompaniment (such as *Sleep*), the other side by the jaunty song often with a tavern background. There is a third type of song, the quasi-mediaeval, which reminds us of his first-rate editing of the lute songs of the Elizabethans and other early music; for this he seemed to have a natural affinity. The three albums recommended above present a good selection of his songs.

WOLF   (a) *51 songs* (Peters, E.G. [H., M.L.])
                       (e) *Eichendorff Lieder*, 2v. (Peters, G.)
                       (c) *Goethe Lieder*, 4v. (Peters)
                       (c) *Italienisches Liederbuch*, 3v. (Peters, G.)
                       (e) *Michaelangelo Sonnets* (Peters, G.)
                       (e) *Spanisches Liederbuch*, 4v. (Peters, G.)
                       (c) *Mörike Lieder*, 4v. (Peters, G.)
                       (e) *Settings from various poets*, 2v. (Peters, G.)

Hugo Wolf (1860–1903) probably excelled all other song writers in his ability to combine words and music into an organic unity, so that the music points and illuminates the words and the latter are not maltreated to fit a preconceived musical pattern. Interest in Wolf's songs, outside his native Austria, was largely stimulated by the incomparable interpretations of Elena Gerhardt and her album of *51 selected songs* (from a total of about 250) should be regarded as a prime necessity despite the fact that demands for this and other volumes of Wolf's songs may be disappointingly slow. Another general selection is a *Baritone or Bass album* (Peters) containing thirty-five songs. The individual albums are all published in the original keys, but the second volume of both the Eichendorff and Mörike songs can be obtained for low voice; only the original setting is available for the other volumes in each set. The *Michaelangelo Sonnets* comprise three songs written for a bass voice. Peters publish two further selections "for lower voice", one of sacred and the other of secular songs.

It must be emphasized that for a Wolf Lied the pianist is not, strictly speaking, an accompanist but rather a musician whose part is as important as that of the singer, so that a very high degree of interpretative skill is required as well as a good pianistic proficiency.

DUETS

Vocal duets are not usually popular unless they are excerpts from operas and musical plays. Where such works are required, the following items are suggested for consideration.

BRAHMS   *14 soprano and contralto duets* (Peters, G.)
             4 contralto and baritone duets (Peters, G.) *or*
             4 duets for contralto and baritone, op. 28 (Augener, E.G.)

These duets can hardly be rated as an important part of Brahms's music, yet they do show his skilful writing for both voices and pianoforte and are likely to prove enjoyable both to performers and listeners. The soprano and contralto duets comprise opus 20, 61 and 66, which comprise three, four and five duets respectively plus the second and third items from the *Four ballads and romances, op. 75* (the other two duets in that particular set being for contralto and tenor and for two sopranos respectively). The Augener edition of opus 28 contains the four items that comprise the work and is to be preferred to the Peters edition which contains items from both opus 28 and opus 75, but neither work complete.

DVOŘÁK   *Moravian duets, op. 32* (Simrock)

A set of 13 duets for soprano and contralto with poor English translations.

MENDELSSOHN *16 two-part songs* (Schirmer, G.E.)

PURCELL   *6 duets for soprano and baritone or contralto* (Augener)

SCHUMANN   *34 duets* (Peters, G.)

This album contains an excellent mixture with duets for two sopranos, soprano and contralto, soprano and tenor, contralto and bass, and tenor and bass. As with Brahms, the vocal duets are not well known and are of less musical value than most of Schumann's solo songs, but they do make useful provision for duettists.

Collection of Songs

DOLMETSCH   (c) *Selected English songs and dialogues* (Boosey)

FELLOWES   (b) *40 Elizabethan songs*, 4v. (Stainer & Bell)

Canon Edmund H. Fellowes was the author of the standard book on the English madrigal composers. This collection has the expert and scholarly editing that would be expected and provides an excellent choice of material.

HARDY   (c) *Songs from Shakespeare's plays*, 2v. (Curwen)

These volumes contain the earliest settings of these famous lyrics.

JEPPESEN   (b) *La flora*, 3v. (Hansen, I.)

Though not as well known as the Parisotti collection (listed on the next page), these three volumes are well selected and edited; English translations are provided for the Italian words, but these are literal translations and appear at the beginning of each volume so cannot be used as an alternative to the Italian words though they are an obvious aid to interpretation. Italian song writers of the sixteenth and seventeenth centuries should be represented in quite small collections of vocal music for their contribution to the art of song-writing has both historical importance and current interest since many of them are still found in the standard repertory.

KEEL   (a) *Elizabethan love songs*, 2v. (Boosey)

The standard of editing may not be so high as that of the similar collection edited by Fellowes, but this is a selection of better-known songs with works by Morley, Campian, Pilkington, etc.

NORTHCOTE   (b) *The New Imperial albums*, 6v. (Boosey)

Of the many collections of songs suitable for different ranges of voice this is probably one of the best. There is one volume each for soprano, mezzo-soprano, contralto, tenor, baritone and bass. There are thirty songs in each volume, written by standard composers and covering a range in period from the sixteenth century to the present day. Arrangement within each volume is chronological and operatic and oratorio excerpts are in a very small minority.

PARISOTTI   (b) *Aria antiche*, 3v. (Ricordi, I.)

Probably the best-known collection of early Italian songs and airs. Only the large collection will require both this set and that edited by Jeppesen since the two collections cover much the same ground.

POTTER   (b) *The reliquary of song* (Schirmer)

A collection of English songs edited by an American, it provides a useful alternative or additional selection to the others listed here.

REIMANN   (c) *Das deutsche Lied*, 4v. (Simrock, G.)

This is a standard selection of early German songs.

SCHUMANN   (d) *Elisabeth Schumann album* (Chester, E.G.)

Vocal Music

A collection of songs from the repertoire of this famous singer—it is suitable for most sopranos. Most of the items included are to be found in one or other of the volumes recommended in this section.

WECKERLIN   (d) *Echos du temps passé* 3v. (Durand, F.)

A collection of early French songs.

WILSON   (a) *Old English melodies* (Boosey)

This collection by Lane Wilson is justly famous. It includes such perennial favourites as *My lovely Celia* (George Munro) and *Phillis has such charming graces* (Anthony Young).

NATIONAL AND FOLK SONGS

Almost every country has produced a number of volumes containing national songs and airs and the list below represents but a small fraction of the available material. For obvious reasons, selections for the Home countries far outweigh others. Collections with songs from more than one country are listed first under "Britain" and England, Ireland, Scotland and Wales have separate entries. Other countries follow in alphabetical order.

Britain

BRITTEN   (b) *Folk-song arrangements*, v. 1 and v. 3 (Boosey)

Though listed by Britten or his publisher as songs of the British Isles these are mainly English folk-songs and have become deservedly popular in these arrangements. This is due in no small part to the gramophone records made by Peter Pears (with Britten himself accompanying at the piano) of several of these songs. The accompaniments themselves are a model of their kind. Britten's second volume in this set of three is of French folk-songs and is listed below.

KIDSON & Shaw   (d) *Songs of Britain*

McMAHON   (d) *New National and folk song book*, 2v. (Nelson)

STANFORD &
SHAW   (a) *New National song book*, v. 1 (Boosey)

BOULTON &
SOMERVELL   (a) *National song book*, v. 2 (Boosey)

These four volumes are listed together because the similarity of titles leads to confusion. The Stanford and Shaw work is sub-titled "A complete collection of the folk-songs, carols and rounds suggested by the Board of Education (1905)" and is a revised edition of the *National Song Book*, edited by C. V. Stanford alone. Geoffrey Shaw was responsible for the revision and the new (1938) edition gives both editors' names on the title-page and amends the title itself. The major differences between the two editions are to be found in the piano accompaniments which are more difficult, but also more satisfying, in the later version. The second volume of the *National Song Book* was edited by Harold Boulton and Arthur Somervell; this has not been revised and is still issued under its original title.

The similarly titled volumes edited by Desmond McMahon have no relationship with the Boosey & Hawkes volumes, though a number of songs appear in both works.

England

BROADWOOD &
   FULLER-
   MAITLAND   (a) *English county songs* (Cramer)

A well-known collection of English folk songs arranged under groups of counties and covering the whole of England. In addition, there are four sea songs.

HATTON &
   FANING   (c) *Songs of England*, 3v. (Boosey)

KIDSON &
   MOFFAT   (b) *Garland of English folk songs* (Ascherberg)

This volume contains sixty songs.

MOERAN   (e) *6 folk songs from Norfolk* (Augener)
   (e) *6 Suffolk folk songs* (Curwen)

Moeran was himself an East Anglian with a great love for that part of the country, which is, perhaps, reflected in these attractive arrangements.

SHARP &
   VAUGHAN
   WILLIAMS, *etc.*   (b) *Selected folk-songs*, 2v. (Novello)

Cecil Sharp has an imperishable place in English musical history because of his efforts to record English folk song before the changing way of twentieth-century life caused its disappearance. He noted down very many songs, and many variants in both words and music, and was ably assisted by a number of people including Vaughan Williams and Holst. The two volumes contain sixty-nine songs in all. The large collection will probably include all ten sets of folk-songs collected by Sharp (also Novello).

THOMAS   (c) *Cryes of old London*, 2v.

Ireland

HATTON &
   MOLLOY   (a) *Songs of Ireland* (Boosey)

HUGHES   (b) *Irish country songs*, 4v. (Boosey)

These arrangements by Herbert Hughes are made with great skill. The same composer has also edited *Historical songs and ballads of Ireland* (Cramer), a

Vocal Music

collection of ten songs that includes such favourites as *The dear little Shamrock* and *Cockles and mussels*.

MOERAN　　　　　(e) *Songs from County Kerry* (Augener)

STANFORD　　　　(c) *Irish melodies of Thomas Moore* (Boosey)
　　　　　　　　(d) *Songs of old Ireland* (Boosey)

These two volumes are good collections (and arrangements) by one of Ireland's greatest composers. *The New National Song book*, listed above, also contains a section of Irish songs.

Scotland

BOULTON,
LAWSON &
　McLEOD　　　　(b) *Songs of the north*, 3v. (Cramer)

HOPEKIRK　　　　(b) *70 Scottish songs* (Ditson)

An excellent American collection in the *Musician's Library* series.

KENNEDY-
　FRASER　　　　(a) *12 selected songs of the Hebrides*, 3v. (Boosey [H.L.]) *or*
　　　　　　　　(c) *Songs of the Hebrides*, 3v. (Boosey)

A number of these arrangements of folk-tunes have become extremely well known; all the famous ones are to be found in the volumes of selections. The library with the larger music library will naturally require the complete edition.

PITTMAN &
　BROWN　　　　(b) *Songs of Scotland*, 2v. (Boosey)

ROBERTON　　　　(c) *Songs of the Isles*, 2v. (Curwen)

Arrangements by the famous founder, trainer and conductor of the Glasgow Orpheus Choir. The first volume of this collection contains the well-known *Westering home*.

Wales

RICHARDS　　　　(b) *Songs of Wales* (Boosey, E.W.)

WILLIAMS &
　SOMERVELL　　(c) *Welsh melodies*, 2v. (Boosey, E.W. [H.L.])

Australia

SUTHERLAND　　*Old Australian bush ballads* ([Melbourne]; Allan)

LETHBRIDGE　　*Australian aboriginal songs* ([Melbourne]; Allan)

There are thirteen songs in the volume of bush ballads. The aboriginal songs number five and the original words (with assistance as to their pronunciation) are given. The editor provides both an English translation and a piano accompaniment.

France

BRITTEN   *Folk song arrangements, vol. 2* (Boosey, E.F.)

TIERSOT   *60 songs of France* (Ditson, F.E.)

Germany

ANDERSEN   *Mein Heimatland* (Schott, G.)

A collection of 212 folk and student songs.

      Album of Bavarian folk songs (Chappell, G.E.)

A cheap but useful volume containing ten songs.

KAPPEY   *Songs of Germany* (Boosey, G.E.)

LEY   *German songs* (Macmillan, G.)

The songs have been selected by Hugh Haworth and the arrangements and accompaniments are by Henry G. Ley. The volume of thirty-four songs has an introduction written in English, but only the original words with the songs themselves.

Hungary

KORBAY   *Hungarian songs*, 2v. (Schott, H.E.)

In the field of folk song, Korbay may be described as the Hungarian equivalent of Cecil Sharp. This is a small collection but contains one or two that have become comparatively well known outside their native country, such as *Had a horse* and *Shepherd, see thy horse's foaming mane.*

Italy

      Bella Italia (Universal, I.G.)

A collection of twenty folk songs, unfortunately without an English translation.

Switzerland

GUND   *Schweizer Volkslieder*, 4v. (Universal, G., etc.)

The first three volumes are devoted to folk songs of the German-speaking area, and the last to the Italian and Swiss-Romance areas. All songs are printed with the original words only.

United States

COPLAND   *Old American songs*, 2v. (Boosey)

Each volume contains five songs and the arrangements are as attractive and musicianly as the equivalent works by Benjamin Britten.

IVES   *Folk songs and ballads*, 2v. (Leeds Music Corp.)

Burl Ives has achieved international fame and popularity as a singer of American songs—both traditional ones and those of recent origin. The two volumes contain many of the songs that this singer has made popular.

Vocal Music

SANDBURG   *The American songbag* (Harcourt, Brace)

A collection of 280 songs, ballads and ditties with introductions to the songs, an index of first lines and some attractive line illustrations. The index is required since the songs are arranged in classified order under such headings as "Tarnished love tales or Colonial and Revolutionary antiques", "Frankie and her man", and the like. "Bandit biographies", for example, contains three songs—on Jim Fisk, Jesse James and Sam Bass.

Special types of song

BOTSFORD   *Collection of folk songs*, 3v. (Schirmer, E. and original)

The first of these volumes is devoted to songs of the Americas, Asia and Africa, the second to northern Europe and the third to southern Europe, providing a useful selection of songs, particularly for countries not otherwise included in the preceding recommendations.

British students' song book (Bayley & Ferguson)
Scottish students' song book (Bayley & Ferguson)

Although these two volumes contain some of the folk and traditional songs that are to be found in some of the earlier volumes recommended, many of the works included are in neither category. While "British" might be taken to include Scottish in its purview, neither volume has a particularly national flavour.

BURLEIGH   *Negro spirituals*, 2v. (Ricordi)

CHAMBERS   *Treasury of negro spirituals* (Blandford)

JOHNSON   *30 negro spirituals* (Schirmer)

The Burleigh arrangements, though now possibly a little dated in the style of accompaniment, are probably the best known in Britain. Each volume contains ten spirituals, and is available in paper covers only. The Blandford edition, with thirty-five well-known spirituals plus seven modern compositions in that style, has been well arranged by H. A. Chambers. The Schirmer edition, with arrangements by Hall Johnson is the edition most likely to be stocked in American libraries.

DEARMER   *The Oxford book of carols* (O.U.P.)

A book usually in great demand a little before Christmas, and then neglected for the next eleven months. Many people appear completely unaware that there are carols for seasons other than Christmas and this volume presents a wide and comprehensive selection for all parts of the year.

SAMPSON &
HARRIS   *The seven seas shanty book* (Boosey)

TERRY   *The shanty book*, 2v. (Curwen)

The collection by Sir R. R. Terry contains sixty-five shanties (or chanteys) compared with forty-two in the single-volume selection.

413

Music Librarianship

COFFIN, Berton. The singer's repertoire (New Brunswick, N.J.; Scarecrow Press.) 1956.

A large work of 839 pages listing some 7,500 songs in classified order. The arrangement is primarily by voice and then by type of song. The author recognizes nine different types of voice from Coloratura soprano and Lyric soprano to Baritone and Bass. For each type of voice the author provides between 71 and 92 lists of songs, so that there are a total of 752 lists, usually very brief.

Each page has five columns across it. The first is for composer, the second for the title of the song, the third for the availability in different keys (i.e. High, Medium or Low setting), the fourth for the voice range needed and the fifth for the publisher. When a song is available in more than one setting (e.g. H., L.), the voice range quoted in the following column is that for the lowest available version—in the example quoted, the range would show the highest and lowest notes to be met with in the arrangement for low voice.

There is considerable repetition throughout the book. A song may be listed for both Coloratura soprano and Lyric soprano, and be found in "Songs for recital", "Songs employing sustained singing", "Atmospheric songs", etc. The work is probably useful to a particular type of singer and will help the music librarian to make suitable suggestions; it may also be used as a guide to accessions of songs suitable for a particular type of voice, but as a general aid to selection the work is of much less use than that listed next.

KAGEN, Sergius. Music for the voice: a descriptive list of concert and teaching material. (N.Y.: Rinehart.) 1949.

An invaluable work, not only to the music librarian but also to singers in general. It is divided into four parts: Songs and airs before the nineteenth century; Songs, nineteenth and twentieth centuries; Folk songs; Operatic excerpts. Each section is sub-divided. The first, for instance, has chapters on English, Italian, French, German songs, etc. Arrangement under each sub-heading is alphabetical by composer. If the composer is an important one in the field of vocal music there is a prefatory note upon his songs in general, and in some cases particular recommendations are made (as well as a warning of songs that the less-experienced singer should avoid). Russian, Scandinavian and Czech composers are normally included only when an

Vocal Music

English translation of a song is available. The classification under individual composers is again alphabetical by title, though complete song cycles are kept together under the title of the cycle itself, e.g. *Winterreise* by Schubert. The information given includes the vocal compass of the song; the tessitura (i.e. the normal range of the song, excluding the occasional extra high or low note); the type of voice best suited to the song (e.g. "Man's voice"; "Heavy voices"; "All voices"; "Not suitable for very low voices"), and Remarks. This last section may deal with the song itself or its translation, e.g. "Spirited and vigorous"; "Animated. In parts demands considerable dramatic intensity. Interpretatively not easy. Demands an excellent pianist", or "The English version is fair". In many cases the publisher of the song is shown, but it must be realized that in Britain a different publisher may have the issuing rights of the same song. The information about the songs is arranged in columns across the page and has similarity with the other volumes in *The field of music* series, of which this is a most distinguished member.

The work is not perfect—it lacks, for instance, an index of composers which would be a most useful adjunct. It omits Welsh folk songs on the grounds that "in the opinion of this writer, it seems preferable to sing them in their native language". Most of us would agree with that statement but not with the decision to omit all Welsh folk songs as a result of it. The length of this annotation gives a clear indication of my view of the value of this book. It should be included in the stock of bibliographies maintained in even small libraries but, unlike many such reference tools, should be made freely available for public use and not retained in the administrative quarters of the library. Its use to the librarian is only equalled by its value to the singer who wishes to extend his or her repertory and who appreciates expert advice and guidance.

KNAPP, J. Merrill, *ed.* Selected list of music for men's voices. (Princeton, N.J.: Princeton U.P.) 1950.

The author is Director of the Princeton University Glee Club and has based his work upon Arthur W. Locke's *Selected list of choruses for women's voices* (Smith College Monographs no. 2; first published in 1927 with a second edition in 1946—a work that I have not been able to see) using similar abbreviations and format but a dissimilar arrangement. Mr. Knapp used two main groups: (1) Octavo [apparently sheet] music, and (2) Music in collections. Each of these two groups is sub-divided and the general arrangement under each heading is alphabetical by composer. Sacred and secular pieces are separated as are those with and without accompaniment.

There are eight groups for Octavo music: I and II, Sacred, unaccompanied and Sacred, accompanied; III and IV, Secular, unaccompanied and accompanied; V and VI, Folk music, unaccompanied and accompanied; VII, Carols and rounds and VIII, Octavo groups. For music in collections only the first four of these groupings are used.

It is possible for a single composer to appear under several of these categories but the index allows one to trace all the works of an individual writer. Unaccompanied songs include those for which the accompaniment is not specified and also those in which it is shown "for rehearsal only".

Examples will show the layout and method adopted:

I—Sacred, unaccompanied

Davies, H. Walford (1869–1941)
Dominus illuminatio mea op. 38 (In the hour of death) (Anon) T T Bar B B   Eng CU 41016

The abbreviations indicate that the setting is for two tenors, baritone and two basses, with English words and published by Curwen. "In the hour of death" is the first line of the anthem.

IV—Secular, accompanied

Holst, Gustav Theodore (1874–1934)
Before sleep (The toil of day is ebbing) (Helen Waddell's Prudentius) T B pf or orch Eng HU GC – ed pf or org BoH Winthrop Rogers Edition 4698

In this case the work is for tenors and basses only; the first arrangement allows either piano or organ accompaniment in an unpublished arrangement of the Harvard University Glee Club while the normal published edition is that of Winthrop Rogers available through Boosey and Hawkes. No indication is given of the differences between Harvard's edition and the published one; the song (the last of six choruses for male voices written during 1931 and 1932) has accompaniment for strings, organ or piano in the Boosey edition.

V—Folk music, unaccompanied

Old Paint (My feet are in the stirrups) (Cowboy song) T T B B Eng arr MB Gx 1511

This indicates that the arrangement is by Marshall Bartholomew and the setting is published by the Galaxy Music Corporation and numbered 1511 in their catalogue.

Very few copies of this volume or of Arthur Locke's can be found in Britain, yet they would seem to offer a useful indication to enterprising choirs of what is available for them. As the examples given above would indicate, many British compositions are included so that problems of importation of copies need not arise.

Vocal Music

A useful British work is the *Catalogue of choral works* . . . published by the National Federation of Music Societies (2nd edn, 1953). It lists, without recommendation or annotation, a total of 510 works by 171 composers; every one of these works has been performed at least once by a choir affiliated to the Association since its inauguration in 1936. The entry indicates the composition of the chorus required, the soloists and the orchestra. A specimen entry is:

TIPPETT, Michael   (1905–)

   A child of our time

   VS. 5s 6d

Schott   75

chorus S.A.T.B.   *soli* S.A.T.B.

orch. 2, 2(CA), 2, 2(CB): 4,3,3,0: Perc. & Strs.

This indicates that the work is published in a vocal score by Schott at a cost of 5s. 6d. and takes 75 minutes to perform. Both soloists and chorus are the usual four voices and the orchestral accompaniment is written for strings, with two each of flutes, oboes, clarinets and bassoons, and a cor anglais and a double bassoon; the brass consists of four horns, 3 trumpets, 3 trombones (and no tuba), and a percussion section completes the necessary orchestra. This book, published at 3s. 6d. is a useful aid to selection for librarian and conductor.

Chapter VIII

MINIATURE SCORES

Although the demand for miniature scores is never likely to be large, the provision of them is highly desirable in a music collection. They are among the cheapest items of music (though binding may well increase the cost by more than 100 per cent) and represent an excellent long-term investment. The normal expectation of life of such a score is high and the likelihood that one will need to be replaced by a later edition is remote though it does happen occasionally.

In Britain, at least, the Second World War seems to have been a period when interest in miniature scores increased rapidly. Since that time this interest has been maintained, if not further heightened, by the ever-growing demand for classical music, and by the spread of gramophone record libraries. Recorded music on disc has sold in increasing quantities since the introduction of long-playing records and a growing minority of buyers and borrowers have discovered the added interest and enjoyment that can come when the performance is followed with the printed score. This growing use has been reflected by a similar increase in the number of libraries that provide miniature scores, though it would appear that several librarians have been disappointed with the results when a few scores have been put into stock. Probably of no other type of music is it truer to say that the supply creates the demand. Where provision is limited to twenty or thirty scores it may be felt that the experiment has been a failure but it must be realized that only a good representative selection will make readers turn first to the library; several disappointments when looking for standard works (which must inevitably happen if the stock is less than a hundred scores) will soon discourage potential users with the result that those scores that are in stock will receive even less use. Even at best, borrowing is not likely to be frequent and the score which is borrowed two or three times in the course of a year may be regarded as being extremely popular.

Miniature Scores

Miniature scores are handy for putting on dispɪay and for British librarians the summer season of B.B.C. Promenade Concerts presents an annual opportunity to bring the section to public notice and also to remind the librarian of gaps in his stock.

The scores may be divided into three major categories—orchestral music, chamber music and vocal music. The first is by far the most popular and it includes such works as symphonies, concert and operatic overtures, concertos, etc. Chamber music scores are much less in demand but the collection that does not include some of the many masterpieces in this field is indeed lacking balance. Suitable provision may be made at modest cost; the score of a Haydn string quartet, for instance, still costs but half a crown or three shillings. The third category, vocal music, includes operas, cantatas, masses and the like. Complete vocal scores are usually expensive and the more-easily-read format of vocal score with piano accompaniment is much more popular with most people. For this reason, the provision of a Bach cantata, a Wagner opera, etc., in miniature score form is not recommended unless the collection is large enough to warrant such a step or there is expressed local demand. Here again, the provision of a gramophone record lending library may well make such a policy justifiable and necessary. Overtures to operas are, of course, part of the normal orchestral repertory in many cases; where this is so the overture is published separately and should be considered for purchase with other orchestral works.

Publishers have been enterprising in their choice of works issued in this form and many composers whose names are rarely encountered, even in the catalogues of long-playing records, are to be found in various publishers' lists. How many readers of this paragraph know anything of Heath, Hegar or Heinrich XXIV of Helstead? All have had chamber music works published in the form of miniature scores and the remainder of the alphabet provides a similar wealth of examples. Better-known names still form the basis of publications and with composers of recognized standing the librarian can rarely make a wrong choice for purchase.

It should hardly be necessary to point out that miniature scores should be shelved in a separate sequence and there are several possible arrangements of the scores. The two most frequently adopted are arrangement by form or alphabetically by composer. The former is the more usual since it agrees with the scheme of music classification in use. On the other hand, there is much to be gained by making the primary arrangement by composer, sub-dividing the scores of each composer by form so that his overtures are together, his string quartets, etc. The usual request from a would-be borrower is for a particular work and both patron and unskilled assistant are likely to find composer arrangement less difficult to follow. The student of chamber music, or orchestral form as exemplified by symphonies, etc., loses by this arrangement but the user interested in the works of a single composer makes a corresponding gain. Libraries that arrange scores by form can try this alternative arrangement for themselves, using the class mark to ensure correct arrangement under each composer. If public and staff reaction is unfavourable to a single sequence of composers then nothing has been lost, since the scores can be rearranged with a minimum of trouble in their original class order. Many classification problems are minimized by the adoption of composer arrangement. The decision as to whether Bach's *Brandenburg concertos*, Bartók's *Concerto for orchestra* and Rachmaninov's *Rhapsody on a theme of Paganini* for piano and orchestra should be classed with general orchestral music or with concertos, or whether Berlioz's *Harold in Italy* for orchestra with viola obbligato should be classified as an orchestral work, a concerto or (from its sub-title) a symphony, becomes of much less importance when primary arrangement is by composer. *Harold* will be near the *Fantastic symphony*, the *Carnaval romain* overture and other works by Berlioz; the patron who has failed to check the class mark in the catalogue will not overlook the work by seeking it in vain among the concertos when it is classed with the symphonies.

Some librarians do not allow miniature scores to be issued for public use until they have been cloth-bound. This is not always necessary. Not only are some works issued in a good, strong format that will last several borrowings (which may take place over a space of years) and which will add some colour to the shelves but at least two of Britain's library binding contractors will bind miniature scores using the original cover stiffened by a board and varnished over. It is efficient, is considerably more economical than cloth rebinding and is certainly more attractive in appearance. In many cases the spine is broad enough for the composer, title and class mark to be shown. This form of binding is not practicable when two or three scores are bound together.

As with other forms of music, there is usually no alternative edition for works still protected by copyright: one must accept or reject the only available version. Earlier classics, however, which are now free from this restriction are often available in two editions and sometimes in as many as four or five. Before 1939, the two editions best known in Britain were those of Eulenburg and Philharmonia, published in Germany and Austria respectively. Since the war, Philharmonia scores have made a limited reappearance but Eulenburg scores (issued from London, New York and Zurich) are freely available. Their chief English rivals are now the "Hawkes pocket scores" of Boosey & Hawkes.

Before the war the introduction to Eulenburg editions was in German only. This is true of many of the reprints but as time passes an increasing number are being issued with the introduction in both German and English, incorporated with the binding immediately after the title-page and without any examples in music type. Hawkes, on the other hand, quote the main themes of a work in their introductions which are (in Britain) usually in parallel English and Spanish texts. These aids, however, are provided in the form of an inserted leaflet which is easily lost. These scores are not, therefore, suitable for issue before rebinding. Prices for alternative editions of the same work are usually just about equal: there is rarely more than sixpence difference in the prices charged by the two publishers. Under present conditions a fair proportion of the scores issued by both firms tend to be out of print for long periods so that choice between them is much more limited in practice than in theory, and unless he is prepared to wait for varying lengths of time, the librarian may find that he has to accept a particular edition of a work rather than the one he would prefer.

In the early nineteen-fifties two foreign firms entered the British market and began to build a collection of standard works in addition to the compositions for which they held the copyrights. Ricordi miniature scores have each a brief introduction (without musical illustrations) in English, French, German and Italian, while the Paris firm of Heugel (whose English agents are the United Music Publishers) offer introductions in English, French, German and Spanish. In both editions the standard of production and editing seems good and prices are approximately standard with those of Eulenburg and Hawkes.

The potential market for miniature scores in the U.S.A. is probably tremendous but it may be doubted if it is sufficiently large in Britain for this duplication to be generally profitable. This is par-

2E   421

ticularly true of a number of popular favourites which have appeared in the Penguin edition at about half the cost of the competitive issues.

Though these Penguin scores are apparently aimed at a music public that had not previously bought miniature scores, the edition is eminently suitable for public library use. The first score was issued in June 1949, in the oblong format that became immediately recognizable. A few works (the earliest of which was *Romeo and Juliet* by Tchaikovsky, the eleventh to be issued) were printed in an upright format because the number of instruments used in the work was too great to allow clear printing in the oblong page shape. The first four scores were printed in the conventional way, but the next fifteen printed the scores to show the notes actually produced by the transposing instruments and not those written by the composer which are apparently in a different key. Readers who find this quite baffling and who wonder what "transporting instruments" are should read the very clear description under this head in *The Oxford Companion to Music* where Dr. Scholes explains this apparent anomaly in a score and recommends the adaptation which was employed by Penguin. However, the firm received some complaints and sales showed signs of falling away, so that in October 1953 Penguin reverted to conventional practice and printed the parts for transposing instruments as written and not as sounded. A glance at the trumpet and clarinet parts of a score will show the problem to be faced by the unskilled score-reader. By April 1956 there were some thirty Penguin scores, representing about thirty-five works since a few volumes included two works within the one cover. The scores were apparently intended primarily for sale in ordinary bookshops with other Penguin books, rather than in music shops; the lack of new additions to the series suggests that the experiment has probably been unsuccessful in achieving the very high rate of sales that such a series needs. Indeed, Mr. Bruce Hepburn (Penguin's Sales Manager) told a 1958 conference of librarians that paper-back miniature scores are "wildly uneconomic".

Another series of miniature score that might be considered separately is the Lea pocket score, published in New York. This firm limits its output to piano and chamber music that is not normally available in miniature form. Examples of its productions are the Bach *48 Preludes and Fugues* and the Mozart *Piano trios*. It is recommended that these scores should not normally be added until the library has got a good nucleus collection of orchestral and chamber music works, though the Lea scores are inexpensive.

In building a representative stock a number of contradictory claims have to be considered and reconciled as far as is possible. First, the stock should contain works by old masters but also by contemporary composers, though scores by living writers will generally be appreciably more expensive than those no longer covered by copyright. Secondly, the stock should achieve a fair balance between orchestral and chamber music as a whole and also between the different types of orchestral and chamber music—symphonies, concertos, quartets and quintets, etc. Thirdly, a fair balance should be struck between the composers of different countries. For contemporary works there may well be a reasonable bias in favour of one's own countrymen. An American list of recommended miniature scores (that prepared by Mary Frances Focke of Cincinatti P.L. under the title "Music buying guide" in the *Library Journal* for 1st November 1951) included such works as Barber's *Overture to "The school for scandal"*, Copland's *Lincoln portrait*, Griffes' *White peacock, op. 7, no. 1* and Roy Harris's *Symphony no. 3*. All (with the possible exception of the last work which has been available on a gramophone record) are virtually unknown in Britain and are not included in the lists that follow—but they could well represent a much better set of purchases than an equivalent number of British works in an American library.

It is usually necessary to build up a collection of miniature scores over a period of years and the temptation to deal with individual forms in each batch of accessions should be avoided. Instead, the librarian should start with a collection that however small does attempt to be representative, in which symphonies are not included at the expense of overtures, or concertos bought to the total exclusion of works for a handful of players. If the first selection was limited to symphonies, for example, then the collection would be completely out of balance and many famous names in music would be missing. It should also be remembered that although the concert-goer may well want the score of a hackneyed work, the student is equally likely to want that of a much less frequently performed work, but one that is, perhaps, of greater historical importance and which may be heard via radio or gramophone though rarely encountered in the concert hall. Both types of demand are legitimate, but general preference while the stock is small should be given to works that achieve some regularity of performance since these are the ones more likely to be in demand. Certain standard works, such as Beethoven's symphonies, are as necessary as a complete Shakespeare or the novels of Jane Austen in the library stock.

Finally, it may be asserted that any work which is available in recorded form has a strengthened claim to inclusion since there are many people who will use a score to follow a recorded performance in order to get a better grasp of the work, particularly if it is new and strange. Where the library includes gramophone records in its stock, selection of new discs and miniature scores should run parallel, if possible. Kent County Education Committee's gramophone catalogue indicates by means of an asterisk all works that are available in miniature score and the score itself may be borrowed at the same time as a record or records, if desired. This is an excellent scheme. In the public library field, Hornsey gives every facility to the user of its gramophone collection to borrow the appropriate scores, while Coventry shelves both types of music in close proximity as a permanent encouragement.

As an introduction to the study and use of miniature scores the most valuable book for the non-professional musician is probably Gordon Jacob's *How to read a score* (Boosey & Hawkes, 1944) which is published in the same format as that firm's pocket scores; this allows the book to be shelved in the same sequence as the scores, if desired. This book includes a chapter on transposing instruments. For the checking and selection of the scores themselves the most useful guide was the *Reference book of miniature scores, with thematic list of the symphonies and chamber music works of the great masters*, published by J. & W. Chester, Ltd. The last edition was published in 1937 and has long been out of print. It cost but a shilling and was wonderful value for money. Owing to the fluctuating prices of imported scores and the tantalizing way in which they are reprinted only to disappear from the market again after a comparatively brief time, the appearance of another edition is highly problematical. This is most unfortunate since the book listed all miniature scores that were available at the time of going to press giving the price of each. No mention of the edition or editions available was made, which was a drawback, but it was obviously valuable to know if a certain work was published in miniature score. The thematic list in the appendix was also useful. A book published in 1955 on similar lines (but at an incomparably greater price) was most disappointing for its omissions, misprints and downright errors. If Chester's can ever be persuaded to publish a sixth edition of their work, librarians should buy a copy at once.

Three minor points should be mentioned. First, a few of the scores published by the Oxford University Press are not, strictly speaking, "miniature" scores but are octavos and are published as such. Because of their greater height they may prove a nuisance to shelve in the same sequence with the other miniature scores. They are not alone in this; the Hawkes pocket scores of Copland's *Third symphony* and Stravinsky's *Sacre du printemps*, for example, are also larger than the great majority of the series and require an outsize pocket in which to carry them. The second point is that Haydn symphonies have been numbered by the normal current method, i.e. by those allotted in the Mandyczewski list. Until quite recently, Hawkes pocket scores have continued to use the misleading numbers of the old Breitkopf & Härtel edition which are far from indicating the correct order of composition. If such a score is in stock, the newer number should be shown on its spine to ensure correct filing with the other works using the current numbering system. Similarly, the symphonies should always be catalogued under these numbers but with the old B. & H. number added if and when applicable, and also the "Salomon" number if it is one of the symphonies published on the occasion of Haydn's last visit to London. These numbers, together with the opening notes of each symphony, can be found in *Grove* and elsewhere. Entries in the lists that follow indicate these numbers for the works recommended. The third point is that scores should normally be bound singly for the greater benefit of patrons. Exception may well be made in the case of chamber music when two or three works form a convenient set or group, such as the three *Rasoumovsky* quartets of Beethoven that comprise his opus 59. Similarly, Haydn wrote several sets of string quartets with six works in each (e.g. opus 1, 2, 3 and 9, etc.) and these, because of their slimness, could be bound in twos or threes. Eulenburg issue some scores in bound volumes; these are not recommended for first choice but are excellent for duplicates, especially for the library with a gramophone record collection.

Although this is the last chapter in the book it was the first to be written and the preceding few pages are a modified version of an article that appeared in *The Librarian* for December, 1951. The miniature scores recommended for purchase were listed in the issue for February, 1952. The number of scores was 250, divided into five groups of fifty, each group printed separately and without annotation. These lists, with one or two very small modifications, have now been arranged in a single sequence. Although there are many more than 250 worthwhile scores it has been thought best to letter these original five lists as (a) to (e) and to show further recommendations at (f) and (g). To that extent, the recommended works have a different suggested priority to those in the preceding chapter. The quite small library should seriously consider buying not only the items marked (a), but also those shown as (b) and (c), and the medium-sized collection will probably find that the 250 scores (selections up to "e") are not sufficient. Annotations have been added for the majority of works, though this has resulted in some repetition in the case of chamber music.

BACH, J. S.   (c) *Brandenburg concertos* (Lea, 2v.)
    *(c) *no. 1, in F major* (Boosey; Eulenburg; Heugel; Philharmonia; Ricordi)
    *(c) *no. 2, in F major* (Boosey; Eulenburg; Heugel; Philharmonia; Ricordi)
    *nos. 1 and 2 published in one volume by Penguin
    (b) *no. 3, in G major* (Boosey; Eulenburg; Heugel; Philharmonia; Ricordi)
    (c) *no. 4, in G major* (Boosey; Eulenburg; Heugel; Penguin; Philharmonia; Ricordi)
    (b) *no. 5, in D major* (Boosey; Eulenburg; Heugel; Penguin; Philharmonia; Ricordi)
    (c) *no. 6, in B♭ major* (Boosey; Eulenburg; Heugel; Philharmonia; Ricordi)
    (b) *Double violin concerto in D minor* (Boosey; Eulenburg; Heugel)
    (b) *Piano concerto in D minor* (Boosey; Eulenburg; Heugel)
    (c) *Piano concerto in F minor* (Eulenburg; Heugel)
    Suites (Overtures)
    (c) *no. 1, in C major* (Boosey; Eulenburg; Heugel)
    (b) *no. 2, in B minor* (Boosey; Eulenburg; Heugel)

Miniature Scores

BACH, J. S.   (a) *no. 3, in D major* (Boosey; Eulenburg; Heugel)

(c) *no. 4, in D major* (Boosey; Eulenburg; Heugel)

(c) *Violin concerto in A minor* (Boosey; Eulenburg; Heugel; Ricordi)

(b) *Violin concerto in E major* (Boosey; Eulenburg; Heugel; Ricordi)

The above selection does no more than indicate Bach's immense importance in the field of orchestral music. The larger collection could usefully add the concertos for two, three and four harpsichords (pianos) as well as miniature scores of the more popular cantatas and the two major choral works. It should be mentioned that the four works listed as "Suites (Overtures)" are known by either title. They are more frequently known today by the name of "Suites" but the other title is equally correct.

BARTÓK   (b) *Concerto for orchestra* (Boosey)

(c) *Piano concerto no. 3* (Boosey)

(g) *String quartet no. 1* (Zerboni)

(g) *String quartet no. 2* (Universal)

(g) *String quartet no. 3* (Philharmonia)

(g) *String quartet no. 4* (Philharmonia)

(g) *String quartet no. 5* (Universal)

(g) *String quartet no. 6* (Boosey)

Both the orchestral works belong to Bartók's last (post-war) period when his music appeared to acquire a serenity lacking earlier. Certainly, both works are comparatively popular, especially the *Concerto for orchestra* which is virtuoso music at its best. If pre-war orchestral music of Bartók is to be represented, a useful choice would be the *Music for strings, percussion and celesta* (Philharmonia) which dates from 1937. Another earlier work is the *Dance suite* (Universal) written in 1923 to celebrate the 50th anniversary of Budapesth. For many critics, however, the string quartets of Bartók are his greatest works and the finest written for this medium since the time of Beethoven. They date from 1908 to 1939, covering most of the composer's working life.

BAX   (d) *The garden of Fand* (Chappell)

(g) *Overture to a picaresque comedy* (Chappell)

(e) *Symphony no. 3, in C major* (Chappell)

(f) *Tintagel* (Chappell)

Bax's music is highly romantic and colourful. The *Garden of Fand* is a tone-poem based upon an old legend, while *Tintagel* has King Arthur as its inspiration. Bax does not appear to have had any particular book or play in mind for the overture which is a lively and attractive work that receives occasional performance. The symphonies are undeservedly neglected; the third was chosen by

427

the British Council for subsidized recording during World War II. Bax is hardly known outside Britain and an overseas librarian might well consider this selection too generous.

BEETHOVEN

(e) *Consecration of the house* (*Die Weihe des Hauses*) *overture, op. 124* (Eulenburg)

*(c) *Coriolan overture, op. 62* (Boosey; Eulenburg; Heugel; Ricordi)

*(b) *Egmont overture, op. 84* (Boosey; Eulenburg; Heugel; Philharmonia; Ricordi)

**Coriolan* and *Egmont* together in Penguin

(f) *Fidelio: overture, op. 72b* (Boosey; Eulenburg; Heugel)

(b) *Leonora overture no. 3, op. 72a* (Boosey; Eulenburg; Heugel; Philharmonia; Ricordi)

Piano concertos

(e) *no. 1, in C major, op. 15* (Boosey; Eulenburg; Heugel)

(e) *no. 2, in B♭ major, op. 19* (Boosey; Eulenburg; Heugel)

(c) *no. 3, in C minor, op. 37* (Boosey; Eulenburg; Heugel)

(a) *no. 4, in G major, op. 58* (Boosey; Eulenburg; Heugel; Philharmonia; Ricordi)

(a) *no. 5, in E♭ major* ("*Emperor*"), *op. 73* (Boosey; Eulenburg; Heugel; Ricordi)

(d) *Piano trio no. 6, in B♭ major* ("*Archduke*"), *op. 97* (Eulenburg)

(g) *Prometheus overture, op. 43* (Boosey; Eulenburg)

String quartets (Lea, 4v; *separately* Boosey; Eulenburg; Heugel; Ricordi)

(b) *op. 18, nos. 1–6*

(a) *op. 59, nos. 1–3* ("*Rasoumovsky*")

(c) *op. 74, in E♭ major* ("*Harp*")

(c) *op. 95, in F minor* ("*Serious*")

(c) *op. 127, in E♭ major*

(c) *op. 130, in B♭ major*

(c) *op. 131, in C♯ minor*

(c) *op. 132, in A minor*

(c) *op. 133, in B major* ("*Grosse Fuge*")

(c) *op. 135, in F major*

428

Miniature Scores

BEETHOVEN
(a) *Symphonies, nos. 1–9* (Boosey; Eulenberg; Heugel; Philharmonia; Ricordi. Penguin nos. 1, 2, 3, 7, 9)

(a) *Violin concerto* (Boosey; Eulenburg; Heugel; Ricordi)

This may be regarded as a representative selection, with complete symphonies, piano concertos, and string quartets, but with many of the other chamber music works omitted as well as some of the less-frequently played overtures and Beethoven's two major choral works.

BERG
(e) *Lyric suite, for string quartet* (Philharmonia)

(b) *Violin concerto* (Universal)

These are difficult works written in the twelve-tone idiom. The concerto has received an excellent recording with André Gertler as soloist and this may provoke some interest in the score.

BERKELEY
(g) *Symphony* (Chester)

BERLIOZ
(f) *Béatrice et Bénedict: overture* (Eulenburg)

(g) *Benvenuto Cellini overture, op. 23* (Eulenburg; Heugel)

(d) *Le carnaval romain, overture, op. 9* (Boosey; Eulenburg; Heugel)

(e) *Le corsair overture, op. 21* (Eulenburg)

(c) *La damnation de Faust, op. 24; three orchestral extracts* (Eulenburg; Heugel)

(g) *Les francs juges* (*Judges of the secret court*) *overture, op. 3* (Eulenburg)

(e) *Harold in Italy, op. 16* (Eulenburg)

(g) *King Lear: overture, op. 4* (Eulenburg)

(c) *Symphonie fantastique, op. 14* (Eulenburg; Heugel)

The overtures are all of the concert type and are not preludes to operas, etc. The three extracts from *Faust* comprise the famous *Hungarian march* which concludes the first act, the *Dance of the sylphs* from Act II and the *Minuet of the Will o' the wisps* from Act III. *Harold in Italy* is a symphony with a major part for solo viola and is nominally based upon Byron's poem.

BIZET
(e) *L'Arlésienne: suites I and II* (Eulenburg)

(f) *Symphony in C major* (Choudens)

BLISS
(e) *String quartet no. 2* (Novello)

(f) *Violin concerto* (Novello)

These are important modern works that have been recorded and which present some difficulty for the listener with a nineteenth-century outlook upon string quartet and concerto writing.

429

BLOCH   (b) *String quartet no. 2* (Boosey)

Bloch is a Jew, born in Switzerland but resident for many years past in the U.S.A. He is one of the few composers to have used his racial inheritance deliberately and to good purpose. It is unfortunate that no miniature score of the piano quintet is available.

BORODIN   (e) *On the steppes of central Asia* (Eulenburg; Ricordi)

                     (f) *Prince Igor: Polovtsian dances* (Boosey; Eulenburg)

                     (g) *Prince Igor: overture* (Boosey; Eulenburg)

                     (c) *String quartet no. 2, in D major* (Boosey; Eulenburg)

                     (a) *Symphony no. 2, in B minor* (Boosey; Eulenburg; Ricordi)

The overture to *Prince Igor* was pieced together by Glazunov from recollections of piano performances by Borodin together with some scraps of themes written on odd scraps of paper; the rest of the opera was similarly retrieved by Rimsky-Korsakov. Without the efforts of these two friends, Borodin's opera would never have been born. The symphony is an attractive and popular work (with distinct references to *Prince Igor* at several points). The string quartet is today rather less popular than it was, and is regarded as rather weak but contains the lovely *Nocturne* as its slow movement.

BRAHMS   (a) *Academic festival overture, op. 80* (Boosey; Eulenburg)

                     (b) *Clarinet quintet, op. 115* (Boosey; Eulenburg; Heugel; Ricordi)

                     (e) *Double concerto, for violin and violoncello, in A minor, op. 102* (Eulenburg)

                     (d) *Piano concerto no. 1, in D minor, op. 15* (Eulenburg)

                     (b) *Piano concerto no. 2, in B♭ major, op. 83* (Boosey; Eulenburg; Heugel; Rircordi)

                     (d) *Piano quintet in F minor, op. 34* (Eulenburg; Heugel; Ricordi)

                     (f) *String quartet no. 1, in C minor, op. 51, no. 1* (Boosey; Eulenburg)

                     (e) *String quartet no. 2, in A minor, op. 51, no. 2* (Boosey; Eulenburg)

                     (e) *String quartet no. 3, in B♭ major, op. 67* (Boosey; Eulenburg; Heugel; Philharmonia)

Miniature Scores

BRAHMS *Symphonies*, 4v. (Boosey; Eulenburg; Philharmonia; Ricordi)

  (a) *no. 1, in C minor, op. 68*

  (b) *no. 2, in D major, op. 73*

  (b) *no. 3, in F major, op. 90*

  (b) *no. 4, in E minor, op. 98*

  (d) *Tragic overture, op. 81* (Boosey; Eulenburg; Heugel; Ricordi)

  (a) *Variations on a theme of Haydn, op. 56a* (Boosey; Eulenburg; Heugel; Penguin; Philharmonia; Ricordi)

  (b) *Violin concerto in D major, op. 77* (Boosey; Eulenburg; Heugel; Penguin; Ricordi)

The works suggested above represent rather less than half of those available in miniature score form; they are, however, the compositions most likely to be requested by music-lovers. The large collection could usefully expand the representation of chamber music.

BRITTEN (d) *Serenade for tenor, horn and strings, op. 31* (Boosey)

  (f) *Spring symphony, op. 44* (Boosey)

  (g) *Variations on a theme by Frank Bridge, op. 10* (Boosey)

  (b) *The young person's guide to the orchestra (Variations and fugue on a theme of Purcell), op. 34* (Boosey)

The opus 10 variations are written for string orchestra, date from 1937, and were one of the first pieces that made Britten an internationally-known figure. The *Spring symphony* is scored for soprano, alto and tenor soloists, mixed chorus, boys' choir and orchestra.

BRUCH (f) *Violin concerto no. 1, in G minor, op. 26* (Eulenburg)

BRUCKNER (e) *Symphony no. 4, in E♭ major ("Romantic")* (Brucknerverlag; Eulenburg; Hinrichsen; Philharmonia)

The invention of the long-playing record has been a boon to lovers of Bruckner for his musical thought loses much of its appeal when chopped up into four-minute instalments required by SP discs. The length of the symphonies has militated against their popularity in Britain but there appears to be a growing audience for his works.

Choice of edition is highly complicated because of the different versions; almost all of Bruckner's symphonies are available in different recensions and it is difficult in most cases to decide which one represents the composer's final

431

intention. The fourth symphony, for example, has had no less than four versions, and the Eulenburg edition, by Hans Redlich, represents a compromise between them. The Brucknerverlag version has the advantage of being "official", but conductors may well use any of the available versions or make their own amalgam.

The reason for these difficulties and confusions has been well explained by Hans Redlich in his book on "Bruckner and Mahler" in the *Master Musician series* (Dent). After the fourth symphony, the seventh is probably the most popular and should be added in the larger collection.

CASELLA   (g) *Italia op. 11: rhapsody* (Universal)

CHABRIER   (e) *Espana: rhapsodie* (Enoch; Eulenburg)

CHAUSSON   (g) *Symphony, op. 20* (Rouart, Lerolle)

COPLAND   (g) *Billy the kid: ballet music* (Boosey)
            (g) *Symphony no. 3* (Boosey)

Two important works by an outstanding contemporary American composer. Though published as "Hawkes pocket scores", an outsize pocket is needed to accommodate either work, as the page size is much larger than normal in this series.

CORELLI   (e) *Concerto grosso, in G minor ("Christmas"), op. 6, no. 8* (Eulenburg; Ricordi)

The *Christmas concerto* is the most popular of the twelve concerti grossi that comprise opus 6. The nickname appears to derive from the pastoral slow movement, and however undeserved the appellation may be, it appears to make for more frequent performance of this concerto than of its companions.

DEBUSSY   (f) *Images* (Durand)
            (d) *La mer: trois esquisses symphoniques* (Durand)
            (e) *Nocturnes* (Jobert)
            (a) *Prélude à l'après midi d'un faune* (Eulenburg; Jobert)

Images is the third set of that title, the two previous series being for solo piano. The orchestral set consists of *Gigues, Iberia* and *Ronde de printemps*; it is the second (and longest) movement that is often played at concerts without its companions. *Nocturnes* also consists of three pieces—*Nuages, Fêtes* and *Sirènes* (the last employing a female chorus, and so making a concert performance rather more difficult and expensive).

DELIUS   (f) *Appalachia: variations on an old slave song* (Boosey)
            (c) *Brigg Fair: an English rhapsody* (Universal)
            (f) *Sea drift* (Boosey)
            (b) *Two pieces for small orchestra (On hearing the first cuckoo in Spring: Summer night on the river)* (O.U.P.)

Both *Appalachia* and *Sea Drift* (the latter a setting of words by Walt Whitman) require a chorus for performance. Both are highly effective but are never likely to achieve the universal popularity of the brief and enchanting *First cuckoo*, which may be regarded as the perfect evocation of the English countryside.

DOHNANYI

(d) *Variations on a nursery tune, for piano and orchestra, op. 25* (Eulenburg; Lengnick)

This is one of the best pieces of musical humour. The English title is itself subject to a series of variations on the fifth word, which may be rendered in different recordings and programmes, etc., as nursery "tune", "rhyme", "theme", "song", etc.

DUKAS

(e) *L'apprenti sorcier* (Durand)

DVOŘÁK

(g) *Carnaval overture, op. 92* (Eulenburg; Lengnick)

(d) *Piano quintet in A minor, op. 81* (Eulenburg)

(g) *Serenade for strings, in E major, op. 22* (Eulenburg)

Symphonies

(c) *no. 2, in D minor, op. 70* (Simrock; Eulenburg)

(b) *no. 4, in G major, op. 88* (Eulenburg; Novello)

(a) *no. 5, in E minor ("From the New World"), op. 95* (Eulenburg; Lengnick)

(b) *String quartet in F major ("American"), op. 96* (Eulenburg; Lengnick)

(c) *Violoncello concerto, in B minor, op. 104* (Eulenburg; Lengnick)

Dvořák wrote nine symphonies and it is the last five which are known as numbers 1 to 5; the three recommended are, in fact, the seventh, eighth and ninth respectively, and it is by these numbers that the works are known in their native Czechoslovakia. The opus 96 quartet is still more often called the "Nigger" quartet in Britain, but this title is slowly giving way to the alternative sobriquet.

ELGAR

(b) *Cockaigne (In London town): concert overture, op. 40* (Boosey)

(d) *Falstaff: symphonic study, op. 68* (Novello)

(b) *Introduction and allegro for strings, op. 47* (Eulenburg; Novello)

(e) *String quartet in E minor, op. 83* (Novello)

(c) *Symphony no. 1, in A♭ major, op. 55* (Novello)

(d) *Symphony no. 2, in E♭ major, op. 63* (Novello)

(a) *Variations on an original theme ("Enigma" variations), op. 36* (Eulenburg; Novello)

433

(c) *Violin concerto, in B minor, op. 61* (Novello)

(c) *Violoncello concerto, in E minor, op. 85* (Novello)

Falstaff is considered by some critics to be Elgar's finest orchestral work but it remains the least popular of the major compositions. Although Elgar is one of Britain's finest composers his works make little appeal in other countries and only the *Enigma variations* have become internationally famous. For this reason the overseas librarian might rightly reduce the recommended selection of scores.

FALLA

(d) *Nights in the gardens of Spain* (*Noces en los jardines de España*) (Chester)

(f) *The three-cornered hat* (*El sombrero de tres picos*): *ballet* (Chester)

Nights in the gardens of Spain is written for piano and orchestra (though the piano is treated as an orchestral instrument rather than a soloist) and is a wonderfully evocative picture of the country. The ballet is a popular one, and the orchestral suite of three dances is a great favourite with concert audiences.

FAURE

(g) *Ballade for piano and orchestra, op. 19* (U.M.P.)

Although the work was originally written for solo piano it is generally considered to be more effective in this second version.

FRANCK

(g) *Le chasseur maudit: symphonic poem* (Eulenburg)

(f) *Piano quintet in F minor* (Hamelle; Eulenburg)

(b) *Symphony, in D minor* (Boosey; Eulenburg; Hamelle)

(a) *Variations symphoniques* (Boosey; Eulenburg; Penguin)

The *Symphonic variations*, Franck's most popular work, is written for piano and orchestra. The symphony is an outstanding example of a work that can be faulted in many respects on critical grounds but which obstinately remains a great favourite in the orchestral repertory. The piano quintet is undoubtedly Franck's most successful piece of chamber music and is one of the best piano quintets in the repertory.

GRIEG

(f) *Holberg suite, op. 40* (Eulenburg)

(a) *Piano concerto in A minor, op. 16* (Eulenburg)

The *Holberg suite* is sub-titled as "in the ancient style" and was written in connection with the 200th anniversary of the birth of the Danish playwright Holberg (1684–1754). The suite consists of five movements written in early dance forms. This version for string orchestra was adapted by the composer from the original piano score—a form in which the work is infrequently performed.

HANDEL

Concerti grossi for strings, op. 6 (Boosey, 12v; Eulenburg, 12v; Lea, 2v; Ricordi, 12v.)

(e) *no. 1, in G major*

HANDEL

(f) *no. 2, in F major*
(e) *no. 3, in E minor*
(e) *no. 4, in A minor*
(e) *no. 5, in D major*
(e) *no. 6, in G minor*
(e) *no. 7, in B♭ major*
(f) *no. 8, in E minor*
(f) *no. 9, in F major*
(f) *no. 10, in D minor*
(f) *no. 11, in A major*
(e) *no. 12, in B minor*
(f) *Music for the royal fireworks* (Boosey)
(e) *Water music suite* (arr. Harty) (Chappell)

The twelve concerti grossi will bind conveniently into two, three or four volumes if considered desirable; the Lea edition is issued in two volumes only. The *Water music* is almost invariably played in the Harty arrangement which is a selection of seven movements from the complete work in F. The score of the complete sequence is available in miniature from both Boosey and Heugel. The remaining movements of the *Water music* (those in D minor) are not available in miniature score. The *Royal fireworks music* is also usually played in the Harty arrangement of four movements only; the recommended score contains the complete work which was written to celebrate the peace of Aix-la-Chapelle.

HAYDN

String quartets
(b) *op. 20, nos. 1–6* ("*Sun*" *quartets*) (Eulenburg)
(e) *op. 33, nos. 1–6* ("*Russian*" *quartets*) (Eulenburg)
(f) *op. 50, nos. 1–6* ("*King of Prussia*" *quartets*) (Eulenburg)
(g) *op. 51, nos. 1–7* ("*The seven words*") (Eulenburg)
(d) *op. 54, nos. 1–3* (Eulenburg)
(a) *op. 64, nos. 1–6* (Eulenburg)
(d) *op. 74, nos. 1–3* (Eulenburg)
(a) *op. 76, nos. 1–6* (Eulenburg)
(c) *op. 77, nos. 1 and 2* (Eulenburg)
Symphonies
(g) *no. 6, in D major* ("*Le matin*") (Eulenburg)
(g) *no. 7, in C major* ("*Le midi*") (Eulenburg; Ricordi)
(g) *no. 8, in G major* ("*Le soir*") (Eulenburg; Ricordi)

(f) *no. 22, in E♭ major ("The philosopher")* (Eulenburg)

(g) *no. 31, in G major ("Horn signal")* (Eulenburg; Ricordi)

(g) *no. 44, in E minor ("Trauer")* (Eulenburg)

(f) *no. 45, in F♯ minor ("Farewell")* (Eulenburg; Philharmonia; Ricordi)

(g) *no. 48, in C major ("Maria Theresa")* (Eulenburg; Ricordi)

(f) *no. 49, in F minor ("La Passione")* (Eulenburg)

(f) *no. 73, in D major ("La chasse")* (Eulenburg)

(g) *no. 83, in G minor ("The hen")* (*Paris set no. 2*) (Eulenburg)

(d) *no. 88 (13) in G major* (Eulenburg)

(b) *no. 92 (16) in G major ("Oxford")* (Boosey; Eulenburg; Heugel; Philharmonia; Ricordi)

(a) *no. 94 (6) in G major ("Surprise"; Salomon no. 3)* (Boosey; Eulenburg; Heugel; Penguin; Philharmonia; Ricordi)

(b) *no. 95 (9), in C minor (Salomon no. 5)* (Eulenburg)

(e) *no. 96 (14), in D major ("Miracle"; Salomon no. 6)* (Eulenburg)

(g) *no. 98 (8) in B♭ (Salomon no. 4)* (Eulenburg)

(f) *no. 99 (3), in E♭ major (Salomon no. 10)* (Eulenburg)

(d) *no. 100 (11), in G major ("Military" Salomon no. 12)* (Boosey; Eulenburg; Heugel; Penguin; Philharmonia; Ricordi)

(b) *no. 101 (4), in D ("Clock"; Salomon no. 11)* (Boosey; Eulenburg; Heugel; Penguin; Philharmonia; Ricordi)

(b) *no. 102 (12), in B♭ major (Salomon no. 9)* (Eulenburg)

(d) *no. 103 (1), in E♭ major ("Drumroll"; Salomon no. 8)* (Eulenburg; Heugel; Philharmonia; Ricordi; Boosey)

Miniature Scores

HAYDN   (a) *no. 104 (2), in D ("London"; Salomon no. 7)*
(Boosey; Eulenburg; Heugel; Penguin;
Philharmonia; Ricordi)

(e) *Trumpet concerto* (Boosey; Eulenburg)

This may be an intimidating list for the librarian yet there are many other important works that could usefully be added—such as further string quartets, symphonies, etc. The quartets, many of which were written in sets of six, will bind three in a volume quite conveniently in such cases. As would be expected, some individual quartets have become much more popular than others sharing the same opus number; it is possibly a coincidence that the best known are often those with nicknames. The fourth of the opus 20 quartets is sometimes known as *The row in Venice*, but it is the fifth which is probably the finest. The second of the opus 33 quartets is known as *The Joke*, the third as *The bird* or *The birds*, and this last has proved the most popular of this set. The fifth and sixth of the *King of Prussia* quartets are nicknamed respectively *The dream* and *The frog*, while the most popular of the opus 64 quartets is number 5, *The lark*. The third and last of the opus 74 quartets is known as *The rider* or *The horseman*, and this is the pick of three fine quartets. Three of the opus 76 works have nicknames—the second, third and fourth which are known respectively as the *Quinten*, the *Emperor* and the *Sunrise*. The *Emperor* derives its name and probably its outstanding popularity from its slow movement; this consists of variations on the theme of the Austrian national anthem, which was Haydn's composition. It is difficult to over-estimate Haydn as a composer of string quartets and the large collection will need to add miniature scores of some of the other works in this form.

Salomon was the impresario who persuaded Haydn to come to London in 1792–3 and again in 1794, and the twelve symphonies that Haydn wrote for these English concerts still bear the enterprising violinist's name. The old Breitkopf numbers are now very rarely used indeed: gramophone records, concert programmes and other media all use the "new" Breitkopf series. Many of the symphonies also have opus numbers; this is one of the rare cases where this form of identification is not used at all.

HINDEMITH   (f) *Mathis der Maler: symphony* (Schott)

(g) *Metamorphosis of themes by Weber* (Schott)

(g) *Nobilissima visione* (Schott)

The symphony is based upon music from Hindemith's opera of the same name, which deals with the life of the seventeenth-century German painter. Hindemith used a similar method with his opera *Harmonie die Welt* and made an orchestral suite out of certain passages. *Nobilissima visione* is a ballet based on the life of St. Francis of Assisi.

HOLST   (a) *The Planets, op. 32* (Boosey)

A suite of seven pieces, excellently scored for large orchestra. Complete performances are not frequent but the fourth movement, *Jupiter: the bringer of jollity*, is the popular favourite.

HONEGGER   (f) *Pacific 231* (Salabert)

(g) *Pastorale d'été* (Salabert)

Though the novelty of *Pacific 231* has long worn thin, it remains an orchestral *tour de force* and Honegger's methods have been copied by many composers of light music who also wish to portray railway engines in motion.

HUMPERDINCK (f) *Hänsel und Gretel: overture* (Eulenburg; Schott)

INDY (f) *Symphony on a French mountain theme op. 25* (Hamelle)

IRELAND (f) *A London overture* (Boosey)

(g) *Mai Dun: symphonic rhapsody* (Augener)

(d) *Piano concerto in E♭ major* (Chester)

The main, perky tune of the *London overture* is based upon a bus-conductor's cry of "Piccadilly". *Mai-Dun* is the old name for the prehistoric camp of Maiden Castle, in Dorset.

JANAČEK (f) *Sinfonietta* (Philharmonia)

This is an exuberant and breath-taking work. Its unconventional scoring calls for no less than twelve trumpets.

KHATCHATURIAN (f) *Gayane: ballet* (Boosey)

(g) *Piano concerto* (Boosey)

KODÁLY (f) *Dances of Galanta* (Philharmonia)

(e) *Hary János: suite* (Boosey; Philharmonia)

The *Dances* were written to celebrate the 50th anniversary of the city of Budapesth. The suite *Hary János* is drawn from the opera of the same name; the hero is a Hungarian Baron Munchausen and the humour of this work makes it a popular favourite with audiences.

LISZT (d) *Piano concerto no. 1, in E♭ major* (Boosey; Eulenburg; Heugel)

(f) *Piano concerto no. 2, in A major* (Eulenburg)

(e) *Les Préludes: symphonic poem no. 3* (Boosey; Eulenburg; Heugel; Philharmonia)

Les Préludes is the most popular (and, therefore, the most frequently played) of the twelve symphonic poems. The two concertos are both virtuoso pieces.

MAHLER (g) *Symphony no. 1, in D major* (Universal)

(b) *Symphony no. 4, in G major* (Universal)

Mahler wrote nine symphonies plus an unfinished tenth. The fourth is the most popular and its last movement contains an important part for soprano soloist. The first symphony was originally entitled the *Titan* by the composer; it is a most unsuitable appellation and was later withdrawn by Mahler though it is still sometimes used. Large music collections could add the fifth and ninth symphonies if fuller representation of the composer is desired.

MARTIN (f) *Petite symphonie concertante* (Philharmonia)

The solo instruments are harp, harpsichord and piano, with string orchestra providing the accompaniment. The work dates from 1944–45 and is generally considered to be one of the most important works written during the decade.

Miniature Scores

MENDELSSOHN
    (g) *Calm sea and prosperous voyage overture, op. 27* (Eulenburg)

    *(b) *The Hebrides (Fingal's Cave) overture, op. 26* (Boosey; Eulenburg; Heugel; Ricordi)

    *(a) *A Midsummer night's dream: overture, op. 21* (Boosey; Eulenburg; Heugel; Philharmonia)

    (b) *A Midsummer night's dream: incidental music, op. 61–5 orchestral pieces* (Eulenburg)

    (f) *Ruy Blas; overture, op. 95* (Eulenburg)

    (e) *String octet, in E♭ major, op. 20* (Eulenburg)
    Symphonies

        (f) *no. 3, in A minor ("Scotch"), op. 56* (Boosey; Eulenburg; Heugel; Ricordi)

        (b) *no. 4, in A major ("Italian"), op. 90* (Boosey; Eulenburg; Heugel; Ricordi)

        (g) *no. 5, in D major ("Reformation"), op. 107* (Broude; Cranz)

    (b) *Violin concerto, in E minor, op. 64* (Boosey; Eulenburg; Heugel; Penguin; Philharmonia; Ricordi)

As the two different opus numbers indicate, the incidental music to Shakespeare's play was written some time after Mendelssohn had composed the overture. The five orchestral pieces include the lovely *Nocturne*, the attractive *Scherzo*, and the famous *Wedding march*. The octet was written when Mendelssohn was only sixteen and is scored for double string quartet.

MOZART
    (f) *Clarinet concerto, K.622*

    †(c) *Don Giovanni overture, K.527* (Boosey; Eulenburg; Heugel; Philharmonia; Ricordi)

    (e) *Horn concerto no. 3, in E♭ major, K.447* (Eulenburg)

    (f) *Horn concerto no. 4, in E♭ major, K.495* (Eulenburg)

    (a) *Eine kleine Nachtmusik (Serenade) in G major, K.525* (Boosey; Eulenburg; Heugel; Philharmonia; Ricordi)

    (c) *Le nozze di Figaro: overture, K.492* (Boosey; Eulenburg; Heugel; Philharmonia Ricordi)
    Piano concertos (Eulenburg)

        (b) *no. 9, in E♭ major, K.271*

* Bound together (Penguin).
† Bound with *Die Zauberflöre* overture in Penguin edition.

MOZART

(f) *no. 12, in A major, K.414*

(g) *no. 14, in E♭ major, K.449*

(d) *no. 15, in B♭ major, K.450*

(e) *no. 17, in G major, K.453*

(c) *no. 20, in D minor, K.466* (Heugel)

(f) *no. 21, in C major, K.467*

(e) *no. 22, in E♭ major, K.482*

(a) *no. 23, in A major, K.488* (Boosey; Heugel; Philharmonia; Ricordi)

(b) *no. 24, in C minor, K.491* (Heugel; Philharmonia; Ricordi)

(g) *no. 26, in D major ("Coronation"), K.537* (Boosey; Heugel; Ricordi)

(f) *no. 27, in B♭ major, K.595*

(e) *Serenade for 13 wind instruments, in B♭ major, K.361* (Eulenburg)

(f) *Serenade for violin solo and orchestra, in D major ("Haffner"), K.250* (Eulenburg)

String quartets (Boosey; Eulenburg; Heugel; Philharmonia; Ricordi)

(b) *in G major, K.387*

(c) *in D minor, K.421*

(d) *in E♭ major, K.428*

(d) *in B♭ major ("The Hunt"), K.458*

(d) *in A major, K.464*

(d) *in C major, K.465*

(d) *in D major, K.499*

(d) *in D major, K.575*

(f) *in B♭ major, K.589*

(f) *in F major, K.590*

(a) *String quintet in G minor, K.516* (Eulenburg; Ricordi)

Symphonies

(g) *no. 25, in G minor, K.183* (Heugel; Ricordi)

(f) *no. 29, in A major, K.201* (Heugel; Ricordi)

(g) *no. 31, in D major ("Paris"), K.297* (Heugel)

(f) *no. 35, in D major ("Haffner"), K.385* (Boosey; Eulenburg; Heugel; Philharmonia; Ricordi)

Miniature Scores

MOZART   (d) *no. 36, in C major ("Linz"), K.425* (Boosey; Eulenburg; Heugel; Philharmonia; Ricordi)

(b) *no. 38, in D major (without minuet, "Prague"), K.504* (Boosey; Eulenburg; Heugel; Philharmonia; Ricordi)

(a) *no. 39, in E♭ major, K.543* (Boosey; Eulenburg; Heugel; Penguin; Philharmonia; Ricordi)

(a) *no. 40, in G minor, K.550* (Boosey; Eulenburg; Heugel; Penguin; Philharmonia; Ricordi)

(a) *no. 41, in C major ("Jupiter"), K.551* (Boosey; Eulenburg; Heugel; Penguin; Philharmonia; Ricordi)

Violin concertos

(g) *no. 3, in G major, K.216* (Boosey; Eulenburg; Heugel; Ricordi)

(f) *no. 4, in D major, K.218* (Boosey; Eulenburg; Heugel; Ricordi)

(d) *no. 5, in A major, K.219* (Boosey; Eulenburg; Heugel; Ricordi)

*(c) *Die Zauberflöte (Magic flute): overture, K.620* (Boosey; Eulenburg; Heugel; Ricordi)

Mozart is a composer whose works can hardly be represented too widely in a collection of miniature scores. There are many lovely works that could be profitably added to the list above, long as the latter might appear. The first six of the ten string quartets listed are known as the "Haydn" quartets because the young Mozart dedicated them to the older composer, and the last three (for similar reasons) are known as the "King of Prussia" set. These nine quartets would conveniently bind into three volumes if required, leaving K. 499 as a single work. There is no symphony no. 37, as the work originally listed as such is now known to have been written by Michael Haydn.

MUSSORGSKY   (e) *Night on the bare mountain* (Boosey; Eulenburg)

(d) *Pictures at an exhibition* (Boosey; Eulenburg)

The *Pictures* are published in the Ravel orchestration, which is the one most frequently used, and quotes the original piano score at the bottom of each page for comparative purposes.

NIELSEN   *Symphonies*

(g) *no. 1, in G minor, op. 7* (Hansen)

* Bound with *Don Giovanni* overture in Penguin edition.

441

    (g) *no. 2 ("The four temperaments"), op. 16* (Hansen)

    (g) *no. 3 ("Espansiva"), op. 29* (Engstrom & Sodring)

    (d) *no. 4 ("Inextinguishable"), op. 29* (Hansen)

    (f) *no. 5, op. 50* (Skandinavisk Musikforlag)

Nielsen is a comparatively recent discovery on the part of British audiences though he died in 1931. The continued efforts of a small band of enthusiasts seems likely to bring these symphonies to the fringe of the regular repertoire. It is worth comment that many Scandinavians rate Nielsen above Sibelius.

PROKOFIEV   (f) *Love of the three oranges, op. 33a: suite* (Boosey)

    (f) *Peter and the wolf, op. 67* (Boosey)

    (g) *Piano concerto no. 3, in C major, op. 26* (Boosey)

    (b) *Symphony no. 1, in D major ("Classical"), op. 25* (Boosey)

    (g) *Symphony no. 7, op. 131* (Boosey)

The Suite is taken from Prokoviev's somewhat unorthodox opera. His first and last symphonies, particularly the former, are the two best known; the large library might also add the fifth and sixth symphonies while the third piano concerto is the one that is most frequently played.

RACHMANINOV   *Piano concertos*

    (g) *no. 1, in F♯ minor, op. 1* (Boosey)

    (a) *no. 2, in C minor, op. 18* (Boosey)

    (c) *no. 3, in D minor, op. 30* (Boosey)

    (f) *no. 4, in G minor, op. 40* (Foley)

    (b) *Rhapsody on a theme of Paganini, for piano and orchestra, op. 43* (Foley)

The second piano concerto of Rachmaninov is probably second in public popularity only to the Tchaikovsky B-flat minor, while the *Rhapsody* has gained much wider audiences since the beginning of World War II. The fact that the eighteenth variation has achieved popularity as a dance tune may be a fair indication of Rachmaninov's melodic skill. It is unfortunate that neither the second nor third symphony is available in miniature form.

RAVEL   *Daphnis and Cloe ballet*

    (f) *Symphonic fragments, set I* (Durand)

    (d) *Symphonic fragments, set II* (Aurand)

    (g) *Ma mere l'Oye [Mother Goose]: suite* (Durand)

    (f) *Piano concerto in G major* (Durand)

    (f) *Piano concerto for left hand* (Durand)

    (g) *Rhapsodie espagnole* (Durand)

Miniature Scores

(g) *Le tombeau de Couperin* (Durand)

(e) *La valse: poème choréographique* (Durand)

The second of the *Daphnis and Chloë* suites contains much better music than the first and appears fairly frequently in concert programmes. *Mother Goose* is an orchestral arrangement of the suite originally written for piano duet, while *Le Tombeau de Couperin* is an orchestral version of four of the six pieces originally written for piano solo. The composer himself made the orchestral versions. *Rhapsodie espagnole* has four movements and is, with the two concertos, the only orchestral music written by the composer for concert performance. *La valse*, a choreographic poem, is a favourite showpiece of orchestral virtuosity, with a genteel touch and a parody on Johann Strauss the younger. The music is for a ballet.

RAWSTHORNE   (f) *Piano concerto no. 2* (O.U.P.)

                       (g) *Symphony* (O.U.P.)

RESPIGHI   (g) *Ancient airs and dances* [*Antiche danze ed arie*]: *three suites* (Ricordi)

                       (f) *The birds* [*Gli uccelli*]: *suite for small orchestra* (Ricordi)

                       (f) *The fountains of Rome* [*Fontane di Roma*] (Ricordi)

                       (g) *The pines of Rome* [*Pini di Roma*] (Ricordi)

                       (f) *Three Botticelli paintings* [*Trittico Botticelliano*] (Ricordi)

Respighi's works can be divided into two very different categories. His tone poems are loud, colourful and often vulgar, but his arrangements for small orchestra of old music are tastefully made and are delightful. The three suites of *Ancient airs and dances* were originally lute pieces by various Italian composers of the sixteenth and seventeenth centuries. *The birds*, perhaps the most popular of Respighi's suites, is an arrangement of keyboard works by English, French and Italian composers of the sixteenth and seventeenth centuries, while the *Botticelli triptych* is a picture in music of three of the famous paintings by the Florentine artist; an original work scored for small orchestra, it sounds in part like a pastiche and is quite different from the tone poem. For many people Respighi is mainly, if not solely, known as the arranger of small piano pieces by Rossini which were made into the ballet *La boutique fantasque*.

RIMSKY-
KORSAKOV   (g) *Capriccio espagnole, op. 34* (Boosey; Eulenburg)

                       (d) *Scheherazade, op. 35* (Boosey; Eulenburg)

                       (f) *Antar* (*Symphony no. 2*), *op. 9* (Eulenburg)

ROSSINI   (c) *Barber of Seville: overture* (Eulenburg; Philharmonia)

                       The silken ladder (*La scala di seta*): *overture* (Eulenburg; Ricordi)

(g) *The thieving magpie [La gazza ladra]: overture* (Eulenburg)

(e) *William Tell [Guillaume Tell]: overture* (Eulenburg; Ricordi)

The Rossini overtures are all to operas and the large library could usefully extend the collection to cover all available scores of opera overtures, for the works are popular with both audiences and orchestras.

RUBBRA (f) *Symphony no. 5, op. 63* (Lengnick)

(d) *Symphony no. 6, op. 80* (Lengnick)

The miniature score recommendations, when originally published in *The Librarian*, included the composer's fourth symphony; these later works have now been substituted as they are more satisfying. The fifth has been recorded. Rubbra is one of the few modern composers who continue to use the symphonic form, and whose skill and resource increase with every new work.

SAINT-SAENS (e) *Carnival of the animals [Le carnaval des animaux]* (Durand)

(g) *Piano concerto no. 2, in G minor, op. 22* (Durand)

(g) *Le rouet d'Omphale [Omphale's spinning wheel], op. 31* (Durand; Huegel)

The second piano concerto is the most popular of the five written by this composer, while the tone poem goes to Greek mythology for its subject. The *Carnival*, for two pianos and small orchestra, was originally written for private amusement and (except for the single movement, *The swan*) was not published until after Saint-Saen's death.

SCHUBERT (e) *Octet in F major, op. 166 (D.803)* (Boosey; Eulenburg; Heugel; Philharmonia; Ricordi)

(e) *Piano quintet in A major ("Trout"), op. 114 (D.667)* (Boosey; Eulenburg; Heugel; Philharmonia; Ricordi)

(c) *Piano trio in B♭ major, op. 99 (D.898)* (Eulenburg; Ricordi)

(c) *Rosamunde (Die Zauberharfe): overture, op. 26 (D.644)* (Boosey; Eulenburg; Philharmonia)

(f) *Rosamunde: entr'actes and ballet music, op. 26 (D.797)* (Eulenburg)

String quartets

(d) *no. 13, in A minor, op. 29 (D.804)* (Boosey; Eulenburg; Philharmonia; Ricordi)

Miniature Scores

SCHUBERT

(a) *no. 14, in D minor ("Death and the maiden"), op. posth. (D.810)* (Boosey: Eulenberg; Heugel; Philharmonia; Ricordi)

(d) *no. 15, in G major, op. 161 (D.887)* (Boosey; Eulenburg; Heugel; Philharmonia; Ricordi)

(d) *String quintet in C major, op. 163 (D.956)* (Boosey; Eulenburg; Philharmonia; Ricordi)

Symphonies

(f) *no. 4, in C minor ("Tragic") (D.417)* (Boosey; Eulenburg; Heugel)

(b) *no. 5, in B♭ major (D.485)* (Boosey; Eulenburg; Philharmonia)

(d) *no. 6, in C major (D.589)* (Eulenburg)

(b) *no. 7 [or no. 9] in C major (D.944)* (Boosey; Eulenburg; Heugel; Philharmonia)

(a) *no. 8, in B minor ("Unfinished") (D.759)* (Boosey; Eulenburg; Heugel; Penguin; Philharmonia; Ricordi)

The octet is written for string quartet, double bass, clarinet, French horn and bassoon. The *Trout quintet* is so named because one movement consists of variations on Schubert's own song of that name. The *Rosamunde* incidental music consists of an overture originally written for another work (*The magic harp*), and of the entr'actes and ballet music. Although they share the same opus number, the works were not written at the same time, which accounts for the considerable difference in the numbers allotted in the Deutsch catalogue. O. E. Deutsch's thematic catalogue is arranged in chronological order, and a check of the works recommended above will show how misleading are the Schubert opus numbers as a guide to the order of composition; the symphonies have no opus numbers at all. The two C major symphonies are sometimes known as the "Great" and "Little" C major, though there is nothing small about the sixth symphony. While the later work is apparently known in most countries as no. 7, usage in Britain is tending towards calling the work "no. 9", allotting the earlier number to a symphony in E major which exists only in sketch form.

SCHUMANN

(a) *Piano concerto in A minor, op. 54* (Boosey; Eulenburg; Heugel; Penguine)

(d) *Piano quintet in E♭ major, op. 44* (Eulenburg; Ricordi)

(e) *String quartet in A major, op. 41, no. 3* (Eulenburg; Ricordi)

445

Symphonies (Boosey; Eulenburg; Heugel; Philharmonia)

(f) *no. 1, in B♭ major ("Spring"), op. 38*

(g) *no. 2, in C major, op. 61*

(d) *no. 3, in E♭ major ("Rhenish"), op. 97*

(c) *no. 4, in D minor, op. 120* (Ricordi)

Schumann wrote only three string quartets and these comprise opus 41; it may be considered desirable to buy all three and perhaps to bind them in a single volume. Although the symphonies are not nearly as successful or popular as the evergreen piano concerto, they continue to appear in concert programmes and gramophone record catalogues and are still effective when well played.

SHOSTAKOVITCH (g) *Piano and trumpet concerto, op. 35*

Symphonies

(c) *no. 1, in F minor, op. 10* (Boosey)

(f) *no. 5, op. 47* (Boosey)

(f) *no. 10, op. 93* (Boosey)

The concerto is a popular work with an uncommon combination of soloists in which the trumpet is definitely the junior partner. The first symphony dates from the nineteen-thirties and is still more frequently played than most of its successors; the fifth has some claims to be considered, while the tenth (first heard in 1955 and the penultimate at the time of writing) has been hailed as showing a return to the composer's best after a long period of disappointing compositions.

SIBELIUS (e) *Finlandia, op. 26* (Breitkopf)

(g) *Karelia: suite, op. 11* (Breitkopf)

(c) *En saga, op. 9* (Breitkopf)

(g) *String quartet in D minor ("Voces intimae"), op. 56* (Eulenburg)

Symphonies

(b) *no. 1, in E minor, op. 39* (Breitkopf)

(a) *no. 2, in D major, op. 43* (Breitkopf)

(e) *no. 3, in C major, op. 52* (Eulenburg)

(c) *no. 4, in A minor, op. 63* (Breitkopf)

(a) *no. 5, in E♭ major, op. 82* (Hansen)

(c) *no. 6, in D minor, op. 104* (Hansen)

(b) *no. 7, in C major, op. 105* (Hansen)

(c) *The swan of Tuonela, op. 22, no. 2* (Breitkopf)

(d) *Tapiola, op. 112* (Breitkopf)

(d) *Violin concerto in D minor, op. 47* (Eulenburg; O.U.P.)

The complete symphonies of Sibelius are necessary to the well-rounded collection as an outstanding modern series of works in this form. The other items give a fair representation of a twentieth-century composer. The *Swan of Tuonela* should correctly be listed under *Four legends, op. 22*, of which it is the second, but this popular work, with its dark and sad cor anglais solo, is the only one of the four movements in the suite that has become generally popular.

SMETANA
    (f) *The bartered bride: overture* (Boosey; Eulen-burg; Philharmonia)

    Ma vlast (My country): cycle of symphonic poems

    (f) *no. 1, Vysehrad* (Eulenburg)

    (e) *no. 2, Vltava (Moldau)* (Eulenburg; Boosey; Ricordi)

    (g) *no. 3, Sarka* (Eulenburg)

    (e) *no. 4, From Bohemia's woods and fields* (Eulenburg)

    (g) *no. 5, Tabor* (Eulenburg)

    (f) *no. 6, Blanik* (Eulenburg)

    (g) *String quartet no. 1, in E minor* ("*From my life*") (Boosey; Eulenburg; Philharmonia; Ricardi)

Only the second and fourth of the six tone poems that comprise *Ma Vlast* are generally known in Britain but the others certainly do not warrant their obscurity. The string quartet is autobiographical, hence its sub-title, and describes in a continuous high wail, in the finale, the onset of deafness that marred the the composer's life.

STRAUSS, R.
    (b) *Don Juan, op. 20* (Eulenburg; Novello)

    (f) *Don Quixote, op. 35* (Eulenburg; Novello)

    (g) *Ein Heldenleben (A hero's life), op. 40* (Novello)

    (a) *Till Eulenspiegels lustige Streiche, op. 28* (Eulen-burg; Novello)

    (g) *Tod und Verklärung (Death and transfiguration), op. 24* (Eulenburg; Novello)

These are the five most popular of Strauss's symphonic poems. Each attempts to tell a story in musical terms and achieve the objective with varying success.

STRAVINSKY
    (d) *The firebird (L'oiseau de feu) ballet: orchestral suite* (Chester)

    (a) *Petrouchka: ballet* (Boosey)

    (e) *Sacre du printemps (Rite of Spring): ballet* (Boosey)

> (g) *Symphonie de Psaumes* (*Symphony of Psalms*)
> (Boosey)

Petrouchka and the *Firebird* are the two most popular of Stravinsky's ballets; both scores have been slightly revised by the composer since World War II though they date back to 1911 and 1910 respectively. The other two works are probably of greater permanent importance, however. The *Symphony* is in three movements and is a choral work with orchestra.

TCHAIKOVSKY

> (d) *Capriccio italien, op. 45* (Boosey; Eulenburg)
> (a) *Casse noisette* (*Nutcracker*): *suite, op. 71a* (Boosey; Eulenburg)
> (g) *1812: overture, op. 49* (Boosey; Eulenburg)
> (d) *Francesca da Rimini: symphonic poem, op. 32* (Eulenburg)
> (g) *Hamlet: overture, op. 67* (Boosey; Eulenburg)
> (a) *Piano concerto no. 1, in B♭ minor, op. 23* (Boosey; Eulenburg; Ricordi)
> (c) *Romeo and Juliet: overture-fantasy* (Boosey; Eulenburg; Penguin)
> *Symphonies*
> (c) *no. 4, in F minor, op. 36* (Boosey; Eulenburg; Philharmonia)
> (b) *no. 5, in E minor, op. 64* (Boosey; Eulenburg; Philharmonia; Ricordi)
> (a) *no. 6, in B minor* (*Pathétique*), *op. 74* (Boosey; Eulenburg; Philharmonia; Ricordi)
> (f) *Violin concerto in D major, op 35* (Boosey; Eulenburg; Ricordi)

TIPPETT

> (g) *Concerto for double string orchestra* (Schott)

An interesting work by a contemporary British composer; it has been recorded under the auspices of the British Council and shows Tippett's excellent use of contrapuntal parts.

VAUGHAN
WILLIAMS

> (d) *Fantasia on a theme of Thomas Tallis* (Boosey)
> *Symphonies*
> (f) *no. 2, in G major* ("*London*") (Stainer & Bell)
> (c) *no. 3* ("*Pastoral*") (Boosey)
> (c) *no. 4, in F minor* (O.U.P.)
> (a) *no. 5, in D major* (O.U.P.)

448

Miniature Scores

(b) *no. 6, in E minor* (O.U.P.)

(g) *no. 7 ("Antartica")* (O.U.P.)

(f) *no. 8, in D minor* (O.U.P.)

(g) *Job* (O.U.P.)

This large representation is a fair reflection of the importance of Vaughan Williams in contemporary British musical life. The non-British librarian may well decide that only the fourth, fifth and sixth will suffice. The first work in this important series is the *Sea symphony*, primarily a choral work set to words by Walt Whitman. *Job* is sub-titled "a masque for dancing" and dates from 1930.

VIVALDI   (f) *Le quattro stagioni (The four seasons), op. 8, nos. 1–4* (Eulenburg)

The Four seasons are the first four of the twelve works published as opus 8 under the title *Il cimento dell' armonia e dell' invenzione (An essay in harmony and invention)* and are probably the best-known works of Vivaldi whose stature as a composer is only now being recognized through the medium of gramophone recordings.

WAGNER   (b) *Die Fliegende Holländer (Flying Dutchman): overture* (Boosey; Eulenburg; Heugel; Philharmonia)

(c) *Götterdämmerung (Twilight of the Gods): funeral march from Act III* (Eulenburg; Philharmonia)

(b) *Lohengrin: preludes to Acts I and III* (Boosey; Eulenburg; Heugel; Philharmonia; Ricordi)

(a) *Die Meistersinger von Nürnberg: overture* (Boosey; Eulenburg; Heugel; Penguin; Philharmonia; Ricordi)

(a) *Siegfried idyll* (Boosey; Eulenburg; Heugel; Penguin; Philharmonia; Ricordi)

(c) *Tannhäuser: overture* (Boosey; Eulenburg; Heugel; Philharmonia; Ricordi)

(c) *Tristan und Isolde: Introduction, and Isolde's love-death* (Boosey; Eulenburg; Heugel; Philharmonia; Ricordi)

(b) *Die Walküre: Ride of the Valkyries* (Boosey; Eulenburg; Heugel; Philharmonia; Ricordi)

The opera titles are given in the original, and the excerpts with their English title—an inconsistent but (I hope) practical arrangement. The *Siegfried idyll* (written as a birthday present for Cosima Wagner on Christmas Day, 1870, and played by Wagner and some friends at the foot of the stairs outside her room) is the only work here which is not an operatic excerpt. The large library could well add further examples, since many of these short extracts are often played in the concert hall and are familiar to many music-lovers who have never seen a complete Wagner opera.

449

WALTON   (f) *Façade: first and second suites* (O.U.P.)

                      (f) *Portsmouth Point overture* (O.U.P.)

                      (b) *Symphony* (O.U.P.)

                      (g) *Viola concerto* (O.U.P.)

                      (g) *Violin concerto* (O.U.P.)

These five works cover some thirty years of the composer's working life- The suites from *Façade* are orchestral arrangements by the composer; the original *Façade entertainment* is a setting of some Edith Sitwell poems which are recited to a chamber orchestra accompaniment.

WARLOCK   (g) *Capriol: suite* (Boosey)

The work exists in three versions. The original (and miniature score version) The for string orchestra; two years later, in 1928, the composer re-scored the wokr for full orchestra but this variant loses much of the charm of the simpler setting. Third and last comes the composer's arrangement for piano duet. The work is nominally based on tunes found in Arbeau's *Orchésographie* (1588). Since both Warlock and Arbeau are pseudonyms and some of the movements have only the barest resemblance to themes in the original work, the suite could well be something of a cataloguer's nightmare. It is simplest (and almost true) to count it as an original work by the twentieth-century composer—and a most attractive one.

WEBER   *Overtures*

                      (g) *Euryanthe* (Boosey; Eulenburg; Heugel; Ricordi)

                     *(c) *Der Freischütz* (Boosey; Eulenburg; Heugel; Philharmonia; Ricordi)

                     *(a) *Oberon* (Boosey; Eulenburg; Heugel; Philharmonia)

These overtures are popular in the concert hall though the operas to which they rightfully belong are very rarely heard. Other Weber overtures (such as *Abu Hassan* and *Jubel*) are very occasionally performed. Mention should be made of the Berlioz orchestration of the piano piece, *Invitation to the dance*; the miniature score is published by Eulenburg.

ABBREVIATIONS

In the preceding pages, the following abbreviations have been used for certain publishers:

Boosey & Hawkes   —   Boosey

Breitkopf & Härtel   —   Breitkopf

Oxford University Press   —   O.U.P.

United Music Publishers   —   U.M.P.

* Bound together in Penguin edition.

Appendix II

INDEX OF WORKS IN PART II

Appendix II

Appendix II

Appendix II

457

Appendix II

Appendix II

463

Appendix II

465

Appendix II

467

Appendix II

Appendix II

Appendix II

Weep you no more; My life's delight; Damask
roses; The faithful shepherdess; Brown is my
love; By a fountainside; Fair house of joy.

op. 6: Come away, death; O mistress mine;
Blow, blow, thou winter wind.

op. 23: Fear no more the heat o' the sun; Under
the greenwood tree; It was a lover and his
lass; Take, o take those lips away; Hey, ho,
the wind and the rain.

op. 30: Come unto these yellow sands; Full
fathom five; How should I my true love
know? Sigh no more, ladies; Tell me, where
is fancy bred?; When daffodils begin to
peer; When that I was; Where the bee sucks;
Who is Silvia?

Appendix II

Appendix II

Appendix II

Appendix II

ABBREVIATIONS USED

cl—clarinet
pf—pianoforte
m.s.—miniature score
tpt—trumpet

va—viola
vc—violoncello
vn—violin
v.s.—vocal score

Appendix III

MUSIC PUBLISHERS

The names and addresses of music publishers are given in an appendix to each number of *The British Catalogue of Music*. The following list gives the English agents of foreign publications mentioned in the preceding pages, and the addresses of some lesser-known British firms. Where no sole agent is indicated, music can be obtained through any English importer or public library suppliers, such as Messrs. J. B. Cramer & Co., of 139 New Bond Street, London, W.1.

Original publisher	*English agent or address*
ANGLO-SOVIET MUSIC PRESS	296 Regent Street, London, W.1.
ARCADIA	24 Great Pulteney Street, London, W.1.
ARTIA, *Czechoslovakia*	Boosey & Hawkes
BÄRENREITER, *Germany*	Novello
BELAIEFF, *France*	Boosey & Hawkes
BORNEMANN, *France*	United Music Publishers
BREITKOPF & HÄRTEL, *Germany*	British & Continental Music Agencies
CARISH, *Italy*	Orchestral music—Chester; otherwise no sole agent
CHOUDENS, *France*	United Music Publishers
DURAND, *France*	United Music Publishers
EDITION DANIA, *Denmark*	Chester
EDITION RUSSE DE MUSIQUE	Boosey & Hawkes
ENGSTROM & SODING	Chester
ESCHIG, *France*	Schott
FOLEY, *U.S.A.*	Schott
FREDERYK CHOPIN INSTITUTE, *Poland*	No sole agent
HAMELLE, *France*	United Music Publishers
HANSEN, *Denmark*	Chester
HENLE, *Germany*	Novello
HEUGEL, *France*	United Music Publishers
HUDEBNI MATICE UNELECKE BESEDY, *Czechoslovakia*	Boosey

INTERNATIONAL MUSIC CO., *U.S.A.*	No sole agent
JOBERT, *France*	United Music Publishers
KALMUS	24 Great Pulteney Street, London, W.1.
KISTNER, *Germany*	Novello
LEA, *U.S.A.*	Universal (Kalmus)
LEDUC, *France*	United Music Publishers
LEEDS MUSIC, *U.S.A.*	4 Denmark Street, London, W.C.2.
LIBER-SOUTHERN	8 Denmark Street, London, W.C.2.
MATHET, *France*	United Music Publishers
MERCURY, *U.S.A.*	Schott
NAGEL, *Germany*	Novello
NORSK MUSIKFORLAG, *Norway*	Chester
ÖSTERREICHISCHER BUNDES-VERLAG, *Austria*	No sole agent
PARAGON, *U.S.A.*	Hinrichsen
RAHTER	Schauer, 239-241 Shaftesbury Ave., London, W.C.2.
ROUART, LEROLLE, *France*	United Music Publishers
ROZSAVOLGYI, *Hungary*	Boosey
SALABERT, *France*	United Music Publishers
SKANDINAVISK MUSIKFORLAG, *Denmark*	Chester
SCHAUER	239-241 Shaftesbury Ave., London, W.C.2.
SCHLESINGER	Sibelius–O.U.P.; others – Hinrichsen
SIMROCK, *Czechoslovakia*	239-241 Shaftesbury Ave., London, W.C.2.
SIRENE, *France*	United Music Publishers
SONZOGNO	No sole agents
UNION MUSICALE FRANCO-ESPAGNOLE	United Music Publishers
UNIVERSAL, *Austria*	24 Great Pulteney Street, London, W.1.
ZIMMERMANN, *Germany*	Novello

Appendix IV

TUTORS

The following list of suggested tutors is offered with considerable reservation, since works of this type are often subject to wide fluctuations in popularity and the accepted work of one decade may be almost totally ignored in the next. Where an asterisk is shown against the name of an instrument, it indicates that other suitable works are listed in *Schirmer's guide to books on music* (Darrell), which receives notice in Chapter II.

*PIANO

Beringer	*Daily technical studies* (Bosworth)
Beringer	*Beringer piano tutor* (Bosworth)
Brée	*The groundwork of the Leschetizky method* (Schirmer)
Howard	*Invitation to the piano* (Ascherberg)
Tausig	*Daily studies* (Schirmer)

See also the section on Piano solo (pp. 296–305) under BACH, J. S.; BARTÓK; CLEMENTI; CRAMER; CZERNY and HELLER.

*ORGAN

Alcock	*The organ* (Novello)
Coleman	*The amateur organist* (O.U.P.)
Ellingford & Meers	*The science of organ pedalling* (Musical Opinion)
Stainer	*The organ* (Novello)

*VIOLIN

Dounis	[*Various*] *studies* (Strad)
Flesch	*The art of violin playing* (Fischer)
Robjohns	*Violin technique* (O.U.P.)
Sevcik	*School of technic* (Bosworth)
Tours & Reed	*The violin* (Novello)

And technical studies by Kreutzer, Mazas, Paganini, Rode, etc.

*VIOLA

Flesch	*Scale system* [adapted for viola] (Fischer)
Sevcik	*School of technic* [arr. viola by Lionel Tertis] (Bosworth)
Tours & Shore	*The viola* (Novello)

*VIOLONCELLO

Stutschewsky	*The art of playing the violoncello* (Schott)
Swert & Sharp	*The violoncello* (Novello)

See also under POPPER (p. 343).

DOUBLE BASS

Lotter	*Practical tutor for the double bass* (Boosey)
Simandl	*New method* (Chester)

GUITAR

McNeil	*Modern guitar method* [6-string guitar with plectrum] (Keith Prowse)
Media	*Spanish guitar tutor* [finger method] (Essex)

Appendix IV

Morales	*Guitar method* [Flamenco style] (Essex)
Ranieri	*Méthode de guitarre* (Cranz)

*RECORDER
Giesbert	*Method for the recorder* (Schott)
Priestley & Fowler	*School recorder handbook* (Schott)

FLUTE
Chapman	*Flute technique* (O.U.P.)
Langey	*Practical tutor for the flute* (Boosey)
Moyse	*Enseignement complet de la flûte* [9 vols. exercises; 12 vols. studies] (Leduc)

OBOE
Adkins	†*Complete modern tutor* (Boosey)
Langey	*Practical tutor for the oboe and cor anglais* (Boosey)
Rothwell	*Book of scales for the oboe* (O.U.P.)
	Oboe technique (O.U.P.)

*CLARINET
Klosé	*Clarinet school* (Boosey)
Jettel	*The accomplished clarinettist* (Weinberger)
Thurston & Frank	*The clarinet* (Boosey)

SAXOPHONE
Eby	*Scientific method for the saxophone* (Francis, Day & Hunter)
Ville	*Universal method* (Fischer)

BASSOON
Adkins	*Complete modern method* (Boosey)
Langey	*Practical tutor for the bassoon* (Boosey)
Oubradous	*Enseignement complet du basson* (Leduc)

BRASS
Standard tutors, by Otto Langey (Boosey) and W. M. Eby (Jacobs)

PERCUSSION
Gardner	*Modern methods for instruments of percussion* (Fischer)

† Out of print at present.

GENERAL INDEX

General Index

General Index

General Index

General Index

General Index

General Index

General Index

General Index

General Index

General Index

General Index

General Index

General Index

General Index